1384

ROADSIDE HISTORY
of NEW MEXICO

Francis L. Fugate 939
and
Roberta B. Fugate

MOUNTAIN PRESS PUBLISHING COMPANY 2
Missoula, 1989

Third Printing, September 1992

Library of Congress Cataloging-in-Publication Data

Fugate, Francis L., 1915-
    Roadside History of New Mexico / Francis L. Fugate and
Roberta B. Fugate.
        p.   cm.
    Bibliography: p.
    Includes index.
    ISBN 0-87842-248-X: $24.95 — ISBN 0-87842-242-0
(pbk.) : $14.95
    1. Historic sites—New Mexico—Guide-books. 2. New Mexico—
History, Local. 3. New Mexico—Description and travel—1981
—Guide-books. 4. Automobiles—Road guides—New Mexico.
I Fugate, Roberta B. II. Title
F797.F55   1989   89-32930
917.89004'53—dc20   CIP

Mountain Press Publishing Company
P.O. Box 2399 • Missoula, MT 59806
Toll Free 1-800-234-5308

Dedication

To Bobbie
who enlivened our early travels through New Mexico

and

To Dempsey
who worried that the road might play out
just beyond every curve.

About the Authors

Francis and Roberta Fugate are well-seasoned travelers. They have traveled in all fifty of the United States and thirty-two foreign countries. In 1949 they arrived in the Southwest with the avowed intention of staying a year; they have been there ever since. The highways and byways of New Mexico are their turf.

Francis Fugate has been a freelance writer in the Western field for more than half a century. In addition to hundreds of articles and short stories, his works include *The Spanish Heritage of the Southwest*. For twenty-five years he conducted classes in Professional Writing at the University of Texas at El Paso. He has served a two-year term as president of Western Writers of America.

In 1977 he left the University to devote full time to writing. His wife Roberta retired from elementary teaching to join him as a collaborator. Their first work was *Secrets of the World's Best-Selling Writer: The Storytelling Techniques of Erle Stanley Gardner* (William Morrow, 1980). Then they acquired a recreational vehicle, which they dubbed "The Writer's Cramp," and settled down to travel writing.

The Writer's Cramp is a common sight on New Mexico highways, and the Fugates are frequent contributors to *American West* magazine.

Foreword

New Mexico became a territory of the United States in 1846 and was admitted to statehood in 1912. Nevertheless, because of association of its name with Mexico, the nation to the south, the State of New Mexico continues to suffer an identity problem. Prospective visitors are frequently told by airline employees and travel agents, particularly in the East, that they will need passports to visit New Mexico. Residents often receive packages plastered with customs declarations; shippers to New Mexico are sometimes charged extra for processing foreign shipments and told that payment must be in "US dollars."

Norma Wheeler, of Deming, ordered a case of spring water from a subsidiary of Coca-Cola in Saratoga, New York. She was informed: "We're sorry, but we will not ship out of the U.S.A." . . . A visitor from California who consulted a doctor in Santa Fe was told that services furnished outside the United States are not covered by Medicare. . . . Jim Lord of Albuquerque wrote to inquire about graduate programs at the University of Texas. The reply said his application should be sent to the Office of Foreign Admissions: "Any questions you may have as a foreign student may be addressed to the International Office."

New Mexico is indeed a part of the United States, the fifth largest in the Union!

For the past forty years we have roamed the state from border to border, from the tops of her mountains to the bottoms of her canyons. We have never been asked to show a passport or an international driver's license, and we have not had to get our U.S. dollars changed into pesos.

Within New Mexico's 121,412 square miles we have experienced a variety of unspoiled scenic beauty and natural wonders equaled in few other areas of similar size. But we cannot tell you about them; they have to be seen. Along the highways and byways, we have met a continuing parade of interesting people, the like of which you'll find no place else on earth. But we cannot tell you about them; you have to meet them.

During those forty years, wherever we have gone, we have probed the history of the area. Some of the oldest history in the United States and some of the newest scientific developments have unfolded, bringing the land about us to vibrant life. We can tell you about these things. However, faced with the pressure of limited space, our problem has been deciding what to leave out. So that you can share the excitement of discovering all we had to omit and more, we are including a "Bibliography for Additional Reading."

We hope that you will derive as much pleasure from reading and using this book as we have experienced during our forty years of traveling and writing.

Francis L. & Roberta B. Fugate

Table of Contents

Acknowledgments

It would be impossible for us to name all of those in a forty-year succession of friends, colleagues, acquaintances, and fellow travelers who have contributed to our knowledge of New Mexico. However, we would be remiss not to recognize some of the special people who have helped us during the past year of collection and consolidation.

First on the list are Matias Montoya and Dennis Salazar of the Cartography Section of the New Mexico State Highway and Transportation Department. They went far beyond the call of duty in helping us surmount the problem of changing highway numbers. Their generous assistance eased our task and improved this book.

For permission to quote we are indebted to novelist Max Evans, of Albuquerque; Bart McDowell, of *National Geographic Magazine*; and Thomas W. Pew, Jr., Editor-in-Chief, *American West*. We thank El Paso artist José Cisneros for use of his map of the Camino Real and drawings portraying Spanish colonial times.

We must recognize David Shindo, of Darst-Ireland Photography, El Paso, for exercising his magic to bring faded photographs back to life. Archivist Al Regensberg, at the New Mexico Records Center and Archives, and Photographic Archivist Arthur L. Olivas, Museum of New Mexico, enhanced this volume by searching their files for historical pictures of early-day New Mexico. Others who contributed in this area were: William D. Ebie, Director, Roswell Museum and Art Center; Charles Cooper, Superintendent, Aztec Ruins National Monument; Jo Smith, Salmon Ruin; Joy L. Poole, Curator, Farmington Museum; Laurance D. Linford, Executive Director, Inter-Tribal Indian Ceremonial Association; Mark Nohl, New Mexico Economic Development and Tourism Department; Gordon Church and Christy Johnson, 1% for Art Program, Albuquerque; Rex E. Gerald, University of Texas at El Paso; and Alma Edmonds, Missouri State Historical Society.

El Paso author-historian Leon C. Metz generously opened his file of photographs. Dr. Joseph P. Sanchez, Director, Spanish Colonial Research Center of the National Park Service, provided early Spanish maps and information from his wealth of lore regarding El Camino Real and New Mexico during the Spanish regime. Special thanks go out to Cesar Caballero and S.H. "Bud" Newman, Special Collections, University of Texas at El

Paso Library, for providing access to many rare volumes and to the Hertzog Collection. Margaret Palmer, publisher of the *Chama Valley Tattler,* was most helpful. Duane W. Ryan, director of Broadcasting, Eastern New Mexico University, came to our rescue when we were lost during our search for information about old bones.

We suspect there is a special place in the Hereafter reserved for librarians who give of themselves to help authors in their quests for information. Surely, Mary Sarber of the El Paso Public Library will someday take over the reference desk in that celestial kingdom; she has been ever-present and ever-helpful during our pursuit. Many librarians across the State of New Mexico have rendered assistance. We particularly want to cite Octavia Fellin, Director, Gallup Public Library; Carmen M. Jaramillo and Barbara Martinez, of the Los Lunas Community Library; and Betty Lloyd, Arthur Johnson Memorial Library, Raton.

This all started as an act of faith on the part of David Flaccus, our publisher, who "turned us loose" on a year-long trek over the highways and byways of New Mexico. Then the job of honing the manuscript into shape fell upon the shoulders of Kathy Spitler at Mountain Press. We feel particularly blessed to have the artistry of cowboy-artist Joe Beeler to provide a setting for this volume.

On behalf of Simon and Pierre, we extend appreciation to Gerry Carpenter for taking care of them while we were away and, thus, adding greatly to their well-being and to our peace of mind.

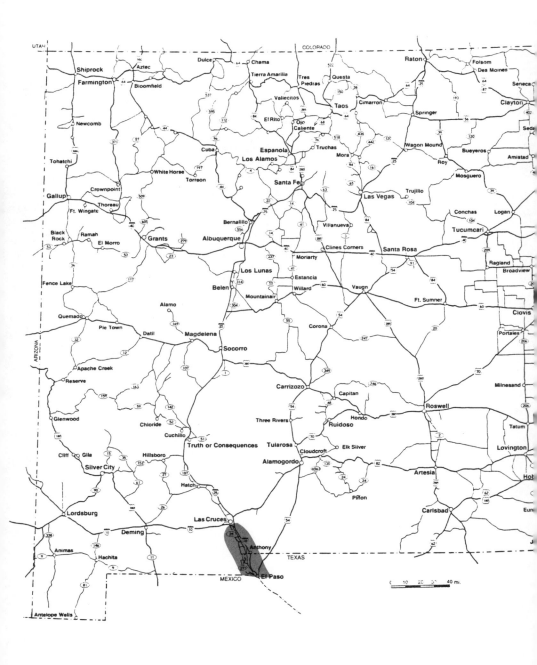

Don Juan De Oñate Trail

During the Spanish conquest and coloniza-tion of New Mexico, the Crown and the Sword were always accompa-nied by the Cross.

— Courtesy José Cisneros

I. Don Juan de Oñate Trail

Don Juan de Oñate has aptly been called the "Father of New Mexico". He was the founder of Spanish civilization in the South-west. He organized and led the first *entrada* of settlers into a harsh unknown land peopled by hostile natives.

After exploratory probes during the sixteenth century, on Sep-tember 21, 1595, Viceroy Luís de Velasco and his friend Don Juan de Oñate signed a contract for the occupation and colonization of New Mexico. Under the agreement, Oñate, a wealthy man, was to pay all expenses of the expedition except for the missionaries; they were supported by the Crown. He was to receive a salary of 6,000 ducats a year and have unlimited power. He would report directly to the Council of the Indies in Spain. As a conqueror and colonizer of new lands, he would have the title of *Adelantado* (governor). He was to have the right of *encomienda,* of exacting tribute from Indian pueblos, usually paid in produce and trade goods. In return, the *encomendero* was charged with defending his subjects and looking after their welfare.

There was no shortage of volunteers for the expedition since all land not in possession of the Indians was to be granted to the settlers, and they were to have the rank of *hidalgo*, the lowest rank of nobility in Spain. They would "enjoy all the honors and privileges that noblemen and *caballeros* [knights] of the Kingdom of Castile enjoy." Whole families enlisted. Many pledged money and supplies in support of the venture, some committed their entire fortunes.

It is usually agreed there were 400 men, including 129 soldiers. A hundred thirty-eight of the men were accompanied by wives and children. Eight priests and two lay brothers went along to convert the heathens. It took eighty-three wagons to cart their supplies and belongings, and they drove a herd of 7,000 head of livestock. It is estimated the train stretched between three and four miles in length.

The trek across the barren Mexican desert was not easy. A shortage of food forced the settlers to eat weeds and roots. They were rained on for seven days. Then they went four days without water. But Oñate's expedition finally reached the southern bank of the Rio Grande—hungry, thirsty, and foot-sore. Poet-soldier Gaspar Pérez de Villagrá wrote about the thirst-crazed horses: "Two of them drank so much that their bellies burst open." The settlers fared little better: "Our men . . . threw themselves into the water and drank as though the entire river could not quench their terrible thirst."

The entourage proceeded up-river to some twenty miles southeast of present-day El Paso, Texas. Because of the spring thaw and rains in the mountains to the north, the river was running too deep and the *bosque* (thicket) was too dense to attempt a crossing at that point. However, there was water to drink and pasture for the horses. Hunters shot ducks and geese, and the settlers caught fish from the river. Villagrá described the tree-shaded river bank as "the Elysian fields of happiness."

Oñate had an altar built under a grove of trees. The priests conducted a solemn high Mass and some of the soldiers presented a drama written by Captain Don Marcos Farfán de los Godos. After a display of horsemanship by the soldiers, Oñate stepped forward to perform the most solemn act of all:

Be it known that I, Don Juan de Oñate, governor, captain general, and adelantado of New Mexico, and of its kingdoms and provinces, as well as those in its vicinity and contiguous thereto, as the settler and conqueror thereof, by virtue of the authority of the king, our lord, hereby declare that:

... I take possession, once, twice, and thrice, and all the times I can and must, of the actual jurisdiction, civil as well as criminal, of the lands of the said Rio del Norte, without exception whatsoever, with all its meadows and pasture grounds and passes.

Oñate planted the royal standard and nailed a cross to a tree. The trumpeters sounded a blast and harquebusiers fired a volley. Every man, woman, and child shouted. Thus, New Mexico was brought under Spanish rule. It would remain a part of the far-flung Spanish empire until September 27, 1821.

The expedition crossed the Rio Grande. Forty Indians armed with bows and arrows showed up to help with the sheep. On May 4 the long caravan strung out along the east bank and headed north toward dreams of riches. It was July before Oñate reached the junction of the Rio Grande and the Rio Chama where he established a headquarters from which to begin colonization.

NM 28, the Don Juan de Oñate Trail, begins at the southern border where Mexico, Texas, and New Mexico meet. From there to Mesilla, the highway along the Rio Grande closely approximates the original trail taken by Oñate's expedition almost four centuries ago. It follows a historic route through the agricultural communities of the verdant Mesilla Valley. The principal crops are cotton, chiles, lettuce, tomatoes, onions, pecans, and grapes.

NM 28 can be reached by taking NM 273 from El Paso through Sunland Park and Santa Teresa to where NM 273 joins NM 28 just south of La Union. The Don Juan de Oñate Trail can also be reached by driving west from Canutillo, Texas, on Texas Highway 259 and crossing the Rio Grande into New Mexico.

NM 273
Sunland Park—Santa Teresa

Sunland Park

Sunland Park is reached by NM 273 from US 85 (Paisano Drive) in El Paso, Texas. Until 1960 Sunland Park was a small village named Anapra, located near the old ford by which Don Juan de Oñate crossed the Rio Grande to head northward into New Mexico along the east bank of the river. The name was changed to help promote a race track which was established there to take advantage of its convenient location on the New Mexico side of the Rio Grande where it garners betting money from El Pasoans. At that time New Mexico allowed race tracks with parimutuel betting; Texas did not.

Along here, a small portion of New Mexico extends across to the east side of the Rio Grande because the river changed its course after the border between Texas and New Mexico was established by the Gadsden Purchase in 1854. This quirk created a bonanza for a few bar owners in El Paso, Texas.

For a number of years, it was illegal in Texas to sell mixed drinks in an open bar. Topers who wanted something stronger than beer had to belong to a private club. A number of watering places opened along a short stretch of New Mexico on Doniphan Drive in El Paso, between Paisano Drive and Sunland Park Drive, another entrance to Sunland Park. They did a brisk business until the Texas law prohibiting the public sale of mixed drinks was repealed.

Close to Sunland Park, atop Cristo Rey Mountain, a massive statue of Christ looks out over the land. The peak was known as Mule Driver's Mountain until Urbici Soler, a Spanish sculptor,

A massive statue of Christ overlooks the racetrack at Sunland Park. —Courtesy New Mexico Economic Development & Tourism, No. 71

erected the statue. It is one foot taller than the Christ of the Andes. A rocky switchback trail will lead the hardy hiker to a spectacular view of Mexico, Texas, and New Mexico. Since robbers have been known to waylay hikers, it is recommended the trip be undertaken only by sizeable groups. During the annual Easter pilgrimage, some of the more faithful crawl up the tortuous road on their knees.

Santa Teresa

Santa Teresa is an unincorporated town some six and a half miles from the Texas border on NM 273. The community grew from the dream of a country club. In the early 1970s, professional golfer Lee Trevino was one of the principal backers in the design and construction of a golf course and country club known as Santa Teresa. Originally, it was touted as an ultra-posh layout with luxury homes and an airport for fly-in golfers.

Trevino withdrew from the operation, but growth continued and the dream began to come true. Then, as residents of nearby El Paso sought to escape urban crowding, real estate developers added homes and condominiums appealing to various economic levels. With the development of an industrial park during the late 1980s, Santa Teresa is on its way to becoming a sizeable town if not a city.

NM 28

La Union—La Mesilla

La Union

La Union is an agricultural community stretching almost a mile west of NM 28. The post office was opened in 1909, but time-worn adobe houses testify that the settlement is considerably older. The population is primarily Hispanic-American, some with ancestral roots reaching back beyond the Treaty of Guadalupe Hidalgo.

Chamberino

Chamberino began shortly after the Mexican War as a refuge for New Mexicans who could choose between citizenship in Mexico and the United States under the Treaty of Guadalupe Hidalgo. It was known as El Refugio and Los Amoles. Until 1854, when the Gadsden Purchase became effective, Chamberino was in Mexico. Then, residents found themselves in New Mexico after all.

The original settlement was located east of the present site. Inundated by devastating floods which washed away most of the adobe buildings, the original site was abandoned in 1886 and the citizens rebuilt on higher ground on the sandy western mesa where the village stands today.

It took eight years to construct the adobe church, San Luís Rey de Francia. Once a month, Father Joseph Lafon would ride horseback from Smeltertown, near El Paso, to say Mass. In 1902, when Monsignor Henry Granjon, the Bishop of Tucson, made a pastoral visit, Father Lafon was on hand. Monsignor Granjon told of his reception:

> The people of Chamberino—men, women, and children, in their Sunday best and joyous—have come to meet us. Wagons whose axle trees cry out under their loads fall in behind us, one after another, on the narrow road, raising a whirlwind of dust. As we advance, other carts emerge from all sides and take their place in the procession. Everyone is outside, and Father L. exults. His flock has been faithful to his order. At a curve in the road he invites me to look behind us. The line of wagons extends as far as the eye can see, half lost in the cloud of dust.

One old man hobbled along pushing a wheelbarrow loaded with a barrel of water, hoping for an opportunity to settle the dust for the distinguished visitor. When it came time for services, the parishioners were disappointed that Father Granjon had not brought his mitre and cross. Father Lafon confided "discreetly" that his congregation believed a bishop without a mitre and cross was "only half a bishop." The bishop noted in his journal: "I resolve to procure for myself a small, light mitre and an aluminum cross, collapsible and transportable."

In the area around Chamberino there has been a recent revival of grape culture which was originally brought to the New World by the Spaniards. Most of the old vineyards were allowed to die out during the Prohibition Era.

La Mesa

This farming community was founded between 1854 and 1857 by Hispanic-Americans and a few Anglo-American pioneers. It was named La Mesa (tableland) after a nearby lava flow called Black Mesa. Following the close of the Mexican War, this part of what is now New Mexico was in Mexico until the Gadsden Purchase became effective in 1854. Settlement here was desirable because the high ground did not suffer from frequent floods which inundated other parts of the Mesilla Valley before flooding of the Rio Grande was brought under control by dams to the north. The first post office opened in 1908. The official name was Victoria, but the residents still called their town La Mesa.

San José Church had been established in 1875. In 1902 Father Granjon found it in a state of ruin. "I cannot resist a feeling of melancholy in the presence of all these things which palpitated with life in the wonderful days of yesteryear."

San Miguel

San Miguel is a *placita* of pink and yellow houses with deep-set windows. The houses almost touch the roadway which is lined with elms, chinaberries, salt cedars, and cottonwoods. The residents are primarily Hispanic-American. The village dates back to the 1850s.

Monsignor Henry Granjon described San Miguel:

> San Miguel is a village of fifty families, living on the fruits of the land, lacking water to irrigate their plantings, and spending four-fifths of the year waiting for a rain that never comes. Thus we find the population, free from any work in the fields, gathered around the church to receive us. Godparents and babies are ready for the confirmation. . . .
>
> Despite their poverty, the inhabitants of San Miguel have gone to some expense for the occasion. The interior of the small adobe church is all newly whitened; the earth floor, which takes the place of flagstones or planks, has been carefully swept and then dampened to guard against the formation of dust by the trampling of the crowd. Neither chairs nor benches have hampered the operation, for one never sees seats in a Mexican church; the men stand, the women kneel on the ground. Curtains hang, freshly starched, at the clear glass windows. The altar disappears under a profusion of painted paper flowers, the product of local art, and above rises a beautiful statue of Saint Michael vanquishing the dragon, imported from France.

Shortly after Monsignor Granjon's visit, a landowner named Telles opened a store and post office and the Post Office Department listed the town by his name until 1917. The original adobe mission church was built in 1880 and torn down in 1926. In its place, a larger church was built of vesicular basalt from a volcanic outcrop on the mesa a mile to the west.

Stahmann Farms

In 1926 Deane Stahmann and his father acquired the Santo Tomas Farm of about 2,900 acres. Only 150 acres were under cultivation. The remainder consisted of sand dunes and bosque.

Stahmann Farms is said to contain the largest pecan orchard in the world. —Courtesy of New Mexico Economic Development & Tourism, No. 15,488

The road to Las Cruces was a winding path through dense mesquite. The Santo Tomas Farm was to grow into the largest pecan orchard in the world.

The Stahmanns cleared and leveled the farm. They acquired more land. In 1936 they began planting pecan orchards. For many years, the Stahmanns "double-cropped" the area between trees by growing cotton, lettuce, and onions. The practice was discontinued as the pecan trees became so large the row crops no longer prospered.

For some fifteen years, during the double-cropping period, passing motorists could see thousands of White Chinese Geese pecking at the ground among the pecan trees. They were weeding the crops and, incidentally, making Stahmann Farms the largest producer of geese of any farm in the world.

Today there are 180,000 trees, planted forty-eight to the acre. NM 28 takes almost three miles to get through the orchard.

La Mesilla

In 1848 the Treaty of Guadalupe Hidalgo established the area west of the Rio Grande occupied by present-day Mesilla as part of Mexico. (In local usage, it is more often called Mesilla or Old Mesilla.) Las Cruces and Doña Ana, on the east bank of the river, were in American territory. Anglo-Americans arrived to claim land in such force that many native Mexicans moved away. Those who preferred to remain in the area but on Mexican soil crossed the river and settled on a small rise in the river valley. The settlement, known as Mesilla (little table), included about half the population of Doña Ana.

In 1853 the Mexican government issued the Mesilla Civil Colony Land Grant and the town was formed. In 1854 the Gadsden Purchase was negotiated, acquiring from Mexico a strip of land south of New Mexico and Arizona which stretched from Texas to California—29,142,400 acres for $10 million—a wedge of level land which would eventually serve as the southern railroad route to the Pacific coast. The erstwhile Mexican residents of Mesilla found themselves in the United States.

The new government honored land ownership under the Mexican land grant. On November 16, 1854, the treaty was symbolically formalized in the plaza at Mesilla. The flag of Mexico was lowered, and the flag of the United States was raised. Officials and soldiers from both governments were on hand to see that it was done right. Local Mexican officials swore allegiance to the new government. Residents who did not want to live under it were "notified to leave and take refuge in Mexican dominions."

Mesilla Plaza as painted during the mid-nineteenth century.

In 1858 Mesilla became a stop on the Butterfield Overland Mail route which linked St. Louis and San Francisco. Waterman L. Ormsby, a reporter for the *New York Herald*, rode the first westbound stage; he described the community. There were more than three thousand inhabitants. He saw "irrigated fields groaning with the weight of heavy crops." But he was not impressed by the cluster of one-story adobe houses; they looked like "miserable dog kennels."

Today, La Posta Restaurant occupies the old Butterfield Overland Mail stage stop in Mesilla. The rooms in the rambling building are labeled to indicate their former usage. This is the only one of the Overland Mail's way stations which is still in use, still serving travelers.

On July 25, 1861, the Civil War came to Mesilla. Lt. Col. John R. Baylor, commanding 258 Texan troops in Confederate service, occupied the village without firing a shot and settled down to await the arrival of Union forces from nearby Fort Fillmore. The "battle" was brief:

> I posted my men in position and awaited the arrival of the enemy. At about 5 o'clock I discovered their cavalry approaching the town by the main road, and soon after the infantry came in sight, bringing with them three howitzers. They formed within 300 yards, and were, as near as I could tell, about 600 strong. A flag was sent in to demand "unconditional and immediate surrender of the Texas forces," to which I answered that "we would fight first and surrender afterward." The answer was followed by the enemy opening on us with their howitzers. After four or five rounds of bombs, grape, and canister, the cavalry formed and marched up within 250 yards, preparatory to making a charge. . . .The cavalry was thrown into confusion and retreated hastily, running over the infantry. In a few moments the enemy were marching back in the direction of their fort.

Baylor forthwith issued a proclamation taking possession of all of New Mexico south of the thirty-fourth parallel of north latitude "on behalf ˙ f the Confederate States of America." He dubbed it the Territory of Arizona: "The city of Mesilla is hereby designated as the seat of government of this Territory." Baylor was appointed governor.

Thirteen months later, in August, 1862, the "California Column," under Gen. James H. Carleton recaptured Mesilla and the surrounding area for the Union.

Following the Civil War, people of the Southwest were ardent in their political attachments. An election could erupt into a pitched battle. Mesilla was no exception. In 1871 José M. Gallegos was candidate for delegate to Congress on the Democratic ticket. Col. J. Francisco Cháves was a Republican candidate. Gallegos scheduled a rally in the plaza on Sunday, August 21. The Republicans arranged a meeting at the same place and time.

All went well until after the meeting when the Democrats started a procession around the plaza with their band playing "Marching Through Georgia." The Republicans paraded in the opposite direction. Collision was inevitable: Nine men were killed and forty or fifty injured in the ensuing imbroglio. Troops from Fort McRae arrived and stayed a week to maintain order.

The Democrats won the election. Many of the Republicans felt so strongly that they would not stay where Democrats were victors. Fifteen families left for Ascensión in Mexico. It is said the Democrats came out of their houses to serenade them out of town singing to the tune of "Marching Through Georgia":

> "Se van, se van los Republicanos
> Para la Ascensión
> Por que los Democratos
> Ganaron la elección."

"The Republicans are going to Ascensión because the Democrats won the election."

In 1881 Mesilla experienced a brief period of excitement. On March 28 Billy the Kid was transferred from Santa Fe to Mesilla to stand trial on several counts of murder. A dwelling was converted into a courthouse, and the trial began on April 8. It took only two days for the jury to find the outlaw guilty of the murder of Sheriff William Brady. On April 15 the judge pronounced sentence decreeing that "the said William Bonney, alias Kid, alias William Antrim, be hanged by the neck until his body be dead."

The execution was set for Friday, May 13. The prisoner had to be transported to Lincoln in the face of a newspaper editor's grim prediction: "We expect every day to hear of Bonney's escape." As Billy the Kid left the Mesilla jail, he described it as the "worst place he had ever struck." With Billy the Kid under heavy guard, the trip to Lincoln came off without incident. The Kid did not get the opportunity to make his last escape from the jail in Lincoln until April 28. That resulted in his death. On the night of July 14, he was killed by Sheriff Pat Garrett.

During its heyday, Mesilla was a bustling community. George Griggs, a lifelong resident, told of activities in his book *History of the*

Mesilla Valley or The Gadsden Purchase. Its prime season began on December 12 with the fiesta of Our Lady of Guadalupe and ended on March 2 with the fiesta of St. Alvino, the patron saint of the town. People came from as far away as Santa Fe, Tucson, and Chihuahua. Ladies came to buy velvet gowns and satin shoes; men came to attend bullfights and street fairs. Mesilla had cock pits, billiard halls, theaters, and even bowling alleys for the entertainment of visitors. There was a flour mill and stores with supplies for the farmers who tilled the rich irrigated farms in the Mesilla Valley.

Griggs cited one firm that sent eighty-three wagons from Kansas City to Mesilla, each loaded with 5,000 pounds of merchandise. That firm paid $30,000 in freight bills on a wagon train containing $126,000 worth of goods which sold within three weeks at a profit of $51,000.

Mesilla's eminence faded in 1881 when the Santa Fe Railroad was routed through Las Cruces instead of Mesilla. Today, Mesilla basks in its historical past. The old buildings around the plaza are still there. They are now occupied by boutiques, gift shops, art galleries, and restaurants.

II. El Camino Real

From a historical standpoint, it is appropriate to enter New Mexico from the south by way of El Camino Real—"The Royal Road" or "The King's Highway"—the oldest, most historic road in the United States. This route was used by all of the early Spanish explorers and colonizers with the exception of Coronado. When the road reached its full extent as an artery of commerce, it stretched fifteen hundred miles from Mexico City through Santa Fe to Taos, Spain's northernmost outpost in the New World.

The road became El Camino Real or "The Royal Road" in 1598 when Don Juan de Oñate claimed the land on behalf of the king of Spain. The designation was analogous to the "US" attached to the numbers of Federal highways, indicating they are supported by the United States government. For the record, a Spanish king never came near New Mexico's Camino Real until September 30, 1987, when King Juan Carlos I visited Santa Fe.

After winning independence from Spain in 1821, the Mexican government decreed the road would henceforth be called El Camino Constitutional, or "Constitutional Highway." In practice, it continued to be known as the Camino Real into the twentieth century.

In an effort to cut down on slave raids to supply labor to mines in northern Mexico, in 1573 the Crown issued a royal *cédula* forbidding any expedition to the north for purposes other than furthering missionary work. In 1581 the Rodríguez-Chamuscado Expedition set out on such a trek; it blazed a trail which would be used for three hundred years.

Fray Agustín Rodríguez organized the expedition along with Franciscan brothers Francisco López and Juan de Santa María. Sergeant Francisco Sánchez Chamuscado headed a military escort of nine soldiers. (*Chamuscado* was a nickname meaning "scorched" or "singed" because of his red beard.) They had nineteen Indian

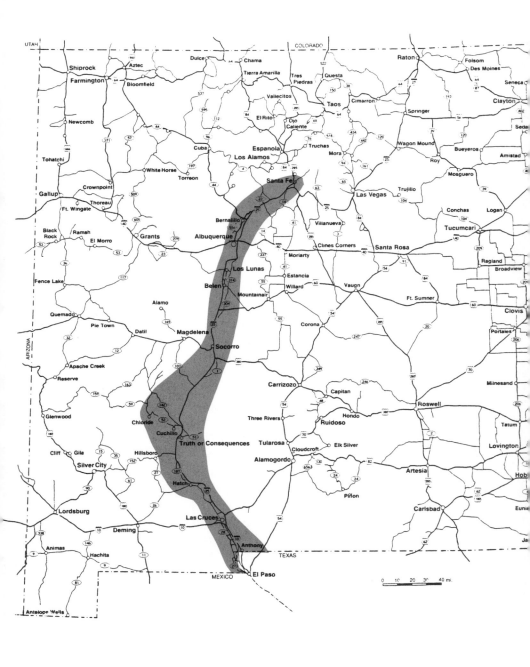

El Camino Real

servants, ninety horses, five hundred head of additional livestock, and a supply of trinkets to be dispensed to the natives as gifts. They crossed the Rio Grande at a ford which they named El Paso del Río del Norte, near present-day Sunland Park, and followed the east side of the river northward.

A short distance below what is now Santa Fe, Fray Juan de Santa María, a priest who dabbled in astrology, decided to return home. The stars did him wrong: He was murdered by the Indians a few days later. The Camino Real had claimed its first victim. When Chamuscado was ready to return, the other two priests elected— against Chamuscado's advice—to remain and continue their missionary work among the Indians. The military escort made it home, except for Chamuscado who became ill and died along the way.

The following year, Antonio de Espejo, a fugitive from justice on a charge of murdering one of his ranch hands, set out to rescue the two priests in the hope of winning a pardon. He was accompanied by two friars. They too crossed the ford and followed the river northward. At Puaray (the ruins are in Coronado State Monument near Bernalillo), they learned that the two priests they had come to rescue had been killed.

In 1598 Don Juan de Oñate and his colonial expedition crossed the ford into New Mexico. As the expedition proceeded north, the pioneering settlers left names upon the land. A terse entry in a journal testifies to the naming of Robledo Mountain, near present-day Doña Ana: "May 21, 1598, We buried Pedro Robledo." While crossing the barren stretch which would later be dubbed La Jornada del Muerto (dead man's route), the expedition ran out of water. A dog belonging to one of the men trotted back to camp with its feet and muzzle wet. Indians back-tracked the dog and found pools of water left by a vagrant desert shower. The campsite became known as Los Charcos del Perillo, (the pools of the little dog), later shortened to Perillo.

As traffic increased, *parajes* or campsites developed at intervals of a day's travel. Many present-day communities started with a name like Paraje de Belén or Paraje de Bernalillo. The late Cleve Hallenbeck, an avid student of the Camino Real, identified eighty-six parajes between the ford across the Rio Grande and Santa Fe. The Oñate expedition established about thirty, the names of which were still in use as late as 1859.

The Camino Real was the umbilical cord of the colonies. It brought companies of soldiers, bands of Franciscan friars, fresh groups of colonists, semi-royal processions of governors—eighty-

In 1536, Alvar Núñez Cabeza de Vaca traced a wandering path across southern New Mexico. In 1540-1542, Francisco Vásquez de Coronado crossed the north-central portion of the state in search of Cíbola and Quivira. In 1581, the Rodríguez Expedition blazed a route between El Paso and Santa Fe which would become known as the Camino Real and serve for three centuries. —Courtesy José Cisneros four of them—along with *commandantes-general* and dignitaries of the Church on inspection tours, and ever-welcome newcomers to relieve officials who had been so unfortunate as to be assigned duty fifteen hundred miles from the luxuries of life in Mexico City. Northbound caravans brought supplies needed by the colonists. Southbound caravans carried raw products of the frontier: buffalo hides, jerked meat, salt, piñon nuts, and Indian slaves to be sold in the mining towns of Chihuahua.

A regular schedule of supply was organized about 1609, subsidized by the Royal treasury. Initially, colonists were forced to be virtually self-sufficient because supplies carried over the Camino Real were intended solely for the use of religious missions and government agencies. By the end of the seventeenth century supply trains were dispatched every year, and some governors and influential private citizens illegally entered private trade by chartering trains to bring merchandise north for resale.

The caravans, called *conductas*, were organized in Mexico City. A round trip required a year and a half—six months for travel each way and six months for unloading, resting, and loading. There would be thirty-two great cloth-topped, iron-tired wagons, each requiring eight strong mules. The lead wagon flew the Royal banner, and the caravan was protected by a detachment of twelve or fourteen soldiers. A "spare parts kit" was specified for each group of eight wagons: 150 extra spokes, 24 tire irons, 500 pounds of tallow for lubrication, 24 pounds of tarpaulin cord, miscellaneous hardware, hammers, saws, adzes, crowbars, and a 27-pound sledge. A surplus of 288 mules was specified, and a small herd of cattle was brought along for food.

As traffic over the Camino Real increased, travelers in a caravan might number five hundred, and several thousand sheep and cattle would be driven in the wake of the cavalcade.

After the Pueblo Revolt of 1680, traffic on the road was closed down until the Reconquest in 1692. About 1750 Royal officials leaned to the belief that they would effect savings by turning the supply trains over to private contractors. A group of Chihuahua merchants, 550 miles south of Santa Fe, dominated the trade. During the 1770s mule packtrains began to be used, rather than expensive wagons. A mule could carry up to four hundred pounds and did not require frequent repair. Wagons were not again used until Americans got into the trade during the 1820s.

The possibilities of trade with the Spanish colonists did not go unnoticed by Americans, but the Spaniards zealously protected

Mule packtrains came into use on the Camino Real in lieu of wagons as an economy measure: mules did not require frequent repair.

—Courtesy New Mexico Department of Development, No. 2291

their monopoly. Mexican independence in 1821 did not stop traffic; it merely changed the politics and eased restrictions upon trade by Anglo traders from the United States. Traders from Missouri could come off the Santa Fe Trail and head on southward over the Camino Real to sell their wares in the more lucrative market in Chihuahua City. They called the stretch between Santa Fe and Chihuahua City the Chihuahua Trail.

Following the peace treaty with Mexico in 1848, developing travel and trade between San Antonio, Texas, and Santa Fe began to demand regular postal communications. In 1849-1850, monthly service was established over a route from San Antonio to El Paso, Texas, and then up the old Camino Real to Santa Fe. A Capt. Henry Skillman carried mail by horseback over the 1,100-mile trek. In 1854 a contract was let for the first coach mail service between the two cities. The El Paso to Santa Fe service was maintained until April, 1860. Officially, it was Route No. 12,851.

Except for the hiatus caused by the Pueblo Revolt between 1680 and 1692, New Mexico's Camino Real was in constant use until 1881 when the Santa Fe Railroad probed southward from Albuquerque to El Paso, Texas.

From the ford across the river near El Paso, the Camino Real followed along east of the Rio Grande to the *paraje* called Robledo between present-day Doña Ana and Radium Springs. There it left the river valley and proceeded across that 90-mile thirst-ridden stretch of desert which earned the name La Jornada del Muerto, "The Dead Man's Route" or "The Journey of Death." The name seems to have come from a German trader, Bernard Gruber, whose body was found in the Jornada about 1670. The place was called *El Aleman*, "The German." To this day, at that spot a railroad siding on the Santa Fe Railroad is called Aleman. Hallenbeck estimated that if all the graves in the ninety miles of the Jornada del Muerto were evenly distributed along the route they would mark the road at 500-foot intervals.

The Camino Real got back to the Rio Grande Valley at Paraje de Fray Cristóbal, near a rock formation which resembled the face of a member of the Oñate expedition named Fray Juan Cristóbal. This old campsite was eventually inundated by Elephant Butte Lake.

At Paraje de Fray Cristóbal, the Camino Real divided for the trip to Albuquerque with a route up each side of the river. At Albuquerque the routes rejoined, went along the east side of the valley as far as Santo Domingo, and then took a northeasterly course to Santa Fe. Old US 85 was indicated on many maps as the Camino Real, but the highway followed the old Spanish road only where it was within the river valley.

Most of today's northbound motorists enter New Mexico at Anthony on I-10, pick up the beginning of I-25 at Las Cruces, and speed on until they reach the Santa Fe exit—a trip which can be driven comfortably in eight hours or so. This route approximates the old Spanish road but it misses the permeating flavor of this historic land.

Visitors who stop along the way at villages which have been bypassed by the freeway will find many which look little different than they did during Spanish colonial days. Thick-walled adobe buildings, some a century or more old, offer welcome respite from summer heat. Laboriously built eighteenth-century mission churches testify to the religious zeal which fired those early missionaries to risk their lives. Or one can stop in the Jornada del Muerto and watch distant mountains shimmering in the heat which boils up from the desert floor and readily imagine how it would be if he were wearing leather pants to ward off spiky plants, a heavy metal helmet, and a thick breastplate—fearful that an Apache might appear from behind the nearest clump of cactus.

Anthony (Exit 160)

Anthony, the southern gateway to New Mexico on I-10, is a town of divided loyalties; it straddles the Texas-New Mexico border. A sign boasts: "The Best Town in 2 States." The town began in 1881 as a Santa Fe Railroad station on the Texas side of the border. The station was called La Tuna, after the Spanish name for the fruit of the prickly pear which was prevalent in the area.

A town grew around the station extending on both sides of the border. A Spanish-American lady named Sabrina had a chapel dedicated to San Antonio on the New Mexico side of the line. When it came time to name the town, Sabrina flatly rejected the name La Tuna and insisted that her patron saint be honored. She had her way.

During the days of the Butterfield Overland Mail, a stage stop, known as the Cottonwoods Station, was located on the Cottonwoods Ranch a little more than a hundred yards northeast of the railroad station at La Tuna.

Berino (Exit 160, west to NM 478)

Berino is a small community identified with the settlement which grew up around the Butterfield Overland Mail station, located on the Cottonwoods Ranch northeast of Anthony. It was cited on maps in 1851 as "Los Alamos" and later translated to Cottonwoods.

Vado (Exit 155, west on NM 227 to NM 478)

Vado has had a variety of names. It was first called Herron, after the first Anglo settlers. It was later changed to Earlham, for the town in Ohio or Illinois from which the Herrons came. Later still, a postmaster called it Center Valley. Vado, meaning "ford," is probably commemorative of an early river crossing at this point.

—— Historical Sidebar ———————————————————

Fort Fillmore

At a site between present-day Vado and Mesquite, Fort Fillmore was established September 23, 1851, by Col. E. V. Sumner, commander of the Military Department of the Territory of New Mexico.

The British exhibited a lively interest in the American West. This picture of Fort Fillmore was published in London in 1854. —London Illustrated News, 1854

The ostensible mission of the post was to protect travelers from Indian attack; however, Colonel Sumner's real purpose was to move troops away from the temptations of Santa Fe. He thought the site on the east bank of the Rio Grande was far enough from the fleshpots of El Paso, to the south across the river in Mexico, and the vineyards of the Mesilla Valley to isolate the soldiers from both women and wine. Additionally, the new post was to be located where soldiers could raise vegetables and forage and thus reduce their cost to the government.

After an inspection tour of the western forts in 1853, Inspector General Joseph K. F. Mansfield judged the program to cultivate "kitchen gardens" a failure; it was in debt more than $14,000: "There are probably many officers and soldiers too who have never had the least practice at planting not even an ordinary garden, and certainly the subject at the Military Academy has never been introduced as one of the essentials of an officer in defence of his country."

Trouble came from within as the Civil War approached. The post sutler was a Southern sympathizer; he openly invited the troops to join the Rebel cause. When the Civil War broke out, many did. Citizens in and around the nearby town of Mesilla, mostly Texans, held a convention in March, 1861, and announced themselves as the Arizona Territory and petitioned for admission to the Confederacy.

On July 23, 1861, Capt. John Robert Baylor arrived at Mesilla with a Confederate force of 258 Texas cavalrymen. On July 25, troops from Fort Fillmore marched on Mesilla and their commander demanded the surrender of the Confederates. During a brief encounter, three Union soldiers were killed and six wounded. The Union force retreated to Fort Fillmore with the undisciplined soldiers attempting to drink up the fort's supply of liquor rather than risk having it captured. The commander surrendered his hangover-plagued force of some 700 the following afternoon.

U.S. troops returned to Fort Fillmore after the Confederates left the Mesilla area; however, the installation was permanently abandoned in October, 1862.

Today, not a trace of Fort Fillmore is visible. There is not even a historical marker to commemorate the ill-fated post.

Mesquite (Exit 151, west on NM 228 to NM 478)

Mesquite was established and named by executives of the Santa Fe Railroad after the desert brush which grew profusely along the tracks. This persistent desert shrub had long been a feature of the landscape. In 1847 a military detachment left El Paso on an expedition against the Apaches. Before leaving the saloons of El Paso, where "Pass Whiskey" was plentiful, they armed themselves with a supply. By the second day out, a portion of the party were so befuddled that they got lost in the jungles of mesquite which grew in the area. When they finally found their way back to the main body of troops, their commander ordered them to make camp, confiscated the rest of their whiskey, and gave them the remainder of the day to sober up.

—— Historical Sidebar ——————————

Bishop's Cap Cave

To the east of Mesquite in the southern extremity of the Organ Mountains, Pyramid Peak or Bishop's Cap Mountain looms up. On the eastern slope, a cave was found which contained a thick bed of sediments. This cave was discovered by Roscoe P. Conkling and excavated in 1929 by the Natural History Museum of Los Angeles County. Conkling told of his find:

In a cave on the eastern flank of this peak, which was filled with sediments to a depth of more than fifty-two feet, fossil remains of the sloth, cave bear, horse, camel, bison, dire wolf, and other mammalian forms of the Pleistocene were discovered, some of which were in close juxtaposition with the skeletal fragments of man, all bearing valuable testimony to the antiquity of man in America.

This find shook the archaeological world. It placed man in New Mexico from 10,000 to 50,000 years ago, coexistent with Ice Age animals.

The dire wolf, also called the great wolf, was a large, ferocious animal with paws larger than a man's hand and massive teeth capable of crushing big bones. All of the bones in the cave except those of the dire wolf had been cracked, presumably to get at the marrow. One human skull fragment had the appearance of having been gnawed.

A ghost story came to light which indicated that Conkling was not the first to find the cave. During the 1880s, two Hispanic-American men from Mesilla were prospecting in the area and using the cave as shelter. Not having any luck at prospecting, they delved into the cave, remembering stories of buried treasure. After unearthing bones and teeth, they were certain they had found the remains of mules which had carried Spanish gold. That night they were sitting in the cave when a black-clad figure entered carrying a candle. The apparition greeted them in Spanish, "*Buenos noches*," and then disappeared. The following morning, the erstwhile treasure-hunters sacked up the bones and headed for home. They consulted a priest regarding the bones, and he advised burying them in the cemetery, which they did.

Les Davis, an archaeologist who has made a study of Bishop's Cap Cave, paints an interesting scenario: Some day far, far in the future, says Davis, an archaeologist is going to be excavating a Catholic cemetery in Mesilla, New Mexico. Along with the remains of nineteenth-century citizens, he is going to find one grave containing Pleistocene bones and thus have material for a scientific paper which can speculate that Ice-Age mammals and man must have survived into the nineteenth century.

To date, Bishop's Cap Cave has not been designated as a historic site. It is located within the Fort Bliss military reservation in an area which is sometimes used as an artillery range. The bones which were unearthed can be viewed in the Natural History Museum of Los Angeles County.

Brazito Battlefield

The site of the only battle of the Mexican War to take place on New Mexican soil is commemorated by a historical marker in the tiny community of Brazito three miles north of Mesquite on NM 478. In December, 1846, Col. Alexander W. Doniphan was marching south along the Rio Grande with about 800 men of the First Regiment of Missouri Volunteers. According to George F. Ruxton, a British traveler who visited Doniphan's camp, it was a rag-tag outfit, ill-prepared to meet an enemy:

> From appearances no one would have imagined this to be a military encampment. The tents were in a line, but there all uniformity ceased. The men, unwashed and unshaven, were ragged and dirty, without uniforms, and dressed as, and how, they pleased. They wandered about, listless and sickly-look-ing, or were sitting in groups playing at cards, and swearing and cursing, even at the officers if they interfered to stop it (as I witnessed).

In his assessment of American character, Ruxton had obviously forgotten lessons learned by the British during the American Revolution. He commented:

Doniphan's Missouri Volunteers were criticized by a British observer as being unsoldierly, but they won battles. —Hughes, 1850

> The American can never be made a soldier; his constitution
> will not bear the restraint of discipline, neither will his very
> mistaken notions of liberty allow him to subject himself to its
> necessary control.

Doniphan's unit was put to the test on December 25, 1846. The day dawned bright and sunny. Some of the soldiers celebrated Christmas by firing their guns and singing "Yankee Doodle" and "Hail Columbia." A soldier noted in his diary: "After a lively breakfast, in fine glee the troops set off for El Paso."

After about eighteen miles, Colonel Doniphan ordered the unit to pitch camp at Brazito on the east bank of the Rio Grande, a place bordered on the east and southeast by a mesquite and willow chaparral. The men scattered to find wood for cooking fires and grass for their animals. To the rear, wagons and stragglers were scattered along the road for miles.

Colonel Doniphan sat down to play three-trick loo with several of his officers and men to determine who would get a fine Mexican horse which had been captured by the advance guard the day before. One of the advance guard galloped up and interrupted the game by telling Doniphan that the enemy was approaching only a short distance away. The colonel laid his hand aside.

"Boys, I held an invincible hand, but I'll be damned if I don't have to play it out in steel now."

Colonel Doniphan had the bugler sound assembly. The men dropped their loads of wood and buckets of water and fell in under the nearest flags. Cartridges were distributed and weapons were loaded. By this time the banners of the Mexican force were plainly visible; sun glinted from their lances and sabers. It was General Antonio Ponce de León with more than 500 regulars reinforced by militia from the El Paso district. They were dividing into two columns to attack the flanks of Doniphan's forces.

Colonel Doniphan spoke to his men briefly: first, words of encouragement, then he reminded them of the disgraceful retreat of the Missouri volunteers during the Florida Indian war nine years before. "Remember Okechobee!"

Shortly a Mexican lieutenant bearing a black flag emblazoned with a skull and crossbones dashed to within sixty yards of the American lines. Colonel Doniphan sent an interpreter forward and received a demand to surrender. In his report of the battle, Colonel Doniphan wrote: "The reply was more abrupt than decorous--to charge and be d---d."

The Mexican dragoons were resplendent in blue pantaloons, green coats trimmed in scarlet, and tall caps plated in front with brass. Plumes of horsehair or buffaloes' tails danced on their caps.

The battle occupied about thirty minutes. The Mexicans' losses were 43 killed and about 150 wounded, including General Ponce de León. The Americans had seven wounded, none killed.

When General Ponce de León reached El Paso after the battle, he was arrested for cowardice and taken to Chihuahua. There he was shown fortifications which had been erected to defend against the invading Americans. He was reported to have responded: "Yes, these are all right; but those Americans will roll over them like hogs; they do not fight as we do."

The general's assay was prophetic. Doniphan's Missouri Volunteers defeated the Mexican forces, 2,000 according to Mexican accounts. Ruxton, the skeptical British military critic, admitted they were "as full of fight as game cocks."

I-25
New Mexico State University
—Santa Fe

New Mexico State University (Exit 1)

University Park, off I-25, is a village which grew up around New Mexico State University. The community was called State College until 1960, when New Mexico State College became a university. The university is located in the V formed by the intersection of I-10 and I-25 as I-25 originates and heads north.

In July, 1887, Hiram Hadley, a Quaker educator from the East arrived in Las Cruces. While dabbling in real estate, he was instrumental in founding Las Cruces College with sixty-four students. In spite of the name, instruction was not even at a high-school level. Some students had to struggle to comprehend *McGuffey's Readers*.

In 1888, the New Mexico Territorial legislature authorized the creation of a land-grant agricultural college "in or near Las Cruces." The movement to acquire the school was backed by local businessmen and politicians, even though some thought it would be better if Las Cruces tried for an insane asylum or a mining school instead.

Politicians pointed out that $50,000 would come from the Territorial government for school construction. Additionally, the Federal government would kick in $15,000 a year. Such a college would be worth "a million dollars" to the Mesilla Valley, they said. Hiram Hadley and the local newspaper editor labored to educate the citizenry through a series of articles: "The What and Why of Agricultural Experiment Stations."

Las Cruces businessmen subscribed a land-grant fund and a site was acquired outside of Las Cruces near a village called Mesilla Park. The "Agricultural College" was scheduled to open January 21, 1890, before construction started on its buildings. Buildings were leased from Las Cruces College for the first year at $25 a month, and the Board of Regents had to spend $119 for desks, tables, and chairs.

"An examination in arithmetic, English grammar, and United States History, as well as other portions of the 'three Rs'" would be required for entrance. The admission fee was $5. Thirty-five students enrolled that first semester. Seventeen classified as "college level"; one came from outside New Mexico. Next semester, the student body consisted of twelve college-level students and forty in the "preparatory department." One enrollee arrived three weeks late from faraway Pennsylvania.

The first bulding on the campus of New Mexico's agricultural college, now known as New Mexico State University, was named Hadley Hall to honor the founder of the school.
—Frost, 1894

During the 1890-1891 year the institution was officially dubbed the New Mexico College of Agriculture and Mechanic Arts and was thus called until November, 1960, when it became New Mexico State University.

Las Cruces was a frontier town with its share of saloons, gambling dens, and brothels. Ardent Quaker Hiram Hadley noted transgressions by students in a record book. They went from bad to worse: "disobedience," "drinking," "disrespectful conduct," "ball bouncing," "smoking in the horse sheds," "assaulting a Chinese laundryman and throwing stones against his door," "being in a saloon."

The school struggled for survival during its first four years as Hadley tried to reach beyond mere agricultural perspectives. He gave the library a goal of 20,000 volumes for "communion with the greatest minds of all past ages."

The burgeoning school persevered and prospered. It became a liberal arts institution and attained university status in 1960. In addition to claiming to have the world's largest campus, 6,250 acres, it boasts one of three full-time planetary observatories in the nation.

Ranking among the top one hundred universities in Federal research and development programs, the university specializes in missile, space, and weaponry research as well as utilization of solar energy.

One of its agricultural programs is unique. Thirty of the two hundred known varieties of capsicum (chile) peppers are cultivated and studied. New hybrids are being developed in order to create milder chiles which will be more acceptable to Eastern palates.

Las Cruces (Exits 3 & 6)

As Mexican colonists came north to settle in the rich Mesilla Valley during the 1840s, Doña Ana became crowded. All of the available irrigated land close to the settlement was occupied. Farmers attempting to work fields further away ran into problems getting back and forth over faint, boggy burro trails that connected clearings among the mesquite and tornillo trees. Lurking Apaches were an ever-present threat. As American soldiers made their headquarters in Doña Ana in 1846, the situation became even more difficult. The only solution was to start a new settlement farther south.

Eight miles south on the Camino Real there was a stretch which had such a bad reputation that nobody would think of stopping. In

1787 travelers found the bodies of several oxcart caravan drivers and erected crosses to their memory. In 1830 the Apaches massacred a party of thirty travelers from Taos and more crosses were added to commemorate the tragedy. In 1846 Susan Magoffin, who had traveled from Missouri with her husband over the Santa Fe Trail and the Camino Real, took note of the area in her diary:

> Yesterday we passed over the spot where a few years since a party of Apaches attacked Gen. Armijo as he returned from the Pass with a party of troops, and killed some fourteen of his men, the graves of whom, marked by a rude cross, are now seen.

This haunted place, sprinkled with sun-bleached crests of death, known simply as *La Placita de las Cruces* (the place of the crosses), was selected by the justice of the peace in Doña Ana as the site for the new village.

The local United States military detachment had the only surveying equipment around. Lt. Delos Bennet Sackett and five men were detailed to lay out the townsite. A rawhide rope was the nearest thing they had to a surveyor's chain. The rawhide stretched and shrunk as it was alternately dragged through irrigation ditches and dried in the desert sun. Consequently, some of the streets were crooked and some of the blocks were not square, but the settlers were not choosy.

Main Street in Las Cruces during the 1890s.
—Courtesy El Paso Public Library

When the measuring was completed, the residents gathered under a grove of cottonwoods (where the Armory now stands) to draw names from a hat to determine which lots they would get. The town of Las Cruces was born. The original townsite centers on Mesquite Street in the eastern portion of town.

The new property owners molded adobe blocks, cut cottonwoods for vigas to support the flat mud roofs, and cleared nearby fields to plant corn, pumpkins, chiles, and beans. A crude adobe chapel was built. Father Manuel Chávez was appointed the first priest, and the more substantial St. Genevieve Church was completed in 1879. (It was demolished in 1977.) Bells for the church were cast locally in a placita in back of a house. Devout parishioners filed past the cauldron of molten metal to throw in jewelry and money to sweeten the voices of their bells.

Las Cruces prospered. In 1852 it became the county seat of Doña Ana County. With the coming of the railroad through town, Las Cruces won out over nearby Mesilla, and building boomed. Houses in both the territorial and Victorian styles sprouted among the old adobes. Some of those century-old houses have been preserved.

Most noteworthy is the Amador (lover) Hotel, built in the 1850s on the corner of Water and Amador streets. The Amador was built by Martín Amador, a Santa Fe Trail stage driver. It was furnished with massive walnut furniture brought from the East by oxcart. The hotel became a rendezvous for officers and men from Fort Selden and Fort Fillmore. Twenty-three girls vied for their patronage. The girls' names were displayed over the doors to their rooms: La Luz, María Esperanza, Natalia, Dorotea, Muñeca. The old Amador Hotel now serves as a museum and a bank.

Doña Ana (Exit 9)

Doña Ana's name goes back to the seventeenth century when a good and charitable woman named Doña Ana Robledo lived in the area. The name is mentioned in an account by Governor Otermín dated 1682. He stayed at Doña Ana on February 4 during his southward flight from the Pueblo Revolt. Then there was another Doña Ana. About a decade later it was reported that the Apaches had become troublesome in the area of Los Organos (the Organ Mountains).They killed three Spaniards and raided a sheep ranch belonging to Doña Ana María Niña de Cordova.

Even if the Apaches ran off all the Doña Anas, the name stuck. In June, 1839, Don José María Costales petitioned for a land grant for 116 colonists at a spot on the east bank of the Rio Grande known as El Ancon de Doña Ana (Doña Ana bend). The grant was approved in July, 1840. Don José did not get his colony of settlers on the ground until July, 1843, when they began digging irrigation ditches and building a church. It was January, 1846, before the Prefect of El Paso got around to formally issuing titles to the settlers. However, the settlers had been busy with their crops.

Tradition tells that when the first official visitor from the Mexican government came he found only four people. The rest were so poor and ragged they were ashamed to come out of their crude adobe homes.

Capt. John T. Hughes, who was with Doniphan's expedition which had just traversed the Jornada del Muerto, noted in his diary for December 23, 1846, "Marched 12 miles—passed through Doñana—obtained fruit & other luxuries." Later he wrote about it:

> Here the soldiers found plenty of grain and other forage for their animals, running streams of water, and abundance of dried fruit, corn-meal, and sheep and cattle. These they purchased; therefore they soon forgot the sufferings and privations which they had experienced on the desert. Here they feasted and reposed.

This illustration of a Texas Ranger helps explain why the New Mexicans were so deathly afraid of the Texans that they would abandon their homes and move to avoid them. Harper's Weekly *described them as "half savages, each of whom is mounted upon a mustang horse. Each is armed with a pair of Colt's navy revolvers, a rifle, a tomahawk, a Texan bowie-knife, and a lasso."*
—Harper's Weekly, 1861

Col. Alexander W. Doniphan spent two days at Doña Ana, resting and buying supplies, before continuing on into Mexico. He also donated a cannon to the village for use as protection against the Apaches.

On February 10, 1847, a Santa Fe trader named Samuel Magoffin passed through Doña Ana, along with his nineteen-year-old wife Susan who had accompanied the trading expedition all the way from Missouri. Susan kept a diary. She noted that some of Magoffin's wagoners "got on a spree." They went into the village, drank too freely of the excellent but powerful wine for which the Mesilla Valley was already famous, and ran off with Doña Ana's cannon. Magoffin prevented an international incident by retrieving the cannon and rendering an apology to the Alcalde.

After the Mexican War, when the area became United States territory, many Texan land speculators came to the village. Sixty dissident Mexican families moved across the river to settle in Mesilla and other communities which were under Mexican jurisdiction. For a while Doña Ana was the county seat of Doña Ana County, but it lost out to Las Cruces in 1852.

Today, the majority of the Anglos are gone and Doña Ana is once more a small Hispanic-American farming community. The old church, Nuestra Señora de la Candelaria (Our Lady of Purification), is about the only visual reminder of the past, but the names of some of those original fourteen families live on in the roster of residents.

Fort Selden State Monument (Exit 19)

Fort Selden was established in 1865 for the purpose of protecting settlers in the Mesilla Valley and travelers on the Camino Real from Apaches.

The fort was built on the Rio Grande across the river from Mount Robledo. During Spanish days there had been a trading post and a presidio at the base of the mountain. The U.S. Army used the mountain to establish a heliograph station by which the troops, using mirrors, could send messages to Fort Bliss, fifty miles to the south, and Fort McRae, some fifty miles to the north. The Apaches used the mountain as an observation post. From it they could look down into the fort and pick a fortuitous time for deviltry.

From a military standpoint, Fort Selden was not a rousing success. Neither was it popular with the wives of officers who were stationed there. Lydia Spencer Lane told of their experiences in her book *I Married a Soldier*:

Ruins of Fort Selden
—Photo by the authors

Our station was a quiet, unattractive place garrisoned by one company of colored infantry and one of white cavalry. The commanding officer's quarters were not nearly finished when we arrived. Just four rooms were ready but larger and better than a tent.... Our porch was made of cottonwood poles covered with brush which formed a fine sanctuary for snakes, scorpions, and centipedes, but they did not annoy us much.

Mrs. Lane used packing boxes for furniture. She kept cows and chickens to supplement government supplies which the fort received from Fort Union, 350 miles to the north. Coyotes killed her chickens. It was unsafe to go more than a mile from the fort. When she did go out she carried a revolver and rode a horse which she believed could outrun any Indian pony. Lydia Spencer Lane shed no tears when Colonel Lane's health made it necessary for them to leave Fort Selden.

Capt. Arthur MacArthur served at Fort Selden in 1884. It was there that his son, Douglas A. MacArthur, learned to ride and shoot before he learned to read or write.

The need for Fort Selden ended when the Santa Fe Railroad extended southward to connect with the Southern Pacific. The post

45

was abandoned and its troops consolidated with those at Fort Bliss, Texas. However, during the Geronimo raids, it was later re-garrisoned by Gen. Nelson A. Miles to mount patrols on the Mexican border. After Geronimo's surrender, it was abandoned for good in 1890.

A contract was awarded to remove the bodies from the fort cemetery for reinterment at Fort Bliss. In exchange for his labor, the contractor received the wooden portions of the buildings. Only the adobe walls were left standing in the hot desert sun to become a historic ruin.

The old fort fell prey to vandals because of a legend that once during an Indian raid the paymaster of the fort buried a payroll of $80,000 in gold and was subsequently killed in the raid. Over the years, clandestine treasure-hunters have literally pock-marked the ruin with holes, particularly in fireplaces. This weakened many walls and caused them to topple.

In 1972 New Mexico took over Fort Selden as a state monument and opened it to the public.

Radium Springs (Exit 19)

Radium Springs is located on NM 185 west of I-25 across the Rio Grande from Fort Selden. During the time when the military post was active, the free-flowing mineral hot springs were frequently visited by soldiers from Fort Selden and became known as Fort Selden Springs.

A farmer moved into the area and called in a driller to sink a water well.

"What'll you have?" the driller asked. "Hot or cold?"

It developed that cold water cost more than hot. Hot water was available between twenty and forty feet. Clear, cold water could be brought in at eighty feet.

Chemical analysis of the water from the hot spring reported 2.57 millimicrocuries per liter of radium activity, enough to satisfy the Post Office Department so that it permitted use of the word *radium* in the town's name, a privilege which has not been accorded to any other community in the nation. The spring ceased to flow, but wells tapped the geothermal, mineral-laden hot water.

During the 1920s, the Radium Springs Resort Hotel was built with bathhouses connected to the wells. There were claims that the water was beneficial for sufferers of arthritis, paralysis, stomach troubles, high blood pressure, eczema, rheumatism, diabetes, and

46

Radium Springs during its heyday as a health resort.

nerve afflictions—claims which were stoutly debated by medical science. Nevertheless, the resort attracted a substantial clientele.

After almost a half-century, the weekend sanitorium fell upon hard times. Recently it has served variously as a resort, a women's prison, and an art center.

Rincon (Exit 35)

Rincon is just off I-25 in a canyon. Rincon (corner) took its life from the railroad. Here, at the southern end of the Jornada del Muerto, the Santa Fe Railroad divided with one branch proceeding south to El Paso and the other going west to Deming. For thirty years, Rincon was a principal trading and business center for railroad shipping. Cattlemen drove their cattle to Rincon to be shipped to market. Today all that remains are a few old buildings surrounded by memories.

Hatch (Exit 41)

With unabashed immodesty, Hatch bills itself as the "Chile Capital of the World." Annually, on the Saturday and Sunday preceding Labor Day, the community stages a Chile Festival to celebrate its fame as a center for production of a large percentage of the nation's red and green chile peppers. The festival is held at the municipal airport. The feature event is a "chile cook-off" during which contestants from far and near vie to produce the hottest and/or the tastiest chile concoctions. Other events include a senior citizens' race, fiddling, watermelon eating, car-stuffing contests, and a *ristra* arrangement competition.

Ristras are strings of chiles which are hung up to dry preparatory for use in cooking. Throughout New Mexico during the harvest season, the entire sides of houses are often covered with flaming red strings of chiles. As city-folk began to prize ristras for decorative use, a lively competition developed in designing ristras, wreaths, and other arrangements from chiles for sale in shops and galleries throughout the Southwest.

It should be noted that in New Mexico chile is "chile," *not* "chili." In 1988, the New Mexico State Legislature emphasized this point by passing a tongue-in-cheek memorial which threatens to deport to Texas any New Mexican caught using the word "chili."

Hatch originated in the 1890s as Hatch's Station, a stop on the Santa Fe Railroad named for Gen. Edward Hatch, commander of nearby Fort Thorn.

─────── **Historical Sidebar** ───────────────────────────

Fort Thorn

Fort Thorn was established in 1853 a few miles northwest of the site of present-day Hatch on the edge of a swamp along the Rio Grande. It was supposed to protect the Camino Real against Apaches and outlaws, but the soldiers spent most of their time on sick call as each succeeding year saw more sickness and fever.

James Augustus Bennett, a 23-year-old private from New York State, was stationed at Fort Thorn. He had joined the army because he thought it might get him to California, but after five years of campaigning he was a professional soldier. Private Bennett's entry in his diary for December 28, 1855, gives an idea of conditions at Fort Thorn:

> Dec. 28—80 men of us under command of Captain Richard S. Ewell left fort: last night camped in the mountains, having traveled 30 miles. In fording the Rio Grande, we lost 3 horses and 2 mules by drowning. We lost 2 boxes of ammunition and some provisions also. Camped beside a small salty lake on a plain. Used some ice for cooking. It is very cold and there is little wood here.

Fort Thorn as it appeared during William W.H. Davis's tour of New Mexico during the 1850s. —Davis, 1857

Fort Thorn was abandoned in 1859, but both the Confederates and Union troops occupied it briefly during the Civil War. No trace of the fort remains today.

Historical Excursion

NM 187
Salem—Caballo Lake State Park

From Hatch, a detour to the north on NM 187 to rejoin I-25 at Caballo Dam will take one through a succession of small farming communities—Salem, Garfield, Derry, and Arrey—and past numerous fields of produce: chiles, cotton, lettuce, onions, and alfalfa.

Caballo Lake State Park

This state park is a recreation area which was developed after the construction of Caballo Dam in 1937-38. Caballo Dam is a secondary storage reservoir on the Rio Grande eleven miles south of Elephant Butte Lake. It was built to re-impound water released from Elephant Butte. An elaborate system of flumes, siphons, and several hundred miles of main canals supplement the main dams and provide irrigation for the Rincon Valley, Mesilla Valley, and the El Paso Valley to the south of New Mexico.

Las Palomas (Exit 71)

One look tells the observer that Las Palomas has seen better days, but her days of glory were exciting times. Nearby ruins of an Indian pueblo testify to prehistoric dwellers. Indians, Spanish colonists, and miners stopped here to soak in hot water that bubbled from springs. The area took its name from the thousands of doves that lived in the cottonwoods along the river and around the springs.

The settlement was founded by the García and Tafoya families who brought numerous peóns with them, only to have to comply with a law releasing indentured workers from their obligation. Las Palomas became the gateway for east-west traffic passing through a gap in the Caballo Mountains.

There was a plaza in the center of town, surrounded by houses. Here early settlers gathered their livestock for protection during Indian raids. Legend has it that Indians came out of the Caballo Mountains with gold nuggets to trade for provisions and fire water. This attracted gold-seekers who used the springs for placer mining, but, when the Pueblo Revolt of 1680 erupted, the fleeing residents destroyed not only the mines but the springs to rob the Indians of water and impede their pursuit.

A story of buried treasure has brought many to the area. During the first half of the seventeenth century when there was an influx of Spanish settlers into New Mexico, one Pedro Navárez, a renegade Spaniard, joined a murderous band of Indians. He was captured in 1649 and taken to Mexico City where he was tried and condemned to death. He turned to religion for consolation and confessed his sins.

Navárez told of a deep cave containing arms, crockery, clothing and harness, and many bars of silver. His directions pointed to the springs near Las Palomas: "In the gap where the sun rises look for the spring; it is very large."

Vicente Vásques, a sacristan to the priest who heard the confession, made copies, presumably hoping to share in discovery of the loot. Copies of this document have been passed down from generation to generation. To date, there has been no report of the treasure having been found. Some who looked reported seeing mysterious lights in the mountains, thought to have been campfires of watchful Indians who guarded the *tesoro de los muertos*, the "treasure of the dead."

Williamsburg (Exit 75)

In 1949 three residential areas adjacent to Hot Springs (now Truth or Consequences) were incorporated into the village of Williamsburg and named after the first mayor, Dr. Thomas B. Williams. One week after Hot Springs voted to change its name to Truth or Consequences, the residents of Williamsburg voted to change the name of their community to Hot Springs. Apparently the discarded name did not bring about the desired results. In 1959 the residents changed the name back to Williamsburg by a vote of 57 to 18.

Truth or Consequences (Exits 75 & 76)

The area around Truth or Consequences was known for its hot springs long before the arrival of Europeans. According to legend, the Indians treated it as neutral ground. They laid aside tribal differences when they came to soak their wounds in the magic waters which flowed from the earth. After the establishment of Fort McRae in 1863, U.S. soldiers came to bask in the curative waters and plaster their aching muscles and wounds with the thick white mud.

In 1884 Fort McRae was abandoned and Sierra County was established. The county commissioners appropriated $400 to build a shelter over a spring which was known as Geronimo Spring. Water bubbled up from sand into a rock-lined pool, overflowed, and formed a slough on its way to the Rio Grande. At that time, the river ran down what is now Main Street as far as the Post Office before veering southwest. In 1907 a cloudburst in the north part of town deposited enough debris to change the river to its present course.

By 1895 the John Cross Cattle Company had acquired the land west of what is now Broadway and built a room over a spring for the benefit of their cowboys. The community was known as Palomas Hot Springs or Palomas Springs, after the thousands of doves that lived in the cottonwoods along the river.

By the time Elephant Butte Dam was completed in 1916, the community had adopted the name Hot Springs and was ready to capitalize upon both the mineral baths and the nearby recreational facility provided by Elephant Butte Lake. In the 1930s, with the increase in automobile travel, Hot Springs become a small resort city.

In 1950 Ralph Edwards, entrepreneur of the popular radio program "Truth or Consequences," put out a call for a town that would agree to officially change its name to Truth or Consequences. In return, the production crew would go to that community to stage a live coast-to-coast broadcast. The New Mexico tourist bureau relayed the news to Burton Roach—local cattleman, state senator, and manager of the Hot Springs Chamber of Commerce:

"Here's a chance to get your mineral baths advertised all over the United States every Saturday night for free."

Roach viewed the opportunity as a bonanza. After all, the community was indistinguishable from the many other towns named Hot Springs. He organized local bathhouse owners and business people to back a city election. The proposition passed, but not without opposition. Some thought the name-change plain foolish; others thought it made cupidity and veneration of show-business personalities too visible. However, a series of elections challenging the change failed. Hot Springs became Truth or Consequences.

True to his word, Ralph Edwards brought his show to town on April 1, 1950, establishing the precedent for an annual Fiesta attended by Ralph Edwards and an assortment of show-business personalities. On the Saturday afternoon of the first Fiesta, the two-mile parade route was lined by 10,000 people. Ralph Edwards commemorated the occasion by breaking a bottle of mineral water over the head of Senator Burton Roach.

If Ralph Edwards visualized his show as being advertised by frequent use of "Truth or Consequences" in newspaper headlines, the exercise was somewhat abortive. Reference to Truth or Consequences is customarily abbreviated to "T or C." Nevertheless, the community is a popular haven for wintering senior citizens and fishermen, and the Ralph Edwards Fiesta in early May continues to highlight the community calendar.

Ralph Edwards continues to bring entertainment personalities to the Truth or Consequences Fiesta: Rusty Burrell, bailiff of "The People's Court"; Gene Bell, tap dancer; Ralph Edwards; Bob Hilton, former emcee of the "Truth or Consequences" television show.
—Courtesy Geronimo Springs Museum

Fort McRae

In 1863 Fort McRae was established about ten miles east of present-day Truth or Consequences to provide protection for travelers over the Camino Real through the Jornada del Muerto. Capt. Albert Pfeiffer was recovering from arrow wounds he had received during a recent encounter with Apaches. Familiar with the hot springs to the west, he believed the waters would have a salubrious effect upon his wounds.

On the morning of June 20, 1863, Captain Pfeiffer, his wife, two servant girls, and a small escort of volunteer soldiers rode to the hot springs. While Pfeiffer was bathing, a band of Apaches drove off the escort, killing two of the soldiers. They killed the women, then turned their bows on Pfeiffer. He swam away with arrows bristling from his body. After the Apaches left, Pfeiffer managed to make it back to Fort McRae by crawling and walking the ten miles.

The Apaches were never caught, but Pfeiffer recovered and lived to establish a reputation as one of the most famous Indian fighters of his day.

Fort McRae was officially abandoned in 1876, but it was kept up for the use of travelers for several years. The ruins of old Fort McRae are now at the bottom of Elephant Butte Lake.

—————————————————————————————

Historical Excursion

NM 51
Elephant Butte– Engle

Elephant Butte Lake State Park (Exit 75)

A movement to build a dam on the Rio Grande started in 1896 when private promoters organized the Rio Grande Dam and Irrigation Company and were granted right of way for a dam and irrigation system on public property. Preliminary construction was started in November, but problems arose. Land owners in the El Paso area took a dim view of the project; they would lose water to upstream irrigation. Mexico, on the south bank, also depended upon the river for irrigation water. The United States Supreme Court intervened on the grounds that the Rio Grande was a navigable stream and could not be blocked.

While floods were washing away the initial breastworks which had been put in place, the Federal Government blocked private enterprise and launched a similar scheme under the auspices of the Reclamation Service. Preliminary surveys started in 1903; an agreement with Mexico to deliver water was signed May 21, 1906; the project was officially authorized March 4, 1907. Actual construction did not begin until 1911. The dam was completed on May 13, 1916.

The dam was 306 feet high, 1,674 feet long, 16 feet wide at the top, and 205 feet wide at the bottom. The resulting lake, covering about 40,000 acres, filled a canyon on the Rio Grande to an average depth of 66 feet. It stretched forty-five miles upstream and was three miles across at its widest point. The shoreline was some two hundred miles long, and the lake had a capacity of 2.2 million acre feet of water. At the time of its completion, the dam was the largest structure which had been constructed in the United States to impound water.

The reservoir was named Elephant Butte Lake because of a hill in the center which resembled an elephant. In addition to providing for irrigation and flood control, the lake became a boon to water-starved New Mexicans as a recreational facility.

Elephant Butte Lake State Park was completed in 1965 to become one of the largest and most popular state parks in New Mexico. It combines boating, fishing, and other water-based sports

Elephant Butte Dam and the butte which prompted its name.

with land activities such as camping, picnicking, and hiking. Concessionaire-operated marinas, boat-launching ramps, rental cabins, restaurants, and stores for boaters, campers, picnickers, vacationers, and fishermen are available. Fish are caught year-around including bass, catfish, pike, and crappie.

Engle

Engle, eleven miles down the road at the end of NM 51, is now a ghost town. Engle began in 1880 as a water-stop and shipping point on the Santa Fe Railroad between El Paso and Albuquerque. It was named for R. L. Engle, one of the railroad surveyors. However, the postmaster misspelled the name when he sent it in to the Post Office Department, and for six months Engle was "Angle" on the official list of post offices.

In 1880 Engle became a supply base for mining activities in the area and blossomed with general stores, hotels, and even an open-all-night restaurant. However, within three years the mining supply business dried up and Engle withered. By 1896 ranchers in the Lincoln area discovered they could drive cattle across the Jornada del Muerto during the wet season, and Engle revived by becoming a shipping center for cattle and a mecca for thirsty cowboys. This lasted until the turn of the century.

By 1901 cattlemen in the White, Capitán, and Sacramento mountains to the east were using closer and more convenient railheads; and the huge Bar Cross Ranch, which had its headquarters nearby, fell victim to drought and overgrazing. Once more, Engle struggled for existence.

Construction of the Elephant Butte Dam brought new life, and Engle advertised itself as "the best town in New Mexico by a dam site." But by 1920 it was all over. The government incorporated most of the desolate Jornada del Muerto into White Sands Missile Range, cutting off travel to the east, and Engle found itself the last stop on a dead-end road.

Today, only a few old buildings remain. Trains will pass on the Santa Fe Railroad, but they seldom stop. However, at Engle a visitor has one of the few remaining unobstructed views of the Jornada del Muerto. One can get a feeling for the loneliness that accompanied early travelers across this desolate stretch.

NM 52
Cuchillo—Chloride

Cuchillo (Exit 89)

Cuchillo, eight miles west of I-25 on NM 52, was founded about 1850 to serve pioneers and ranchers. Cuchillo is Spanish for "knife," but in New Mexico the term was extended to describe a geological outcropping or sharp ridge. During the gold rush days in this area, Cuchillo was the headquarters for freighting and stagecoaches. Horses were changed and passengers allowed to rest. Often the stages had military escorts when the Apaches were on the warpath.

The bar and general store, occupying a territorial style building, has been in continuous operation since it opened in 1850. It still has the original scales, cash register, and display cases.

Winston

The village about twenty-five miles up NM 52 from Cuchillo was formerly a mining community named Fairview. In June, 1881, a building boom was underway: twenty-five buildings were being constructed. By 1883 the population reached 500. Frank H. Winston had opened a mercantile establishment in 1882, and the name of the town was changed, perhaps as a testimonial to his faith in the community.

Winston has been called the "little town that refused to die." Even after the mines failed in the 1890s, the town managed to survive. Flurries of mining activity still occur from time to time, but ranching is the mainstay of the community.

Chloride

In 1879 a mule skinner named Henry Pye, who hauled freight to military posts, was traversing this area. He saw some ore he thought was silver where Chloride now stands. He took a sample, had it assayed, and found he had made a strike. As soon as he completed his contract with the government, he returned with a party of friends to develop claims.

Within six months, the area grew from a tent camp to a full-fledged town. The name Chloride was given because of the charac-

Rough and ready prevailed in early mining camps. The sign partially hidden under the trees reads: DINING TENT MEALS 50¢.

—Courtesy New Mexico Department of Development, No. 2510

ter of the ore. Pye did not live to enjoy his wealth; a roaming Apache killed him and several settlers. The town grew to 500 residents who patronized eight saloons, three general stores, three restaurants, two butcher shops, a newsstand, a lumberyard, an assay office, a boarding house, livery stable, post office, and the Pioneer Stage Line. Today, it is truly a ghost town.

Historical Excursion

NM 142
Placita—Monticello

Placita

NM 142, reached from Exit 89 off I-25, leads up the Alamosa River valley to Placita and Monticello. During the mid-1880s, farms and ranches were the mainstay of Placita (little plaza), located on

57

the Alamosa River. The community was subjected to many Apache raids before the Indians were brought under control. Today, some of the original adobe homes are still standing, along with the San Lorenzo Church.

Monticello

The ranching and farming community of Monticello, some three miles up the road from Placita, was settled in 1856. Originally called Cañada Alamosa, it was headquarters for the Southern Apache Agency before establishment of the Ojo Caliente Apache Reservation in 1874.

One faction of historical investigators maintains the town was named by John Sullivan, a freighter from Monticello, New York, who became the first postmaster in 1881. Another group says a prospector from Virginia wanted to commemorate Thomas Jefferson's estate in the Old Dominion. Perhaps both are right.

Because of frequent Indian raids, houses in the community were built around a square to form a fortress for protection. The square still stands. Mass is still celebrated in the San Ignacio Church. A gas pump and a sign proclaiming La Alamosa Bar is the last of the business establishments which once flourished in Monticello.

—— Historical Sidebar ——————————————

Ojo Caliente

This adobe military installation never reached the status of a fort. It was established by Executive Order, April 9, 1874, as headquarters for the Warm Springs Apache Reservation. In 1875-76 it was home for 1,500 to 2,000 Apaches, but by 1877 most of the Indians had returned to their old homelands. Some 450 who remained were transferred to the San Carlos Reservation in Arizona.

In the spring of 1877, Geronimo and his warriors escaped from the San Carlos Reservation and were camped at the hot springs three miles above the old Ojo Caliente post. San Carlos Agent John Clum took eighty of his Apache police to Ojo Caliente. He secreted sixty of them in the buildings and sent word to Geronimo that he wanted to talk to him about surrender. Geronimo appeared with a hundred warriors and saw Clum on the parade ground with only twenty men.

No. 176—Council between General Crook and Geronimo.

Capt Roberts   Geronimo   Nana   Lieut Maus   Three Interpreters   Capt Bourke   Gen Crook

During a council between Gen. George Crook and the Apache chiefs, Geronimo and Nana, an uneasy peace was fashioned. The participants broke off negotiations long enough to pose for a photograph.
—Courtesy El Paso Public Library

The defiant and boastful Geronimo succumbed when surrounded by the eighty Apache police who poured from the buildings, rifles at the ready. Geronimo was taken back to San Carlos in chains, captured for the first and only time.

Three weeks later, Geronimo escaped again. After that he surrendered only when he wanted to go back to the reservation for regular meals.

In the fall of 1879, the Apache leader Victorio and his band of Chiricahuas, accompanied by a few Mescaleros, attacked the garrison at Ojo Caliente, killing eight troopers of the 9th Cavalry and capturing forty-six horses. Units of the 9th Cavalry trailed Victorio into Mexico, but the wily Apache eluded his pursuers.

Ojo Caliente continued to be occupied until Victorio was killed in an ambush in the Tres Castillo Mountains of Mexico in 1880. In the spring of 1882, the post was abandoned.

Fort Craig (rest area: milepost 113)

Memory of Fort Craig and the Civil War battle at Valverde is kept green by historical markers at the Fort Craig Rest Area.

59

In 1851 Fort Conrad was built about thirty-five miles south of present-day Socorro. Its mission was to protect travelers on the Camino Real through the Jornada del Muerto. Poorly located, from the beginning it was a useless "hard-luck post." In 1854 it was abandoned and its troops moved to Fort Craig, nine miles south.

In 1863 troops from Fort Craig were defeated by Confederate forces during the Battle of Valverde, seven miles away. Union soldiers, under Col. Edward R. S. Canby, retreated back to Fort Craig as the Confederates advanced upon Albuquerque. Later, Canby led his troops in a siege upon the Confederate garrison at Albuquerque, forcing withdrawal of Confederate forces to Texas.

Also in 1863, the Navajos were raiding the settlements along the Rio Grande. On July 4, they attacked Fort Craig. Most of the troops were away on a scouting mission. The few guards remaining at the post had been engaging in an Independence Day celebration; however, they rallied sufficiently to drive off the Indians, who contented themselves with stealing sixteen hundred sheep that were grazing nearby.

An 1874 report described Fort Craig:

> The post was designed for two companies. The barracks are two in number, built of adobe, in the form of a hollow square, each enclosing a placita. Each barrack consists of two dormitories fifty-one by twenty by twelve and two-thirds feet, with a wide hall extending from the front of the buildings to the enclosed court in the rear. . . .
>
> In one corner of the guard room is a trap door opening upon a stairway that leads down to the cells where prisoners are kept in solitary confinement. The cells are six in number, three on each side of the passage ten inches wide, and four feet ten inches high, giving a cubic space of seventy-six feet. Eight augur holes, and chinks around the doors are the only means of admitting air and light into the cells. The whole amount of air and light admitted into the dungeons passes through two openings not to exceed four feet square. The cells are seldom occupied.

Capt. Jack Crawford, the renowned marksman and "Poet Scout," operated the post-trader's store at Fort Craig in addition to his duties of trailing marauding Apaches. His wife ran the officer's mess. Because of a shortage of help on the frontier, Crawford's daughter Eva was often required to remain out of school to wait tables. She was the victim of boorish behavior on the part of one Lieutenant Dwyer, the post bully; but Captain Jack's daughter was not one to be put upon.

"You eat exactly like a hog," she told ill-mannered Lieutenant Dwyer.

"I'll thank you to keep a civil tongue in that sassy face of yours. Remember you are speaking to an officer—"

"I'm glad you didn't say 'gentleman'!" snapped Eva as she left the dining room.

The next morning as she served breakfast, the officers made faces and pushed their bowls of oatmeal away. Eva gathered up the bowls and retreated to the kitchen, afraid her behavior the day before had insulted the officers. But she found a ten-dollar gold piece in each of the bowls.

They explained that it was a bonus for her having to endure Lieutenant Dwyer. Not long after, Dwyer was court-martialed.

Fort Craig was deactivated in 1885. Captain Jack remained as custodian for several years, warning vandals and thieves off the premises with shotgun pellets. In 1895, after spending fifteen years at Fort Craig, Eva got married and moved to El Paso, Texas.

The crumbling adobe ruins of Fort Craig have recently been donated to be rebuilt as a historic site.

—— **Historical Sidebar** ————————————————————

Valverde Battlefield

The first major battle of the Civil War on New Mexican soil took place at Valverde on February 21, 1862. It was a fight between friends. Edward R. S. Canby, commander of the Union forces, had been a close friend of Henry H. Sibley, commander of the Confederate forces, while they were cadets at West Point. When Sibley got married, Canby served as his best man.

On February 12, Sibley's invasion force of some 2,000 Texans had reached a point about seven miles south of Fort Craig. Canby's garrison at Fort Craig consisted of 3,810 men—regulars, Colorado and New Mexico volunteers, and "about 1,000 hastily- collected and unorganized militia."

Feeling his force was not strong enough to attack the fort, Sibley attempted to lure Canby out of the fort for a fight in the open. Canby declined the challenge, and Sibley camped two miles east of the fort where ridges of volcanic flow concealed his troops and protected them from the fort.

On the night of February 20, Canby sent out a detachment to harass the Confederates and keep them from occupying high ground overlooking Fort Craig. Capt. James "Paddy" Graydon led a raiding party. He lashed wooden boxes of 24-pound howitzer shells on the backs of mules, then sneaked them through the darkness toward the Confederate camp. When within range of the pickets, he fired the fuses, hazed the mules toward the Confederate lines, and headed for Fort Craig. Instead of continuing on course toward the Confederate camp, the mules turned back to follow Graydon and his raiders. The Union party beat a hasty retreat with shells exploding close behind them.

The next day, the forces met in combat, across the Rio Grande northwest of Fort Craig. There was bravery aplenty on both sides. Later, Private Ovando Hollister, in his book *A History of the First Colorado Regiment*, told how the Fifth Texas Lancers charged the Colorado Volunteers, who were commanded by Capt. Theodore H. Dodd:

> Each was armed with a lance, the blade three inches wide and twelve long—the shaft nine feet. A red guidon was tacked to each where it would drink the blood of a man impaled on it, and coming in three columns at full speed, they looked as if the Devil has set them on end. . . . Capt. Dodd said to his men, "They are Texans. Give them hell." And they did. Some came near enough to be transfixed and lifted from their saddles by bayonets, but the greater part bit the dust before their lances could come in use. Of the entire force, three men returned unhurt, and a pile of forty-two dead horses marked the termination of their career for months.

The Texans were armed with a variety of weapons which included squirrel rifles, bear and sportsmen's guns, single- and double-action shotguns, revolvers, and Bowie knives.

"For the first time, perhaps, on record," said General Sibley, "batteries were charged and taken at the muzzles of double-barreled shotguns, thus illustrating the spirit, valor and invincible determination of Texas troops."

With the collapse of the left of the Union line, Canby withdrew his forces behind the protection of the adobe walls of Fort Craig. Both Union and Confederate troops were too weakened to resume hostilities. Sibley prepared his forces for a march up the Rio Grande. On March 2, 1862, he raised a flag over the plaza at Albuquerque and took possession of the town in the name of the Confederate States of America.

NM 1
San Marcial—
Bosque del Apache

San Marcial

To go past the site of San Marcial to the Bosque del Apache Wildlife Refuge, take Exit 124 off I-25 and turn left on NM 1 (old US 85).

San Marcial had an early beginning and a disastrous ending. Sometime after Spanish settlers returned northward following the Pueblo Revolt of 1680, a community began forming on the east bank of the Rio Grande. It appears on early maps as Paraje (campground or stopping place). By 1848, after the American occupation, the colony was dubbed La Mesa de San Marcial, usually shortened to San Marcial. In 1866 the town was wiped out by a flood, and the inhabitants moved across the river to the higher west bank. In October, 1880, the Santa Fe Railroad reached San Marcial and the town was on its way to becoming an important link in transcontinental transportation.

By the 1920s, San Marcial was a thriving ranching and farming center, with a railroad division point. Its population had grown to several thousand. There were hotels, even a Harvey House restaurant. All went well until September, 1929, when the Rio Grande went on another rampage. The residents of San Marcial received warning barely in time to evacuate before the roiling river roared in to inundate the town. Locomotives, cars, and homes were swept away or buried. The first floors of most business buildings were filled with silt.

Today, hardly a trace of San Marcial is left.

Bosque del Apache National Wildlife Refuge

Seven miles farther down NM 1, the population of the Bosque del Apache National Wildlife Refuge is teeming. It consists of cranes, herons, geese, ducks, and many other species of migratory and permanent birds. The Bosque provides habitat for some 295 bird species and over 400 different mammals, reptiles and amphibians, such as mule deer, rattlesnakes, soft-shell turtles, and porcupines.

The refuge was established in 1939 by the U.S. Fish and Wildlife Service for the primary purpose of preserving the whooping crane. By 1940 the population of whooping cranes in North America was down to seventeen. Biologists had discovered the problem. Few young could survive the long migration route from northern British Columbia to the Texas Gulf Coast. An experiment was launched.

Whooping cranes' eggs were placed in sandhill cranes' nests to see if sandhill cranes would accept the chicks. Sandhill cranes ended up serving as foster parents to whooping cranes, and now both species spend winters in the Bosque del Apache Refuge. Up to four and a half feet high, the whooping crane is North America's tallest bird with a wingspan measuring as much as seven feet. Bird watchers and photographers come to see them in November and March as they fly to and from their winter home in New Mexico.

Although the refuge was established primarily for the sandhill crane, it also is home for endangered bald eagles and peregrine falcons. Those species almost died off during the 1960s when their food supplies became contaminated by the pesticide DDT. The use of DDT was banned in 1972, and the endangered birds are making a slow comeback.

A self-guided automobile tour of the wildlife refuge takes about an hour and a half, but an enthusiast armed with a camera, binoculars, and a "bird book" can spend from daylight to dark. The Semipalmated Plover is a spring and fall visitor, but a sharp-eyed observer may spot the shy Black-tailed Gnatcatcher year-around; they nest locally.

San Antonio (Exit 139)

In 1629 two zealous Spanish padres, Fray Antonio de Arteaga and Fray García de Zuñiga, founded a mission and built a church and monastery at a Piro pueblo on the west bank of the Rio del Norte. Mission San Antonio de Senecú would serve as a Christian lodestar to the Piros and a haven to travelers at the last southern stop on the Camino Real before venturing the dreaded Jornada del Muerto.

On January 23, 1675, Apaches swept out of the desert and destroyed the mission. The few survivors fled south, leaving only the name of the village to grace a stop on the Santa Fe Railroad which, two centuries later, replaced the Camino Real.

Today, San Antonio lays claim to being the site of the "first Hilton Hotel." Hotel magnate Conrad Hilton was born in San Antonio. His mother turned the family's adobe house near the railroad station into a hotel. Young Connie and his brother Carl had the job of meeting trains and lugging the bags of guests across the street. Later, Conrad Hilton wrote:

> . . . Carl and I met every train, at midnight, at three in the morning, at high noon. We hustled. We carried luggage and trunks and showcases.
>
> I can't honestly say I fell in love with the hotel business as it was practiced by the Hilton family in 1907, or began to dream of the Plaza or the Waldorf. It was a case of urgent necessity and soon we were making a name for ourselves and, more important, at $2.50 a day with meals, a profit.
>
> Only once did I give serious thought to a future in the hotel business and then strictly as a bellboy.
>
> A man tipped me five dollars.

Later, Hilton would say: "We all worked hard, and no one harder than my mother. I wouldn't take a million dollars for what those days taught me."

Much of old San Antonio remains. The Owl Bar, a state historical site, is a popular stopover for travelers off I-25. Ruins of the old Hilton house are at Sixth and Main streets.

Laborcita—Luis Lopez

Two rural villages, Laborcita and Luis Lopez, are located just east of I-25 between San Antonio and Socorro on NM 1. In Spanish, *labor*, the Latin word for work meant tilling and plowing. In New Mexico the term was extended to include the land which was tilled: Laborcita ("little farm"). Thus, this cluster of small farms by the Rio Grande was called Laborcita. For a time it was also called River View because of its outlook on the river.

The roots of Luis Lopez are imbedded deep in the history of the land. Luís López was the name of a Spaniard who had a hacienda or ranch in the area during the seventeenth century. Luís López's ranch served as a campground for travelers on the old Camino Real.

Socorro (Exit 147)

Socorro has been steeped in New Mexico history since Don Juan de Oñate stopped off during his entrada on June 14, 1598. The site was then occupied by Pilabo, the northernmost Piro Indian pueblo; the Oñate documents called it "Piloque." Oñate was in advance of the main body of colonists. The caravan, still struggling through the desert behind him, was in desperate need of provisions. Of the Piro

Indians, Oñate said, they "gave us much corn." The pueblo was renamed Socorro (succor, help) to commemorate the gift.

While Oñate continued north, two priests remained behind to do missionary work among the Indians. Fray Alfonso was so successful that he became known as "The Apostle of Socorro." The two priests built a modest church, to be replaced by a larger structure between 1615 and 1626. Here Fray Zuñiga and Fray Antonio de Arteaga planted the first grapes to be raised in New Mexico.

Most of the Spanish governors of New Mexico exploited the natives by forcing them to work without pay for service rendered. This was done under the guise of leading them to the white man's civilization and teaching them mechanical skills whereby useful articles of commerce could be produced. These items were sent south to Parral and Sonora for sale with profits accruing to the governor's account. Export items shipped south over the Camino Real included deerskins, blankets, woolen stockings, piñon nuts, leather jackets, shirts, breeches, and buffalo skins. The Indians could protest such exploitation and make claims for compensation.

There was a "minimum wage" under the Spanish administration. Governor Bernardo López de Mendizábal (1661-64) aroused the ire of the settlers when he raised the established rate of pay for Indian labor from one-half real per day to one real and food. But Governor López was not against augmenting his salary as governor by commandeering labor and trade goods for personal gain. Perhaps this was to be expected. Each governor had to pay an income tax consisting of one-half of his first year's salary.

Indian claims for compensation at the end of Governor López's term in office show some of the activities of the residents of Socorro. Thirty-six Indians claimed pay for spending two weeks transporting piñon nuts to a warehouse in Senecú; sixty-three had worked three days carrying salt from the east bank of the Rio Grande to Socorro. And there was the matter of making thirty pairs of stockings for the governor's account.

In late 1681, after the Pueblo Revolt, Governor Don Antonio de Otermín returned to the north in a half-hearted attempt at reconquest. He reached Socorro in November and found the community abandoned and the church profaned. He burned what supplies and provisions were left to keep them from falling into the hands of rebel Indians. He was unsuccessful in negotiating peace. The Indians had "returned to idolatry" and were unwilling to accept the resumption of Spanish rule. On January 2, 1682, Otermín gave up his attempt to reassert Spanish rule and started back toward El Paso.

Ten years later, on August 21, 1692, Don Diego de Vargas set out from El Paso for the reconquest of New Mexico. His force consisted of sixty Spaniards and a hundred friendly Indians. The odds were staggering. He was entering an area populated by from twenty-five to thirty thousand Indians. Several factors led to de Vargas's success. Leaders of the revolt had become oppressive rulers; despite firmly entrenched Indian beliefs, many found it hard to forget the teachings of the friars; and, having tasted the amenities of civilization, they were loathe to return to their former primitive state. Within four months de Vargas restored twenty-three pueblos to Spain's empire and to the Christian fold—all without firing a shot or drawing a sword.

By September, 1693, de Vargas was back in El Paso gathering an expedition for resettlement. He was not as lucky this time; his force met with resistance. The battle to occupy Santa Fe was short, but it took most of 1694 to subdue the remainder of the pueblos.

During the recolonization, the former residents of Socorro did not return. Except for travelers and caravans on the Camino Real, Socorro was deserted and dormant until 1816 when the Spanish Crown awarded land to twenty-one families by the Socorro Grant.

The settlers depended upon agriculture and raising cattle and sheep. They settled on the hillside and valley floor, irrigating their crops from mountain springs and the Rio Grande. There were fields of wheat and corn, vineyards and orchards, and pastures. As protection from the Apaches, they built adobe houses facing a central courtyard.

Like so many communities in New Mexico, Socorro has a buried treasure story. During the days before the Pueblo Revolt, the Spaniards had the Indians mining silver in the area, and much of the silver was used for church embellishments: a solid silver communion rail, a tabernacle, and vessels used in the Mass. At word of the Pueblo Revolt, these were supposed to have been buried. Numerous expeditions have attempted to find the treasure, but none has reported success.

During the second quarter of the nineteenth century, life in Socorro settled into a leisurely if not lazy agrarian pattern, punctuated by occasional Apache raids and the arrival of travelers on the old Camino Real, now usually called the Chihuahua Road by the Santa Fe traders. Socorro was the last stop before or the first stop after crossing the Jornada del Muerto, and the residents learned to profit from their position.

On September 28, 1841, prisoners of the ill-fated Texan-Santa Fe Expedition stopped in Socorro. George W. Kendall, chronicler of the group's trek from Santa Fe to Mexico City, was not favorably impressed by the citizens of Socorro:

> As Salazar [the nefarious Captain Damasio Salazar who was in charge of the guard for the prisoners] had to make a demand on the alcalde for corn and meal enough to sustain us across the long and dreary waste [the Jornada del Muerto] yet to travel, we were permitted to remain in Socorro until the following day. That the inhabitants of this frontier town were a pack of thieving, cheating, swindling scoundrels, we ascertained beyond a doubt before we had been in the place two hours. I remember perfectly well that a small party of us paid for a supper twice in this place, and that, because we would not pay for it a third time, the master of the house became very indignant.

On December 15, 1861, George F. Ruxton, a British traveler, visited Socorro. He also viewed the community with a highly critical eye:

> The next day we passed through Socorro, a small, wretched place, the first settlement of New Mexico on the river. . . .The population of Socorro was wretched-looking, and every countenance seemed marked by vice and debauchery. The men appear to have no other employment than smoking and basking in the sun, wrapped in their serapes; the women in dancing and intrigue. The appearance of Socorro is that of a dilapidated brick-kiln, or a prairie-dog town; indeed, from these animals the New Mexicans appear to have derived their style of architecture.

The smelter at Socorro during its heyday as a mining town. —Ritch, 1885

The 1850s brought changes. Fort Craig was built some twenty miles to the south, and Socorro became an "army town," a trading center and rendezvous for officers and men from the fort. After the Civil War erupted, freighting and storing supplies created a bustle that completely transformed the village.

Silver was discovered—or rediscovered—in the Magdalena Mountains to the west in 1867, and Socorro began a period of steady growth. In 1880 the Santa Fe Railroad arrived, and shortly after that the Billings Smelter and stamping mill was constructed west of town. It took a steady stream of wagon trains, some as long as 200 wagons, to serve the mines. By the early 1890s, Socorro was the largest town in the state with a population of more than 5,000. Almost 3,000 miners made Socorro their trading, gambling, and drinking center. Some say there were forty-four saloons; others put the number at only thirty.

In either case, a strong hand was needed to maintain law and order. Socorro had Elfego Baca.

Elfego Baca was born in 1865 in Socorro. According to the story, his nineteen-year-old pregnant mother was playing baseball with some girls. She jumped for a high ball, came down with a thump, and Elfego joined the ball game.

Elfego Baca displayed a gun he had stolen from Pancho Villa. Villa was offering a reward of $30,000 for Baca, dead or alive.
—Courtesy New Mexico State Records Center & Archives

Elfego Baca became a legend in his own time and a folk hero after his death. He had a quick draw and deadly aim. He established his reputation at the age of nineteen when he held eighty Texas cowboys at bay for thirty-three hours. He killed four of them and wounded eight, coming through the fracas without a scratch.

Baca accumulated nine notches on his gun; he was tried and acquitted three times on murder charges. He served as a sheriff, U.S. marshal, district attorney, school superintendent, mayor, and bouncer in a Mexican gambling casino. He read law in the office of a Socorro judge and was admitted to the New Mexico bar in 1894. He was admitted to practice before the United States Supreme Court in 1919.

His practice of law was directed primarily toward helping defendants of Mexican ancestry who were being harassed by Anglo prosecutors. He arrived at the decision which would shape his life while awaiting trial for murder after his epic gunfight. He decided that he wanted "to be an A No. 1 peace officer, likewise a criminal lawyer. I wanted the outlaws to hear my steps a block away from me."

Baca proved that he had achieved his goal soon after taking office as sheriff of Socorro County. The grand jury handed down indictments against a goodly collection of the county's hardcase criminal element. Warrants were issued, and Baca's deputies were arming themselves in preparation for going out to make arrests. Baca stopped them. He dictated a letter to be sent to each of the accused:

> I have a warrant here for your arrest. Please come in by March 15 and give yourself up. If you don't I'll know that you intend to resist arrest, and I will feel justified in shooting you on sight when I come after you.

The accused heard his footsteps. One by one, they appeared in the sheriff's office to surrender their guns.

Elfego Baca died in 1945 at the age of eighty. In 1958 Walt Disney assured him folk-hero status by releasing a movie entitled *The Nine Lives of Elfego Baca*.

In 1893 Socorro began to suffer a series of reverses. That was the year Congress demonetized silver. The market price of silver plummeted, Socorro's smelter shut down, and many mines closed. In 1895 weather added to Socorro's woes. The arroyo in Blue Canyon flooded and destroyed the lower town. Agricultural activities continued, but a succession of floods and droughts during the 1920s and 1930s ruined wheat crops and the Crown Flour Mill closed.

In its day, the Windsor Hotel in Socorro was one of the finest hostelries in New Mexico. —Ritch, 1885

However, one vestige of Socorro's mining glory lived through the bad times to prosper. In 1893 the New Mexico School of Mines opened. Less than three miles from the campus an entire mountain provided its students with a laboratory containing all the conditions of mining: shafts, tunnels, drifts, stopes, winzes, and rises. The State Bureau of Mines and Mineral Resources became a department of the college.

Socorro is a living museum of New Mexican architecture. Adobes from the resettlement period are represented. Then came the period of "territorial architecture" which lasted from the U.S. conquest of Mexico through the Civil War and Indian campaigns. With the coming of the railroad and mining during the 1880s and 1890s, Victorian and Queen Anne styles became popular, characterized by red brick and gingerbread. Many houses have been maintained in their original condition or have been recently restored. The historic section of Socorro is sufficiently compact that it can be covered by a walking tour.

Lemitar (Exit 156)

Lemitar is another small farming community just off I-25. The community is, in a manner of speaking, a town which lost its place in history. For many years, Lemitar was thought to be the site of Teypana, the Indian pueblo at which Coronado camped in 1541. However, during the early 1980s archaeologists from the University of New Mexico uncovered the old pueblo thought to have been visited by Coronado south of Socorro—quite a distance from Lemitar.

Polvadera (Exit 163)

The traveler will not find Polvadera on most maps, but it is on the ground. Spanish customs are still preserved in this tiny hamlet. Bright red ristras of chiles decorate the houses during harvest time.

The town's name is a corruption of Spanish *polvareda* (dusty). According to the story, the Lord told the people that if it did not rain by August 10 the place would be a desert. It did not rain, and the town was named Polvadera. August 10 is fiesta day, in honor of San Lorenzo, the patron saint; it is said to always bring rain.

San Acacia (Exit 163)

San Acacia, between I-25 and the Rio Grande, is a farming and ranching community on the Santa Fe Railroad. It was named for San Acacio, who was customarily represented by the *santeros* (image carvers) as crucified and dressed in a Spanish military uniform. San Acacio was a Roman soldier who was martyred because of his faith during early Christian times. The change of the final *o* to *a* is believed to have resulted from confusion of the saint's name with *acacia*, a variety of tree.

Alamillo (Exit 163)

Alamillo (little cottonwood) is opposite San Acacia on the east side of I-25. Early in the seventeenth century, the Franciscans established a mission, Santa Ana de Alamillo, at a Piro Indian pueblo which was located here. The inhabitants did not join in the Pueblo Revolt of 1680. Most of them fled south and did not return during the resettlement. During his attempted reconquest in 1681, Governor Otermín drove out the remaining inhabitants and burned the village.

In 1800 the government sponsored a resettlement program. Sixty-two families were located at Alamillo, subsidized with farm equipment and provisions to last until the first harvest. Each family received a yoke of oxen and a supply of corn. The people were granted exemption from the customary tithes for five years. The cost, not including the corn, was 1,330 pesos, drawn from a "gratuity fund." The governor expected repayment within a year, in the hope that other resettlement projects could be financed with the fund. The governor's hope was not realized.

Bernardo (Exit 175)

This "town" now consists of a store and a filling station east of I-25 (Exit 175) at the intersection with eastbound US 60. It had an active post office from 1902 until 1919.

The mountains to the west are the Ladrón Mountains, also called Los Ladrones (the thieves). They served as a hideout for Apache and Navajo horse thieves and, later, for American rustlers. One of the Americans had a ranch in the area which he supplied by raiding towns along the Rio Grande. He was said to have had a confederate in Socorro who was thought to be a simpleton but who kept him supplied with information to abet his rustling activities.

Historical Excursion

NM 304-314
La Joya—Los Padillas

Rio Abajo District (Exit 169)

At La Joya, I-25 enters the Rio Abajo district. About 1650, during the Spanish administration, the area north of Santa Fe was designated as the Rio Arriba (upper river) district, and the area to the south was Rio Abajo (lower river). Initially, the Rio Abajo stretched from a paraje or campground on the Camino Real between Santa Fe and Albuquerque known as La Bajada to La Joya de Sevilleta in the south. A county in north-central New Mexico was named Rio Arriba in 1852. No county was designated Rio Abajo; however, the area along the Rio Grande valley from Albuquerque south to La Joya is still generally known by that name.

This area was the breadbasket of New Mexico during the Spanish colonial period. It was also the residence of some of the wealthiest and most influential of the early colonists. Many of the families living in the Rio Abajo today proudly trace their names back to the original colonists.

La Joya

When the Spanish arrived at what is today La Joya (the jewel), there was a Piro Indian settlement on the site; it became a stopover for caravans on the Camino Real. In 1598 Don Juan de Oñate called it *Nueva Sevilla* (New Seville), later changed to *Sevilleta* (Little

Seville). Apaches drove the Piro Indians out, but between 1626 and 1630 Franciscan fathers rounded up the remnants of the tribe, resettled the place, and established the mission of San Luís Obispo de Sevilleta.

When Zebulon Pike was being escorted through New Mexico as a prisoner, he stopped at La Joya on March 10, 1807. It was still called Sevilleta, which Pike spelled "Sibilleta." He described the village in his diary: "a regular square, appearing like a large mud wall on the outside, the doors, windows, etc., facing the square, and is the neatest and most regular village I have yet seen."

Later during the nineteenth century, the name was changed to La Joya de Sevilleta and subsequently shortened to La Joya.

La Joya State Game Refuge

In 1973 the Nature Conservancy bought much of the old Sevilleta Grant east of the Rio Grande and turned it over to the U.S. Fish and Wildlife Service which administers it as the Sevilleta National Wildlife Refuge.

Abeytas

Abeytas was founded in the late 1700s by descendants of Don Diego de Veitia, of Basque origin, who came to New Mexico after the reconquest of 1692. One of his grandsons married into a Rio Abajo family, and a group of families formed a community known as Plaza de Abeytas. In 1910 Gregorio Abeytas, from Abeytas, was a member of the board of directors for a formal organization of the Belen Land Grant.

Las Nutrias

Governor Antonio de Otermín reported being in Las Nutrias in 1682 during his retreat southward after an abortive attempt at reconquest following the Pueblo Revolt of 1680.

In 1764 Governor Don Tomás Velés Cachupín granted a petition for a settlement south of Tomé, and the following year thirty families located at San Gabriel de las Nutrias. The site they selected for a plaza was unsatisfactory. It had poor drainage and was too far from the river for inhabitants to secure water for washing. They moved closer to the river. They neglected to built a sufficiently compact settlement for defense against the Apaches, and the village had to be abandoned.

Sabinal

Sabinal was populated in the 1770s by fifty-one families, 214 persons. Don Fernando de la Concha, governor from 1787 to 1793, was somewhat ahead of his time in attempting to establish an Indian reservation policy. He negotiated with a band of Apaches and settled them on land near Sabinal. He provided a weekly ration of corn and meat. But the Apaches soon reverted to their hostile ways and were not subdued until the campaigns of Generals George Crook and Nelson A. Miles in the 1880s.

Turn

This site was originally occupied by a settlement named Casa Colorado (red house), sometimes spelled with a final *a*. In 1788 Governor Fernando de la Concha was returning from the Gila, and he found a missing horse herd here. It also served as a stage stop between Albuquerque and Socorro.

A rancher named Conant renamed the town Turn because of a sharp curve in the road.

Bosque

Bosque was founded during the eighteenth century as a settlement of *genízaros*, captive or Christianized Indians. Later, it was settled as a community by a number of farming families: Abeytas, Bacas, Chávezes, Montaños, Pinos, and Zamoras. Today, some of the small farms around the community are still owned by descendants of those early settlers.

The early Spanish settlers borrowed their irrigation system from the Pueblo Indians. Individual fields were made viable by *acequias* (irrigation canals), connected by the *acequia madre* (mother ditch). The *acequia madre* was dug and maintained by the community. Individual farmers dug and maintained the smaller *acequias* to their fields. During times of drought, the *mayordomo de la acequia* (overseer of the ditch) became a man of considerable power. He decreed how long an *acequia* gate could remain open and, thus, how much water a farmer could have.

Jarales

Jarales is reached by the Old Mill Road off NM 304. This quiet rural village is crisscrossed by irrigation ditches for the alfalfa fields. The center of the village has shifted during the past years depending upon where the post office, the grocery store, or the local bar was located.

Belen

The history of Belen began in 1740 when Captain Diego de Torres and thirty-two other settlers received a royal land grant. The formal transfer took place on November 15, 1740, with the usual ceremonies attendant to the bestowal of a Royal land grant. Captain Torres acted as grantee on behalf of the settlers.

Nicolás Durán de Cháves, alcalde of Albuquerque, acted as a representative of the Superior Council of the Royal Treasury. In the presence of three witnesses, Cháves performed the official act of putting Torres "in possession of said lands with all their uses, customs, privileges and appurtenances to him, his heirs and successors." Testimony of a government official during subsequent litigation over the land grant described the ceremony:

> I took him by the hand, led him upon the land; he pulled grass, threw stones, spilled water, and said to the bystanders who accompanied me:
>
> "Gentlemen: Be you my witnesses that this possession is taken without any opposition."
>
> "How good; how how good; how good. May it profit you," they answered.
>
> For which reason I, the commissioned judge, maintained him in possession.

Officially, the grant was known as Nuestra Señora de Belén (Our Lady of Bethlehem).

In 1746 twenty families of *genízaros* disputed the land grant on the grounds that the land included Indian pueblos which had been occupied continuously prior to the coming of the Spaniards and should, therefore, be returned to the Indians. At a subsequent hearing, Captain Torres testified he had invited approximately twenty families of *genízaros* to move into the homes of the settlers. The Indians were destitute, hungry, and had no place to live. They were taken in as a Christian act. Other witnesses branded the Indians as fugitives from their masters, odious people, vagabonds, thieves and knaves. The Viceroy in Mexico City apparently ruled in favor of the settlers, since they continued in possession of the land.

In 1856 Belen was beset by internal strife over the division of the town into two sections: Plaza Vieja (Old Town) and New Town. The former, composed of the old settlers, had tradition and the old church on its side. New Town, composed primarily of farmers, had a new irrigation ditch and great plans for the future. Father Paulet, a young priest who sometimes went about the Lord's work armed with six-shooters, solved the problem. The old church was in ruins;

a new church would be built in New Town. The new church was completed on November 19, 1860, with the bell from the old church, which had been brought over the Santa Fe Trail, installed in one of its two towers.

When the Civil War came to New Mexico, Belen remained loyal to the Union with the men organizing themselves into volunteer companies. However, the volunteers did little but watch when some 400 Confederate cavalrymen galloped through town in March, 1862.

With the coming of the Santa Fe Railroad in 1880, Belen changed from a sleepy Spanish farming community to a bustling town. Local merchants contributed heavily to building the railroad, assuring that it would pass through Belen. It did, complete with railroad shops, a roundhouse, an ice plant, and employees. With connections to Denver, Chicago, El Paso, and Los Angeles, the town began to advertise itself as "The Hub City" after the Belen cutoff linked Belen to Amarillo in 1907.

In 1972 Belen lost the last vestige of one of the eight plazas which had formed the original town, the Bacaville post office and general store. The old building was badly damaged by a flood in 1969. It was demolished under a city program to do away with abandoned and unused structures.

The coming of the freeway during the 1960s brought Albuquerque within easy reach of many residents of Belen's trade area, but it did not dampen the spirit of this bicultural, bilingual city where old Spanish customs still exist side by side with modern conveniences.

Los Chavez

In 1738 Don Nicolás Durán y Chávez, son of a captain under de Vargas during the reconquest of New Mexico in 1692, petitioned for a land grant in the area now occupied by Los Chavez. According to his petition, he had nine sons and cattle and sheep. He lived in the area of Isleta and had no place to pasture his stock without infringing upon the land of the Isleta Indians.

The town began as a typical rectangular plaza of adobe structures with doors and windows facing to the center for protection from Indian raids, as recommended by military authorities in Santa Fe:

> . . . building the towns in form of a quadrangle, with at least twenty families in each, the houses in form of a fortress, the small ones with two ramparts, the larger ones with four and, between, embrasures for *escopetas* [muskets] when needed.

It is not advisable to erect *torreónes* [towers] as was the ancient usage, because experience has taught us that the enemy seeks protection under these walls and tunnels under them and sets fires. . . .

The Chávez grant prospered. By 1790 there were six different plazas housing seventy-eight households. Each plaza had a commandante. Nineteen soldiers were listed on the census: three mounted on horseback, sixteen on foot. One of the horseback soldiers was armed with an *escopeta*, the other eighteen had bows and arrows. The census even listed a teacher, the only teacher listed by name in the 1790 Rio Abajo census. Today, the original plaza, Plaza de los Gabaldónes, where the Galbadón family lived, is known as El Dorado Estates.

Members of the Chávez family have had illustrious careers. Three served as governors of New Mexico: Francisco Xavier Chávez (1823), José Antonio Chávez (1828-31), Mariano Chávez (1835). José Francisco Chávez, son of Don Mariano, was elected to Congress in 1865 and served three terms. The late Senator Dennis Chavez always maintained ties to his family heritage; he originated most of his major political campaigns from his home town, tiny Los Chavez in the Rio Abajo.

Tomé

This little village took its name from Tomé Domínguez de Mendoza, who had a hacienda nearby in the days before the Pueblo Revolt of 1680. He did not return after the reconquest, but his name remained on the town which was founded as a land grant to J.

The mission church at Tomé has long been a focal point of faith in the Rio Abajo. —Courtesy El Paso Public Library

Barela and others in 1739. A mission was founded in 1750, Nuestra Señora de la Concepción. Services were conducted by a priest from Albuquerque. In May, 1776, Fray Francisco Atanasio Domínguez visited the mission on an inspection tour. There were 135 families, numbering 727 persons. Father Domínguez wrote a detailed description of the mission and its furnishings:

> The chapel is adobe with thick walls, with the outlook and door to the west. It is 36 varas long, 8 wide, and the same high, with fifty-eight wrought beams. There is no choir loft. Two windows to the south on the Epistle side, and a little belfry with a cracked bell. The main door is like that of the missions with a wooden lock and key. There is no cemetery.
>
> Its furnishings as follows: In the center of the upper wall there is a niche like an arch containing a middle-sized completely carved image in the round of Our Lady of the Conception. She has imitation lace on the edge of her mantle. Her wardrobe consists of six silver reliquaries, an escutcheon and medal of the same, a small reliquary and five medals of bronze, an ordinary rosary set in silver, another silver one. She has a crown of gilded cardboard on her head. Fine pearl earrings in her ears. Around her neck two strings of ordinary pearls. On her wrists bracelets of black jet. On her fingers twelve silver and copper rings.

1. Jesuit / Franciscan
2. Alb / Surplice and Cassock
3. Amice
4. Cincture
5. Maniple
6. Stole
7. Chasuble
8. Cope

Missal with Stand

Chalice, paten and purificator

Veiled chalice with burse

Chalice, pall and purificator

Cruets

There is a set of vestments consisting of a white satin chasuble with all accessories; amice, alb, cincture, purificator; chalice with paten and spoon, all of silver, small silver vials for the holy oils, which came from the King and are kept in a little tin-plate box; glass cruets on a Puebla plate.

During those days, life in Tomé was not easy. On May 26, 1777, Fray Andrés García, the Albuquerque priest who served Tomé, noted in his burial book that he interred twenty-one settlers of Tomé who had been massacred by the Comanches. On June 3, 1778, there were thirty more burials.

If there is anything to the legend for which Tomé was designated "The Town of the Broken Promise," perhaps one of those raids was in retribution for a deception practiced by Ignacio de Vaca.

According to the story, a Comanche chief visited Vaca. Vaca had a daughter named María and the chief had a son of about the same age. The children became friends, and the Comanche proposed that they marry when they reached the proper age. Señor Ignacio de Vaca agreed, thinking to insure friendship between the Indians and the settlers.

The Comanche departed and, as time passed, the Vaca family forgot the promise. In fact, María was betrothed to a local boy. Then word came that the Comanches were coming, prepared for the wedding between the chief's son and Vaca's daughter. Vaca went to the cemetery, dug a fresh grave, and mounted a cross on it. When the Comanches arrived, he wept over the grave as he told the chief of the sad and untimely death of his daughter.

The chief learned of the false story and returned with a war party. Many were killed and wounded in the ensuing fight. María was taken hostage and married to the chief's son. The story usually ends on the note that María and her Comanche husband lived happily ever after.

Tomé is now a quiet village, free of Indian raids. It is now best known in the Rio Abajo for an impressive Easter sunrise procession to the top of Tomé Hill.

Valencia

Valencia is one of the oldest Spanish settlements in the Rio Abajo. It was the site of a sixteenth-century hacienda belonging to Francisco de Valencia, a lieutenant general for the Rio Abajo in the middle of the century. Apparently none of the Valencias returned to settle after the Reconquest, but the name continued.

Valencia had its share of Indian problems. On October 26, 1846, the Mormon Battalion stopped by on the way south to buy some pack blankets at the Otero store. Señor Otero was not in a good humor, and he was not inclined to sell his blankets at a bargain. He had lost between five and six thousand sheep to Indians the day before and two of his shepherds had been killed. He had spent the previous night riding to Indian villages trying to hire Indians to pursue the marauders.

On another occasion, José Sanchez, a ten-year-old boy was carried away by Apaches during a raid. He was held captive for a number of years. One night when the Indians were drinking and dancing in celebration of a victory, José stole one of their fastest horses and headed for Valencia. He rode all night with Indians in hot pursuit. When the horse gave out, he hid in a cedar clump until the Indians gave up their search. He finally made it back to Valencia. His mother was so grateful that she crawled on her knees from Valencia to the church at Tomé to give thanks to Nuestra Señora de la Concepción.

During the Territorial period the first county seat of Valencia County was located at Valencia where it remained until 1852 when it was moved to Tomé.

Los Lunas

Los Lunas is on the San Clemente Grant, granted to Don Felix Candelaria in 1716. Shortly after that, the Luna family laid claim to the grant and took possession of it.

On June 9, 1779, Antonio de Luna was killed by Apaches. Since he died intestate, a detailed inventory of his belongings was made so that his children's share of his estate could be determined. That inventory is in the Spanish archives. It gives an insight into the belongings of the early settlers:

> . . . one tract of land in said place of Los Lunas; 13 cornfields, small ones and large ones; three rooms of an adobe house; two small houses and one house lot; five pictures of 3 handbreadths painted in oil colors with their frames and one Infant Jesús in sculpture of 3 fingerbreadths; one hoe of medium weight; one plow with equipment; one medium-sized kettle and one iron griddle, both very old; one mortar; one spit; two benches; one pair of trousers of scarlet cloth and one jacket of black cholula cloth; one old cloak of *Queratano* cloth; one pair of useless blunderbusses; one branding iron; one horse and one mule; one cart; four oxen; two cows with calves; four bulls two years old; eight calves one year old; 600 breeding ewes and 412 lambs born in that year.

All was appraised at 3,607 pesos. In accounting for the property, the widow reported that the hoe had worn out; she had paid the trousers for four masses, the receipt for which she had lost; she had given the jacket for twelve masses and the horse for twenty masses; the cloak was worn out in service; she sold the mule for one yoke of oxen; the cart was entirely useless; 300 sheep had died because of carelessness and the plague of lice; she had given 40 ewes as a burial fee for her deceased husband; 118 were lost by the *major-domo* of the herd, "which he still owes"; 2 oxen were killed by Indians; one ox she gave for the shroud.

A later Antonio—Antonio José Luna, born in 1808—is often referred to as the "Father of Los Lunas." He was a sheepman and a political leader.

Through a union of the Luna and Otero families the Luna-Otero Dynasty was born, two powerful Republican families which would control and dominate the future of Valencia County for a century. They made their money by embarking on a bold venture for the time: selling sheep in California. They could receive from $10 to $15 a head in California, as opposed to fifty cents on the local market. During one large overland drive in the 1850s, it was estimated that they moved more than 50,000 sheep.

Don Antonio José was a hard bargainer. In 1880, the Santa Fe Railroad wanted right of way through the Luna property. The tracks were headed squarely at the Luna hacienda. Don Antonio José agreed to relinquish the property if the railroad would build a new house to his specifications. Legend has it that the family then made several trips to the South to create the design. Whether this is true or not, the house is Southern Colonial in style, even though it is built of adobe.

Antonio José Luna's Southern Colonial mansion is built of adobe.
—Photo by the authors

Because Don Antonio José died in 1881, his oldest son Tranquilino was the first to occupy the Luna Mansion. The home has been restored and now operates as a restaurant.

Peralta

Although Peralta was named after residents of the same name who settled in the area in the late seventeenth century, it was on occasion referred to as "Plazeres," "Placeres," and "Los Placeres."

George Kendall recorded a stop in 1841 by the Texan-Santa Fe Expedition prisoners on their long trek to Mexico City:

> After leaving Albuquerque, we continued our march through a succession of cultivated fields and pastures until we reached a small rancho called Los Placeres, and here we were encamped for the night. Nothing was given us to eat, and on complaining to Salazar that we were hungry, he pointed to the spot where his mules and horses were feeding and said that the *grazing was excellent*! Because many of the prisoners swallowed the corn given them by the women raw, the fellow called them wolves and pigs.

Peralta was the scene of the last battle of the Civil War to be fought in New Mexico. Henry Connelly, the wartime governor of New Mexico, had observed the defeat of Union forces at the battle of Valverde. He hurried back to Peralta, where he had a hacienda, and distributed his cattle, merchandise, and equipment to the people of Peralta, lest they fall into the hands of the Confederates.

When the opposing forces met it was at Governor Connelly's hacienda, and it was more of a skirmish than a battle. The Confederate forces were in retreat following defeat at Glorieta. The Union commander allowed the Confederate forces to slip away, principally because the Union army was so short on supplies that they could not have fed the captives had they captured the entire Confederate force.

Bosque Farms

Early Spanish settlers of the Bosque Farms area called it Bosque de los Pinos, but its history dates back to the Tewa Indians who settled in the valley about 1500. Today, it is an incorporated village of more than 3,000.

In the first quarter of the twentieth century, Eduardo Otero owned some 28,000 acres of the area for grazing cattle and farming. But much of the land had a high water table and too much alkali for successful farming. Otero was instrumental in getting the Middle

Rio Grande Conservancy District to dig canals to drain excess water. Otero sold some of his land, and the U.S. Government used about 28,000 acres for rehabilitation of farm families who were wiped out in the Dust Bowl of Northern New Mexico, Texas, and Oklahoma in 1934-35.

The land was divided into tracts and sold to those who had their names drawn at a public drawing on May 1, 1935. The Works Progress Administration worked the Bosque Farms area to clear trees, level land, make adobes, and build homes. When settlers arrived they lived in two-room shacks and tents until their permanent homes were constructed.

Farming was difficult in the alkaline soil. By 1939 many residents had turned to dairying. Federal Security loaned money for the purchase of cows, and thirty-one dairy barns were built in Bosque Farms. It became known as the "Heart of the Rio Grande Dairy Land."

Isleta Pueblo

Today the Isleta Pueblo occupies the same place along the Rio Grande that it occupied when it was visited by Capt. Hernando de Alvarado, a soldier in Coronado's expedition who came that way in 1540. This historic pueblo was a stopping place for practically every Spanish explorer and conquistador who passed through New Mexico. The Spanish word, meaning "islet," was given to the place because its location was once a delta or small island. The Indian name was *tsugwevaga* (kick flint) for a kicking race the Indians played using a piece of flint or obsidian.

Fray Agustín Rodríguez stayed at Isleta in 1581. He reported a population of 1,500 housed in 123 two- and three-story houses.

Initially, the people of the Isleta Pueblo did not take part in the Pueblo Revolt of 1680. Spanish colonists in the vicinity took refuge in the pueblo before their flight to El Paso. But when Governor Otermín arrived a few days later, he found the pueblo completely deserted; the Indians had joined the rebels. The pueblo remained deserted until 1709 when Fray Juan de la Peña induced fugitive bands of Indians to return to their pueblos. This was the founding of the present pueblo.

The church was built about 1613 and dedicated to St. Anthony of Padua. It was seriously damaged during the Pueblo Revolt but not completely destroyed. When de Vargas reached the pueblo on October 30, 1692, he found it in ruins "except for the nave of the church, the walls of which are in good condition." The old mission

Turn-of-the-century photograph of Isleta Pueblo with the mission church in the background. —Courtesy New Mexico Department of Development, No. 2807

required extensive repairs during the first decade of the eighteenth century, but it was the same basic structure in the same location as had been built in 1613. Thus, the Isleta church has a strong claim to being the oldest church in New Mexico.

During his inspection tour in 1776, Fray Francisco Atanasio Domínguez thought the Indians were being weaned to Spanish customs. He noted: "I say that they are well inclined to Spanish customs, for many use mattresses on their beds, and there are many bedsteads."

Isleta Pueblo has one of the most fascinating ghost stories in New Mexico. In 1756 Fray Juan José Padilla died and was interred beneath the altar in a wooden coffin. In 1826 priests discovered that Fray Padilla and his coffin had literally risen from the grave up through the dirt floor. The priest's body showed little sign of deterioration. He was immediately reburied, but not before it became general knowledge in the pueblo that Fray Padilla's ghost was out looking for sinners.

In 1889 Fray Padilla again came to the surface, his body still in an excellent state of preservation. When he put in another appearance in 1962, he was reburied beneath a thick slab of concrete. The scientific explanation is that the high water table beneath the church floats the coffin to the surface during unusually wet years, but this has convinced none of the devout of Isleta Pueblo that Fray Padilla is not on the prowl in search of sinners.

By the time of the Civil War, the Isleta Pueblo was one of the wealthiest pueblos in the state. It had a reputation for loyalty to the government. In 1862, when Confederate forces invaded New Mexico, Ambrosia Abeyta, a native of Isleta, loaned the Union commander $18,000 in species, taking only a receipt for the money. Abeyta's loan was forgotten after the war. Finally, twelve years later, he took his case to Washington and laid it before President Grant. He received payment immediately.

A few Indians still tend farms along the river; however, better wages have attracted most of the population to jobs in Albuquerque and Belen. The pueblo ranks fourth in New Mexico in tribal land with 211,000 acres. Like at most of the modern Indian pueblos in New Mexico, bingo games are conducted.

The Isleta Pueblo is located thirteen miles south of Albuquerque near I-25. It can be reached from NM 304 or I-25, Exit 209.

Los Padillas

The Padillas settled in the Rio Abajo in 1705 after the Reconquest. The community close by the Isleta Pueblo was originally known as San Andres de los Padillas. It became a prosperous farming area. In 1846 Susan Magoffin visited Mariano Chávez, a well-to-do Mexican whose house was in the midst of a corn field, "well furnished with handsome brussles carpet, crimson worsted curtains, with gilded rings and cornice, white marble slab pier tables—hair and crimson worsted chairs, candelabras."

Albuquerque

Albuquerque is a sprawling city. During more than two and a half centuries, it has expanded from a tiny Spanish village to cover the flood plain cut by the meandering Rio Grande and climb up onto the surrounding mesas. Albuquerque now contains about one-third of the population of the state. Centrally located at the intersection of I-40, the main east-west freeway, and I-25, the principal north-south route through the state, Albuquerque is at the crossroads of New Mexico.

To read Albuquerque's earliest history, you do not go to a library or visit musty archives. You pack a picnic lunch and drive west on I-40 to Exit 155. Take NM 45 (Coors Road) north. Turn left on Atrisco Road and go to Petroglyph State Park. There, for hundreds of years, the lava flows from five extinct volcanoes to the west were hunting grounds for Paleo-Indians. As they waited for game or feasted on the spoils of their hunts, they chipped records of their lives and beliefs in the rocky formations around them.

Conservationists wage a continuous battle in their efforts to save the thousands of prehistoric petroglyphs in the Albuquerque area from the inroads of real estate developers. —Photos by the authors

In all, there are more than 10,000 drawings: gesturing men, whimsical faces, birds, snakes, animals, and unidentifiable designs. Unfortunately, we do not yet have a Rosetta stone by which we can translate the enigmatic messages. Scattered spear points and bones from butchering sites testify to the activities of very early man. Some authorities, such as Frank Hibben who excavated Sandía Cave in the 1930s, say hunters roamed the area as early as 17,000 B.C. Other anthropologists say it was later. We do know that permanent settlements of the Tewa people were scattered about the land presently occupied by Albuquerque as early as 1350 A.D. In 1980, residents of Los Ranchos, on the north edge of Albuquerque, unearthed a pueblo village while digging a swimming pool.

The Spaniards began exploration of the area in 1540. Rumors of seven cities as big as Mexico City, rich in gold and silver, only forty days to the north, were circulating in New Spain. In 1539, Viceroy Antonio Mendoza sent Friar Marcos de Niza and a Moorish slave named Estévan northward to investigate.

Fray Marcos dispatched Estévan ahead with a party of friendly Indians to report on what he found. Since the Moor could neither read nor write, he was instructed to send back crosses to show:

> . . . . information of a rich, peopled land, . . . if the thing was of moderate importance, he send me a white cross the size of a hand; if it was something great he send me one of two hands; and if it was something bigger and better than New Spain, he send me a large cross.

When a messenger brought back a cross the size of a man, Fray Marcos did not take time to go investigate. He rushed back to tell the viceroy that he had discovered the fabled Seven Cities of Cíbola, replete with riches.

Mendoza sent Francisco Vásquez Coronado at the head of an expedition of more than three hundred Spaniards and eight hundred Indians to explore the wonders of Cíbola. Fray Marcos de Niza went along as a guide. By the time they reached the area now occupied by Albuquerque, Coronado had found nothing but mud houses. He had dubbed Fray Marcos "The Lying Monk" and sent him back to Mexico City.

Coronado and his men spent the winter of 1540-41 at Kuaua, near present-day Albuquerque (see Coronado State Monument). Before he gave up and returned to Mexico, a party ranged as far east as present-day Kansas without finding the golden cities. Spanish exploration and colonization continued apace, but a community was not established at the site of Albuquerque until 1706.

In 1706 Francisco Cuervo y Valdés, the provisional governor of New Mexico, decided to establish a villa in the Rio Abajo district, south of Santa Fe. He named it La Villa de San Francisco de Alburquerque, after the viceroy of New Spain, who held the title "Duke of Alburquerque." As a result, Albuquerque is called "The Duke City." Early in the eighteenth century, after Americans came, the r was dropped from "Alburquerque," probably because the Anglos had difficulty with Spanish pronunciation.

Governor Cuervo founded the villa on February 7, 1706, with a contingent of twelve families, and wrote to tell the viceroy and the king about it after the fact. This was against the law. A villa, the highest classification of Spanish towns, could not be established without permission from the viceroy. However, the viceroy approved the settlement, probably because Cuervo had named it after him. He did stipulate that no more villas were to be established without permission and that the name was to be changed to San Felipe de Alburquerque, after the patron saint of King Philip V of Spain.

Rather than receiving appointment as permanent governor of New Mexico as he had hoped, Cuervo ended up in Mexico City to face an investigation of his activities in founding San Felipe de Alburquerque. He had lied about the size of the town; he had claimed there were thirty-five families in the community, more than the thirty required to establish a villa.

Despite Cuervo's somewhat tarnished reputation, Albuquerque has elevated him to a place of honor. In 1988, the City Council declared April 23 to be "Founder's Day." That was the date in 1706 that Cuervo wrote his superiors certifying that he had founded Albuquerque. A statue of Cuervo was dedicated, and New Mexico

historian Marc Simmons polished up Cuervo's reputation: "A villa was needed in this area, so he got busy and did one. The resources and population for something like this were pretty slim. He did some corner-cutting."

In 1706, when the villa was founded, ten soldiers were stationed nearby for protection against Indians. Governor Cuervo withdrew the detachment in 1707 and the settlers began to be plagued by Indian depredations. When they complained to the governor, he said he had less than sixty soldiers to guard all of New Mexico; they could not expect preferential treatment.

By 1779 the authorities in Santa Fe were tired of complaints about Indian attacks. An order was issued to the settlers to construct houses in a defensible plaza and move into them. Adobe houses were built around the church, butting one against the other with entrances toward the center. During Indian attacks, livestock was herded into the plaza and a gate was closed; women and children went into the church and men mounted the roofs of the adobe houses with such weapons as they had. Instead of living on their farms and ranches and going to church on Sundays, the settlers lived in the plaza near the church and went to their fields

89

every day. This was the beginning of that section of Albuquerque known as Old Town.

By 1790 the old church on the west side of the plaza had deteriorated to the point of ruin. A new church was built on the north side of the plaza by genízaros from Tomé and Belen in 1793. The San Felipe Neri Church still stands in the Old Town plaza.

The first picture of Albuquerque through American eyes came from Lt. Zebulon Pike in March, 1807, as he was being escorted down the Camino Real on his way to Mexico. In Albuquerque he was entertained by Father Ambrosio Guerra at a lavish dinner. He was waited upon by six beautiful girls whom the priest said he had purchased from Indians as infants. The next day, as Pike left Albuquerque, he was impressed by the sight of farmers irrigating their fields.

During the eighteenth century, except for Indian raids, the citizenry of Albuquerque led a sedentary and uneventful existence, broken only in the fall by the annual assembly of merchant convoys destined for Mexico. Besides farming, the principal occupations were weaving hosiery and blankets and making shoes.

In September, 1821, New Mexico gained independence from Spain. In Albuquerque, about the only immediate change was renaming the plaza to *Plaza de la Constitución*. However, Albuquerque shortly began to profit from the flow of traffic over the Camino Real as merchants went east over the Santa Fe Trail to buy merchandise in the United States. A profitable trade developed with Mexico.

After a bloodless occupation of Santa Fe on August 18, 1846, Gen. Stephen Watts Kearny headed down the Rio Grande in pursuit of Governor Manuel Armijo. Instead of a defending army, the troops met vendors attempting to sell grapes, melons, and eggs. In Albuquerque, they were greeted by a twenty-gun salute and the residents became American citizens as Kearny administered an oath of allegiance.

Before leaving for the conquest of California, Kearny established a contingent of dragoons in Albuquerque to protect against Navajo raids. The soldiers' efforts were largely futile; however, Albuquerque profited from the activity as dragoons chased up and down the Rio Grande Valley in pursuit of Indians. Anglo traders and European immigrants arrived to compete with Hispanic storekeepers.

In 1857 Lt. Fitzgerald Beale came through Albuquerque on a project to survey and build a wagon road to the west. Beale was also engaged in an experiment to test the use of camels in the southwestern desert, and New Mexicans were treated to a parade of hump-backed beasts and their colorfully dressed Greek and Turkish handlers. The Camel Brigade was quartered for three days in the army's corrals near the plaza.

Gen. James Carleton, Commander of the Military Department of New Mexico, was not above lining his own pockets. His wife Sophia acquired twelve buildings just west of the church in the plaza. The military rented these for $105 a month, a nice supplement to the general's salary.

In March, 1862, as the Civil War approached Albuquerque, the meager Union forces had no choice but to retreat in the face of the advancing Confederate force. They burned the stores of military supplies to keep them from falling into the hands of the Confederates. The supplies were stored in Sophia Carleton's buildings.

The Confederate victory was short-lived. Union forces in New Mexico were supplemented by volunteers from Colorado. On March 28 they met the Confederates at Glorieta Pass east of Santa Fe. A resounding defeat forced the Southern troops to retreat to Albuquerque. There, after losing a brief artillery duel, the Confederate commander deemed discretion the better part of valor.

As the Confederate forces abandoned Albuquerque, they buried eight mountain howitzers in a garden near the plaza. These cannon were excavated thirty years later with the help of the former Confederate officer who buried them. Four were retained by Albuquerque for display in the plaza, and four were given to the Colorado Historical Society in appreciation of Colorado's aid in defeating the Confederates.

In Albuquerque the scars of the Civil War, both physical and political, healed quickly. A more pressing issue was control of the Indians, but Col. Kit Carson had been assigned to handle that. His force of First New Mexico Volunteers included some men from Albuquerque; however, by 1863 most Albuquerqueans were giving their attention to less warlike pursuits, such as passing ordinances in an attempt to clean up the town:

> All houseowners or heads of families within the city limits of the town of Albuquerque, shall have especial care that their servants do not cast dirty water, sweepings, ashes or kitchen residue in front of the plaza, roads, streets, or alley-ways.

In May, 1872, John H. Beadle, a *Cincinnati Commercial* correspondent visited New Mexico. In the resulting book, *The Undeveloped West; or Five Years in the Territories*, he viewed New Mexico as a "sterile" wasteland occupied by backward people. He judged nine-tenths of the Territory "totally barren or fit only for pasturage." But when he got to Albuquerque, it was a different story. He found the Rio Grande valley an oasis; the river was comparable to the Nile. "Albuquerque is the coming town of New Mexico, if it has a coming town, which I am much inclined to doubt."

He observed, "An American cannot live here as a farmer; he cannot compete with the natives. They can live too cheap." Beadle was right on this score. Most of the Easterners who came to New Mexico following the Civil War were merchants and artisans. They learned Spanish, or married someone who could speak it, and went into business. The town emerged from the 1870s as a leading commercial center of the Southwest with a population of 2,135.

By the middle of June, 1879, representatives of the Santa Fe Railroad were inquiring about land in Albuquerque for right of way and shops, and by the end of the year the tracks were only eighty miles away. A few Albuquerqueans were against it, particularly those who were engaged in wagon freighting, but that did not stop the flow of progress that had been in the planning stage since the 1850s when Lt. Amiel W. Whipple had surveyed the 35th parallel across New Mexico for a possible transcontinental railroad route.

On April 22, 1880, the entire population of Albuquerque turned out to celebrate the arrival of the railroad. Before the speeches were over, Albuquerque had been cited as the "Central City of New Mexico," the "Queen City of the Rio Grande," and the "Chicago of the West." Barrels of wine were situated in the plaza with tin cups chained to them, and the celebration lasted well into the night.

The first "businessman" to locate by the railroad was Peter "Shorty" Parker. During the night following the ceremonies, he preempted a six-foot square of land at the intersection of Railroad Avenue and the tracks. He brought a suitcase full of liquor and a supply of beer which he deposited in a hole in the ground to keep it cool. Shorty upended an old barrel to serve as an impromptu bar and offered either whiskey or beer at two-bits a drink.

The railroad tracks ran across the sandy plain of the ancient river bottom some two miles east of the plaza. The cluster of buildings around the plaza was connected by an umbilical cord called Railroad Avenue (today's Central Avenue). The depot was nothing but a boxcar, but the New Mexico Town Company, a real-estate subsidiary of the railroad, got busy developing the area and the price of lots escalated. By 1881 the business district of New Town was well underway.

In spite of a mule-drawn streetcar line down the center of

Railroad Avenue, Old Town did not prosper. There was a post office named Albuquerque at either end of the streetcar line, and a postal inspector decided the one in Old Town should be closed to solve the problem of two towns with the same name. The Post Office Department responded to the consequent public outcry by designating the old plaza as Armijo and naming the area around the railroad Albuquerque. In 1886 the names were again changed: to New Albuquerque and Old Albuquerque. It was well into the twentieth century before the two areas grew together.

As usual in Western communities, the railroad brought gamblers, shady ladies, bunko artists, and outlaws. Saloons sprouted with names ranging from the White Elephant for the elite of Albuquerque to the Bucket of Blood which was patronized by railroad section hands. Mexican monte, faro, roulette, chuck-a-luck, fan-tan, keno, craps, and stud poker games gathered in all available loose change; "soiled doves" hung around, hoping to lure barroom patrons to nearby brothels for "a good time" before the gamblers got all their money.

Saloon licenses and fines for creating disturbances at the gaming tables went a long way toward relieving residents of the burden of taxation. Municipal officials were not above lining their pockets. One judge had a penchant for three-card monte. When he ran out of money, he would have his deputy bring in someone guilty of "disorderly conduct." The judge would hold a trial on the spot, levy a fine of however much money the "guilty party" had, and continue with his game.

Albuquerque suffered a series of outlaws, including Billy the Kid who shot up a bar in Old Town. There were street fights, murders, and hangings. When justice was deemed too slow, masked vigilantes raided the jail with ropes in-hand. There were two triple hangings as "dastardly culprits" were simultaneously "lynched into eternity." For the legal hanging of a town marshal who was convicted of murdering an innocent citizen, a gallows was constructed from plans published in the *Scientific American*. The newspaper reported that the marshal was "Jerked to Jesus."

The finer side of Albuquerque was developing in the midst of the rough times. There were numerous private schools, but public education did not come until 1891 after the Territorial legislature passed a bill authorizing local districts to issue bonds to pay for school buildings.

The University of New Mexico was located outside of town on a barren mesa, and the first building was completed in 1892, a red brick structure that somewhat resembled Victorian architecture. In 1901 Dr. William George Tight arrived from Ohio to head the burgeoning institution. He took a unique view of architecture. He believed it should spring from the local culture instead of being borrowed from afar. Amidst a storm of criticism, he instituted Pueblo architecture: flat-roofed adobe buildings with projecting vigas, decorated with Indian symbols. One building intended for social meetings was circular, constructed below ground level, and entered by a ladder from the roof, modeled after a ceremonial kiva at Santo Domingo Pueblo. He even "pueblo-ized" that first old red brick building by knocking off gables and cornices and plastering the outside with earthen stucco.

Many Albuquerqueans took a dim view of Dr. Tight's "reversion to the primitive"; they saw pueblo architecture aplenty in rural Indian communities. It was wryly suggested that the faculty should wear Indian blankets and feathered headdresses. Despite the fact that Dr. Tight was fired because of his radical ideas, the Pueblo-style architecture of the University of New Mexico persists to this day.

On July 4, 1882, a local saloonkeeper named Park A. Van Tassel staged a balloon ascension, inflating his 30,000-cubic-foot balloon with coal gas from the Albuquerque Gas Works. The local population went without lights for two days so that gas could be diverted to the balloon. The ascension was a rising success. Afterwards, Van Tassel assumed the title "Professor" and went on a world tour. Sometime later, he and his balloon dropped into the ocean off Hawaii, and Professor Van Tassel was presumed to have been eaten by sharks.

Professor Van Tassel's watery fate did not dampen Albuquerque's

The first building on the campus of the University of New Mexico before it was "pueblo-ized" by Dr. Tight. —Frost, 1894

enthusiasm for balloons. That 1882 ascension was a precursor of the future. Today, Albuquerque claims the title "Balloon Capital of the World," and not without reason. During the annual International Balloon Fiesta in October, more than four hundred balloonists from all over the world congregate.

By the turn of the century, Albuquerque had surpassed Santa Fe as the commercial center of the Territory. During the 1890s, the Commercial Club, predecessor of the Chamber of Commerce, had been advertising to lure new investors and residents to the area. Real estate promoters began to boom the joy of suburban living. On August 3, 1905, a somewhat chilling advertisement appeared in the *Albuquerque Morning Journal*:

> Have a nice garden, raise your own chickens, keep a
> horse and a cow. Bring up a big family.
> Be independent . . .
> Enjoy life while you live
> For you will be dead a long time.

With the development of New Town, Old Town gradually deteriorated as residents moved to locations more convenient to their work. By the Depression of the 1930s, the area had decayed to the point that the county welfare office located in Old Town to be close to its clientele. The historic plaza did not really come into its own again until after the middle of the twentieth century when it was discovered as a tourist attraction.

Today, hotels advertise their distance from Old Town or the time it takes their guests to reach the old plaza which is ringed by boutiques, galleries, and gift shops. Indians spread their wares on the sidewalk under the portales of buildings and do a brisk business selling turquoise and silver jewelry to visitors who come from across the nation.

During the first quarter of the twentieth century, health care became a major industry in Albuquerque. Capitalizing on its high altitude with thin atmosphere which reduced pressure on the lungs, low humidity, and mild climate, the city became a mecca for tubercular patients. A local physician was quoted as saying that Albuquerque would be ruined if a cure for tuberculosis was discovered. Many from colder climes elected to stay in Albuquerque after their affliction was cured or arrested, and the city was enriched by professional people, businessmen, artists, journalists, and musicians.

In the 1920s, America's love affair with the automobile launched

The plaza in Albuquerque's Old Town.
—Courtesy New Mexico Economic Development & Tourism, No. 656

a burgeoning ·tourist industry, and Route 66 brought a steady stream of vacationers to tourist courts, filling stations, and restaurants along the route which ran right through the central business district. The Depression turned that stream of travelers into impecunious hitchhikers and poverty-stricken escapees from the Dust Bowl of the Middle West. The central downtown business district began to decline, and Albuquerqueans joined the nation in a hardscrabble effort to overcome financial disaster.

Somehow, Albuquerque weathered the hard times. In 1935 local businessmen staged a three-day celebration of Albuquerque's half-century as an incorporated municipality. The *Albuquerque Journal* trumpeted the purpose of the fiesta: "to end the Depression blues and turn Albuquerqueans' thoughts to the future." However, few were really sure that the Depression was over until 1939 when Conrad Hilton displayed enough confidence in the city to open a spanking new ten-story hotel in the downtown area.

In 1940 Albuquerque's population stood at about 35,000. Old Town was not considered a part of the city until 1949 when it was annexed to increase the population in preparation for the 1950 census. By 1955 the population had exploded to 175,000. The growth took place during and after World War II as the city became a center for military training, war-oriented industries, and weapons research.

With Kirtland Air Force Base, Sandia Base, and Sandia Labora-

With Kirtland Air Force Base, Sandia Base, and Sandia Laboratories, Albuquerque was launched on a high-tech course. Contracts for atomic research, additional weapons research, and work on solar energy brought more and more contracts and more and more people. As new subdivisions and industrial complexes developed in outlying areas, shopping centers sprang up, and the downtown area was drained of people and capital.

Historic buildings, including the Alvarado Hotel which had stood by the railroad tracks since 1902, were bulldozed into parking lots in the forlorn hope that urban renewal and more parking spaces would lure business back to the downtown area. Albuquerque businessmen did not develop a feeling for saving remnants of the city's past until low-interest loans for that purpose became profitable under the National Historic Preservation Act of 1966.

During the 1970s, nostalgia began to merge with a renewal of interest in the past, and seeking out old Victorian and Queen Anne homes for restoration became an "in" thing for those who could afford it. Conrad Hilton's hotel was returned to its former glory. A program was launched to define historical residential districts as Albuquerqueans began to realize the losses their city had suffered in the interests of economic gain.

Historical Excursion

NM 556
Alameda—Algodones

The leisurely traveler should take NM 556 (known locally as "Old Highway 85") north out of Albuquerque to visit Alameda, Rio Rancho, Corrales, Sandía Pueblo, Bernalillo, Coronado State Monument, and Algodones. Through the northern suburbs of metropolitan Albuquerque the old and the new are interspersed in startling contrast.

Alameda

Prior to the arrival of the Spaniards, the site of Alameda was a Tiguex pueblo near the ruins of a pre-Columbian Indian village. About 1641 the pueblo was reported to have a "fair church and friary" with an organ, but it was judged to have "poor provision for public worship." A mission dedicated to Santa Ana ministered to "400 souls." The pueblo was abandoned and burned after the Indian revolt of 1680.

The land occupied by Alameda was granted to Francisco Montes Vigil in 1710. Vigil arrived in New Mexico as a colonist from Zacatecas. Vigil sold his land grant to Captain Juan Gonzáles in 1712, and Gonzáles developed the community. Eight families were living in Alameda in 1744. By 1774 the population had increased to sixty-six families, 388 "people of various classes and walks of life." A small chapel had been dedicated to San José.

Today, modern commercial establishments line the highway, but side roads to the east and west lead to truck farms, alfalfa fields, and the cottonwood groves for which the town was named.

Rio Rancho

During the early 1960s, the desert around Albuquerque was scarred as numerous entrepreneurs used bulldozers to scrape vegetation from large areas of land and gouge networks of broad furrows to represent future streets. Scatterings of model homes were constructed; then advertisements in Eastern newspapers, particularly during the snow-plagued winter months, were designed to lure potential retirees to the "Sunbelt." Dinner parties were staged in New York and other Eastern cities with slide-shows and movie presentations to persuade investors to fly to New Mexico to bask in the sun and take bus tours of the sites of their future homes. Rio Rancho is one of the more successful results of such a promotion.

Prior to 1960, the site of Rio Rancho was open grazing land, part of the Thompson Ranch which had been carved from the eighteenth-century Alameda Land Grant. AMREP Corporation, out of New York, promoted the development. Initial investors who were brave enough—or perhaps farsighted enough—to occupy one of the barren, wind-swept lots found themselves shoveling sand instead of snow. Rattlesnakes were more common than neighbors.

But the community persevered and grew as it attracted not only Eastern "snowbirds" but high-tech employees who wanted to escape the bustle of life in metropolitan Albuquerque. Today there are more than 10,000 people living on paved streets in neat suburban bungalows and townhouses.

From Alameda, Rio Rancho is reached by taking NM 45 (Corrales Road) across the Rio Grande to NM 528.

Corrales

By continuing on NM 45, Corrales Road, from Alameda, one finds a definite contrast to Rio Rancho. Corrales was once part of the Alameda Land Grant. Captain Juan Gonzáles, who bought the grant in 1712, dug a sizeable ditch in 1720 to irrigate farms and fields. In the early days two communities were strung along the Rio Grande. The northern village was called Santa Rosalía de Corrales (Upper Corrales); the southern, San Ysidro de Corrales (Lower Corrales). During a survey of missions in 1776, Fray Francisco Atanasio Domínguez found ten families (42 persons) in Upper Corrales and twenty-six families (160 persons) in Lower Corrales.

The name "Corrales" apparently derived from extensive corrals which were built along the river. For a while the Post Office Department insisted that the community be called Sandoval, but the village remained Corrales to its residents. The Post Office Department capitulated to local preference.

During recent years, Corrales has attracted artists, writers, and sculptors. At least one of the old Spanish haciendas from the 1700s, Casa San Ysidro, has been restored to its former glory. The San Ysidro Church, built in the 1860s, is on the National Register of Historic Places; restored and protected, it now serves as the Adobe Theater.

The town is an admixture of architecture: old Spanish home-steads and recent adobes equipped with boxy solar units. Unpaved rural lanes still impart a pastoral atmosphere. There are small res-taurants, galleries, and shopping centers instead of sprawling malls. Visitors from Albuquerque come in the spring to see fruit trees in bloom and in the fall to buy pumpkins, apples, corn, and other produce.

Sandía Pueblo

Sandía (watermelon) was not the Indians' name for their pueblo. They called it Nafiat, "dusty place." It was constructed about 1300, probably by Anasazi migrants from what is now Arizona.

With a population of some 300 and a reservation of only about 24,000 acres, Sandía is one of the smallest of New Mexico's pueblos. The reservation extends from Bernalillo on the north to Alameda on the south and from the Rio Grande on the west to the Sandia Mountains on the east. Its proximity to Albuquerque provides employment for members of the Indian community.

When Coronado's expedition arrived in 1540, the Dusty Place was a thriving community of some 3,000, at that time more than two centuries old. During a two-year stay, the Spaniards meted out harsh treatment and virtually destroyed the pueblo. After the Spaniards left, the Indians rebuilt—only to have other Spaniards return as colonizers.

Fray Estévan de Perea founded the San Francisco Mission at Sandía in 1610 or 1611. Father Perea was a zealous defender of the faith; he was primarily responsible for bringing the dreaded Inquisition to New Mexico. Penalties for not accepting the white man's god were severe; kivas were raided, ceremonial objects were burned, and Indians were hanged or sold into slavery.

It is small wonder that the Indians of Sandía joined wholeheartedly in the Pueblo Revolt of 1680. Their pueblo became a headquarters for the rebels. The Indians piled hay in the church and burned what was to them the primary symbol of Spanish rule.

One story has it that a group of Indian maidens plotted to beguile a party of Spanish soldiers and kill them while they were sleeping off their orgy. With or without this ploy, the Indians soundly defeated the Spaniards who fled south of the Rio Grande to regroup and plan for Reconquest.

The Indians at Sandía rebuilt their pueblo and worshiped their gods, troubled only by the raids of other tribes. It was twelve years before the Spaniards returned under Don Diego José de Vargas. Other pueblos might capitulate to the return of Spanish rule, but Sandía Pueblo had had enough.

They picked up bag and baggage and scattered to other pueblos. A substantial group trekked more than two hundred and fifty miles westward to the land of the Hopis. The Hopis welcomed them. They were having trouble with the Navajos and needed good fighters. The Indians from Sandía built a new home in what is now Arizona. They called it Payupki.

But they were not happy. The Hopis' gods were different; their language was different. The Tewas from Sandía became homesick. After sixty-two years, in 1742, Fray Juan Miguel Menchero convinced them to return to the ruins of their old home. Under petition from Father Menchero, the Spanish administration in Santa Fe set aside land and renewed the old grant for the pueblo.

Spanish priests were now more lenient. They asked the Sandía Indians "to try" their religion. An informant reported: "Some of us did. Some of us went back to our old gods; they worked better." For a while Indians in neighboring pueblos viewed the Sandía Indians with suspicion; they mixed Hopi gods with their religion.

Today, the Sandía Indians are zealous of their ancient cultural heritage. Kivas and other ceremonial structures remain in the center of their pueblo. Understandably, they do not allow photography in the pueblo, even for a fee.

Bernalillo

Prior to the coming of the Spaniards, Bernalillo (little Bernal) was the site of prehistoric Tiguex pueblos. It is still not uncommon to find shards of thirteenth-century pottery around town. Excavations for new buildings have revealed archaeological sites of major importance.

By 1674 there were a number of large haciendas along the river. The largest was that of the González-Bernal family. Don Diego de Vargas stayed at Bernalillo during the Reconquest and founded the town in 1695. When de Vargas died in 1704, his will read: "If His Divine Majesty shall be pleased to take me away from the present life, I desire and it is my will that a Mass be said while the corpse is present in this town of Bernalillo."

By 1776 Bernalillo had became an important trading center. There were twenty-seven families, eighty-one people. Trade continued during the American period. In 1871 Nathan Bibo established the Bernalillo Mercantile Company. The "Merc" became headquarters for a mercantile empire. An inventory from early days included: coffins, harnesses, overalls, tractors, Studebaker wagons, brass bells, feathers, beads, spittoons, coal buckets, loggers' hooks, nails, cook stoves, horseshoes, fringe and ticking for shawls, shells for heishi, blue cornmeal, native herbs, hides, pelts, bolts of cloth, and dolls.

When the Santa Fe Railroad came through Bernalillo, officials started negotiating for land on which to build yards and shops. José Leandro Perea was the largest landowner in town. He liked the village as it was. He priced his land so high that the railroad elected to go twenty miles south to build its facilities in Albuquerque.

Bernalillo is still dominated by Hispanic families, and Spanish customs dating back two centuries are still observed.

Coronado State Monument

Coronado State Monument is on NM 44 northwest of Bernalillo. It can also be reached from I-25 by taking Exit 242 and driving three miles on NM 44.

Toward the end of February, 1540, an army of 336 Spanish soldiers; 100 Indian allies and slaves; and horses, mules, and other livestock left the frontier town of Compostela, Mexico. They marched northward in search of the legendary Seven Cities of Cíbola. The

A gentle warning keeps visitors on the paths at the Coronado State Monumemt.
—Photo by the authors

Captain General of this expeditionary army was Francisco Vásquez de Coronado.

When Coronado came up the Rio Grande Valley in 1540, he found a group of Indian pueblos between Isleta and present-day Bernalillo. He called this region the Tiguex Province because the inhabitants spoke a common language, Tewa. This was the most densely populated part of the Southwest seen by the Spaniards.

Hernando de Alvarado told of their arrival at the pueblo of Kuaua on September 8, 1540:

> ... we went to a river [Rio Grande], which we named *Nuestra Señora* because we reached it the evening before her day in the month of September. We sent the cross, by a guide to the villages in advance, and the next day people came from twelve villages, the chief men and the people in order, those of one village behind those of another, and they approached the tent to the sound of a pipe, with an old man for spokesman. In this fashion they came into the tent and gave me the food and clothes and skins they had brought, and I gave them some trinkets, and with this they went off.

We owe the sharp-eyed Pedro de Castañeda, chronicler of the expedition, for much detail concerning the everyday lives of pueblo Indians during the sixteenth century:

> They all worked together to build the villages, the women being engaged in making the mixture and the walls, while the men bring the wood and put it in place. They have no lime, but they make a mixture of ashes, coals, and dirt which is almost as good as mortar, for when the house is to have four stories,

they do not make the walls more than half a yard thick. They gather a great pile of twigs of thyme and sedge grass and set it afire, and when it is half coals and ashes they throw a quantity of dirt and water on it and mix it all together. They make round balls of this, which they use instead of stones after they are dry, fixing them with the same mixture, which comes to be like a stiff clay. . . .

The young men live in the estufas [kivas], which are in the yards of the villages. They are underground, square or round, with pine pillars. . . . The floor was made of large, smooth stones, like the baths which they have in Europe. They have a hearth made like the binnacle or compass box of a ship, in which they burn a handful of thyme at a time to keep up the heat, and they stay in there just as in a bath. The top was on a level with the ground. Some that were seen were large enough for a game of ball. When any man wishes to marry, it has to be arranged by those who govern. The man has to spin and weave a blanket and place it before the woman, who covers herself with it and becomes his wife. The houses belong to the women, the estufas to the men. If a man repudiates his woman, he has to go to the estufa. It is forbidden for women to sleep in the estufas, or to enter these for any purpose except to give their husbands or sons something to eat.

Castañeda included a detailed account of the Tewas' method of grinding corn:

. . . They keep the separate houses where they prepare the food for eating and where they grind the meal, very clean. This is a separate room or closet, where they have a trough with three stones fixed in stiff clay. Three women go in here, each one having a stone, with which one of them breaks the corn, the next grinds it, and the third grinds it again. They take off their shoes, do up their hair, shake their clothes, and cover their heads before they enter the door. A man sits at the door playing on a fife while they grind, moving the stones to the music and singing together. They grind a large quantity at one time, because they make all their bread of meal soaked in warm water, like wafers.

The conquistadors occupied the pueblo of Kuaua during the winters of 1540-41 and 1541-42, using it as a headquarters from which to search for the riches of Quivira. At first the Tigua people welcomed the visitors and submitted to their demands for food, shelter, and clothing—even to the point of turning a village over to the interlopers. However, the demands of the army and the actions of individual soldiers became unbearable, and the Indians staged a revolt against the Spanish invaders during the winter of 1540-41.

The results were disastrous. Two villages were destroyed and many Indians were killed to serve as "an example."

Coronado returned to Mexico in the spring of 1542 after traveling more than 4,000 miles through country never seen by Europeans. Coronado had prepared the way for further expeditions and eventual colonization of the Southwest by the Spanish, but his expedition was deemed a failure. He had found mud houses and grass huts instead of the Seven Cities of Cíbola. His plunder consisted of a few small copper bells but no gold and no jewels. On his return to Mexico, he was brought to trial for mismanagement of the army and cruelties inflicted upon the native people. He was exonerated of the charges, but his contributions to European settlement of the New World went unrecognized during his lifetime.

After returning to Spain, Gaspar Pérez de Villagrá, who was a member of the expedition, wrote *Historia de la Nueva México*, which was published in Alcala, Spain, in 1610. He told about the quarters occupied by the Spaniards during their stay in Kuaua:

> On the walls of the rooms where we were quartered were many paintings of the demons they worship as gods. Fierce and terrible were their features. It was easy to understand the meaning of these, for the god of water was near the water, the god of the mountains was near the mountains, and in like manner all those deities they adore, their gods of hunt, crops, and other things they have.

Prehistoric mural in the "painted kiva" at the Kuaua Pueblo ruins in Coronado State Monument. —Courtesy Museum of New Mexico, Neg. No. 44483

Almost four hundred years later, when archaeologists excavated the ruins of Kuaua, those paintings of "demons" were discovered, one of the finest examples of prehistoric art in the United States. In the "painted kiva" there were eighty-five layers of adobe plaster. These were carefully removed. Seventeen layers were found to contain multi-colored murals: masked kachinas, flowing springs, cloud symbols and rain, the river, seed and corn, life on earth and after life, and the animals prized by hunters. They have been preserved.

The two Tiguex pueblos, Kuaua and Puaray, were built about 1300; they were abandoned at the turn of the sixteenth century. The people moved in with Tewa kinsmen at Sandía Pueblo, three miles south of present-day Bernalillo. Today, Sandía and Isleta pueblos are the only two remaining of the old Tiguex Province. It is interesting to note that at the time of abandonment the entirety of Kuaua was not occupied. The Tewas would build new houses on the outskirts of their pueblo, letting the older sections deteriorate. Obviously, urban decay is not a new social phenomenon.

In 1934 archaeologists began to probe the rubble. Excavation and restoration took five years. Now the partially restored ruins of Kuaua and Puaray on the bank of the Rio Grande show visitors what life was like from 1300 to 1600. The area was declared a state monument on March 7, 1935. The 400th anniversary of the entrada of Coronado was celebrated in 1940 with the Coronado Cuarto-Centennial, which included dedication ceremonies at the monument.

Algodones

This small Hispanic community was once a local trading center. Now, it is sometimes listed as a "ghost town," a fact which is stoutly disputed by local residents, many of whom trace their ancestry back to the original settlers. They raise alfalfa and garden crops. In the fall, houses are festooned with ristras of chile peppers hung out to dry.

The mission Church of San José is the focal point of community life. Algodones honors its patron saint on June 19, rather than on March 19, the traditional feast day, in order to assure better weather for the procession. The procession, made up of little girls in First Communion dresses and boys in acolyte vestments, assembles around the statue of St. Joseph at the church. From there, the procession snakes through town, picking up people at each house where the participants stop to sing.

During the 1800s, Algodones was a stop on the road to Santa Fe.
—Beadle, 1873

Sandia Peak Aerial Tramway (Exit 234)

The exit leads to Tramway Boulevard and the Sandia Peak Aerial Tramway. The tramway climbs 3,819 feet over a 2.7-mile course, billed as the longest in the western hemisphere. The observation deck on Sandia Peak is 10,360 feet above sea level. It provides a spectacular 11,000-square-mile panorama. The trip up from rugged desert terrain on the west side to lush mountain foliage on the east side goes through four of the earth's seven life zones, said to be biologically equivalent to a trip from Mexico to Alaska. Bighorn sheep, deer, chipmunks, and squirrels are common; occasionally one sees a Golden Eagle soaring past.

San Felipe Pueblo (Exit 252)

San Felipe Pueblo, west of I-25, had two previous locations. It was at the foot of Tamita Mesa when Coronado visited in 1540. It is believed to have been named by Castaño de Sosa when he passed through New Mexico in 1591. Later, it moved to the northern summit of Black Mesa, west of the present location; and, shortly after 1700, to its present location on the mesa overlooking the Rio Grande. The present church was built about 1706. During Fray Francisco Atanasio Domínguez's pastoral visit in 1776, there were ninety-five families numbering 406 people.

San Felipe is a "traditional pueblo" where the people engage in the old ceremonials. The most notable takes place on May 1, the feast day of St. Phillip. A Green Corn Dance is held. Hundreds of men, women, and children in symbolic costumes participate in rhythmic dances throughout the day, accompanied by a great chorus of male voices. Over the centuries dancing feet have worn the plaza into the shape of a huge bowl.

Historical Excursion

NM 22
Domingo—Cochiti Lake

Take NM 22 via Exit 264 to experience the contrasts between two ancient Indian pueblos and a modern retirement and vacation community complete with a golf course.

Domingo

This little community to the east of NM 22 on the Santa Fe Railroad was once called Thornton. Though it has a depot, trains no longer stop. Early in the century a branch of the Bernallilo Mercantile Company did brisk business as a trading center for surrounding pueblos.

Santo Domingo Pueblo

Santo Domingo Pueblo is just west of NM 22. The original pueblo, to the west of the present site, was washed away about 1700. It was the scene of the martyrdom of three priests during the Pueblo Revolt of 1680; Francisco Antonio Lorenzazana, Juan de Talaban, and José Montes de Oca were murdered on August 10. A week later, during his retreat from Santa Fe, Governor Otermín found their bodies, clad in their robes and buried under a pile of earth in the mission church.

Zebulon Pike was impressed by the church during his visit in 1807:

> After we had refreshed ourselves a little the captain sent for the keys of the church. We entered it, and I was much astonished to find enclosed in the mud-brick walls many rich paintings, and the Saint (Domingo) as large as life, elegantly ornamented with gold and silver. The captain made a slight inclina-

Clown dancer in the Corn Dance at Santo Domingo Pueblo in 1890. The Corn Dance is still an annual event at the pueblo. —U.S. Bureau of Census, 1890

tion of the head, and intimated to me that this was the patron of the village. We then ascended into the gallery, where the choir are generally placed. In an outside hall was placed another image of the saint, less richly ornamented, where the populace repaired daily and knelt to return thanks for benefactions received, or to ask new favors. Many young girls, indeed, chose the time of our visit to be on their knees before the holy patron.

The Santo Domingo Indians are known for their expertise as traders, and they supplement farming incomes by handcrafts: pottery, jewelry, and woven rugs. They celebrate the feast day of St. Dominic with ceremonials on August 4.

Peña Blanca

José Miguel de la Peña was one of the first to settle in this area. From 1777 to 1780 the settlement was referred to as Rancho de José Miguel de la Peña; later it became Rancho de la Peña Blanca, perhaps because of the whitish cliffs of Peralta Canyon. The land grant, awarded in 1745, was in litigation thereafter with both the Santo Domingo and the Cochiti pueblos claiming the land.

Nevertheless, Peña Blanca grew to be a bustling farming community. Until 1876 it was the county seat of Santa Ana County, one of the original counties into which the Territory of New Mexico was divided. During the 1880s Adolph Bandelier used it as a headquarters while he was studying nearby pueblos, at which time he judged there were a hundred families there. On July 24, 1930, a disastrous flood inundated the entire town, destroying many houses and fields.

Fray Angelico Chavez, a highly respected author and talented artist, served at the Church of Nuestra Señora de Guadalupe. Fray Angelico painted the Stations of the Cross on the walls of the church. After he finished many citizens of the community found themselves portrayed on the walls of the church.

Cochiti Pueblo

This small Keresan pueblo has occupied the same site on the west bank of the Rio Grande since 1250 A.D. The first European visitor was Fray Agustín Rodríguez in 1581. The Mission of San Buenaventura (Saint of Good Fortunes) was built between 1625 and 1630, but the church's fortune was not so good; it was burned during the Pueblo Revolt.

When the Reconquest began, the Cochiti people fled to a mountain stronghold named Cieneguilla. After de Vargas conquered Cieneguilla most of the Indians returned to Cochiti to help construct a new mission. It is still standing.

Cochiti Pueblo is known for its unique drums and the quality of its pottery. The pueblo's most famous ceramic figure was popularized by Helen Cordero: The Storyteller, a grandfather or a grandmother with children clinging to and climbing on their bodies in various poses. Most of the pueblo's residents commute to jobs in Santa Fe, Bernalillo, or Albuquerque.

Cochiti Lake

After the construction of a massive earthen dam to impound the waters of the Rio Grande, developers obtained a long-term lease on land from the Cochiti Pueblo for the development of a retirement and vacation community. The lake is a popular recreational area.

La Bajada (Exit 259)

Even during its heyday, few took note of La Bajada (off NM 16 west of I-25). Now only a scattering of adobe ruins, it was once a freight depot and trading center. In the 1920s, Frank H. Trego, an early motorist, viewed it from a distance: "The little pueblo of La Bajada looked like a group of tiny brown boxes on the sandy plain at my feet."

However, few who wrote about traveling the Camino Real failed to take note of La Bajada (the descent) Hill, visible west of I-25. Freighters had to wind down the face of the black basalt cliff, bracing their wagon wheels with boulders when they stopped. In 1872, John H. Beadle, a *Cincinnati Inquirer* correspondent, wrote of La Bajada:

> ... Crossing the high *mesa*, level as the sea, we approach an irregular line of rocks, rising like turrets ten or twenty feet above the plain, which we find to be a sort of natural battlement along the edge of the "big hill." Reaching the cliff we see, at an angle of forty-five degrees below us, in a narrow valley, the town of La Bajada. Down the face of this frightful hill the road winds in a series of zigzags, bounded in the worst places by rocky walls, descending fifteen hundred feet in three-quarters of a mile.

During the Tin Lizzie era, motorists carried water to pour into boiling radiators and later boasted about how far their cars made it up in high gear. Model-T Fords often backed up the hill to take advantage of the more favorable gear ratio. In 1911 the hill was conquered. Governor William J. Mills reported on building "New Mexico Scenic Highway, or Camino Real" from Raton to Santa Fe: "One of the most beautiful pieces of road engineering in the Territory is La Bajada Hill."

An afternoon shower in the mountains can turn a dry wash into a roaring torrent. —Courtesy El Paso Public Library

La Ciénega (Exit 271)

During the eighteenth and nineteenth centuries, El Rancho de las Golondrinas was a day's travel from Santa Fe on the Camino Real. It was the first night's stop for southbound travelers or the last night's before Santa Fe for those going north. The ranch was acquired as a Royal purchase in 1710 by Miguel Vega y Coca. The original ranch buildings have been restored.

Today, El Rancho de las Golondrinas (Ranch of the Swallows) is operated by a charitable trust as a living museum to depict the essential elements of Spanish colonial culture. The original ranch buildings have been supplemented by bringing vintage log and adobe cabins from other northern villages of New Mexico. There is a molasses mill, a wheat field with a threshing mill, a blacksmith shop, a wheelwright, and a water wheel to power a functional grist mill.

Near the mill is a morada, a chapel once used by the Penitentes. Overlooking the small valley a chapel houses San Isidro, patron saint of farmers. Volunteers in authentic early costumes demonstrate wool carding, spinning and weaving; soap-making, plastering, and other household activities. The wheelwright and blacksmith are busy at their tasks. During the first weekend in May, there is a religious procession, folk dancing, traditional music, food, and other entertainment.

Santa Fe

On July 11, 1598, Don Juan de Oñate arrived at a Tewa pueblo on the west bank of the Rio Grande about thirty miles north of present-day Santa Fe. The Indians called their pueblo *yoong ghay,* (down at the mockingbird place). The Indians either abandoned the pueblo or were driven out by the Spaniards—the record is not clear. In any case, the Spaniards moved in and christened the place San Juan de los Caballeros.

The settlers set about building a more permanent settlement across the river at the confluence of the Rio Grande and the Chama River. It became known as San Gabriel del Yunque, generally cited as the first capital of New Mexico. It was occupied some time before Christmas, 1600. While the settlers were building San Gabriel, Oñate was out investigating pueblos and searching for gold. At each pueblo, he either subjugated or converted the Indians.

Some Indians, such as the Ácomas, resisted Spanish encroachment; some deserted their pueblos at the approach of the intruders;

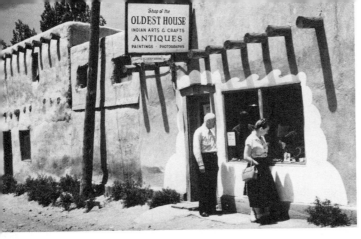

Santa Fe claims to have the oldest house in the United States, the last remnant of the Pueblo of Analco, dating from about 1200 A.D. It has been added to over the years; the annex now houses a gift shop.
—Photo by the authors

and some stayed to listen to an oft-repeated sermon delivered by the missionaries who accompanied Oñate: The King of Spain owns the world and everything in it. If you submit to him and become good Christians you will be brothers to the white men and they will protect you from your enemies. If you refuse, disaster will visit you in this world and eternal damnation will be your fate in the next.

It is doubtful the Indians grasped the religious concept of purgatory. The immediate presence of fire-belching artillery was more meaningful than any threat of vague future doom. Many reasoned they had nothing to lose by taking the oath of allegiance; being on good terms with another god could do no harm. Oñate's missionaries were able to report an increasing number of converts from heathenism.

In the meantime, all was not going well back at San Gabriel. The settlers were disappointed with the barren land. Most, like Oñate, were fortune hunters, and they had found no fortunes. As early as August, 1598, a group of malcontents was discovered plotting to defect and return to New Spain. On November 24, 1601, when Oñate got back to San Gabriel after a five-month campaign, he found that the majority of the colonists had taken advantage of his absence to desert.

In the face of open rebellion, Oñate tried to resuscitate his waning fortunes and reputation by finding the fabled pearl fisheries supposed to be in the Gulf of California. He returned empty-handed, and an order was issued for his suspension in 1607. He forestalled this by resigning. The viceroy appointed one of Oñate's captains, Juan Martínez de Montoya, as *ad interim* governor until the question of whether to abandon New Mexico altogether could be decided.

In 1608 King Philip issued an order to vacate the province of New Mexico and withdraw all Spaniards. However, the viceroy had sent Fray Lázaro Ximénez and Fray Isidro Ordóñez northward to investigate and bring back a firsthand report. Their account told of converting 8,000 Indians to the faith. A committee of theologians and jurists recommended retaining the faraway province. It would not be fair to surrender the converts to heathenism. The fact that Fray Ordóñez and Fray Ximénez exhibited specimens of genuine silver ore probably weighed heavily in the decision. The King remanded his order and took New Mexico under Royal patronage.

Thirty charges were lodged against Oñate, ranging from trivial acts of maladministration to harsh treatment of the Ácomas. He was convicted on twelve of the charges, banished from New Mexico forever and from New Spain temporarily, stripped of his titles, and fined. It was years before he obtained relief and was granted a niche in history for founding a new kingdom for the Crown and reaping a harvest of souls for the Cross.

Under Royal patronage, the governor was to be appointed for a four-year period either by the King or by the viceroy of New Spain with the King's approval. All provincial officials, including the friars, were paid by the Crown.

Don Pedro de Peralta was the first governor. His orders were to establish a new capital at a more central location and move the people from San Gabriel. Thus, La Villa Real de la Santa Fé (The Royal City of Holy Faith) was founded in 1610 on the ruins of an abandoned Tanoan Indian village at the foothills of a chain of mountains which would eventually be called the Sangre de Cristos (Blood of Christ).

When Peralta came to Santa Fe he planned a walled city laid out around a palacio which would serve as a fortress and a seat of government. The Palace of the Governors was constructed in 1610-1612, the oldest governmental building in the United States.

It was a larger structure then than it is now. There was a military chapel at the east end for soldiers of the garrison. The guardhouse was at the opposite end. The palace proper contained the residence of the governor and his family, governmental offices, and council chambers. To the rear were the patio, servants' quarters, barracks for soldiers, stables for cavalry and household horses, a parade

This early-day photograph of the Palace of the Governors predates repair and restoration. —Courtesy New Mexico Department of Development, No. 1467

ground, and other accessories of the citadel. The presidio to the rear extended about two city blocks, and the entire establishment was surrounded by a wall.

After the Indians drove the Spaniards from New Mexico in 1680, they used the buildings and constructed their own pueblo around three sides of the plaza. Twelve years later, after reoccupying Santa Fe, de Vargas put the palace in order and it again became the seat of Spanish government. By 1810 it had fallen into a dilapidated state and Governor José Manrique requested permission to make repairs. Permission was granted, but he was ordered to spend no more than thirty pesos on the job. In 1885 a modern state capital was built and state offices were moved, but the palace continued as the governor's residence until 1909 when it was turned over to museum use.

The section now facing the plaza is what remains of the original palace. None of the old log and earthen roof is left, but during the renovation in 1910 a section of the original adobe walls was left exposed. The lower part consists of courses of adobe, the type of wall constructed by Indians before the Spaniards came. The upper part is built of sun-dried bricks, adobe mixed with straw and laid with mud mortar, a building technique introduced by the Spaniards and still in use in the Southwest. At this point, the wall is fifty-eight inches thick.

Governor Peralta's administration was plagued by the outbreak of bitter conflict between church and state which continued unabated until the Pueblo Revolt. The majority of the Spanish settlers, including governors and civil officials, viewed their situations as an opportunity to enrich themselves.

The Franciscans, charged with administration of New Mexico's missions, resented interference of Spanish laity with their attempts to convert Indians. The priests' favor in this world and their place in the next was based upon the number of souls they could garner for the Kingdom of God. The Franciscans took the part of their Indian converts and criticized the abuses of Spanish settlers and officials. In rebuttal, the latter pointed out that the Franciscans were growing rich by having Indians tend their herds and flocks.

This constant bickering weakened Spanish administration and the Indians lost respect for those on both sides of the internecine conflict. Most Indians looked upon Christianity as an additional belief superimposed upon their own faiths, and they rankled under hangings, floggings, and torture as the Spaniards tried to stamp out their "heathen practices." The controversy culminated in revolt.

In 1680 the Indians rebelled. An Indian medicine man named Popé organized the revolt. For five years he laid plans among leaders in the northern pueblos. Hostilities began on August 9, 1680. From Taos to Isleta, with the exception of Santa Fe, the countryside was devastated and depopulated. Churches were burned and profaned; fields and homes were plundered; about four hundred Spaniards—men, women, children, and clerics—were killed.

The idea of revolt was so far from the mind of Governor Antonio de Otermín that the rebels won a complete strategic surprise. On August 13, by the time he got around to giving orders to prepare for siege, the enemy was closing in on Santa Fe. Some 1,000 Spaniards barricaded themselves in the governor's quarters. Livestock and supplies were brought into the compound. Only a hundred men were capable of bearing arms. They were stationed on the roof. Two pieces of artillery were planted in doorways. On the morning of August 15 the Indians came, sacking houses on the way.

The leader, an Indian named Juan, was induced to come in to parley with Governor Otermín. He bore Spanish arms and wore a red sash. The governor chided him for his rebellion, and Juan replied that it was too late for talk. Juan returned to his warriors. They applied torches to the roof of San Miguel Church, which had been built in 1610, and the roof fell in.

During the ensuing conflict, the Spaniards won a few brief victories, but the Indians eventually cut off the water supply which flowed through the palace from Santa Fe Creek, and on August 21 Otermín faced mounting thirst with a decision to abandon La Villa

Real de la Santa Fé. The Indians let them go. The Spaniards retreated to El Paso, gathering fugitive settlers and Christianized Indians along the way. After one abortive attempt at reoccupation, Otermín gave up. The Indians were free of their Spanish masters.

Indians held Santa Fe for twelve years. An Indian governor occupied the Palace of the Governors. The chapel was turned into a kiva where they worshipped gods of their choice. The Indians cleansed those who had been converted to Catholicism by washing their bodies with yucca juice. However, dictatorial excesses developed among the Indian leaders, and the cooperation which had made the revolt possible began to disintegrate.

To the south Don Diego José de Vargas Zapata y Luján Ponce de León y Contreras was appointed governor of New Mexico by a Royal cedula in 1690. The new governor's reputation as a soldier and administrator was almost as long as his name. Nevertheless, recruits for a force to accomplish the Reconquest of New Mexico were hard to come by. Most of those who had experienced the Indian uprising eschewed promises of land, weapons, food, and other favors along with the rank of *hidalgo*.

Finally, on August 21, 1692, de Vargas crossed the Rio Grande and headed north with a meager contingent of soldiers and a hundred Indian auxiliaries. Following the east bank of the Rio Grande and crossing the Jornada del Muerto, he found pueblos along the way abandoned. He arrived at Santa Fe on September 13. The old palace and the dwellings were occupied by Tanos and Tewas who refused to move out despite peace overtures.

However, the Indians had taught the Spaniards well. De Vargas cut off the water supply. This brought submission on the part of the Indians and promise of absolution by de Vargas, and on September 14 he raised the Royal standard and took formal possession of the villa.

Every year, on that date, de Vargas is still honored in Santa Fe. After his bloodless triumph, de Vargas returned to New Spain to recruit colonists. He came back in 1693. This trip was not as easy; the Spaniards met opposition at many pueblos.

On this occasion, he carried a small statuette, *La Conquistadora*. Tradition holds that de Vargas, a very devout man, attributed his successful Reconquest to the Virgin Mary through *La Conquistadora*. The statue is kept in the Cathedral of St. Francis. Every June on Corpus Christi Sunday, *La Conquistadora* is the focal point of a procession to the Rosario Chapel commemorating the Reconquest.

La Conquistadora stands on a gilded altar in the St. Francis Cathedral. The statue, which has been in Santa Fe since 1693, is carried through the streets in an annual public ceremony commemorating the Reconquest of Santa Fe in 1692. —New Mexico Economic Development & Tourism, No. 47,566

On September 16, 1712, a number of the citizens of Santa Fe met with the City Council to formulate plans for a fiesta to commemorate de Vargas' reconquest of the villa "so that in the future the said fourteenth day be celebrated, with Vespers, Mass, sermon, and procession through the Main Plaza." Thus was instituted what is touted as the oldest community celebration in the United States.

Initially, the fiesta was primarily a religious celebration, then observance lapsed. It was not reinstituted until 1912 when the Santa Fe *New Mexican* announced in the July 4 issue:

> The plans for the De Vargas pageant and Plaza Fiesta tomorrow are all complete. . . .
> The Plaza Fiesta will open prosaically with the rummage sale and will wind up poetically in the evening in the brilliantly illuminated Plaza. . . .

The St. Francis Cathedral was built under the auspices of Archbishop Lamy to serve the needs of the Spanish-speaking people of Santa Fe. It was the first church between Durango, Mexico, and St. Louis, Missouri, to attain the status of a cathedral. The cornerstone was laid in 1869. It was stolen a few days later and has not been seen since. — Courtesy New Mexico Department of Development, No. 1488

There will be plenty to eat and to drink. Refreshments will be served and that at modest figures, on the east side of the Plaza. At the northeast corner will be the unique Mexican booth and on the NW corner the Indian booth. Between them will be the candy booth where homemade candy will find ready buyers, and the cigar booth that will prove attractive to the men.

The next attempt was in 1916 when the Chamber of Commerce took over. The *New Mexican* reported, "It is about time local activities should be directed toward the permanent establishment on a large scale of some distinctive annual celebration or fete that will be a typical Santa Fe affair and bring crowds from 'all over'."

The celebration gradually took on a carnival atmosphere with cowboy-rodeo-Indian-Mexican influence. A historical pageant representing de Vargas' entry into Santa Fe was supplemented by a "Hysterical Pageant," a satirical parody of history. The Santa Fe Fiesta continues annually in mid-September and has grown in stature and reputation to the point that it does indeed "bring crowds from 'all over'." The pageant is opened by burning a gigantic statue of Zozobra, Old Man Gloom, as a symbol to participants and spectators that they should cast aside their cares and dedicate themselves to joy and merrymaking.

Members of the mechanized 111th Cavalry of the New Mexico National Guard mounted horses and rode into Santa Fe in 1940 during the four hundredth anniversary of Coronado's exploration. —Courtesy New Mexico Economic Development & Tourism, No. 47,531

According to Thomas James, an American merchant, the Santa Feans were uncertain as to what to do with independence from Spain after they got it. James arrived on December 1, 1821, and received permission to sell goods at retail. The Mexicans asked him for advice as to how independence should be celebrated. He told about it in his book *Three Years Among the Indians and Mexicans*:

On the fifth of February a celebration took place of Mexican Independence. A few days before this appointed time, a meeting of the Spanish officers and principal citizens was held at the house of the Alcalde to make arrangements for the celebration. They sent for me, asked what was the custom in my country on such occasions, and requested my advice in the matter. I advised them to raise a liberty pole, hoist a flag, and fire a salute for each Province. They counted up the provinces or states, and discovered that Mexico contained twenty-one, including Texas. They said they knew nothing of the rule of proceeding in such cases and desired me to superintend the work. I sent out men to the neighboring mountains for the tallest pine that could be found. They returned with one thirty feet long. I sent them out again, and they brought in another much longer than the first. I spliced these together, prepared a flag rope, and raised the whole as a liberty pole, about seventy feet high.

There was now great perplexity for a national emblem and motto for the flag, none having yet been devised, and those of Spain being out of the question. I recommended the eagle, but

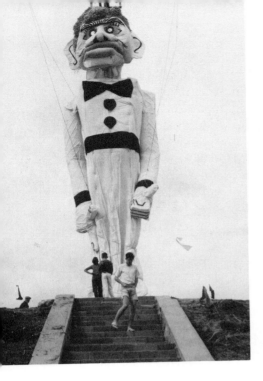

Santa Fe's annual pageant celebrating the Reconquest of New Mexico begins by the burning of Zozobra, "Old Man Gloom." —Courtesy New Mexico Economic Development & Tourism, No. 593

they at last agreed upon two clasped hands in sign of brotherhood and amity with all nations. By day on the morning of the fifth I was aroused to direct the raising of the flag. I arose and went to the square, where I found about a dozen men with the Governor, Don Facundo Melgares, all in a quandary, not knowing what to do. I informed the Governor that all was ready for raising the flag, which honor belonged to him. "Oh, do it yourself," said he, "you understand such things." So I raised the first flag in the free and independent State of New Mexico. As the flag went up, the cannon fired and men and women from all quarters of the city came running, some half-dressed, to the public square, which was soon filled with the population of this city.

During the Mexican administration, trade increased over the Santa Fe Trail. As Anglo-American traders engaged in a lively business, Mexican officials lined their pockets. Governor Manuel Armijo told James J. Webb, a trader, how the system worked. The governor wanted to buy a pair of sorrel horses from Webb, and Webb was trying to import four wagonloads of merchandise.

"Well, young man, I will be liberal with you," said Governor Armijo. "You know that the legal duties on your goods would amount to from $1,800 to $2,000 a wagonload, and I allow you to enter them at seven hundred and fifty dollars a wagon, and if you want to take them to Chihuahua or any interior market, I give you the manifest for them and certify that all import duties have been paid. Now this, young man, is stealing, but we do all the stealing and divide with you, giving you much the largest share of booty. I will give you the duties on one load of goods for the sorrels, and you must pay seven hundred and fifty dollars a load for the balance."

As they neared Santa Fe, wagoners cleaned up and put on their finest clothes in preparation for the debauchery which was available on and around the plaza. Saloons, dance halls, and gaming establishments fronted on the plaza and the streets leading away from it. Gambling, a Spanish passion, was heightened by the arrival of American adventurers.

Doña Gertrudis Barceló, known as "La Tules," became wealthy dealing monte. She also became a social and political force in the community. A newspaper reporter described her as "the supreme queen of refinement and fashion in the republican city of Santa Fe."

Mexican administration was punctuated by a revolt of the northern pueblo Indians in 1837 during which a force of some 2,000 occupied Santa Fe on August 9. They elected a Taos Indian as governor, appointed Indians to governmental posts, and seized the property of former political figures. The occupation was short-lived. In January, Governor Manuel Armijo defeated the rebels and executed the Indian governor and his leaders.

In 1841 the ill-conceived Texan-Santa Fe Expedition invaded the territory, jeopardizing Mexican control. Governor Armijo quashed the threat and reaped the undying hatred of Texans for the barbarous cruelty practiced upon the Texan prisoners.

That invasion was repulsed, but the Americans were coming. It was only a matter of time.

The expansionist drive of Manifest Destiny was bringing them ever closer. Mexico broke off diplomatic relations with the United States in March, 1845, following the annexation of Texas. By Act of Congress on May 13, 1846, a state of war was recognized. On June 30 the Army of the West set out for New Mexico over the Santa Fe Trail.

By August 15, Gen. Stephen Watts Kearny was on a roof-top in Las Vegas claiming New Mexico on behalf of the United States. In the meantime, on August 13, Capt. Philip St. George Cooke and James W. Magoffin, a Santa Fe trader, had met under a flag of truce with Governor Manuel Armijo. Magoffin's wife was Mexican. He was an old hand in the Santa Fe trade. He also knew Armijo. Magoffin reported on the meeting in a letter to the Secretary of War:

> I found many of the rich of the Department here, also the militia officers, with whom I had ample intercourse. I assured them the only object of our Govmt. was to take possession of New Mexico as being a part of the territory annexed to the U.S. and to give peace and quietude to the good people of the country which gave them entire satisfaction.

The meeting must have made a deep impression on Governor Armijo; on the following day he executed his last will and testament. There have been rumors that a satchel of gold changed hands, but no proof has ever come to light. We do know that Magoffin later presented a bill for $50,000 to the United States for his services. He collected $30,000.

For whatever reason, Armijo canceled his plans to personally lead Mexican troops against General Kearny at Apache Pass in defense of Santa Fe. He departed for the south with a personal bodyguard of a hundred dragoons.

On the afternoon of August 18, Kearny marched into Santa Fe without firing a shot. After hoisting the Stars and Stripes over the ancient Palace of the Governors, General Kearny gave an order to two lieutenants to make a reconnaissance of the town and select a site for a fort.

Two days later he was furnished a map. The fort was to be located on low rolling hills about six hundred yards from the palace. Construction plans were completed the next day. Work started on August 23 and the first U.S. Army fort in New Mexico was completed by the end of September. It was named Fort Marcy for Secretary of War William L. Marcy.

The fort was an irregularly shaped earthwork nine feet high with parapets and loopholes to allow a field of fire in all directions. It was surrounded by a moat. Inside was a powder magazine and a two-story log blockhouse. Troops were garrisoned in buildings down the hill north of the palace.

The troops were needed in January, 1847, to put down a rebellion in Taos. During the next few years they were called upon to recover stolen cattle; defend wagon trains; fight Navajos and Apaches and negotiate peace treaties with them; hang Indians, New Mexicans, and renegade Anglos; and drum a deserter out of the service after giving him fifty lashes, shaving his head, and branding a D on his hip.

During 1853, Inspector-General Col. Joseph K. F. Mansfield conducted an inspection of forts in the Department of New Mexico. He estimated the population of the Territory at 50,000 Spanish-speaking residents, about 10,000 Indians located in twenty-eight villages, and only a "nominal number" of persons from the States. He placed the population of Santa Fe at a thousand. "There are probably not over six females from the States in Santa Fe," he commented. In the whole Territory there were only two schools: one a Catholic school for children of the more influential families, and a Baptist school in Santa Fe operated by Rev. Henry Smith, "who has 12 or 14 scholars."

"I doubt if the population will think seriously of taxing themselves to support a State government for many years to come," Mansfield wrote. In actuality, a bill providing for statehood was introduced in almost every Congressional session between 1849 and 1910.

Colonel Mansfield did not approve of the language employed by teamsters:

> I must here remark as to the profanity of the citizen teamsters as a general thing. If there is any thing shocking to the moral sense, it is the awful and hearty swearing bestowed by them on their mules. On the most trifling occasion, the whole vocabulary of "billingsgate" is poured out to the annoyance of every person within hearing. I have no doubt this evil can be corrected by making it a matter of sufficient importance to be noticed by wagon masters and others in authority.

There is no evidence that Colonel Mansfield improved the language of teamsters, either citizen or military.

In 1851 most of Fort Marcy's troops were moved to Fort Union. Lt. Col. Edwin Vose Sumner was named commander of the Military Department of New Mexico in April, 1851. He did not look favorably upon Santa Fe:

> I reached Santa Fe, on the 19th of July and assumed command of the Department. My first step was to break up the post at Santa Fe, that sink of vice and extravagance,.and to remove the troops and public property to this place (Fort Union).

Fort Marcy was deactivated in 1867. The adobe began to crumble and the moat filled with sand. However, troops remained in quarters near the plaza, occupying more than a dozen buildings. Fort Marcy was permanently abandoned in 1894. Today the site of the original fort as well as the Pueblo Indian ruin which occupied the hill before the arrival of the Spaniards are covered by townhouses.

Santa Fe would suffer one more military occupation. Early in March, 1862, fresh from victory at the Battle of Valverde, Confederate forces were approaching Santa Fe—Texans eager to avenge the indignities wrought upon prisoners of the Texan-Santa Fe Expedition. Union quartermaster Maj. J. L. Donaldson, commanding a small force of troops, deemed it advisable to retreat to Fort Union.

Before evacuating the capital, Donaldson torched two warehouses of supplies and ordered the flag pole cut down so the Confederates would not be able to raise their flag on it. The warning *"Tejanos! Tejanos!"* rang through town.

On March 10, the vanguard of the Confederate army arrived to hoist the Stars and Bars over the governor's palace. The ancient villa was formally occupied by Gen. H. H. Sibley on March 13. His proclamation promised "absolute amnesty to all citizens who have, or may within ten days lay aside their arms and return to their homes and avocations." Then Sibley turned his attention to the business of trying to capture Fort Union and sorely needed supplies.

The outcome of the Battle of Glorieta changed his plans. The Confederates abandoned Santa Fe, leaving behind a surgeon and a few attendants to care for sick and wounded soldiers. On April 12, Union forces returned. The Santa Fe *Gazette* commented that the only mementoes left by the retreating Confederates were copies of Sibley's proclamations and empty champagne bottles. The flag of the United States was raised over the plaza. The occupation lasted less than a month.

The marker at the end of the Santa Fe Trail has long been a popular photographic subject. —Courtesy New Mexico Development & Tourism, No. 73

Santa Fe again settled down to the business of serving as a focal point of Territorial government and entertaining travelers, many of whom were now tourists who came via the Santa Fe Trail and the old Camino Real. Books and articles began to appear in the East about the ways of people in this quaint far-Western city.

With the expansion of railroads across the continent during the 1870s, freighters and stagecoaches began to disappear. In 1879, utilizing part of the old Santa Fe Trail, the Santa Fe Railroad crossed Raton Pass and headed toward Santa Fe. However, it was found that construction of a main line through town would involve an expensive uphill run from Glorieta Pass to Santa Fe. Consequently, the Santa Fe junction was located at Lamy, eighteen miles south. A spur was built into town. Service was discontinued over the spur in 1926. Ironically, the railroad which took its name from the Ancient City did not provide direct service to the community.

The railroad brought prosperity to Santa Fe as it made trade goods easier to come by. With the arrival of modern building materials and millwork from the East, architectural fashions deviated from the dull earthen tones of the Spanish-Pueblo style which had dominated the scene for two and a half centuries. The "territorial style" was created, and some builders used Victorian and Queen Anne design books. The town's first bank was housed in a Greek temple.

Beginning in the 1880s and continuing into the twentieth century, Santa Fe's salubrious climate combined with her historical background to attract musicians, artists, writers, and photographers. Archaeologists came to make Santa Fe headquarters while they unearthed ancient Indian cultures.

On January 6, 1912, President Taft formally proclaimed New Mexico the forty-seventh state of the Union.

During the 1940s, with the development of scientific laboratories at nearby Los Alamos, scientists came to live. The 1960s brought flower children to the plaza. With the value of the tourist-dollar becoming more and more evident, fear grew that modernization would ruin Santa Fe's historical integrity. In 1957 a Historical Zoning Ordinance was passed prohibiting new structures in the downtown historical district in styles other than Spanish-Pueblo or territorial style. The ordinance describes "Old Santa Fe style":

> With rare exceptions, the buildings are of one story, few have three stories, and the characteristic effect is that the buildings are long and low. Roofs are flat with a slight slope and surrounded on at least three sides by a firewall of the same color

This drawing of the Catron Building on the Plaza at Santa Fe shows the structure in Victorian splendor as it was completed in 1891. —Frost, 1894

and material as the walls or of brick. Roofs are never carried out beyond the line of the walls except to cover an enclosed portal, the outer edge of the roof being supported by wooden columns. Two-story construction is more common in the Territorial than in other sub-styles, is preferably accompanied by a balcony on the level of the second story. Facades are flat, varied by inset portals, exterior portals, protecting *vigas* or roof beams, *canales* or waterspouts, flanking buttresses and wooden lintels, architraves and cornices, as well as doors, are frequently carved and the carving may be picked out with bright colors.

After passage of the Historical Zoning Ordinance, portales were constructed around the plaza to hide Victorian architecture with "Old Santa Fe style." The second story of the Catron Building still shows Victorian influence. —Photo by the authurs

A sharp-eyed observer will note many fine old Victorian buildings which have been stripped of their gingerbread and had their facades concealed by mud-colored adobe plaster and territorial trappings in order to conform to "Old Santa Fe style."

During almost four centuries of history, the Royal City of the Holy Faith has had many visitors and sojourners, stretching from the hippies of the 1960s to today's movie stars and millionaires who seek anonymity behind dark glasses and high walls; from Billy the Kid to Governor Lew Wallace, who spent a goodly portion of his term in the Palace of the Governors writing *Ben Hur*.

In 1987 King Juan Carlos I and Queen Sofia of Spain paid a ceremonial visit to Albuquerque and Santa Fe, the first visit of Spanish royalty to New Mexico. Eight-year-old Georgia Bennett shook hands with the king and expressed surprise: "It felt like a human hand." King Juan Carlos presented ceremonial canes to the governors of the nineteen Indian pueblos which had once been claimed as part of the sprawling Spanish empire.

Over the years since the American occupation of Santa Fe in 1846, there has been a turnaround in the attitude toward Indians. Pueblo Indians, once looked upon as something of a nuisance, are now encouraged to wear their most colorful native costumes and display their pottery, jewelry, and weaving for sale under the portales along the front of the Palace of the Governors. Architects deftly imitate the once-scorned "mud huts," and the thought of

King Juan Carlos and Queen Sofia, of Spain, in the La Conquistadora Chapel of St. Francis Cathedral during their visit to Santa Fe in September, 1987. —Photo by Robert H. Martin, courtesy Museum of New Mexico, Neg. No. 138627

straightening one of Santa Fe's narrow, crooked streets is greeted with horror. Writing in the *New Mexican* in 1952, Oliver LaFarge summed up the street problem:

> Santa Fe is very old and hence the streets are very tired. It is an old Spanish custom to apologize to a street when you bump over a rut. That rut may well have been started by one of De Vargas' men trailing his pike as he walked along. Treat it with respect. If you don't, it will bust your springs for you.

Today, Santa Fe is a visitor's mecca. About twelve million people come each year to experience the City of Holy Faith. It can be a cultural experience, a shopping binge, a history lesson, or pure entertainment. Almost every building in the downtown section is emblazoned with a historical marker, and there is a multitude of museums, galleries, and exhibits. Entertainment spans a spectrum from rodeo to opera. Lodgings range from posh hostelries to recreational vehicle pads, and some two hundred eating establishments await the hungry traveler, serving everything from Indian fry bread to gourmet cuisine.

Perhaps the most apt comment about Santa Fe was uttered by a tourist from New Bedford, Massachusetts, as he negotiated with a banker to cash a check so that he could stay longer: "There is so much more than we came to see."

Las luminarias, or festival lights, are widely used in New Mexico, particularly on Christmas Eve. The origin of the lights dates back to fires shepherds were keeping for warmth, light, and protection on the night angels appeared to tell them the Christ Child was born. Luminarias *are a legacy to Spanish-speaking people from Spain and Mexico. Formerly, they were fires of piñon or other pungent wood around the homes and churches, along streets, and even on flat roofs. On Christmas Eve large buildings and entire neighborhoods are sometimes outlined by* luminarias. *The illustration is of the New Mexico State Land Office on Christmas Eve.* —Courtesy New Mexico Econmic Development & Tourism, No. 801

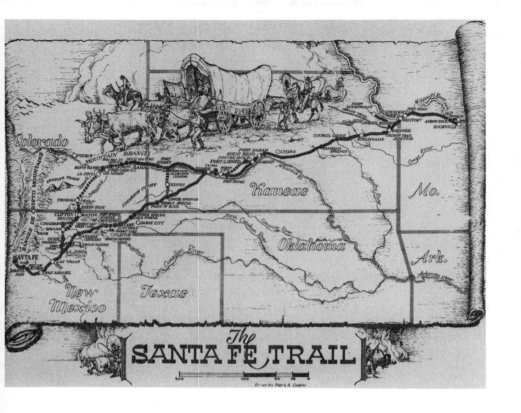

The Santa Fe Trail

III. The Santa Fe Trail

The Santa Fe Trail, stretching from Missouri to Santa Fe, was a prime contributor to the Anglo-American invasion of New Mexico and eventual statehood. The movement started in 1806-07 with Lt. Zebulon M. Pike's western expedition. After capture by the Spaniards, Pike claimed he was in Spanish territory because he was lost; he had mistaken the Rio Grande for the Red River. Pike was escorted to Santa Fe, then through New Mexico to Chihuahua, and finally sent back to the United States by way of Louisiana.

Pike's journal was published in 1810. It attracted attention to trade opportunities in the northern Spanish provinces where manufactured goods were scarce and expensive. Trappers, "mountain men" as they were called, led the invasion into Spanish

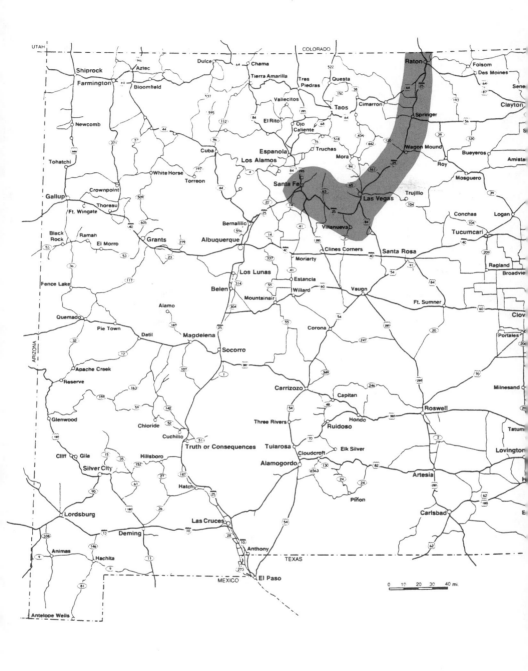

The Santa Fe Trail

territory. Some were arrested and jailed. Others made deals with pliable officials, married natives, or became "citizens" in order to trap beaver from the streams. After 1821, with independence from Spain, the republican government of Mexico did not have sufficient troops to patrol its frontiers.

On June 25, 1821, William Becknell, of Franklin, Missouri, advertised in the *Missouri Intelligencer* for men to accompany him to the southern Rockies "for the purpose of trading for Horses and Mules and catching Wild Animals of every description." On August 18, he departed with a packtrain of trade goods. Near Raton Pass he met a party of Mexican soldiers and was escorted to Santa Fe where, instead of being jailed, he discovered American traders were now welcome. Instead of trading with Indians for horses, mules, and pelts, he sold his meager supply of calico and other goods at a handsome profit.

In January, 1822, Becknell made a triumphant return to Franklin. Legend has it that upon arrival he slit a rawhide bag and let bright silver Mexican coins shower into the street. One townsman claimed a return of $900 on an investment of $60.

By spring, Becknell was ready for another trip, this time with three freight wagons and a packtrain loaded with $5,000 worth of merchandise. On his second trip he took a shorter route, braving the heat over a fifty-mile waterless stretch of the Cimarron Desert, proving that the Great Plains could be crossed by a caravan.

Becknell's success opened a floodgate as eager traders organized caravans to follow his trail. As traffic increased, the Kiowas and Comanches viewed the well-stocked caravans as a windfall. In 1825 Missouri Senator Thomas Hart Benton pushed a bill through Congress authorizing $20,000 to negotiate a treaty with Indians for a right of way and $10,000 to survey and mark the trail. The money was wasted. The Kiowas and Comanches paid no attention to the treaty which was negotiated with the Osage and Kansa tribes, and herds of buffalo stomped the mounds of earth which marked the trail into oblivion. In 1828 military escorts began to accompany the caravans through Indian territory, but this stopped in 1830 when Congress went on an economy kick. The traders were left to protect themselves.

Each caravan elected a "captain," and most carried artillery pieces which were manned by amateur cannoneers. In *Commerce of the Prairies*, Josiah Gregg, the chronicler of the Santa Fe Trail, described the confusion which resulted during an Indian attack:

From the opposite ridge, at the distance of a mile, a swarm of savages were seen coming upon us at full charge, and their hideous whoop and yell soon resounded through the valley. Such a jumbling of promiscuous voices I never expect to hear again. Every one fancied himself a commander and vociferated his orders accordingly. The air was absolutely rent with the cries of "Let's charge 'em, boys!"—"Fire upon 'em, boys!"—"Reserve! don't fire till they come nearer!"— while the voice of our captain was scarcely distinguishable in his attempts to prevent such rash proceedings. As the prairie Indians often approach in this way, Captain Stanley was unwilling to proceed to extremities lest they might be peacefully inclined. But a popping salute and the whizzing of fusil balls over our heads soon explained their intentions. We returned them several rifle shots by way of compliment, but without effect, as they were at too great a distance.

A dozen cannoneers now surrounded our artillery, which was charged with canister. Each of them had, of course, something to say. "Elevate her; she'll ground," one would suggest. "She'll over-shoot, now," rejoined another. At last, after raising and lowering the six-pounder several times, during which process the Indians had time to retreat beyond reach of shot, the match was finally applied and—bang! went the gun, but the charge grounded midway. This was followed by two or three shots with single ball, but apparently without effect; although there were some with sharp eyes who fancied they saw Indians or horses wounded at every fire. We came off equally unscathed from the conflict, barring a horse of but little value which ran away and was taken by the enemy.

Indian attack upon a Santa Fe Trail caravan. —Tassé, 1878

All of the graves along the trail did not result from Indian attacks. Illness, accidents, and hardship took their toll. Robert Morris Peck, who served at Fort Leavenworth during the 1850s, noticed that many of the graves had slanting cross pieces. Old hands informed him that when the crossbar was slanted it indicated the individual had "died with his boots on"—a violent death. If the cross piece was at a right angle the occupant of the grave had "died on the square," a natural death.

The Mexican government established customhouses and charged a duty of $500 per wagon, regardless of size. It was estimated the traders had to pay from $50,000 to $80,000 a year in duties and bribes. The traders responded by using larger wagons and stocking goods of greater value and smaller size. Many avoided duties entirely by transferring their loads to mules and bypassing Santa Fe to go on south to markets in Albuquerque, El Paso del Norte, Chihuahua, and Sonora. Blankets were smuggled past customs by using them to cover merchandise.

The wagons carried a miscellaneous stock: cloth, ribbons, shawls, hose, shirts, thread, combs, buttons, spoons, scissors, costume jewelry, knives, files, padlocks, and hardware of all kinds. Indians preferred to trade their produce for bottles rather than money. Traders bought liquor in Missouri, drank it along the way, and saved the bottles to trade for goods worth more than the cost of the liquor. Buffalo rugs, furs, wool, and coarse Mexican blankets were often carried on return trips.

During early years of the trade, Pittsburgh-made Conestoga wagons were used. They cost about $200 each. Pulled by eight mules or oxen, they covered ten to fifteen miles a day. Later, larger Murphy wagons were used. They were made in St. Louis. Three feet wide and sixteen feet long with five-foot wheels in the back, they carried about 5,000 pounds and required ten or twelve mules or oxen. Caravans of more than a hundred wagons were commonplace. In Indian territory, they traveled in four parallel columns to facilitate forming a square for defense in the event of Indian attack. The trip to Santa Fe took two or three months.

The fastest time over the Santa Fe Trail was five days and sixteen hours, a horseback ride from Santa Fe to Independence, Missouri, accomplished by Francis X. Aubry to win a $1,000 bet. Aubry was a French-Canadian trader who previously had established several records on the trail. He left Santa Fe on September 12, 1848, and rode into Independence on September 17. He used a series of fresh mounts. On one occasion, when a horse collapsed under him, he

Francis X. Aubry, "Skimmer of the Plains" —Courtesy Alma Edmonds, Missouri State Historical Society

walked twenty miles to the next station. He had to strap himself into the saddle for the last two days. He arrived in Independence with blood seeping from his tortured haunches. In recognition of his ride, Aubry was dubbed the "Skimmer of the Plains." His feat has yet to be equaled for sheer physical fortitude.

In May, 1846, the United States declared war on Mexico, and the Santa Fe Trail became a military road as Stephen W. Kearny and Alexander W. Doniphan marched invasion forces into New Mexico. With victory and annexation of the Southwest to the United States, travel over the Santa Fe Trail increased. During the summer of 1848, Col. William Gilpin, commander of Fort Mann, Kansas, located on the trail just west of present-day Dodge City, counted some 3,000 wagons, at least 12,000 people, and 50,000 head of livestock heading west. It is no wonder that ruts are still visible in portions of the land which have not yet been subjected to plowing.

Both of the routes to Santa Fe presented difficulty. The longer route over Raton Pass avoided Indians and the heat of the Cimarron Desert, but the pass was often clogged with snow and the road was a tortuous climb. Susan Magoffin's account, *Down the Santa Fe Trail*, recorded travel through the pass at the rate of a half a mile an hour.

In 1866 Richens Lacy Wootton, known as "Uncle Dick," blasted out twenty-seven miles of reasonably smooth road over the pass. He installed a gate of heavy chains to insure payment of toll and charged $1.50 per wagon and a nickel a head for livestock. It was a

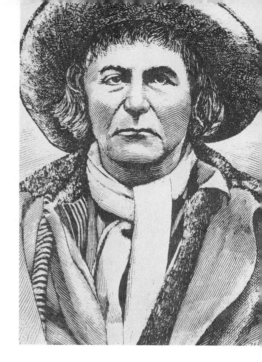

Richens Lacy "Uncle Dick" Wootton.
—Conard, 1891

profitable business. Old-timers told of his carrying whiskey kegs full of silver dollars into the bank. When the railroad came, Uncle Dick released his right to the pass for a lifetime pass on the railroad and $25 per month worth of groceries for the rest of his life.

On the shorter Cimarron Cutoff, there was little water and grass was scarce, the temperature could reach 120°. Indians were never far away from the trail. More often than not, wagons arrived at Santa Fe in such a poor state that they could not stand a return trip.

As railroads pushed westward, so did the jumping off point for the Santa Fe Trail. In 1878 the Santa Fe Railroad surmounted Raton Pass. Two years later the tracks reached Lamy, the station for Santa Fe, and the old Santa Fe Trail was on its way to becoming a memory. On February 9, 1880, when the first train reached Santa Fe (the track was later used only for freight), it was welcomed with speeches and cheers, and a headline in the *New Mexican* announced: "The Old Santa Fe Trail Passes Into Oblivion."

But it hasn't!

In May, 1987, President Ronald Reagan signed a bill making the Santa Fe Trail a National Historic Trail, bringing it under the jurisdiction of the National Park Service for interpretation and marking.

On the Santa Fe Trail wagons traveled in parallel columns to facilitate forming a square for defense in the event of Indian attack. —Gregg, 1844

The southbound motorist on I-25 enters New Mexico on the Santa Fe Trail, over the pass where Uncle Dick Wootton had his toll road. Between present-day Springer and Watrous, a large rock formation which is shaped like a covered wagon looms into view. This landmark on the trail gave its name to the town of Wagon Mound. Here the Cimarron Cutoff joined the main trail. One can visit Fort Union, which was established to guard both forks, and stop off to see the plaza in Las Vegas where caravans used to marshal for the last leg of the 800-mile trek into Santa Fe. On the sixty-mile run from Las Vegas to Santa Fe, I-25 follows the old Santa Fe Trail with little deviation. Along the way, knowledgeable localites can show you century-old ruts made by the Conestoga and Murphy wagons.

I-25
Cañoncito—Raton

Cañoncito at Apache Canyon (Exit 294)

This trading post was located where the Santa Fe Trail entered Apache Canyon near Glorieta Pass. Here, an adobe ranch house was the last stop on the trail before travelers reached Santa Fe. The site was a bastion of defense during the Mexican War and a battlefield during the Civil War.

In 1846, when Gen. Stephen W. Kearny was advancing upon Santa Fe, Governor Manuel Armijo massed 6,000 troops at Apache Canyon for the defense of New Mexico; however, the governor elected not to fight. He fled to Chihuahua and the Mexican forces retired in disarray. Kearny and his Army of the West marched into Santa Fe and raised the United States flag over the plaza in front of the governor's palace without firing a shot.

This site was also the location of a decisive action during the Civil War. On February 21, 1862, Confederate Gen. H. H. Sibley defeated the Union Forces at the Battle of Valverde. The Union forces, reinforced by Colorado and New Mexico volunteers, met the Confederates on March 26 at Apache Canyon.

The Battle of Apache Canyon lasted about three hours. In the evening, representatives of the two forces met under a flag of truce and agreed to put off further fighting until eight o'clock the next morning so that they could bury their dead and tend to the wounded.

The Union forces were headquartered at Pigeon's Ranch, the largest hostelry on the Santa Fe Trail between Las Vegas and Santa Fe. It was named for Alexander Vallé, its French-American owner who had a peculiar style of dancing at fandangos; he cut fancy "pigeon's wings." The Confederates were encamped at the western end of the pass at Johnson's Ranch.

The next morning, the fighting resumed between ten-thirty and eleven o'clock. The Battle of Glorieta Pass lasted for about six hours. Alexander Vallé put it, "Ze foight six hour by my vatch, and my vatch was slow!"

During the battle, Maj. John Chivington, of Colorado, and Lt. Col. Manuel Chávez, of New Mexico, led a small force to climb the mountainside above the battle and find the Confederate supply train at Johnson's Ranch. They burned the supplies with only one casualty, a man who was wounded by exploding ammunition. Essentially, the Confederate forces had won on the battlefield but lost the battle at Johnson's Ranch. Their supplies were gone.

The next morning, both sides spent the morning burying their dead and tending to their wounded. The Confederates had no picks or shovels, so when the Federals finished they loaned their tools to the Confederates.

Unable to fight without supplies, General Sibley retreated southward, ending attempts by Confederate forces to conquer New Mexico. The battles at Glorieta Pass and Apache Canyon have been called the "Gettysburg of the West."

The battle is re-enacted annually on Father's Day. In 1987, on the Monday following the re-enactment, the owner of adjacent property was digging a foundation for a house. His backhoe unearthed two bodies. He stopped immediately and contacted the state archaeologist. In all, there were thirty-one bodies, dressed in Confederate uniforms. He had found the long-sought Confederate cemetery, a mass burial of soldiers killed during the battle.

Glorieta (Exit 299)

The village of Glorieta (meaning "bower" or "arbor"), just off I-25, was founded in 1879 while the Santa Fe Railroad was under construction as a trading center and loading point near the highest point in Apache Canyon. In 1880 Glorieta had a moment of glory as an end-of-track town. The population swelled to 200. There was a railroad depot, saloon, post office, general store, lumber mill, hardware store, blacksmith shop, and restaurant. A theater was called the Metropolitan Opera House; grand balls were held in the two-story Palace Hotel or Glorieta House. Not even vestiges of Glorieta's heyday remain.

Glorieta Baptist Conference Center (Exit 299)

During the late 1940s, Baptist interests acquired an 880-acre ranch near Glorieta as the site for a conference center. Two years were spent constructing facilities, and 1,417 attended the first conference August 7-13, 1952. The conference center now covers 2,500 acres in the midst of the Santa Fe National Forest and serves various religious and educational organizations.

The Glorieta Baptist Conference Center is visited by from 60,000 to 70,000 people a year. It hosts conferences, retreats, and workshops for a variety of nonprofit organizations. Contrary to the implication of its name, the organizations do not have to be Baptist or even religious.

Rowe (Exit 307)

This farming community was established on the Santa Fe Railroad in 1876 along with the coming of the railroad. It was named for a railroad contractor.

NM 63
Pecos National
Monument—Cowles

Pecos National Monument (Exit 307)

The ruins of this ancient pueblo and its mission church were a landmark known to every traveler on the Santa Fe Trail. Today it is reached by NM 63 about four miles from I-25.

About 1100, Pueblo Indians living in the Rio Grande drainage area began spreading eastward over the Sangre de Cristo Mountains and settling in scattered villages along the streams. By 1450 the Pecos Valley Indians had congregated in a multistoried quadrangular pueblo built around a central plaza on a rocky ridge. It had 660 rooms for living quarters and storage and numerous subterranean kivas for ceremonial purposes.

The Indians raised corn, beans, and squash in irrigated riverbottom fields. They gathered wild plants and hunted game. Unable to grow cotton in their high river valley, they traded with Indians along the Rio Grande for cotton fibers or cloth.

When Coronado visited the pueblo in 1540 he was welcomed "with drums and flageolets, similar to fifes" and shown the shaggy skins of "humpbacked cows." There were almost 2,500 inhabitants in the pueblo he called Cicuyé. Upon Coronado's departure in search

When Lt. James W. Abert visited Pecos Pueblo he was told that a huge serpent which lived in the kiva required the annual sacrifice of a virgin.
—Emory, 1848

of the elusive wealth of Quivira, Fray Luís de Escalona volunteered to remain to Christianize the Indians of Cicuyé, thereby becoming New Mexico's first martyr for the sake of the Cross.

The next Spanish visitor was Antonio de Espejo, in 1583. He coerced the people of Cicuyé into furnishing supplies and serving as guides. Consequently, when Gaspar Castaño de Sosa arrived late in 1590, he was met with a shower of arrows and rocks. His men took the pueblo by storm with arquebus and sword and, understandably, Sosa was unable to convince the Indians that his intentions were peaceable. The Indians stole away during the night and Sosa left four days later.

After Oñate's arrival, Franciscans established a mission, and the church, Misión de Nuestra Señora de los Angeles de Porciúncula, was built between 1617 and 1620. It included a church and a convent containing a carpenter shop, weaving rooms, tanneries, a place for religious instruction, and living quarters. The Franciscans were determined to replace the Indians' economic, religious, and political way of life with that of the Spaniards.

During the seventeenth century, the Pecos Pueblo declined in population because of attacks by Comanches and Apaches, and in 1768 an epidemic of smallpox left only 180 survivors. In 1805 mountain fever further reduced the population to 104. It was abandoned in 1838 when seventeen survivors joined their kindred at Jémez. Thus ended life in what had once been the largest pueblo in all of New Mexico.

Ruins of the mission at Pecos Pueblo. —Photo by the authors

In 1869 the beams of the church were removed and used as corral posts, and the adobe of the pueblo gradually crumbled under attack by the elements. In 1915 Phillips Academy, of Andover, Massachusetts, began excavation and restoration under pioneer archaeologist Alfred V. Kidder. In 1965 Congress authorized establishment of Pecos National Monument.

—— Historical Sidebar ——————————————————

The Bogus Bishop of Pecos Pueblo

On May 29, 1760, Bishop Pedro Tamarón y Romeral arrived at the Pecos Pueblo on a pastoral visit. He was accompanied by a priest and a black servant. The party stayed until July. At least one member of the congregation paid close attention to Bishop Tamarón's activities. By September, Agustín Guichí, a carpenter, was ready to stage an elaborate masquerade.

Guichí made himself a bishop. He designed and cut pontifical vestments. He fashioned a mitre out of parchment and colored it with white earth. He made a long cape and a surplice such as the bishop wore at confirmations out of cloaks. He fashioned a pastoral crosier from a reed.

Guichí made an imitation of a Franciscan habit for another Indian so that he could play the part of the priest who accompanied the bishop, and he painted a second Indian black to represent the servant. Thus attired, on September 14, 1760, about one o'clock in the afternoon, the three mounted asses and rode into the plaza of the pueblo where they had arranged to have the residents assembled. All of the Indian women were kneeling in two rows.

The make-believe bishop went among them distributing blessings. Then Guichí and his facsimile priest went to an arbor in which they had previously prepared two seats. The "priest" stood up and announced in a loud voice that the bishop ordered them to approach and be confirmed. The Indians lined up. Guichí used water to make a cross on the forehead of each. After that ceremony a meal which had been prepared for the occasion was served. They followed the meal with a dance.

The next day the Indians again came to the arbor to hear "Bishop" Agustín say Mass. After Mass he distributed pieces of tortillas in imitation of communion. Then they had another dance.

After repeating the masquerade on the third day, Agustín Guichí and his two companions returned to the workaday business of

141

tending their crops. Undoubtedly, had it not been for a bear, Bishop Tamarón would have had some difficulty arriving at a fitting punishment.

While resting under a cedar tree, Guichí was attacked from behind by a bear. The animal tore the skin from the top of Guichí's head, mangled his right hand, and bit him about the breast. The sorely wounded man was taken to his house where he admonished his son:

"I have committed a great sin, and God is punishing me for it. And so I order you that you and your brothers are not to do likewise."

Fray Joaquín Xerez, the pueblo missionary, was summoned and Guichí confessed his sin through an interpreter. Before the carpenter died, Father Joaquín gave him the holy oil of Extreme Unction. He interred the body on September 21.

When Bishop Tamarón heard about the affair, he ordered an investigation. There were nine witnesses, three of them Spanish soldiers from the Royal presidio in Santa Fe. They had been in Pecos on escort duty and witnessed the burlesque. Finally, Bishop Tamarón was ready to issue a statement:

> The Most High Lord of Heaven and Earth willed this very exemplary happening so that it should serve as a warning to those remote tribes and so that they might show due respect for the functions of His Holy Church and her ministers, and so that we might all be more careful to venerate holy and sacred things; for the punishment that befell does not permit its noteworthy circumstances to be attributed to worldly coincidences.

Pecos

Founded about 1700, this community was known as Levy until 1883. During the 1920s and 1930s, the town's economy was closely tied to mining with more than 600 miners employed by the American Metals Company. During summers, the Santa Fe Railroad's Super Chief and El Capitan brought Easterners to spend their vacations at dude ranches which were strung along the Pecos River.

Today, Pecos serves primarily as a supply source for visitors to recreational facilities in the area and an overnight stop for visitors to the Pecos National Monument. Terrero

Cowles

In 1900, Cowles was established as a hunting and fishing resort at the end of the road. It has been there ever since.

South San Ysidro—
North San Ysidro (Exit 319)

South San Ysidro is located on the Pecos River. North San Ysidro is one mile north of the river. Both of these tiny hamlets were named in honor of St. Isidore the Farmer, who lived at Madrid in the eleventh century. San Ysidro is honored in New Mexico during May when his image is often carried through the fields as a blessing for crops.

San José

The roots of this tiny community just south of I-25 reach back to the beginning of the eighteenth century. On November 25, 1794, Governor Don Fernando Chacón approved grants of land along the Pecos River for fifty-two families who were obligated to build fortified plazas and secure firearms within two years. The land grant contained placitas named San José, San Miguel del Bado, El Gusano, Bernal, La Cuesta, Las Mulas, El Pueblo, and Puertrecito. Most have faded with time.

San José remained to be a camping site for Gen. Stephen W. Kearny on his march from Las Vegas to Santa Fe.

Historical Excursion

NM 3
San Miguel del Bado—Villanueva

NM 3 (Exit 323 off I-25) follows the Pecos River between I-25 and Villanueva State Park. It is a winding road through a series of picturesque rural and historic communities.

San Miguel del Bado

San Miguel del Bado (St. Michael of the Ford) is frequently shortened to "San Miguel," particularly on maps, and Bado is often spelled "*Vado.*" San Miguel is one of the oldest towns in New Mexico.

History tells that San Miguel was founded in 1794 by a group of peaceful Indians who were ostracized by their tribes because they converted to Catholicism. The town grew as the Christianized Indians were joined by Spanish herders and farmers. In 1806 the Indians built a stone church under the direction of Padre José Francisco Leyba, the first resident priest. It still stands with walls three feet thick and twenty feet high. Its bells contain gold and silver from coins and jewelry donated by the faithful. Padre Leyba completed his service in San Miguel and was buried under the floor of the church on the gospel side of the altar.

In 1821 on his first trip to Santa Fe, William Becknell stopped in San Miguel. He learned that local officials were giving him permission to go on to Santa Fe, thus inaugurating the Santa Fe Trail. Mexican officials were not long in establishing a customhouse at San Miguel to collect duties on goods transported over the Santa Fe Trail, and it soon became one of the most important way stations on the trail. At the peak of commerce, San Miguel had more than 2,000 residents. James Josiah Webb, who plied the Santa Fe Trail from 1844 to 1847, told how the customhouse worked:

> Messrs. Colburn and Smith took possession of the goods and wagons at San Miguel and entered them and passed through the customhouse without any trouble beyond the usual small annoyances from the customhouse officers, which were usually satisfied by small loans of money which were never paid or expected to be, and small presents of some kind to which they would take a fancy, generally amounting to twenty-five to one hundred dollars according to circumstances and number of wagons entered.

James Josiah Webb also recorded a visit from Father Leyba on one of his trips through San Miguel:

> They had a good supper, with a good supply of liquors for the entertainment of their reverend guest, of which he partook quite freely and became rather hilarious. On leaving camp, he mounted his pony and rode around the camp at the fastest run of his horse (two or three times), and coming to the road leading to town, struck off on it, raising his hat with a grand flourish, and gave us the parting "*Adios!* Goodbye! Go to hell!" and went off satisfied and happy.

In 1841 members of the ill-fated Texan-Santa Fe Expedition were captured and held prisoners in San Miguel before being forced to walk to Mexico City.

The Texan-Santa Fe Expedition resulted from an attempt on the part of Mirabeau B. Lamar, president of the Republic of Texas, to fulfill a dream of extending the western boundary of the republic to the Pacific Ocean. There was also need to bolster the flagging finances of the young republic. Lamar believed it could be done by cutting into the commercial trade which was being monopolized by the Missourians.

Lamar raised funds to organize and equip the expedition. He invited merchants to go along. He believed the people of New Mexico would welcome political and commercial relations with Texas.

On June 21, 1841, Lamar bid goodbye to a motley group as they left a camp near Austin, Texas. It consisted of a military escort of 270 men, nine merchants with $200,000 worth of merchandise, several officials of the Texas government, assorted servants, and George Wilkins Kendall, editor of the New Orleans *Picayune*, who was going along for a lark.

News of the commercial invasion had reached Mexico City. Technically, Texas was still at war with Mexico, since the Texan declaration of independence had not been recognized. The New Mexican governor in Santa Fe was warned to have no contact with the Texans; to meet them at a distance in order to keep dissident New Mexicans from cooperating with the invaders. This suited Governor Manuel Armijo fine. His political stock was at a low ebb, and he needed an opportunity to save his country.

Before reaching New Mexico, the Santa Fe Expedition got lost, ran short of rations, and was harassed by Indians. They were reduced to eating prairie dog and horse meat. On September 15, an advance party of five, including the New Orleans editor, were arrested and forced to walk fifteen miles to San Miguel where they were locked up over night in a small room off the plaza. The next day they were started on a sixty-mile march toward Santa Fe for an interview with Governor Armijo.

Late in the afternoon, about thirty miles from San Miguel, the approach of Armijo was heralded by a trumpet blast. When the governor asked who they were, Capt. William Lewis announced they were traders. Armijo grabbed him by the collar of his dragoon jacket and dragged him to the side of the mule he was riding. He pointed to the Texan star on the buttons of the jacket:

"You need not think to deceive *me*; no merchant from the United States ever travels with a Texan military jacket."

Armijo retained Captain Lewis, who said he could speak Spanish, as an interpreter, and ordered that the other four walk back to San Miguel, almost thirty miles. When they protested against walking because they had already walked ten leagues that day, the general replied:

"They are able to walk ten leagues more. The Texans are active and untiring people—I know them; if one of them *pretends* to be sick or tired on the road, *shoot him down and bring me his ears!* Go!"

The party reached San Miguel the following day. From their cells, Kendall and his three companions watched as two Texans who had attempted to escape were led out onto the plaza and shot. Captain Lewis elected to save his own hide. He led the Mexicans to the main body of the expedition and convinced the Texans they would be safe if they surrendered.

Kendall watched as the remainder of the prisoners were brought to San Miguel. He also watched the wagons and stores that belonged to the expedition being distributed. The traitorous Captain Lewis was given a share in payment for his part in bringing about their surrender.

The treatment of the members of the Texan-Santa Fe Expedition inscribed a black page in Mexican history. Armijo did not execute his prisoners. After parading them in the plaza at San Miguel, he sent them on a march over the Camino Real, through the Jornada del Muerto, to Mexico City so that Santa Anna, the despot president, could see and know the valor of his governor.

On the march, they were guarded by two hundred soldiers, some armed with muskets, others with bows and arrows or clubs. The guards were commanded by Capt. Damasio Salazar, "the greatest brute among Armijo's officers." He rode George Kendall's pack mule, which had been confiscated upon his arrest; Kendall walked. Often their day's ration consisted of nothing but an ear of corn. At Valencia, south of Albuquerque, one of the prisoners died in his sleep. Salazar ordered his ears cut off as evidence that he had not escaped and had his body thrown in a ditch. John McAlester, a volunteer from Tennessee, collapsed from exhaustion. He was shot and the party marched on. As prisoners died or were killed, their ears were added to the string on a buckskin thong. George Kendall reported that the only kindness along the way was shown by women who pitied their plight and occasionally provided food.

After reaching El Paso del Norte, south of the Rio Grande, the prisoners received somewhat better treatment, but they still had to walk as they were taken deep into Mexico and held, often in chains, in the Mexican fortress of Perote. The last of the prisoners was released in June, 1842.

The passage of the Texan-Santa Fe Expedition did not dampen San Miguel's importance as a way station on the Santa Fe Trail. It grew and prospered and was, for a while, the county seat of San Miguel County. The county seat was moved to Las Vegas in 1864, the community for which San Miguel had provided the first settlers in 1835.

San Miguel's importance as a trade center did not diminish until the railroad passed through Las Vegas and traffic on the Santa Fe Trail petered out. Most of the old buildings are gone now, victims of flood, fire, and time. Nevertheless, the town is a national historic district, and the old church is well worth a visit.

Villanueva

Villanueva, hidden in the curves of the narrow two-lane road, was founded before the turn of the century and originally called Cuesta (hilltop). It was here that George Kendall and the other four members of the Texan-Santa Fe Expedition were captured by Capt. Damasio Salazar.

In 1890, when the U.S. Post Office was established, a petition was circulated to change the name of the town. Residents vied to have the town perpetuate their family names. More Villanuevas than Aragóns signed the petition, and the name stuck.

The stone church in the middle of Villanueva dates from 1818. Within is a 265-foot embroidered tapestry which stretches around the walls. The tapestry was embroidered by women of the village. It depicts the history of the community, starting with Coronado, and includes various explorers and religious figures who came through the valley in search of gold and souls. Their efforts garnered more souls than gold here.

The tapestry also portrays the death of a priest, the arrival of nuns to teach school, the construction of the church, and—finally— the paving of the road through the community. The tapestry was hung in the church in 1976 and is proudly exhibited by the priest who lives in the rectory next door.

NM 3 continues on through Villanueva State Park and connects up with I-40 about twenty miles farther on.

Bernal (Exit 330)

Prior to the turn of the century, this community was the first stop on the stage run between Las Vegas and Santa Fe. Its stone and adobe church, Capilla de Santa Rita de Casia, was built in 1916; it has three belfries but only one bell.

Starvation Peak is just east of Bernal. History has it that 120 Spanish colonists—men, women, and children—took refuge near the summit from attacking Indians; all starved to death.

Tecolote (Exit 335)

Salvador Montoya established Tecolote in 1824 as a trading point on the Santa Fe Trail. Later, Tecolote became one of a chain of supply posts for the U.S. Army during the Indian campaigns, 1850-1860, furnishing corn and forage. Extensive stables and a headquarters building were constructed in the village. Ruts of the Santa Fe Trail are visible in the area.

Romeroville (Exit 339)

Romeroville has had its moment in the sun, but it did not happen recently. The town was founded in 1880 by Don Trinidad Romero, a rancher and member of the U.S. Congress whose father had earlier established a highly successful freight and mercantile business in Las Vegas. Don Trinidad built a $100,000 mansion in Romeroville and entertained many prominent citizens including President and Mrs. Rutherford B. Hayes and General William T. Sherman.

After Romero's death, the mansion became a sanatorium and later a dude ranch. It burned in 1932.

Las Vegas (Exits 343, 345, 347)

Archaeologists have verified that the Folsom Man hunted in the vicinity of present-day Las Vegas as far back as 10,000 years ago. Pottery fragments, arrowheads, and dated timbers show Pueblo Indians in the area from about 1200 to 1300, followed by nomadic Comanche buffalo hunters in the 1500s. Spanish explorers visited the site in 1541 as Francisco Vásquez de Coronado and his party crossed the Gallinas River after an abortive search for riches in an Indian village named Quivira in present-day Kansas.

In 1821 Luís María C. de Baca tried his hand at ranching. He petitioned the Mexican government for a land grant on the Rio Gallinas for himself and his seventeen sons. Indian raids made the area untenable.

Las Vegas owes its birth to the Santa Fe Trail. C. de Baca's ranch petered out, and in 1833 San Miguel del Bado citizens obtained a grant under the condition that they erect a plaza for protection against the Indians and as a meeting and market place. This community, originally named Nuestra Señora de los Dolores de Las Vegas (Our Lady of Sorrows of the Meadows), became the Mexican port of entry for caravans that had traveled the Santa Fe Trail from Missouri, and a thriving commerce began to develop.

Initially the business boom did little to upgrade the appearance of the community. Dr. Adolphus Wislezenus, a German naturalist, described the town in his *Memoir of a Tour to Northern Mexico* as "100 odd houses and poor dirty-looking inhabitants."

In 1846, at the advent of war with Mexico, Gen. Stephen Watts Kearny arrived at the plaza. He climbed a rickety ladder to a rooftop and announced:

> I have come amongst you by the orders of my government, to take possession of your country and extend over it the laws of the United States. We come amongst you as friends, not as enemies; as protectors, not as conquerors. . . . Henceforth I absolve you from all allegiance to the Mexican Government. . . . I shall not expect you to take up arms and follow me to fight your own people . . . those who remain peaceably at home, attending to their crops, and their herds, shall be protected by me in their property, their persons, and their religion. . . . But listen! He who promises to be quiet and is found in arms against me, I will hang!

All of the citizens of Las Vegas were not in the audience. The women and children had run away to hide among the rocks at El Creston, a stony ridge behind town. The women were afraid of being raped by the soldiers. Additionally, there was a rumor they would be branded on the cheeks with the letters US, like the *Americanos* marked their horses.

General Kearny took his Army of the West on to Santa Fe. Las Vegas continued to serve as a way station on the Santa Fe Trail and as a seat of military operations in the area until nearby Fort Union was built in 1851 to protect caravans on the trail from Indian raids.

Business continued to boom, and the Santa Fe Railroad, the first to penetrate the Territory of New Mexico, was approaching. In 1879 a railroad representative solicited pledges from local businessmen to build a station. Alas! Donors discovered the rails would pass through open country a mile to the east.

Buildings mushroomed along Railroad Avenue by the tracks. "New Town" grew, and the area around the old plaza became known as "Old Town," as it is to this day. July 4, 1879, was a day of

FRANK LESLIE'S
ILLUSTRATED
NEWSPAPER

9, 1879.   FRANK LESLIE'S ILLUSTRATED NEWSPAPER.   385

In 1879 Frank Leslie's Illustrated Newspaper *devoted a front page to the arrival of the railroad at Las Vegas.*
—Author's collection

celebration and speech-making in Las Vegas. Two locomotives arrived, "handsomely decorated with United States and Mexican flags," and the railroad was declared "completed and open to the public." *Frank Leslie's Illustrated Newspaper* chronicled the event:

> Las Vegas, which lies about forty miles southeast of Santa Fe, and nearly one hundred miles south of the Colorado line, is a brisk, enterprising and growing town, and now that it is supplied with railway communication with the outside world, will no doubt speedily become one of the important centres of population in the Territory. Its present population is made up of Mexicans, Indians, and representatives of various nationalities, nearly all of whom speak the Spanish tongue.

Indeed, the railroad brought more business and more people, the latter including what has been described as "one of the worst gangs of cut-throats and rascals that ever inhabited the West."

What is now Church Street in Old Town was known as Sodomia and La Calle de la Amargura (The Road of Suffering and Bitterness). It was flanked by bawdy houses, dance halls, and saloons.

Murder and robbery were common. Respectable citizens were aroused, and vigilantes got busy. A windmill derrick in the center of the plaza became a favorite gibbet with dangling bodies a frequent morning spectacle. On April 8, 1880, a notice appeared in the newspaper:

> To Murderers, Confidence Men, Thieves: The citizens of Las Vegas have tired of the robbery, murder, and other crimes that have made this town a by-word in every civilized community. They have resolved to put a stop to crime, if in attaining that end they have to forget the law, and resort to speedier justice than it will afford. All such characters are therefore hereby notified, that they must either leave this town or conform themselves to the requirements of the law, or they will be summarily dealt with. The flow of blood must and shall be stopped in this community, and the good citizens of both old and new towns have determined to stop it, if they have to H A N G by the strong arm of force every violator of the law in this country—VIGILANTES

The vigilantes had their way. In 1888 the town physician, Dr. Francis A. Atkins, could report there had been only one death from a gunshot wound. *Harper's Weekly* announced, "it would be hard to find a more quiet and law-abiding community in the far West."

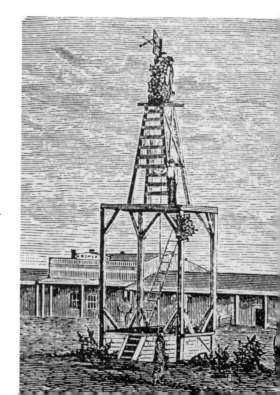

Vigilantes hung outlaws from the windmill derrick in the Las Vegas Plaza. It was torn down after citizens complained about contamination of the water. —Wilson, 1880

As the railroad and attendant businesses pumped money into the town and brought in building materials and architectural fashions from the East, construction went from simple adobe buildings to more elaborate structures, many of which have survived in spite of frequent fires during the early days.

In 1880 Don Benigno Romero raised $25,000 to build an elegant, three-story brick hotel facing the plaza, the "Belle of the Southwest." Along with Las Vegas, the Plaza Hotel suffered good times and bad. During the 1890s the town became a haven for tubercular patients; sanitariums opened and guests filled the Plaza. Those in rooms facing the old square had varying views. On occasion they saw the bodies of outlaws who had been killed by vigilantes. Then in 1899 came the raucous reunion of Teddy Roosevelt with his Rough Riders, most of whom had come from New Mexico. On that occasion, Roosevelt declared: "All I shall say is if New Mexico wants to be a state, you can count me in, and I will go back to Washington to speak for you or do anything you wish." It was not that simple. President William Howard Taft finally announced New Mexican statehood on January 6, 1912.

However, in 1900, at the apogee of its development, Las Vegas was the largest town in New Mexico. "New Town" was officially East Las Vegas and had a post office to prove it.

In 1913 Las Vegas was on its way to becoming—briefly—the motion picture capital of the United States. Romaine Fielding, one of the most popular film stars of the day, arrived to make movies. Because of an argument with the Plaza Hotel, he leased the entire establishment, and it was renamed in his honor. After making seven pictures, including *The Golden God*, a futuristic saga of a labor revolution predicted for 1950, Fielding left town. The 5,000 extras who had participated in a cavalry charge through the streets of Old Town helped spend the $50,000 the movie company left behind. The Plaza Hotel took back its old name, but one can still see "Hotel Romaine" emblazoned on the west wall in faded white letters.

In 1915 Tom Mix came to Las Vegas to participate in a rodeo called "The Cowboys' Reunion" and stayed to make movies: *Never Again, The Rancher's Daughter*, and *The Country Drugstore*. The latter two were pioneer "Westerns," and Tom Mix went on to become one of the nation's most popular actors.

During the 1960s and '70s the State Motion Picture Promotion Bureau was busy, and scenes were filmed in Las Vegas for *Easy Rider, Convoy, Sweet Hostage, Liza's Pioneer Diary*, and *Charlie Siringo*.

The Plaza Hotel was the leading hotel until the Santa Fe Railroad built the luxurious brick Castañeda alongside the railroad track in 1898 for lease to the Fred Harvey System. Over the years, the Plaza Hotel suffered physical deterioration. Nevertheless, it was listed on the National Register of Historic Places. In February, 1982, Wid and Katherine Slick arrived on the Las Vegas scene to ramrod rehabilitation of the aging structure. Architectural documentation and historical studies assured accuracy. Thirteen months and $2,000,000 later the Plaza reopened, again reflecting Victorian splendor.

Historic preservation and restoration caught on in Las Vegas, and many of the buildings around Old Town Plaza have been restored, as well as a goodly number of fine old Victorian homes. The first synagogue in New Mexico was constructed in Las Vegas, a building later to be taken over by the Newman Club.

Historical Excursion

NM 65
Montezuma—El Porvenir

Montezuma

Montezuma is located six miles northwest of Las Vegas on NM 65. The principal attraction is its old hotel and thermal springs. A strong case can be made for this site as the fountainhead of the modern tourist industry in the United States.

As early as 800 A.D. Indians from the Pecos Pueblo came to soak in water that is 110° to 140°. Later, Hispanic settlers in Las Vegas frequented the springs to bathe in the curative waters and bury themselves in warm mud. By 1846, when New Mexico became a U.S. territory, a small bathhouse had been constructed and a fee was charged for a dip in the springs. Wagon caravans on the Santa Fe Trail often detoured to stop and let their passengers soak away the dust and aches accumulated during the long ride from Missouri.

The property passed through a succession of owners, and a story was circulated, reputed to be a legend of the Pecos Indians, that Montezuma had visited the springs to take advantage of their curative powers. Some of the owners advertised "The wonderful effect of these springs in curing Syphilitic and kindred diseases, Scrofula, Cutaneous diseases, Rheumatism, etc."

In 1879 the Santa Fe Railroad bought the Las Vegas Hot Springs Company and built a two-story stone bathhouse. Water from the springs was piped into fourteen bathrooms. The following year a 75-room establishment was built and dubbed the Montezuma after the famed Aztec emperor; the railroad laid a spur track from Las Vegas. Fred Harvey managed the hotel. He catered to a wealthy clientele, importing fruit and vegetables from Mexico and serving such delicacies as green turtle and sea celery. There were carriages and saddle horses for the guests; a park was built with rustic bridges, an archery range, and tennis and croquet courts to provide the guests with entertainment between baths.

After a series of fires, the facility was successively rebuilt, each time larger until it became a multistoried, turreted, balconied castle with more than 300 rooms. The Santa Fe Railroad promoted the hotel across the nation, attracting an impressive guest list: Theodore Roosevelt, Ulysses S. Grant, Rutherford B. Hayes, Kaiser Wilhelm, influential Army generals, and thousands of well-heeled train travelers. Emperor Hirohito topped a list of Eastern nabobs.

The Montezuma was closed on October 13, 1903. It was sold to the Young Men's Christian Association for $1. The facility, often dubbed a "white elephant," passed through a series of owners until it fell into the hands of the Archdiocese of Santa Fe. It operated as a seminary from 1937 until 1972 when it was abandoned. In 1977 the old vacant castle had a moment of glory. It was briefly reopened to serve as the setting for a motion picture entitled *The Evil*.

An illustration of the Phoenix Hotel, known locally as the Montezuma, from a Santa Fe Railroad publication. —Atchison, Topeka, and Santa Fe Railroad, 1887

After a decade of crumbling decay, the historic 110-acre site was purchased in 1981 by the Armand Hammer Foundation for ten million dollars. The foundation spent millions more to rehabilitate the castle for use as the American branch of the United World College.

El Porvenir

In 1905, because of the beauty of a site up the right fork of the Gallinas River, Margarito Romero, a Las Vegas merchant, built a resort hotel which he called El Porvenir. Guests came from Las Vegas in carriages and got room and board for $7.00 a week. After the original building burned, he built another.

NM 65 ends at the base of Hermit's Peak. In 1863 Giovanni Maria Augustini arrived in Las Vegas. Augustini was an Italian who left Italy as a non-comforming Catholic. He had taken a vow to serve others while seeking solitude for himself. He became known as the Hermit, living in a cave on Owl Peak, redesignated Hermit's Peak.

His diet was principally mush. He carved religious emblems which he exchanged in Las Vegas for cornmeal. He carried a staff adorned with a small bell so people could hear him coming and insisted upon sleeping on the floor when he accepted hospitality. He left Las Vegas in 1867; later he was stabbed to death in Mesilla.

His devotees in Las Vegas formed the Society of the Hermit, and Margarito Romero promoted annual pilgrimages to the El Porvenir resort and to the Hermit's abode on Hermit's Peak.

Watrous (Exit 364)

There was a Spanish settlement at the confluence of the Sapello and Mora rivers. It was called La Junta (junction) or Rio La Junta. Samuel B. Watrous, an American trader, arrived in 1848 and built a house and trading post. In 1851, with the establishment of Fort Union only eight miles away, Watrous began to supply some of the fort's needs, and his place became a rendezvous for soldiers stationed there. With the arrival of the Santa Fe Railroad, it became a shipping point and a service center for nearby farmers and ranchers.

Valmora (Exit 364)

An extensive tuberculosis sanatorium-village was opened in 1916 at Valmora, now on NM 446, as the climate in New Mexico began to gain a reputation for having a therapeutic effect upon victims of the dreaded malady. Accommodating some sixty patients, the sanatorium had a central hospital and residential cottages for convalescents. The facility is no longer operative in that capacity.

Historical Excursion

NM 161:
Fort Union National Monument
(Exit 366)

Once the largest post in the Southwest, Fort Union was an important commissary depot. It was Army headquarters for the Northern Military District of New Mexico. It was established in 1851 a few miles north of a private fort which had been built in 1849 by an Englishman named Alexander Barclay on the Santa Fe Trail near Watrous, eighteen miles from Las Vegas.

The outer walls of Barclay's fort were in a 64-yard square with circular towers on two corners. Inside were several one- and two-story adobe buildings and sheds for horses. The Army apparently considered buying the fort. Barclay demanded $20,000. An Army inspector hazarded that Barclay "would probably take $15,000. The rent he fixes at $2,000 per annum."

The War Department passed up the deal in favor of a site at the foot of the mesa opposite Gallinas Mountain, even though Inspector General Joseph K. F. Mansfield wrote, "It is too close under the Mesa for a tenable position against an enterprising enemy, unless the immediate heights can be occupied by a block house." The enemy was enterprising, as Mansfield also reported: "On my arrival at the post, I found Major Carleton was absent and had been for two days with most of his command after a party of Indians who had committed depredations on his horses." The post had other problems. It was eight miles from firewood and the closest water was a spring that sometimes caused diarrhea.

The first fort was built of pine logs covered with earth and lumber. The place was not fortified; it was merely a cluster of buildings, but it had an arsenal. Some of the men and the families who accompanied them had to spend the winter of 1851-52 in tents until buildings were constructed. In 1861, against the threat of Confederate invasion, a new fort was built about a mile away from

Ruins of Fort Union.
—Courtesy New Mexico Economic
Development & Tourism, No. 28

the old fort, a Star Redoubt. It was a large eight-pointed earthwork. The Confederate attack did not materialize. In fact, Fort Union was the only fort in New Mexico that did not fall to the Confederate army.

By 1863 a new, more substantial fort of adobe and bricks was built nearby, and the far outpost on the Santa Fe Trail began to evidence many of the satisfactions provided by centers of civilization: stores, a theater, a church, the first Masonic Lodge in New Mexico, a regimental band, and general social activities for both officers and men. During construction it employed more than a thousand smiths, teamsters, carpenters, and laborers. Fort Union furnished troops and supplies for the forts down the Rio Grande and along the eastern edge of New Mexico.

In its prime, Fort Union was a vast collection of storehouses which held supplies sufficient for a full year, stables for 1,000 horses, bins for two million bushels of grain, yards upon which to stack 2,000 tons of hay, work and repair shops, offices, a hospital, a guardhouse, officers' quarters, barracks for 400 soldiers, and camps for civilian laborers. By 1882 it had cost the government $300,000. The peak population was 3,000. Fort Union brought a boom to farmers and ranchers in the Las Vegas area by providing a market for meat, grain, hay, and flour.

Discipline at the fort was strict, but life was fairly easy when the troops were not chasing Indians. The soldiers organized fraternal lodges, attended chapel or schools, put on plays, and worked in gardens in their spare time. But there were problems. Trooper McMann was an example.

A report by the Fort Union commander, Lt. Col. Henry Ellis, told about him: A man "of gigantic strength, a horse thief, deserter, sneak thief, a hypocritical scoundrel in general":

> Just previous to the departure of Major Alexander and the cavalry companies at this post he broke through the walls of the Military Prison and partly succeeded in breaking down the wall of the Cavalry corral apparently endeavoring to Steal horses, not succeeding in this he left the Post unhindered. . . .
>
> At daylight, the ground being soft, I struck his trail and sent a Sergeant and some mounted men in pursuit. They captured him at a Mexican town some ten miles from here in a state of semi-nudity, he having sold his clothes. He was brought back to the Post when he attacked and nearly succeeded in overpowering the entire Guard, and would have done so had he not been brought to submit by repeated blows by the butt end of their pieces.

Finally, Trooper McMann delivered the crowning insult, and Colonel Ellis had him transferred from Fort Union:

> A few days afterwards while passing the Guard House, I met him going to the rear. With one hand he drew a pocket handkerchief from his pocket and waved it at me in an insolent manner, at the same time placing the thumb of his other hand upon his nose, he gyrated the rest of his fingers into the air in a manner usually intended to be particularly exasperating.

By the 1880s, military action had shifted to southern New Mexico and Arizona where Apaches were on the warpath. Railroads were bringing freight and settlers into New Mexico, and the Santa Fe Trail no longer needed protection. Fort Union was abandoned in 1891. A caretaker detail remained to maintain the buildings until April 1, 1894, when the site along with the improvements on it were relinquished to the landowner.

The old post deteriorated as settlers from miles around came to help themselves to doors, windows, lumber, roofing, vigas, bricks, hardware, and anything else that could be pried loose, leaving

Ruts made by wagons on the Santa Fe Trail are still visible near Fort Union. —Courtesy New Mexico Economic Development & Tourism, No. 70

naked walls and rows of brick chimneys to the mercy of the elements.

It was not until the 1950s that voices were raised in behalf of the stabilization and restoration of old Fort Union, particularly as "The Cradle of Free Masonry in the Southwest." On June 28, 1954, President Dwight Eisenhower signed a bill authorizing the National Park Service to accept the Fort Union site and develop it as a national monument. The facility opened to the public on June 8, 1956.

From the junction of I-25 and NM 161, it is an eight-mile drive to the Fort Union National Monument.

—— **Historical Sidebar** ——————————————————

Sodom on the Mora

Some 125 years ago, Loma Parda was a serious contender as the most sinful town in the Southwest. Located only five miles southwest of Fort Union on the bank of the Mora River, it furnished bars, dance halls, and bordellos for the entertainment of bored soldiers who whiled away their time waiting for Indian threats which seldom materialized.

Soldiers would sneak off to town and be absent for days. Shootings and stabbings were common occurrences. The town became known as "Sodom on the Mora." One lieutenant with a reputation for drinking and gambling returned from Loma Parda without his hat and pants. Commanders at Fort Union repeatedly declared the town off limits to no avail.

In 1866 Maj. John Thompson, the post commander, sent a sergeant and three soldiers into town to arrest any personnel who were loitering. They did not return. The major went to investigate. He found his patrol in jail. The mayor refused to release them.

Business from the fort was so thriving that one resident of Loma Parda operated a buckboard taxi between the fort and town. In 1872 Texan cattlemen suspected their cattle were being rustled by residents of Loma Parda. They went to investigate. The confrontation resulted in a gunfight which left two dead and the mayor wounded.

After the abandonment of Fort Union in 1894, Loma Parda gradually faded. Today a few ruins remain on private property.

Wagon Mound (Exit 387)

The community was formed in 1850 by stockmen who were attracted by the luxuriant pasturage in the region. Initially the town was called Santa Clara, but in 1859 it took the name Wagon Mound after a rock formation which resembled a covered wagon. This formation had long been a landmark on the Santa Fe Trail. It was located where the Cimarron Cutoff of the Santa Fe Trail rejoined the main branch.

This was also a place frequented by both plains and mountain Indians who came to fight each other, hunt buffalo, or raid travelers on the Santa Fe Trail. Despite Indian depredations, prior to the coming of the railroad, the town developed a brisk business as a shipping point on the Santa Fe Trail for farm and orchard produce from the nearby Canadian River valley. However, flooding in the valley devastated fruit production and ended the trade. Then Wagon Mound developed as a corn and bean farming center. In spite of the fact that beans are no longer raised in the area, Labor Day is still annually celebrated as Bean Day.

One unscrupulous local merchant did a thriving business establishing beginners as sheep ranchers and then foreclosing on them when the market declined.

Wagon Mound is still essentially a farming and ranching community.

The rock formation known as Wagon Mound was a landmark on the Santa Fe Trail. —Courtesy New Mexico Economic Development & Tourism, No. 803

Springer (Exit 412)

Springer originated on the Cimarron River with the coming of the Santa Fe Railroad in 1879, organized by Charles Springer, a rancher near Cimarron, and his brother Frank, a lawyer for the Maxwell Land Grant. With the arrival of the railroad, Springer became a shipping point for cattle which were driven in from the eastern plains of New Mexico and the Texas Panhandle.

In 1882 Springer was named the county seat of Colfax County. By 1897 there were more than fifteen hundred people in Springer. After a bitter political fight, the county seat was moved to Raton. During the following year about five hundred residents moved away from Springer.

Springer survived. Annually it hosts the Colfax County Fair in early September. In addition to traditional contests such as tractor-pulling, a cow-chip-throwing contest arouses spirited competition.

Maxwell (Exit 426)

In 1841 the Mexican governor, Manuel Armijo, issued a vast land grant to Charles Beaubien, a French trapper, and Guadalupe Miranda of Taos. The land grant was the largest single holding of land in the Western Hemisphere. It covered 1,714,764.93 acres of minerals, timber, and pasture in parts of southern Colorado and

161

Lucien Bonaparte Maxwell.
—Conrad, 1891

New Mexico. The grant was the subject of much litigation. Its legality was finally approved by the U.S. Congress on June 21, 1860, and later confirmed by the Supreme Court; nevertheless, its validity continued to be a subject of controversy.

Lucien B. Maxwell, a hunter and trapper who came to New Mexico from Kaskaskia, Illinois, about 1849, married Beaubien's daughter, Luz. After Beaubien's death in 1864, Maxwell bought out the other heirs for $3,000. New Mexico towns within the land grant included Springer, Maxwell, French, Raton, Vermejo Park, Ute Park, Eagle Nest, and Elizabethtown.

Maxwell's principal interests were gambling for high stakes, breeding fine horses, acquiring exquisite furnishings for his mansion, and serving as *grande patrón* to the Mexicans and Indians who worked hundreds of acres and tended his vast sheep and cattle holdings. He sold beef cattle and forage to Army posts and to the Ute Indian Agency.

Maxwell did business on a "hand-shake" basis. He outfitted would-be ranchers with stock, land, and seed with which to supplement the rich grama grass that grew on the lava-capped land. When he was pressed for cattle or forage to fill his Army contracts, he called the ranchers together and asked for his share. No accounting was asked for; he took each at his word. It is said he was always well paid, overpaid if the year had been good.

In later years, Maxwell sold his holdings to an English syndicate, a land-promotion outfit which sent brochures back East and to England showing large cargo ships going up the Cimarron and Canadian rivers. Maxwell got his property back and shortly thereafter sold it to a Dutch syndicate for about three million dollars.

The town of Maxwell was established during the late 1880s by the Maxwell Land and Irrigation Company, part of the Dutch syndicate which was surveying the prospects for irrigation in the area. The community began with a general store, a saloon, a hotel, and a livery stable. For some ten years, beets were grown in the area, another of Lucien Maxwell's projects, and a sugar refinery was located just outside the city limits.

The adjacent Maxwell National Wildlife Refuge (via NM 505) is the winter residence of Canadian geese and bald and golden eagles. Hunting is not permitted on the refuge, but the lakes contain bass and trout for fishermen.

Raton (Exit 450)

Early travelers on the Santa Fe Trail elected the northern route west from Bent's Fort (near the present site of La Junta, Colorado) over the Raton Pass and south to Fort Union to reduce the threat of Indian attack and take advantage of the availability of water. Until the advent of Richens Lacy "Uncle Dick" Wootton, it took heavily laden wagons up to five days to negotiate the tortuous pass.

Uncle Dick Wootton was one of the most colorful of the West's characters. He was born in Virginia in 1816. At the age of eighteen while he was working on a Mississippi cotton plantation he heard stories of adventures in the West. This led him to Independence, Missouri, the starting point of the Santa Fe Trail. From there he embarked on a trapping expedition which took him to Bent's Fort.

Wootton organized a "rapid-transit" stagecoach line between Santa Fe and Independence, Missouri. The trip took fourteen days; the fare was $250 one-way. Passengers were fed pork and beans. No stops were made at night, and the passengers had to sleep sitting up.

After the American occupation of New Mexico he received permission to establish a toll road over the pass. He blasted out twenty-seven miles of wagon road and, at his ranch house just north of the New Mexico-Colorado line, he stretched heavy chains across the road to insure payment of toll. The usual charge was $1.50 for wagons.

Switchbacks on the Santa Fe Railroad over the Raton Pass.
—Thayer, 1888

Over the years, Uncle Dick's road was used by freighters, soldiers, emigrants, outlaws, and Indians. He did not charge Indians because he did not believe they would understand the toll system and he wanted to avoid angering or delaying them. From all others he collected—by diplomacy or, as a final resort, by a club.

The old Raton pass road can be reached from Raton by way of Moulton Avenue.

The community which became Raton was a government forage station and watering place on Willow Creek between the Wootton Ranch at the pass and the Canadian River to the south. It was called Willow Springs until 1880 when the Santa Fe Railroad arrived and decided to locate its repair shop at the southern base of Raton Pass.

Within a year the population reached 3,000. Coal deposits, ranch land, and railroad interests combined to make Raton a prosperous town. Originally, the town grew near the railroad tracks along First Street. There was even a reading room, offering railroaders a sedate—and cheaper—alternative to the entertainment provided in the saloons across the street. It was not until the automobile

164

became the main form of transportation that Second Street became the principal thoroughfare.

Like other frontier towns, Raton had its share of violence, lynchings, shoot-outs, and vendettas. However, Raton was not without cultural refinement. There were theaters and an opera house. During the 1880s, Raton was a stop on the theatrical circuit. New Mexico's first public high school was founded in 1884.

Cultural attainment was not without controversy. The elaborate Shuler Theatre was completed in 1915. At one point during its construction, protest became so strong that city officials fled across the state line to Trinidad to escape irate citizens. However, by the time of its opening the Shuler had become a source of civic pride. Today, designed in European rococo style and boasting near-perfect acoustics, the building is a showplace. The lobby is decorated with murals depicting local history, painted as a WPA project by Manville Chapman in the 1930s. Restoration began in the 1970s and continues today with community support. The Shuler Theatre houses the Raton Chamber of Commerce.

The five blocks of Raton's original townsite on First Street have been designated as a historic district, containing some seventy buildings which are of interest for their architectural styles and colorful past. The area is sufficiently compact for a walking tour.

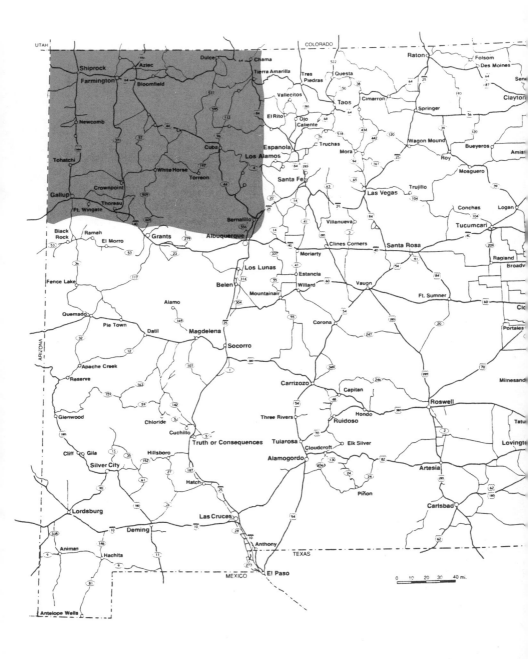

Land of the Anasazis

IV. Land of the Anasazis

About 5500 B.C. civilization was burgeoning in the northwestern corner of New Mexico. The people chipped stone points for projectiles and killed game wherever they could find it, they emulated the beasts by gathering fruits and nuts, they built hearths to contain fires, and by 700 B.C. they had learned to fashion crude sandals to protect their feet and to make baskets in which to gather and store food. Archaeologists have called these early residents Basket Maker I.

During the next thousand years or so—from about 700 B.C. to 450 A.D.—they improved their weaponry by developing spear throwers (atlatls) and darts. In addition to gathering wild seeds and nuts, they were cultivating maize and squash. They were weaving sandals, bags, aprons, and robes. They lived under overhanging rocks and, in some cases, built circular pit houses. This was the Basket Maker II stage of development.

Toward the end of the Basket Maker III period—between 450 and 700 A.D.—they were learning to make ceramic containers. A bow and arrow had replaced the atlatl and dart. They had domesticated turkeys and were combining feathers and fur into warm, fluffy blankets.

The Anasazis diet included corn, beans, and squash. Seashells and turquoise pendants, imported from far-away northern Mexico and the Pacific Coast, indicate they had time to worry about appearance and indulge themselves with luxury items.

These were the ancestors of today's Pueblo Indians. Archaeologist Alfred V. Kidder applied the word *anasazis*, derived from a Navajo term for "enemy ancestors." The translation was later softened to mean "ancient people."

The Anasazis were relatively small with dark brown skin. Their features showed traces of Asiatic characteristics their ancestors had brought across the Bering Strait as they followed herds of mammoths, mastodons, tapirs, big-horned bison, sloths, camels, and horses—all now extinct. In short, they looked much like today's Pueblo Indians.

Following the Basket Maker periods, the Anasazis' life style evolved in the direction of what has been called the Pueblo culture. Initially, it was characterized by rectangular aboveground rooms, as opposed to pit houses, and the architecture subsequently developed into multistoried complexes containing as many as 800 rooms with numerous kivas or ceremonial chambers, indicating an elaborate social structure and formalized religious practices.

When Coronado arrived in 1540, he found descendants of the Anasazis living in adobe and masonry structures which were arranged in communal groups. He called them *pueblos*, "towns" or "villages" in Spanish. The name stuck.

The Pueblo culture reached its peak in 1132 with Chaco Canyon at the hub of a socioeconomic system which included some seventy outlying colonies connected by a network of roads. The ruins of this apogee of the Anasazi development are preserved in Chaco Canyon in the Chaco Culture National Historical Park. The northwestern corner of New Mexico is literally seeded with remains of the Anasazi life style. Some have been excavated, stabilized, and placed on exhibit for visitors to see. Some have been preserved for future generations in an unexcavated state. Still others are yet to be located.

This "saddle cradle," for use on horseback, was drawn from a photograph by Charles F. Lummis.
—Harper's Young People, 1854

There is an intriguing footnote to archaeological studies of the development of the Anasazis from Basket Maker to Pueblos.

Somewhere in the Western Hemisphere, well before the dawn of recorded history, some ingenious aborigine invented the cradle board or baby carrier. This marvelously convenient device could be carried on the mother's back, hung on a tree branch, propped against a rock, carried on horseback, or laid on the ground—a portable day-care center which required no manpower.

As archaeologists penetrated the mists of time, artifacts revealed that the first baby carriers were crudely woven platters of flexible sticks and withes, covered with animal skins. Such were the models discovered in the caves of the Basket Makers.

On the basis of early exploration, archaeologists deduced from a radical difference in head shape that the Pueblos were a new race of broad-headed people who had moved into the area and merged with the Basket Makers or overran them. But the scientists had to revise their thinking.

After a study of more skeletal remains and artifacts, it became evident that this was not the case at all. As the Basket Maker culture blended into the Pueblo culture (as people learned to make pottery, grow better crops, and improve their dwellings), Indians started making cradles out of wood; literally, they became cradle *boards*, and no padding was used under the babies' heads. The back of the infant's head flattened, the sides bulged, and a broad, deformed head resulted. It turned out the "new race" the archaeologists had envisioned was simply the result of a prehistoric beauty fad.

US 666
Gamerco—Shiprock

Gamerco

US 666 leads to the north off I-40 through the vast Navajo Indian Reservation. A few miles north of Gallup, the highway passes Gamerco, the vestigial remains of a coal-mining town which flourished from 1921 until 1950. The name of the town was coined from "Gallup American Coal Company." During its heyday as a mining town, workers immigrated from all over Europe. Sub-bituminous coal was mined. Shafts probed as deep as 400 feet, and there were thirty miles of track underground.

Navajo Indian Reservation

The southern border of the Navajo reservation is about ten miles north of Gallup, and US 666 continues through the reservation for almost a hundred miles to the Colorado border. The Navajo Nation has a population of more than 120,000. The reservation, the homeland of the Navajos, comprises about 14,000,000 acres of desert country, some of which is spectacularly beautiful, stretching into Arizona, Colorado, and Utah.

For comparative purposes, the reservation is roughly the combined size of Vermont, Massachusetts, and New Hampshire. Most of the land is suitable for grazing sheep, goats, cattle, and horses; an irrigation project is underway to increase tillable acreage. Rent from coal, oil, gas, and uranium resources provides supplemental income to the tribe.

When the Spaniards arrived in New Mexico, the nomadic Navajos were regularly carrying on trade with the pueblo dwellers. They exchanged hides, dried meat, and tallow for corn, blankets, and other goods made by the sedentary Indians. In order to convert the Navajos to Christianity, the Spaniards attempted to impose civilization upon them, to get them to live like the pueblo tribes. The freedom-loving Navajos did not understand the white man's God, particularly when He allowed the Spaniards to seize their children to be sold into slavery.

As a result, the Navajos waged war against and plundered the resources of the Spaniards. Further, they urged dissatisfied Pueblo Indians to revolt against their oppressors. After the Pueblo Revolt of 1680, the Navajos retreated into their homeland and adopted

Navajo hogans still dot the landscape. —Photo by the authors

many of the practices of the Pueblo Indians. They learned the art of weaving. They raised crops and tended sheep, becoming largely self-sufficient. During the next hundred years, their numbers increased as their industry freed them from the threat of periodic famine. They lived in hogans, round beehive-like structures which still dot the landscape. But they did not forget how to wage war.

Thus the Americans found the situation. During two and a half centuries, the Spaniards and the Mexicans had been helpless against the Navajos. They were raiding settlements along the Rio Grande from Santa Fe to Socorro at will. On July 4, 1863, they stole 1,600 sheep from under the very noses of soldiers at Fort Craig.

After numerous unsuccessful attempts on the part of the Americans to make peace with the Navajos and to gain control of the New Mexico frontier, Brig. Gen. James H. Carleton became commander of the Department of New Mexico on September 18, 1862. He evolved a plan: The Navajos were to be rounded up in the Bosque Redondo, a 40-square-mile area surrounding Fort Sumner, far from their homeland, and taught the ways of the white man. He picked Col. Christopher Carson for the job. Carleton gave Kit Carson instructions:

> The Indian men are . . . to be killed whenever and wherever you can find them: the women and children will not be harmed, but you will take them prisoners. . . . If the Indians send in a flag and desire to treat for peace, say to the bearer; [they have broken] their treaty of peace, and murdered innocent people and run off their stock: that now we are going to punish them for their crimes, and that you are there to kill them wherever they can be found. We have no faith in their broken promises and we intend to kill enough of their men to teach them a lesson.
>
> I trust that this severity in the long run will be the most humane course that can be pursued toward these Indians.

Carleton's plan worked up to a point. In 1864, with a force consisting of New Mexico Volunteers and Ute Indians, Colonel Carson invaded Canyon de Chelly, the Navajo stronghold. He administered a defeat and captured their leaders. He herded a large part of the Navajos to the Bosque Redondo reservation. From that point on, the experiment was doomed to failure.

There was not enough firewood to supply the Indians' needs. Insects destroyed the first corn crop. Instead of supplying flocks of sheep so Navajo women could weave their own blankets, cheap shoddy blankets were purchased in the East or Middle West and issued to the Indians. Schooling proved to be a farce because neither children nor adults could see the value of education. Carleton's hope that the Navajos would be self-supporting within a year was not realized. Cost to the War Department for supporting the Navajo prisoners during the 18-month period from March 1, 1864, to October 1, 1865, was $1,114,981.70. Gen. William T. Sherman wryly commented that the United States could better afford to send them to a New York hotel for room and board.

Without waiting for ratification of a treaty, on June 1, 1868, under the war powers of the Federal government, General Sherman issued an order for them to be returned to their homeland in northwestern New Mexico and northeastern Arizona. They arrived at Fort Wingate on July 22 after a 35-day trek from the Pecos Valley. They have occupied the reservation to this day.

Not wanting a repetition of the Bosque Redondo experience, most of the Navajos practiced restraint toward the property of others.

Trading posts became the most necessary and influential institution of the reservation system. The trader was usually the only white man in the native community served by his post. The post was more than a store. It provided banking service. It was an information center and community meeting place. The agent gave business advice, personal counsel, and medical help. He was often called upon to bury the dead.

Navajo Indian "slave blankets" represent another product of the loom by this remarkable tribe during the classic period of weaving, about 1860. Slave blankets were produced by Indian women enslaved by army officers. Patterns were often laid out in advance, contrary to the Navajo method. This blanket of the wedge-weave design is in the collection of the Laboratory of Anthropology, Santa Fe. —Courtesy New Mexico Economic Development & Tourism, No. 14,516

The Arbuckles' Coffee premium card for New Mexico portrayed a mountain man. Arbuckles' Coffee was tremendously popular with the Navajos. They drank prodigious quantities, strong and black, boiled with sugar in the pot. They would have nothing but Arbuckles' Ariosa. They asked Indian agents for Hosteen Cohay — *literally, "Mister Coffee."*—authors' collection

As US 666 proceeds north through the reservation, tribal routes branch off, leading to small communities and trading posts. In the past, prior to paved roads and pickup trucks, the Navajos were almost totally dependent upon local trading posts. They were the sole gathering places. This is no longer the case. The pickup truck has mobilized the Navajo. They can easily reach the large communities around the reservation for shopping, trade, and socialization; and the merchants court their trade, as is evidenced by commercials in the Navajo language on radio stations broadcasting to the Navajos.

—— Historical Sidebar——————————————————

The Navajo Code Talkers

During World War II, the Navajos made a unique contribution to the United States war effort. A group known as the Navajo Code Talkers was recruited to serve with the Marines in the Pacific to send radio communications in a code derived from the complex Navajo language. Using the code, a three-line message in English could be encoded, transmitted, and decoded in twenty seconds. It took sophisticated military coding machines half an hour to perform the same task.

One of the code talkers explained how it was done: "You had to be able to use English and Navajo pretty fast. Everybody was shooting at each other, and you had to be on the ball."

The Japanese were never able to break the code. After the war a Marine officer gave a testimonial: "Were it not for the Navajos, the Marines would never have taken Iwo Jima."

Tohatchi

Tohatchi (scratch for water) was called Little Water by the first white settlers. It earned the name Tohatchi because water was obtained by simply scraping below the top soil in arroyos. The community grew up around a United States Indian Service School which was established in 1896. It was built upon the ruins of a pre-Columbian pueblo.

Chuska Peak looms up just northwest of the village. It is sacred to the Navajos. Rainmaking ceremonies were performed on the mountain. When rain was needed, a medicine man collected turquoise beads from each family; he left them on Chuska Peak while praying to the gods. Except for a medicine man, the mountain is off-limits to traditional Navajos.

Sheep Springs

A trading post and a headquarters of Navajo tribal government is located here. The Navajo governmental system consists of a tribal chairman and a tribal council. Councilors are selected from each of the fifty-six chapter houses which form social and governmental units throughout the reservation.

NM 134 leads southwestward to a particularly beautiful part of the reservation. The Navajos maintain public campsites at Blue Lake and Todachene Lake. The road continues through Crystal to Navajo, where there is a large tribal lumbering operation.

Newcomb

The community was originally called Nava, from the first syllables of "Navajo." In 1914 Arthur J. Newcomb and his wife Frances purchased the trading post. The U.S. Bureau of Indian Affairs built a day school with housing for teachers and employees. Numerous pre-Columbian ruins in the vicinity of Newcomb have yielded excellent specimens of Pueblo pottery: corrugated, white-and-black, and red-and-black of the pre-Mesa Verde type.

A tribal road loops twelve miles southwest to Toadlena (water bubbling up). The community was settled and named by the Navajos many years ago. A government Indian boarding school and trading post are located at Toadlena. The location was probably selected because of the many springs on the mountain slope.

—— Historical Sidebar ——————————————————————————

Shiprock Peak

Aficionados of Western movies have seen Shiprock from every possible angle, but there is no substitute for driving along US 666 and watching it sail majestically up 1,100 feet out of the desert floor. To geologists it is a perfect example of a volcanic neck with radiating dikes; they say it originated more than 3,000,000 years ago. But to the Navajos it is a sacred symbol of their creation and, hence, of their claim to their homeland.

They call the great rock tse bida' hi (sa-bit-tai-e), "the rock with wings." There are three versions of the Navajo creation legend. The one heard most often is that a great bird brought the people from the north and the bird was turned into stone when its mission was finished. Others tell that the Navajos crossed a narrow sea from beyond the setting sun. They landed among unfriendly peoples, but the Great Spirit sent a stone ship to carry them to this spot. In smoky kivas, medicine men have a another version: the Navajos were cast up from the earth at this very spot, and the massive stone ship is a symbol of their voyage.

_____

Shiprock

The town which took its name from the geological landmark is located some ten miles to the northeast of the peak. Originally, the community was called Needles. Navajos in the area lived in widely scattered family groups tending separate flocks of livestock. In 1903 Shiprock was created as a headquarters for the Northern Navajo Indian Agency to consolidate Indian administration and tribal business.

Almost every year since 1903, the Navajo nation has held a fair at Shiprock, highlighted by arts and crafts exhibitions and a rodeo. Traditionally, older men wear black flat-brimmed hats with domed crowns and silver hatbands, jeans, silver concho belts, and boots. Navajo women wear what is often called traditional Navajo dress.

Prior to 1863, Navajo women wore black and red hand-woven blanket dresses. During incarceration of the tribe at Fort Sumner, Navajo women began to copy the long dresses and full skirts of the wives of U.S. Army officers. Today, their traditional dress reflects those nineteenth-century styles, consisting of calico or satin broom-stick-pleated skirts topped by velvet blouses.

Indian Agent William T. Shelton arrived at Shiprock in 1904. He operated a 300-acre model farm in connection with a school. He told a reporter about his mission:

> The Navajo boys are taught practical farming in a scientific way. I have put little ideas into their heads about living as white people do, and I want to keep them here and teach them intense farming by irrigation, where they can take a small piece of land and make a living on it, and to encourage the boys and girls to get married when they are old enough.
>
> Another effort I have made is to keep the girls from being sold to old Indians for wives. The marriage custom of the Navajos has always been to buy and sell their wives. The old men would pay better prices for the young girls than the young bucks could pay. Until I got it broken up, they would take three or four wives and keep them all at the same hogan.

Things have changed since 1904. With the opening of oil and gas production in the Four Corners area in 1957, the nearby Rattle-snake Oil Fields began to produce some of the highest-grade oil in the nation, and the Navajo tribe was receiving royalties in excess of

The discovery of oil on the Navajo reservation stained the beauty of the land. —Courtesy New Mexico Department of Development, No. 2559

In July, 1949, the governors of New Mexico, Colorado, Utah, and Arizona dined at the Four Corners, each sitting in his own state. —Courtesy New Mexico State Records Center & Archives

a million dollars a month. Navajo boys and girls are now taught more than how to make a living on a small piece of land. While many Navajos are content with the traditional styles of life and work on the reservation, others choose to work off the reservation, staffing nearby power plants, stores, and professional offices.

—— Historical Sidebar ————————————————————

Four Corners Monument

By a quirk of highway planning, in order to reach the extreme northwestern corner of New Mexico one must leave the state. The Four Corners Monument, the only place in the United States where four states meet, is reached from Shiprock via US 64 across the Arizona border to Teec Nos Pos and thence northward on US 160 to get back into New Mexico to the monument.

The first benchmark for the point where New Mexico, Arizona, Utah, and Colorado join was set in 1875. Today, the marker consists of a somewhat unspectacular cement slab with the state lines joining at the center. Names of the four states and their state seals are implanted in the concrete.

In 1949 the governors of the four states had lunch on the slab, each seated in his own state while passing food to his neighbors, on the theory that breaking bread together would make cooperation on mutual problems easier. However, their camaraderie did nothing to solve the monument controversy.

In 1868 a survey was made along the 37th parallel to establish the boundary between Colorado and New Mexico. Subsequent surveys proved that the boundary had been established a hundred yards south of where it should have been. The U.S. Supreme Court ruled in 1925 that the boundary should stand in accordance with the erroneous survey of 1868.

This leaves the Navajos and the Utes—ancient enemies—in hot dispute over the 100-yard-wide strip of land. The Navajos' treaty with the United States established their reservation boundary at the 37th parallel. The treaty with the Utes established the boundary of their reservation at the New Mexico-Colorado line. The Government has given the same piece of land to both tribes.

The monument has become a popular stop for individuals with a yen to be photographed at the only spot in the nation where four states join. The attraction is operated as a concession by the Ute Mountain Indians. The marker is surrounded by booths from which Indians sell curios and snacks to visitors.

US 64
Waterflow—Monero

Waterflow

This small farming and mining community grew during the first quarter of the century. It took its name from a bounty of rivers; the San Juan, Animas, and La Plata rivers flow through the town. The post office was established in 1920. However, the community has been the site of the Hogback Trading Company since 1871.

Fruitland

Prior to 1877, the community was called Olio. The postmaster, Columbus John Moss, got the name from a dictionary: "a mixture; hodge-podge; a miscellaneous collection." He said it seemed appropriate since the community was made up of Navajos, Spanish-Americans, Mormons, and Anglo-gentiles.

In 1877-78 a Mormon colony joined other settlers. At first the newcomers called the town Burnham to honor Mormon Bishop Luther C. Burnham, but Burnham and James R. Young became interested in growing fruit. In 1891, while Young was the postmas-

The Fruitland Trading Post was established about 1886 by the Fruitland Trading Company. —Four Corners Tourism Council

ter, he registered the name of the town as Fruitland, presumably to publicize their agricultural enterprise. The Fruitland Trading Post had been established about 1886.

Farmington

Because of its location at the confluence of the San Juan and Animas rivers, Navajos who pastured sheep in the area called the location To-Tah (Where-the-rivers-are-divided). The first Anglo settlement, called Junction City, was on the south side of the river. As more settlers arrived, mostly from Colorado, they built on the north side of the river and Junction City ceased to exist. The town was originally called Farmingtown, but the *w* was dropped in 1879 when the post office was named.

During its early days as a farming and ranching center, the community had a full share of characters. Farmington's first resident preacher arrived in 1885. When he refused to drink with cowboys in a local saloon they shot holes in the floor around his feet. He not only remained in his spot until they stopped shooting but he remained in the community for many years.

The Miller store was one of the earliest in Farmington.
—Courtesy of Farmington Museum

Robert Oliver Hanna lived in Farmington. Hanna's principal claim to fame was that he was one of two photographers who took pictures of Billy the Kid. The familiar close-up of the outlaw's face was Hanna's. After a stint as a trapper and photographer near Silver City, he came to Farmington.

Hanna was a roly-poly man who enjoyed a daily draught of whiskey. In addition to practicing photography he was a trapper and a taxidermist. In the latter activities he used skunk oil. Hanna had suffered from rheumatism which he believed he cured by the use of skunk oil. Consequently, during the winter, before going out to service his traps, he rubbed skunk oil and tallow on his face to ward off sunburn and chapped skin. Anyone who came to his house to have a picture taken was met by the odor of rendering skunk oil.

About 1907 Willis Martin purchased a small power mill and got a 25-year franchise to furnish electricity to Farmington: "Street lamps to be lighted during the dark of the moon and on cloudy nights." One irate lady objected to a pole being set in front of her house. After the hole was dug, she got into the hole and sat all day. A worker succeeded in implanting the pole the next morning before she came out to resume her vigil. After the advent of electric irons,

Mr. Martin had to operate his plant two mornings a week so that women could do their ironing.

In the late 1940s, with the discovery of oil and gas in the area, Farmington became a center for New Mexico's oil, gas, and uranium industries. The city made a transition from agricultural dominance to industrial dominance.

Salmon Ruin

Located two miles west of Bloomfield, just off US 64, Salmon Ruin is unique in that it has been protected from vandals and treasure hunters. During the 1800s, George Salmon homesteaded the land containing the ruins of a pueblo which was built and occupied between 1088 and 1095. Salmon built his ranch house on the border of the ruins. The old adobe house, outbuildings, and an orchard still stand.

Salmon Ruin was a colony or "outlier" of the Chaco Canyon complex some fifty miles to the south. Built in the shape of a C, the "apartment complex" stretches 430 feet along the back wall and 150 feet along the arms. The two-story structure contained 250 rooms, arranged in groups as family living quarters. There was a great kiva in the plaza and at the highest point a ceremonial chamber or "tower kiva."

The imported sandstone was quarried from four to thirty miles away, and timbers for *vigas* to support the massive roofs were brought from as far away as southern Colorado. The residents were basically agriculturists. They grew corn, beans, and squash and

This petroglyph in Crow Canyon, southeast of Salmon Ruin, clearly shows the corn symbol with two ears on the stalk. —Courtesy of Jo Smith, Salmon Ruin

supplemented their crops with wild plants and game: rabbit, deer, elk, mountain sheep, and wildcat.

By the middle 1100s, after about sixty years of occupation, the pueblo was abandoned by its Chacoan occupants. The next residents came during the early thirteenth century, pottery makers sometimes referred to as "Mesa Verdians." This group was somewhat less neat than their predecessors.

They divided some of the larger rooms with clumsy partitions and built circular walls within others to make small kivas. Instead of burying garbage they threw it into an unused room, sometimes along with the bodies of their dead. The pueblo was abandoned for the last time during the latter half of the century when a severe drought, 1276-1299, afflicted the northern Southwest.

About 1250 a kiva roof collapsed, killing some fifty children. Archaeologists speculate that the children had climbed onto the roof to escape a fire. Although a tragedy for the Indians, the result was a bonanza for modern archaeologists. It sealed samples of food and ceremonial equipment in a time capsule to be opened in the twentieth century.

In 1969 the San Juan County Museum Association learned the Salmon property was about to be sold to a developer. Subsequently, the county bought the land and county residents passed a bond issue to establish the San Juan County Archaeological Research Center at Salmon Ruin.

Full-scale excavation began in 1972 and continued through 1978. A million and a half artifacts have been removed and retained at the site, along with excavation records, for study by students and candidates for advanced degrees.

Bloomfield

Settled during the late 1870s, the community was initially called Porter, but when it came time to establish a post office Bloomfield was selected in honor of an early settler. Bloomfield had the dubious distinction of becoming the headquarters of the notorious Stockton gang.

Port Stockton arrived in Bloomfield from the Lincoln County War with fifteen notches on his gun. Initially he was made a peace officer, but he quickly proved that he could not be trusted to point his gun in the right direction. He reverted to his outlaw ways; he organized a gang which terrorized the area. He shot a barber who cut him slightly while shaving him; he seized a widow's ranch while she was visiting relatives. Members of his gang robbed stage-coaches and stole cattle at will. They opened a butcher shop in Durango, Colorado, to dispose of rustled livestock.

As ranchers and residents mobilized against the scourge, the affair became known as the Stockton War. After the outlaws were eliminated, at gunpoint rather than in court, Bloomfield settled down to become an agricultural center.

Dulce

This small town on the Jicarilla Apache Indian Reservation was established about 1883. It was named "sweet" or "candy" after a spring of sweet water in the area. It is the trading center of the Jicarilla Reservation. Some 2,000 members of the Apache tribe live in or near this mountain community, and tribal offices are located in Dulce.

The nearly 1,000,000-acre reservation is widely touted as one of the last unspoiled hunting lands for trophy deer, elk, turkey, cougar, and waterfowl.

Lumberton

This community is a ghost left by the lumbering industry which sprang up in the Chama Valley following the coming of the railroad in 1881. E. M. Biggs, the largest sawmill operator of the period, bought a 40-acre ranch, laid out streets, and sold lots in 1884. The community was originally called Amargo (bitter", after the taste of the water in the river. The town was named Lumberton about 1894 because of the many sawmills in the area.

Hundreds of square miles of forest were decimated as timber was harvested and shipped to Colorado or used on the spot to cut railroad ties. Old-timers report that in the 1920s the area from Lumberton to Chama was a forest of rotting stumps. Around the turn of the century, the Fleek and Henderson Tie Company was making 400 hand-cut railroad ties per day and advertising that fifty more tie cutters were needed.

In those days, timber was considered an expendable commodity. After all the timber was harvested from an area, a company would move on to another location. By the end of World War I, the region around Lumberton was devastated and the lumbering industry waned.

Monero

Coal was discovered in the Monero area during 1881-82 as the tracks of the Denver and Rio Grande Railroad were being laid west of Chama en route to Durango. Mines opened and a village grew along the railroad, populated principally by Italian miners.

The name means "money" in Italian. However, one early settler said the name was supposed to have been Minero, Spanish for "miner," but a typographical error was made in sending the name to the Post Office Department. The town had a one-room school, a store, a saloon, a Catholic church, and a Penitente morada. The population reached a peak in the 1930s. There were two large mines and several smaller ones being worked twenty-four hours a day.

Miners were paid $2 per ton. They could work as many hours per day and as many days per week as they wanted. A good miner could mine five tons of coal a day, but if he ran into dirty coal, he had to clean it on his own time. Two or three tons a day was average.

By the 1960s, the mines were closing down. Natural gas lines had been installed in the area and trains stopped running to Monero. Today, the village is a ghost town with only a few buildings left standing.

US 550
Flora Vista—Cedar Hill

Flora Vista

Settlers from Colorado had already built log cabins among the cottonwoods in what would be called Flora Vista by 1877. The little ranching and farming community grew. An abandoned cemetery of some thirty unmarked graves gives mute testimony that times were tough.

There is little there to help the historian reconstruct life in the community. Frontier pioneer settlers had neither the time nor the materials to erect permanent markers. They were too busy dealing with the violence, tragedy, and hardship which filled the cemeteries.

One of two marked graves is that of Eva M. Garren, age twenty. Eva died in 1887 during a scarlet fever epidemic. She left a husband and two small girls, one only a few days old. A yellow newspaper clipping says: "She suffered a great deal until death relieved her pain. She was attended by Grandmas Crouch and Hartly, who did everything to relieve her." The marker on the grave provides a key to an attitude which helped make life on the Western frontier bearable:

"ANOTHER LINK IS BROKEN IN OUR HOUSEHOLD BAND,
BUT ANOTHER LINK IS FORMING IN A BETTER LAND."

Aztec

Early in the 1880s, after the Lincoln County War, George and Frank Coe rented land in the San Juan Basin. They planted wheat and brought in the first commercially-manufactured threshing machine. Phoenix-like, a community was arising on the bank of the Animas River amidst the ruins of ancient Indian pueblos. The Spaniards called the river Rio de las Animas (River of Lost Souls), perhaps in memory of lingering spirits among the ancient ruins.

John Koontz ran a general store where people brought mail to be picked up by stagecoach. When it came time to make application for a post office, the settlers borrowed the name of the Indian ruins just across the river.

In addition to being the county seat, Aztec was a trading center for farmers and ranchers. In 1950 the economy was sparked by the oil and gas industry. In 1963 the city earned the All America City Award by building a nineteen-mile road to the Navajo Dam Recreation Area without U.S. Government assistance. Businesses donated supplies, men and women volunteered labor, and children held fund-raising drives to help meet expenses.

Aztec Ruins National Monument

Near the present-day town of Aztec, the Animas River flows through a slender valley lush with cottonwoods and willows. Farmers have long made a good living raising crops in the fertile bottom lands. The earliest were the Anasazis, the "Ancient People" from the Colorado Plateau. During the twelfth century they lived in scattered clusters up and down the river.

Tree-ring dating tells that they came to the Aztec Ruins National Monument site between 1106 and 1124 and built a large, multistoried pueblo on rising ground overlooking the river, the West Ruin. After 1115 only an occasional room was added, perhaps for new couples as the population grew.

The Great Kiva of the Aztec Ruins National Monument, a large circular room used for ceremonial purposes 800 years ago, was restored in 1934. The masonry structures were built by ancestors of present-day Pueblo Indians, erroneously called "Aztec" by early settlers.
—Courtesy National Park Service

The pueblo resembles the great houses built at Chaco Canyon a half a century before, an E-shaped compound with hundreds of rooms on three levels and more than two dozen kivas including the great kiva in the plaza, apparently for community-wide ceremonies. (The great kiva was excavated in 1921 and restored in 1934, the only restored great kiva in the Southwest.) Masonry work follows the Chacoan practice of alternating courses of large rectangular sandstone blocks with bands of smaller stones.

The pueblo was abandoned about 1175 or 1200, perhaps because of drought or area-wide misfortune. There is no evidence the residents were driven away. It lay deserted until about 1225 when people of the Mesa Verde culture arrived and took up residence. They did some remodeling and built new dwellings, the East Ruin.

The Mesa Verde Indians made pottery, beadwork, and textiles and traded their wares over a wide area. After fifty years or so, they too abandoned the town during the latter 1200s when there were shifts of population throughout the region.

The pueblo was left to crumble. The first Anglo visitor of record was Dr. John S. Newberry, a geologist. In 1859, before the coming of vandals and pothunters, he found walls twenty-five feet high. By the time anthropologist Lewis H. Morgan arrived in 1879, a quarter of the pueblo's stones had been carted away by settlers to be used as building materials. In 1916 the ruin came under protection of the American Museum of Natural History. On January 23, 1923, it was declared a national monument.

Cedar Hill

In 1877, as homeseekers moved across the southern Colorado boundary into the Territory of New Mexico, squatters' rights were established on the cedar-speckled slopes that would be officially become known as Cedar Hill when the Denver and Rio Grande Western Railroad came past.

A Dutchman named Bushelberger planted grapes and dug a reservoir from which to irrigate his vineyard. He made wine and established a race track on Bushelberger Mesa. Men brought their horses from miles around. One pioneer told about it: "Under the influence of old Bushelberger's wine, the men tested their horses' speed on old Bushelberger's track."

Gamblers placed their money on a blanket under the watchful eye of a stakeholder. Bets ran into hundreds of dollars as Bushelberger poured his wine. It was a frontier counterpart to modern-day Las Vegas.

NM 371
Bisti Badlands—Crownpoint

Bisti Badlands

The Bisti Badlands evolved from an ancient lake bed. Over eons, wind and water have carved grotesque formations, dressed in muted browns, blacks and grays accented with purples, yellows and whites against a deep blue sky. Here prehistoric monsters once roamed and died among 100-foot palms. The Bisti Badlands and De-Na-Zin, a fossil forest of 2,720 acres, are under care of the Bureau of Land Management which warns visitors: "No matter what time of the year you go, carry water and fill your gas tank."

Lake Valley

The site of this small community three miles west of NM 371 is thought to have been on the extensive prehistoric road network which extended to outlying Anasazi settlements from the Chaco Canyon complex to the east. There are numerous archaeological sites in the vicinity.

Crownpoint

This community on the eastern edge of the Navajo Indian Reservation is the scene of famed auctions held by the Crownpoint Rug Weavers Association. Auctions are held on several evenings during the year, usually on Fridays. They take place in the school gymnasium and are attended by amateur and professional buyers alike.

On the afternoon of an auction, Navajos submit their rugs for inspection by the association to make certain they are authentic and to note whether commercial yarns and dyes have been used. Prices vary according to size, designs, thread count, and yarns and dyes which have been used.

A Navajo pictorial-design blanket such as this museum piece depicting the arrival of cowboys, longhorn cattle, and the railroad would incite spirited bidding at the Crownpoint auction. —Courtesy New Mexico Economic Develpment & Tourism, No. 14,517

Standing Rock—Coyote Canyon

Those who wish to experience a portion of the Navajo reservation which is accessible but comparatively untrammeled by modern civilization can take the tribal road between Crownpoint and US666 to the west. It goes through Standing Rock and Coyote Canyon.

NM 44
El Huerfano Trading Post
—Santa Ana Pueblo

El Huerfano Trading Post

The turnoff for the Bisti Badlands is at El Huerfano Trading Post, named for Huerfano Mesa which the Spaniards called "orphan" because it stood alone. To the Navajos it is *dzil naodili*, where the Changing Woman raised her sons, Monster Slayer (*Naayee Neezghani*) and Child Born of Water (*To Bajschini*), the Twin War Gods of the Navajos.

Blanco Trading Post

Blanco Trading Post serves as a general store for residents in the area. However, its principal business comes from its location at the intersection with NM 57, the turnoff to Chaco Canyon.

NM 57
Chaco Culture National Historical Park

Familiarly known as Chaco Canyon and often called the "Stonehenge of the West," the complex of Indian ruins located along Chaco Wash in the San Juan Basin represents the highest point of Pueblo pre-Columbian civilization in the United States.

About 8500 B.C. passing hunters in search of Bison antiquus (nothing like latter-day buffalo) used caves along the canyon walls for shelter and left projectile points, hide scrapers, and stone knives. By 1000 B.C. nomadic peoples were staying long enough to grow domesticated crops. Archaeologists call them Basket Maker II.

In 500 A.D. people were huddling in colonies, living in pit houses, shielded from the elements beneath roofs of clay and logs. About two centuries later the Anasazis arrived and introduced above-ground pueblos. By 1030 a real building boom was on. Chaco Canyon became the center of a religious, cultural, and economic movement.

Accomplished architects directed the use of stone and adobe. Before they were through the Chacoans had built thirteen major installations and hundreds of smaller communities in the canyon. The largest, Pueblo Bonito, was a multistoried apartment house containing 800 rooms and 30 kivas.

There were artists among the Chacoans. They painted and carved on the canyon walls; they decorated the walls of rooms and kivas with murals; they painted pieces of wood; they sculpted in wood, stone, and clay; they made ornaments of shell, turquoise, and other rare materials; they wove baskets and textiles and painted pottery. Anthropologists have not called their culture the "Chaco Phenomenon" without reason.

Pueblo Bonito was the largest Anasazi complex in Chaco Canyon. —Courtesy New Mexico Economic Development & Tourism, No. 806

The latest thinking is that the huge complex in Chaco Canyon was similar to a modern convention center to which people from outlying communities came to worship, to trade, or to participate in festivals of some kind. During the peak building period, from 1075 until 1115, some seventy communities were scattered over the 25,000-square-mile San Juan Basin. These outlying pueblos were connected to Chaco Canyon by a 1200-mile network of roads. Building stopped in 1132, and the area was virtually abandoned by 1150.

After the American occupation of New Mexico, Navajos began committing depredations against American settlements, and in 1849 a punitive force camped in Chaco Canyon for several days. 1st Lt. James H. Simpson was so impressed by the array of massive masonry structures that he wrote a description which documented seven of the major ruins. By 1888 the Bureau of American Ethnology developed an interest.

On March 11, 1907, Chaco Canyon National Monument was brought under National Park Service administration. In 1980, the area was renamed the Chaco Culture National Historical Park.

During its height as a center of Anasazi culture, all roads may have led to Chaco Canyon; however, the same cannot be said today. One should check weather and road conditions before setting out. However, the splendid display of ruins and artifacts in Chaco Canyon is well worth the trip.

Cuba

Originally part of the San Joaquin del Nacimiento Land Grant, established in 1769 for thirty-six families, the community was called Nacimiento (nativity). It was resettled in 1879 by the McCoy and Atencio families.

As a ranching center it became noted for brawls, bootlegging, cattle stealing, and gunfights. As late as the first quarter of the twentieth century, travelers were warned not to get caught in Cuba overnight. During the early 1930s homesteaders were told, "It's purty good country in a way. But nothin'll grow, though, and it's shore hard on hogs and women." Times have changed; today, tourists are urged to stop and enjoy Cuba's alpine setting en route to vacations in the mountains.

NM 197-509-605
Torreon—Milan

A hardy motorist with love for mountain and desert landscape and a desire to be alone can take NM 197 southwest out of Cuba through Torreon to Pueblo Pintado (Painted Pueblo), a lonely trading post in Chaco Canyon at the junction with NM 509. NM 509 continues through White Horse, along the Continental Divide, and connects with NM 605 to I-40 at Milan. The trip covers almost 125 miles of varied desert scenery.

NM 96-112
La Jara—Youngsville

La Jara—Regina

Both of these small rural communities on NM 96 were established in 1911. The name of Regina was imported from Canada. Logging was more important than agriculture until the early 1950s when tractors scarred the land to remove the native piñons and cedars and prepare the ground for planting.

Gallina

This tree-shaded settlement beside a creek of the same name was settled in 1818. The post office was not established until 1890. The most remarkable feature of the area is the nearby ruins of the Gallinas towers; they have been called New Mexico's lost cities.

In 1934 a cowboy named Joe Arellano noticed piles of stone scattered over the canyons and mesas, some square and some round. He thought he might find gold in those lost cities. All he got for his efforts were a few pottery vessels and a fine for digging on government land. He did, however, attract the attention of archaeologists to the area.

Excavations revealed a series of ruins along the Gallina River from Cuba to El Vado. There were subsurface pit houses, single-unit houses, cliff dwellings, and large stone towers. Towers in any form are not common to the Southwest, but there were hundreds of them. They were built with crude blocks of sandstone held in place by adobe mortar, often more than thirty feet high, entered from openings in the roofs.

Everywhere there was evidence of violence, death, and destruction wrought by unknown invaders. Every community in the widespread complex had been attacked and burned. Skeletal remains revealed that one middle-aged warrior fell clutching his throat. He had arrows in his neck and arm. A young boy had been in a tower when it was fired. Though struck in the hip by an arrow, he had apparently tried to climb the ventilating shaft. The lower half of his body was burned; the upper half was preserved by the heat. Ten skeletons were found in one pit house, arrows deeply imbedded in their backs and stomachs. Others had gaping axe wounds in their heads. Even more mystifying, the fingers of some had been sliced off at a peculiar angle, leading to the supposition they were tortured prior to being killed.

The questions—Who did it? When? Why?—remain a mystery. The arrows were similar to those made by the Gallinas themselves.

Coyote

Leading into Coyote, NM 96 passes through a valley of lush orchards. The sides of the valley are red cliffs studded with boulders. Coyote, named for Coyote Canyon, has red dirt streets. Farmers and ranchers have eliminated most of the coyotes which gave the community its name.

Youngsville

This farming and ranching community was established early in the twentieth century. The post office was opened in 1914. The old village church contrasts with more recent dwellings.

NM 96 continues on to intersect US 84 north of Abiquiú.

NM 595
Lindrith

The scenery along NM 595 from NM 96 to Lindrith rivals Bryce Canyon. Sandstone mounds have been weather-worried into myriad wrinkles, and the land is stained in stripes of rainbow colors.

The farming and ranching community was named for Lindrith Cordell in 1915 when his stepfather and mother established a post office and store on their homestead. Subsequently, oil was discovered, resulting in the construction of a small oil refinery.

NM 112
El Vado

If one has the leisure and the fortitude to endure a rough road, NM 112 from its intersection with NM 96 to El Vado is a rewarding experience. Sage-grown flats are dotted with Indian paint brush. Small canyons slash the flatness. There are cedar-covered ridges, knolls of piñons and tall sage. It is a quiet, beautiful country. El Vado is a tiny resort community on the edge of El Vado Lake. NM 112 continues to connect with US 84 near Tierra Amarilla.

San Ysidro

Today little is left of this old community which was settled in 1699. In 1786 Antonio Armenta and Salvador Sandoval were awarded a land grant which was two miles wide and twelve miles long. In 1930 much of the farming land was given to the Zia Pueblo.

NM 4
Jémez Pueblo—White Rock

Jémez Pueblo

At San Ysidro, take NM 4 north off NM 44 for five miles north to Jémez Pueblo. This pueblo was established after the Reconquest of New Mexico. Spanish domination did not set well with the Jémez people. During the seventeenth century, in order to exert firmer control, the Spaniards convinced them to abandon their remote villages and settle in three pueblos: Astiolakwa, Gyusiwa, and Patoqua.

In 1680 all three pueblos joined the Pueblo Revolt and the Indians retreated to mountain strongholds. During the Reconquest, de Vargas attacked them in a series of short, murderous battles. With many of their women and children held captive in Santa Fe, the Jémez surrendered and built a new town called Walatow on the Jémez River, a day's walk south of Gyusiwa. This is today's Jémez Pueblo, where pottery is still made in the traditional manner, using only natural colors and painting ancient Jémez designs with yucca leaf brushes.

Ruins of San Diego de Jémez mission, founded in the seventeenth century at the ancient Gyusiwa pueblo. —Courtesy El Paso Public Library

The Jémez reservation covers 88,000 acres. The pueblo proper is a rambling community of low adobe buildings most of which surround a wide central plaza. A few of the residents work at state and federal jobs in Albuquerque but most who are not involved in arts and crafts still tend farms along the river or raise cattle and sheep.

Vallecitos

In 1768 Paulin Montoya and five other heads of families established themselves at Vallecito with Santo Torĭbo as their patron saint. The community occupied a narrow little valley only four miles long, hemmed in by high mesas and pink rimrock. Like in many old Spanish settlements, dwellings and the culture of the occupants centered around the plazas. As more settlers arrived another plaza started. There was Upper Vallecito with San Antonio as the patron saint and Lower Vallecito with San Toribio presiding.

In 1935 a reporter visited Vallecitos and noticed a large number of fair-haired, light-complexioned, blue-eyed, Spanish-speaking people in the community—unusual in New Mexico where Mexican and Indian ethnic backgrounds predominate. The reporter was informed, "We are all *primos*." The residents claimed to be "cousins" who traced their ancestry back to the Spanish *conquistadores*.

Cañon

The post office in this tiny turn-of-the-century community lasted only two years, 1902-03. However, during the summer it is occupied by a substantial population of Jémez women selling fry bread and other Indian delicacies from roadside kiosks to motorists bound for the resort area around Jémez Springs.

Jémez Springs

Today, this small community is primarily a resort centering around the geothermal spring which provides bubbling, sulfur-laden water to a public bathhouse and heat for the municipal buildings. However, things have not always been so serene. Early in the century, Jémez Springs was the scene of range wars, vigilante activities, and gambling enterprises. Texas gunslingers came to Jémez Springs to test their mettle, and local ranchers and bartenders gained a reputation for throwing them out of saloons.

Jémez State Monument

This archaeological site contains ruins of Mission San José de Jémez at Gyusiwa Pueblo, founded by a Franciscan missionary in 1617. The pueblo was abandoned in 1622 because of Navajo raids. In 1627 Fray Martín de Arvide gathered the scattered Jémez Indians and the pueblo was resettled. They joined the Pueblo Revolt but later settled on the present Jémez Reservation. Gyusiwa was a Tewa word meaning "place at the boiling waters."

Bandelier National Monument

The disastrous drought of the late thirteenth century broke up many ancient Pueblo Indian centers in the Southwest, forcing the survivors to move to locations where the water supply was more constant. The later flowering of Pueblo culture occurred in the upper Rio Grande Valley. The numerous ruins of Bandelier National Monument are characteristic of this phase of Pueblo development.

Several groups settled on the canyon-slashed slopes of the Pajarito Plateau where the consolidated volcanic ash called tuff permitted them to dig caves for protection from the elements. About two miles of cliff ruins extend along the base of the northern wall of Frijoles Canyon. Masonry houses built with vigas braced into the cliffs (talus houses) were from one to three stories high, and many had rooms gouged from the cliff faces. Tree-ring dating places the earliest inhabitants during the late twelfth century. For 300 years settlements grew. On the valley floor the Indians constructed great multistoried communal houses called Tyuonyi and Tsankawi.

The cliffs of Frijoles Canyon are honeycombed with the caves of prehistoric inhabitants. —Photo by the authors

Tyuonyi was built around a central plaza with only one entrance. This fact, plus a zigzag pattern of post holes found in the floor, indicate the builders were concerned with defense. It had about 400 rooms and was three stories high in places. It was home for about 100 people who entered their dwellings by holes in the roof. In time of danger, they could pull up the ladders after them. Tree-ring studies show there was a drought during the mid-1500s. By 1580 all but a few stragglers were gone.

While they were there, the Indians grew corn, beans, and squash. (Studies of pollen in the soil has helped determine the types of plants.) They wove cotton cloth on vertical looms which were anchored on posts from floor to ceiling. And they had tobacco.

In June, 1943, a bowl was unearthed in an ancient room at the base of the high north cliff in Frijoles Canyon. In the bowl an archaeologist found dry brown leaves that looked like tobacco. Subsequent tests proved that it was indeed tobacco. J. W. Hendron put the substance to the ultimate test and reported his findings in *New Mexico* magazine:

> I puffed and drew in the smoke and exhaled it through my nostrils.
>
> Although I was smoking probably the oldest specimen of cultivated tobacco in America, I noticed nothing unusual except a faint dizziness.
>
> Except that my "makin's" were two and a half centuries old, my cigarette looked like tobacco, smelled like tobacco, and tasted like tobacco.

Ruins of the communal house at Bandelier National Monument.
—Photo by the authors

The residents of Bandelier were also hunters. Their hunting shrine—Shrine of the Stone Lions—is on the path leading out of the settlement: two catlike stone animals surrounded by a circle of rocks. Even today, worshippers from Cochiti and San Felipe pueblos come to sprinkle cornmeal on the lions, paint their noses red, and place deer antlers between them.

From 1880 until 1886, Swiss-born Adolph Francis Alphonse Bandelier, anthropologist and historian, studied the ruins of New Mexico, particularly the ruins which now bear his name. Bandelier was a determined explorer. He lived in a kiva and explored the ruins from end to end. He wrote numerous scientific reports. In addition he wrote *The Delight Makers*, a novel of the prehistoric Pueblo Indians. It was based upon eight years of study of the ruins and of the manners, customs, creeds, and rites as they had been passed down to the Indians in living pueblos in the vicinity. Bandelier told why he had written a piece of fiction: "By clothing sober facts in the garb of romance I have hoped to make the 'Truth about the Pueblo Indians' more accessible and perhaps more acceptable to the public in general." Published in 1890, *The Delight Makers* was quickly recognized by anthropologists and archaeologists as a classic of both science and literature.

As in other Southwestern ruins, the study of Bandelier National Monument has combined the talents of many specialists: archaeologists (people who investigate ancient cultures), ethnologists (people who study the way cultures live), climatologists (scientists who study climate), dendrochronologists (tree-ring dating analysts), paleobotanists (scientists who study ancient plants), and ecologists (people who study the environment).

Bandelier National Monument was proclaimed a national monument February 11, 1916. It is perhaps the most diverse archaeological site in the state, including petroglyphs, caves, talus houses, cliff houses, kivas, and communal houses. A tour can last from forty-five minutes to two days.

White Rock

Planned originally in 1948 as a construction site for work at Los Alamos, White Rock was a cluster of prefabricated buildings. It has since grown into a middle-class settlement inhabited by people who work at Los Alamos.

Zia Pueblo

Zia Pueblo has perched on the 300-foot lava-covered hill north of the highway since before the arrival of the Spaniards. In 1540 Coronado sent García López de Cárdenas here to obtain hide cloaks to keep the Spaniards from freezing during the coming winter. Cárdenas reported that there were about a thousand whitewashed houses trimmed in bright colors.

Juan de Oñate visited in 1598 and shortly thereafter priests arrived to construct a mission. They employed forced labor as they worked on behalf of the Cross. The Zia people joined the revolt of 1680, killing the resident Spaniards and burning the church. In 1688 Domingo Cruzate came back. He found a force of 3,000 defending the pueblo. He attacked. After two days 50 Spaniards were wounded and 600 Indians were dead; the pueblo was in flames. Most of the Zias fled to the mountains, but Cruzate succeeded in capturing 70 prisoners who were taken to El Paso and sold as slaves.

By the time Diego de Vargas arrived in 1692, Zia refugees had returned to the remains of their village. They signed an oath of allegiance to the Spaniards and converted en masse to Catholicism. Their conversion was commemorated by erecting a large wooden cross on the plaza; it is still standing. The Zias also assisted de Vargas in battles against other pueblos. According to some, the Zias are still considered social outcasts because of their treasonous collaboration.

The Zia reservation consists of 112,000 acres of poor land. Most of the adults work off the reservation in Bernallilo or Albuquerque. The mission which they attend at the north end of the village, Nuestra Señora de la Asunción de Sía, is the same structure which was built in 1692. Below the village are a number of modern HUD homes which are occupied by the younger inhabitants of the pueblo.

The Zia sun symbol was adopted by the State of New Mexico as the official symbol of the state. In an official capacity, it graces the state flag, highway signs, uniforms, and public buildings; unofficially, it has spread across the state to decorate and advertise everything from hamburger stands to massage parlors.

Santa Ana Pueblo

The old village which the Spaniards knew as Tamayo, was located on the north bank of the Jémez River against the cliffs of Black Mesa. There they built a mission church about 1600 and, like most of the Spanish missions, it was destroyed during the Pueblo Revolt. The pueblo was reoccupied after the revolt; however, the re-

Church at Santa Ana Pueblo, probably built shortly after the Spanish reconquest of New Mexico. —Courtesy New Mexico Economic Development & Tourism, No. 423

occupation did not last. The U.S. Census for 1890 found the old pueblo deserted. The 11th Census, published in 1894, reported: "A complete removal is made in March. . . . The cats alone remain, prowling like gaunt specters over the roofs and through the deserted streets." Things haven't changed much since 1890; Santa Ana Pueblo is still that way except for a few weeks out of the year.

Today, the Santa Ana Indians live in modern houses in Ranchitos. They send their children to Head Start and to schools in Bernalillo. They farm and they work at jobs in Bernalilo and Albuquerque. However, there are no kivas at Ranchitos. As the winter solstice nears and at other times important to their tribal heritage, the people move to Tamayo. First the medicine societies go, followed later by the remainder of the pueblo, to take part in week-long ceremonies.

Political and religious life is highly structured in this pueblo. The Santa Anans are born into clans which dictate their affiliation to one of two kivas, the squash and the turquoise. A *cacique*, somewhat comparable to a priest, oversees the community. He holds his office for life. He appoints a war priest and others to administer activities of the pueblo. A tribal council deals with the outside world as the Santa Ana Pueblo continues on its traditional conservative way.

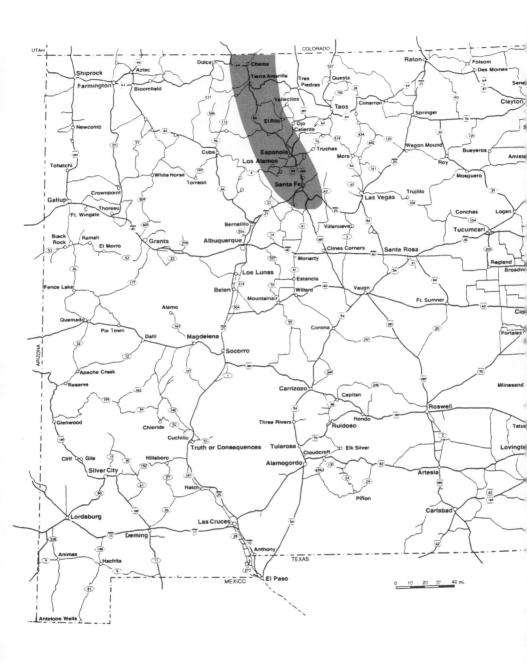

Old Spanish Trail

V. Old Spanish Trail

Spanish exploration and colonization of North America resulted in two long lines of settlements, one strung northward along the Rio Grande Valley and the other up the Pacific Coast. If Spain could make a connection between the missions of California and the colonial settlements of New Mexico, it would not only strengthen domination of a vast empire, but it would forge a profitable trade link.

The problem was a 1200-mile stretch of desert and mountain landscape, slashed by rivers, interrupted by the chasm we know as the Grand Canyon, and populated by hostile natives. In 1765, under orders from Governor Tomás Velés Cachupín, Juan María de Rivera went on a prospecting and trading expedition northwestward from Santa Fe into the land of the Utes. He found silver-bearing ore in a southwestern Colorado mountain range which he called La Plata, but his principal achievement was opening a route for traffic in furs and Indian slaves. That route was the eastern end of what would become known as the Old Spanish Trail.

Fray Silvestre Vélez de Escalante had served the Cross at the Zuñi Pueblo and traveled extensively in western New Mexico. He became convinced that the only practical way to form an alliance with the California missions was by avoiding the forbidding arid land, the great gorge of the Colorado River, and the hostile Hopis. He would go through the Ute country to the northwest.

On July 29, 1776, he set out from Santa Fe with Fray Francisco Atanasio Domínguez and ten men. They spent the first night at Santa Clara Pueblo on the Rio Grande, only nine leagues (2.63 miles) from Santa Fe. The next day, they went up the Rio Grande Valley to the mouth of the Chama River and along the Chama to Abiquiú.

Thus, Abiquiú became the jumping-off point for the trail to California. After a day of preparation, which included a Solemn Mass to ask protection of the patron saints, Fray Escalante and his party set out on a journey which would last five months and cover some 2,000 miles. They went up the Chama Valley for some five miles before turning north to avoid the river canyon. After thirteen miles, they camped on the Arroyo Seco (Dry Stream). The next day they took the old traders' trail along Arroyo Seco, across Cebolla (Onion) Creek to camp on the Rio de las Nutrias (Beaver River).

The next day they again took to the Chama River Valley and followed it to the vicinity of present-day Tierra Amarilla and Chama. Their route took them past Horse Lake, the site of Lumberton and Dulce. The latter is now Jicarilla Apache territory. West of Dulce they turned northwest and entered Colorado near Arboles. Modern US 84 closely approximates their route, but travel along the smooth macadam ribbon of US 84 is a far cry from the trail the Spaniards trod.

The Old Spanish Trail was a pack-mule route, perhaps the longest, crookedest, most tortuous trail in the nation. No wagon ruts marked it, but it served devout priests, trappers, traders, explorers, slave dealers, homeseekers, horse thieves, and warring Indian parties. Piute children were captured for sale to New Mexicans. (A girl brought $150 to $200, a boy less.) As early as 1823, a herd of 400 burros and mules were brought from California to be driven over the Santa Fe Trail to Missouri.

The trip between Santa Fe and Los Angeles took about three and a half months. There were annual caravans. The last was a Mexican mule packtrain in the spring of 1848. After the Mexican War the old trail was supplanted by southern routes which could accommodate wagons.

US 84-285
Tesuque—Chama

Tesuque

Located east of US 84-285, the village of Tesuque dates from 1740. It was named for the nearby Tewa pueblo. The name derives from a Tewa term meaning "spotted dry place" because the river disappears and reappears in the sand. It is now an art center, particularly in the area of woodcarving.

Tesuque Pueblo as it appeared during the 1880s. —Ritch, 1882-3

Tesuque Pueblo

In 1540 Hernándo de Alvarado, of Coronado's expedition, was the first European to visit the pueblo. At that time, it was located about three miles east of its present site. The pueblo was founded about 1300. The people believe their ancestors originated in an underworld to the north beneath a lake known as Sandy Place. They were allowed to populate the Southwest after trial by fire.

On August 9, 1680, warriors at Tesuque struck the first blow in the Pueblo Revolt, killing a Spanish civil servant named Cristóbal de Herrera.

Tesuque does not have a reputation even today for being an exceptionally friendly pueblo; however, highway signs invite passing motorists to stop in and play bingo.

Historical Excursion

NM 502
San Ildefonso Pueblo
—Los Alamos

San Ildefonso Pueblo

Ancestors of the residents of San Ildefonso came from the Anasazi community of Mesa Verde by way of the communities at

Frijoles Canyon (Bandelier National Monument). The present village began about the turn of the seventeenth century. As was the case with most of New Mexico's pueblos, the San Ildefonso Indians participated in the Pueblo Revolt. Perhaps they had better reason than most.

In 1676 the Tewa leaders were accused of bewitching a priest and other Spaniards. Wholesale arrests followed, and more than forty Indians supposedly confessed. They were arrested and sold into slavery. Four more were executed. During the Pueblo Revolt they killed a priest and his assistant while they were holding services at the altar. In 1696 the Indians revolted again and killed two more missionaries. They surrendered only after the Spaniards cut off their food supply.

San Ildefonso is perhaps best known to the rest of the world for the distinctive incised black pottery which was developed by María Martínez and her husband Julian. It is highly prized by collectors.

Los Alamos

Ashley Pond, a wealthy Detroit businessman, believed that hard work and outdoor activity provided the best education for adolescent boys. In 1918 he established the Los Alamos Ranch School at the site of present-day Los Alamos. Young men came to the West to live in log cabins, study the classics, and do ranch chores. By 1942 the school was doing well; however, that would be its last year. The United States government needed a place to develop an atomic bomb.

Gen. Leslie Graves was in charge of the Manhattan Project. He named Robert Oppenheimer to head the research team. Then the two set out to find a site. It had to be remote. It could not be near either seacoast nor an international border. The Pajarito Plateau filled the bill. The ranch school was informed that the government needed its property for military purposes. February, 1943, was the final graduation ceremony.

Thousands of people arrived secretly to build and man the laboratory-community which grew at the end of a torturous road to the top of the mesa. Those who came knew only that they were going to New Mexico. They were told to check in with "personnel" in an office at 109 Palace Avenue in Santa Fe.

They found themselves living behind fences. Guard towers ringed the establishment, and entrance was by badge only; outgoing letters were opened and censored. They ate in a dining room at

Fuller Lodge, the old dining and recreational hall for students at the Los Alamos Ranch School.

The scientists and employees could not reveal the nature of their work, even to their spouses and families. Indeed, some did not know what they were doing; they knew only of specific tasks to which they had been assigned. Eventually, residents in the surrounding area became curious about the clandestine activities within the fence.

The atomic bomb was code-named "Fat Man." By July, 1945, it was ready for testing. The bomb was cautiously transported to a test site in a barren desert sixty miles from Alamogordo. On July 16, 1945, the explosion took place which is still reverberating around the world.

After the war, Los Alamos made a transition to a peacetime scientific community. The land reverted to private ownership; the temporary laboratory buildings were replaced with permanent concrete structures. Research activities were diversified.

Today, there are no guards, and one does not need an identification badge to enter. The Los Alamos Chamber of Commerce welcomes visitors from an office in Fuller Lodge. The Los Alamos Historical Society has been piecing together history of the area; it maintains a museum in one of the old ranch school buildings.

One can spend half a day wandering through the Bradbury Science Museum, named for Norris Bradbury, one of the original Los Alamos scientists.

With its activities no longer a secret, in 1949 Los Alamos entered a float in Española's Oñate Fiesta parade advertising its part in the development of the atomic bomb. —Courtesy New Mexico Department of Development, No. 2836

Española

This spritely farming and ranching community was founded some time after the middle of the nineteenth century. The post office was established in 1881. In 1887, Franklin Bond, a Canadian merchant, began construction of an adobe house trimmed with Victorian gingerbread decorative flourishes. Over the years, Bond added to the two-roomed structure until it became a rambling building. The house became Española's city hall in 1957.

Española long served as a shipping point for fruit, stock, and other farm produce grown in the Española Valley. Today, it is a turnoff for travelers bound for Los Alamos or the Puye Cliff Dwellings.

Oñate's first colony, San Gabriel, was located at the juncture of the Rio Grande and the Chama River, in the Española Valley. No ruins have been pinpointed, and historians have long debated the exact location. Española has grabbed the honor, claiming to be the first capital of New Mexico. Local historians maintain that Española is a shortened version of San Gabriel de los Españoles, the full name of Oñate's first colony.

Historical Excursion

NM 30
Santa Clara Pueblo

To reach Fray Silvestre Vélez de Escalante's first stop on the Old Spanish Trail, take NM 30 south from Española for about two miles. Santa Clara Pueblo was constructed early in the fourteenth century by a wandering clan of Anasazis from the Four Corners area. The Tewa name was K'hapoo ("where roses grow near the water"). It was here in 1540 when Coronado's expedition came past.

The Puye Cliff Dwellings, an Anasazi village built between 1400 and 1450, are within the Santa Clara Reservation eleven miles west of NM 30. Until 1981, an annual arts and crafts fair was held at Puye. In 1981 lightning struck and killed several fairgoers; the fair was canceled, perhaps because the tragedy underlined an earlier warning. During archaeological excavations in the 1930s, several workers had heard ghostly voices: "Don't take me from this ground." Some workers who continued digging mysteriously died.

The Puye Cliff Dwellings date back to Anasazi days.
—Courtesy New Mexico Economic Development & Tourism, No. 805

Abiquiú

Abiquiú has been compared to Salem, Massachusetts. One author noted, "A witch lurked behind every adobe wall, and a wizard was doling out love potions that kept husbands home at night."

The community was first settled about 1744 on the abandoned ruins of an old Tewa pueblo on the bank of the Chama River. The first settlers consisted of a few Spaniards and *genízaros*, Indian captives whom the Spaniards had rescued, captured, or purchased from their captors. The *genízaros*, who had been baptized whether they wanted to be or not, are sometimes referred to as "Hispanicized Indians." After a series of Ute attacks, the *genízaro* settlers marched to Santa Fe, camped on the plaza, and demanded that the governor give them a safer place to live.

The governor mocked their fears, called out his soldiers, added more displaced persons to the ranks of the *genízaros*, and sent the lot back to Abiquiú along with Fray Juan José de Toledo to minister to their spiritual needs. The exceedingly zealous Fray Toledo found himself in a hotbed of laziness, sin, and, worst of all, wizardry and idolatrous worship.

Soldiers were sent door-to-door to root out those engaged in sorcery. Eight culprits were convicted of witchcraft and sentenced to serve as "house servants" to a prominent Spanish colonist. Fray Toledo's cook, one Juachinillo, was a ringleader of the sorcerers. The priest began to suffer stomach trouble, loss of appetite, and insomnia—all of which he attributed to the machinations of his cook. The situation had the makings of a musical comedy. While the friar was in Santa Fe trying to get help from the Holy Office in rooting out sin and sorcery, his parishioners were back in Abiquiú stealing his sheep, corn, and linens.

From its beginning, Abiquiú was a trading center. When the Utes were not raiding the village, they brought deerskins to trade for guns, horses, flour, corn, and an explosive distillate known as "Taos Lightning." A horse was worth twenty deerskins. In 1776 Fray Francisco Atanasio Domínguez arrived in Santa Fe from Mexico City on two missions: to conduct an inspection of clerical activities in New Mexico and to discover a route that would link New Mexico with the recently founded province of California. Father Domínguez enlisted Fray Silvestre Vélez de Escalante, reputed to know much about western trails.

On August 1, they struck out from Abiquiú on a 2,000-mile trek. Winter caught the party before they reached California, but they laid the groundwork for a trade route which would eventually become the Old Spanish Trail between Santa Fe and Los Angeles.

Ghost Ranch

The Ghost Ranch Living Museum is located in the Carson National Forest. It features mammals, birds, and reptiles housed in natural environments. The visitors' center is a worthwhile stop. As one tourist noted, "It's a great place for children if you can pry them away."

The nearby ranch from which the facility took its name was once a working ranch dating back to 1766. It is now an adult study center operated by the United Presbyterian Church. The ranch took its name from the *brujas* or witches which were said to haunt the canyons on the ranch.

Canjilon

Just off US 84 on NM 115, the ranching village Canjilon was reportedly settled by descendants of de Vargas in 1774. An unpaved forest road leads on to Canjilon Lakes. The lakes were originally created by beaver dams. The dams have been strengthened and the lakes enlarged by the forest service.

Cebolla

The post office of this small ranching community dates from just after the turn of the century, but the town was settled about 1880. Cebolla, Spanish for "onion," came from wild flowers of the onion family. Old-timers tell that so many grew along Onion Creek that the smell permeated the entire valley.

Historical Excursion

NM 573
Tierra Amarilla—Los Ojos

Tierra Amarilla

The townsite was filed in 1832 and named Los Nutrias after the many beaver in the area. The land was originally a Mexican land grant to Manuel Martínez, his children, and other settlers. However, settlement was delayed because of raids by Utes, Jicarilla Apaches, and Navajos. It did not become a permanent settlement until after 1846 when U.S. troops arrived.

It was renamed Tierra Amarilla after the yellow earth in the vicinity. It has been the county seat of Rio Arriba County since 1880. In 1967, Tierra Amarilla made headlines in newspapers across the nation because of a shootout at the courthouse.

Land-rights activist Reies López Tijerina headed a movement called Alíanza Federal de los Mercedes (Federal Alliance for Land Grants). He argued that land around Tierra Amarilla belonged to descendants of the original grantees; the federal government and other owners had obtained land by fraudulent means. Tijerina and his followers invaded the courthouse, and a deputy sheriff was wounded during the resulting conflict.

The New Mexico National Guard was called out for a manhunt which employed tanks and helicopters. Tijerina was jailed but was later found innocent of charges stemming from the affair. The following year, Tijerina ran for governor on the People's Constitutional Party ticket, but his name was removed from the ballot because of earlier convictions for legal violations.

Fort Lowell

During the 1860s, northern New Mexico, particularly around Tierra Amarilla, was plagued by the Utes of southern Colorado. In 1867 Fort Lowell was constructed nearby to protect settlers in the area. By 1869 the Utes were deemed to have been "pacified" and the post was abandoned, despite protests of local citizens.

On two occasions after that, troops returned when the Utes threatened trouble. In 1872 the fort was reoccupied as an Indian agency headquarters, and it served nearby Ute and Apache tribes in that capacity until 1881.

Today, nothing remains of the old adobe buildings. A historical marker on US 84 commemorates the post.

Los Ojos

This village, settled in 1860, was the home of Francisco Martínez, son of Manuel Martínez, the original land grant recipient. Camp Plummer, the predecessor to Fort Lowell, was near Los Ojos. The Mercure-Abeyta House is located in Los Ojos, a "Spanish Victorian" structure with two-foot-thick adobe walls and gingerbread decoration. The house was built in the mid-1800s at which time it had a flat roof. A pitched roof and the Victorian decoration were probably added about the turn of the century by Scandanavian artisans who came to the area in response to a land development scheme.

Brazos

Los Brazos, meaning "branches," is located where the two main branches of the Chama River meet. The community was settled in the early 1860s.

La Casa de Martínez, the Martínez house, was once owned in sections by three different people at the same time. It is a 19-room house with two-foot-thick adobe walls and massive log vigas. The oldest section was built in 1868 by Fernando Martínez, an early settler who raised sheep. When his first son was married, Fernando gave him the sitting room as an apartment and built on a second section in 1888. The family grew and so did the house. By 1912 it had three sections, each owned by a different person, located on communally-owned land.

Parkview

This community, a few miles south of Chama off US 84 on NM 95, was settled in the late 1870s. In 1876, land developers from Santa Fe and Chicago laid out the town and sold property to immigrants, including a number of Scandanavians. The developers built a toll road over which the immigrants could travel to their property from Fort Garland, Colorado. During 1877, a crude trail was built from the east over Cumbres Pass so that pioneers could drag their belongings, livestock, and wagons over the mountain. Later, this crude road would be used to bring in railroad construction materials.

In 1880 when the railroad was under construction more Scandanavians came and were employed by the railroad as tie cutters. NM 95 proceeds on to the recreation areas around Heron Lake and El Vado Lake.

Chama

The village of Chama began in the late 1870s with sheep and cattle ranching and came of age in 1880 during the construction of the Denver and Rio Grande Railroad.

Gen. William Jackson Palmer was the driving force behind the project to forge a link from the east to the gold and silver camps in southwestern Colorado's San Juan Range. The curves necessary to negotiate the winding valleys through the mountains would be torturous. This problem was solved by narrow-gauge track, rails only three feet apart. Not only were they cheaper but they could be more easily bent around mountains than standard-gauge which were four feet eight and a half inches apart. After three surveys, the 10,015-foot Cumbres Pass route was selected, the same road used by immigrants to Parkview.

The timing could not have been worse. There were plenty of laborers during the winter of 1879-1880, but they had their minds on dreams of fortunes to be found in the goldfields toward which the railroad was reaching. The turnover was at the rate of 1,000 workers a month. At one point, officials said they were employing 35,000 men to survey, grade, build bridges, blast tunnels, cut ties, lay tracks, and drive spikes. They were advertising for more, as far away as Montreal, Canada.

Chama was a booming, rowdy, exciting place to be. Saloons and gambling houses provided both entertainment and work. Wages were high and groceries were expensive. The 1880 census toted up a population of more than a thousand. The post office opened for business on December 12 of that year, and the railroad arrived two months later. Chama was a "railroad town."

Between Antonito, Colorado, and Chama, trains snaked around a triple-curve on a single mountain slope. The curve was known as "The Whiplash." The route bored through 300-foot tunnels, negotiated rickety wooden bridges, and edged through Toltec Gorge, along the rim of the Rio de los Pinos Valley.

From 1880 until the 1930s was Chama's heyday. There were 50,000 head of sheep in the Chama Valley during the 1920s, according to one authority. Harvesting lumber was big business. Then, there was coal in addition to traffic to and from the goldfields.

But the Depression of the 1930s brought disaster. The forests had been reduced to rotting stumps, many sheepmen had gone broke during the winter of 1931-1932, trucks and paved highways were putting railroads out of business, and the line over the Cumbres Pass was becoming an economic burden to the Denver and Rio Grande Railroad.

In 1967 the railroad petitioned to abandon the historic line that tied Chama to Antonito. A cry went up across the nation: "Save the Narrow Gauge!" But there were no solutions to the problem. However, in 1970 the Colorado and New Mexico legislatures voted, at the eleventh hour, to purchase the sixty-four miles of track and right of way. Thus was born the Cumbres and Toltec Scenic Railroad.

During the first five years of operation it introduced more than 100,000 passengers to a ride on "a real steam train," pausing to take water from old wooden water tanks and to allow passengers to take photographs of mountain scenery and each other. Now, reservations are advised, particularly during September and early October when leaves are taking on their fall colors.

Chama is still a "railroad town."

Toltec Tunnel on the Denver & Rio Grande near Chama.
—Ritch, 1885

An 1806 Spanish presidio soldier. Shortly after the turn of the century, Spain attempted to change its soldiery over to wearing military uniforms more nearly like the Napoleonic styles which were in vogue in Europe at that time. The presidio soldiers in New Mexico would have no part of it. By 1806 they had reverted back to buckskin and rawhide fashions.

—Courtesy Dr. Joseph Sanchez, National Park Service

VI. Domain of the Mountain Men

In Europe, from the Middle Ages on, furs embellished the richest fabrics and served as a background for the finest jewels. Kings and noblemen wore sable, ermine, and fox. Those farther down the social scale had to be content with martin, otter, and squirrel. Beaver pelts came to be sought for hats, and the wealth and social prominence of a wearer was indicated by the height of his hat.

As the French and the English invaded North America and pushed across the continent, the harvest of furs was a primary goal of economic exploitation. In the north the Hudson's Bay Company sought to dominate the world trade in furs. In the south the Louisiana-based Company of the Indies hoped that prairies, covered by bison and streams teeming with beaver, would pay off

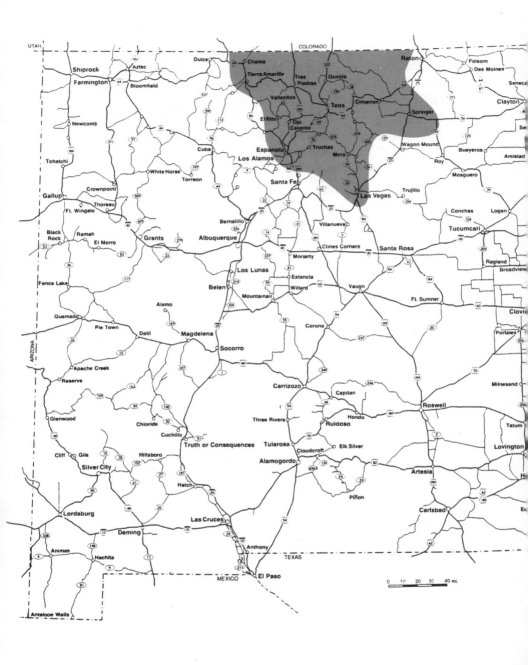

Domain of the Mountain Men

obligations which plagued Louis XIV. In the United States John Jacob Astor amassed a fortune by organizing various fur companies to push across the United States in advance of civilization.

It was a different story in New Mexico. The Spaniards came to a land where the mountain streams were alive with beaver, a ripe crop awaiting harvest. The reasons for their failure to capitalize upon this potential are hazy. Even if fashion in Spain placed little value on furs because of the mild climate, the Spaniards must have been aware of their value elsewhere in Europe.

During the seventeenth century, under the *encomienda* system, from time to time governors would place levies on pueblos for antelope, deer, and buffalo hides. To meet the demands, the primarily agricultural Pueblo Indians gave the Plains Indians maize in exchange for skins. The Spaniards bundled these up and shipped them south over the Camino Real. But there was little if any effort on the part of the Spaniards to deal in "fine furs."

There was no lack of interest among Anglo traders and trappers. American traders recognized the potential of the New Mexican market. Even though governmental officials in the Spanish province were hostile to American trade, natives welcomed traders because of a shortage of consumer goods. Indians on the fringes of New Mexico saw more slave hunters than Spanish traders; they too were interested in traders from the United States. In 1822 a Ute Indian was reported to have told an American trader: "Come over among us and you shall have as many beaver skins as you wish. The rivers are full of them. Their dams back up the water in the rivers."

In 1822, at St. Louis, Maj. Andrew Henry and Gen. William H. Ashley formed a partnership which in time came to be known as the Rocky Mountain Fur Company. They employed no traders; they built no permanent forts; they used no Indian trappers. Instead they hired daring young men who knew the rifle and the steel trap, men who would harvest furs wherever they could be found in spite of rival trappers and hostile Indians. The company held an annual rendezvous in some mountain valley to which the trappers brought their year's catch to trade for a year's wages in goods and a new outfit.

During the spring and fall, these trappers caught beaver, in the winter they hunted and traded with Indians, during the summer they explored for new beaver streams to conquer. They had no reason to return to settlements or sleep under a roof until the beaver trade played out, and few believed that would ever happen. These hardy explorers, daring fighters, and skilled hunters became known as "mountain men" because they lived year-around in the Rockies. Robert Glass Cleland dubbed them "This Reckless Breed of Men."

There was some penetration of the Spanish trade barrier; however, as long as Spain held New Mexico, attempts to trap beaver from the streams of the southern Rockies were thwarted. News of Mexican independence reached Santa Fe in September, 1821, and the governmental policy toward traders changed abruptly. They were welcomed as long as they paid taxes and "other charges." The latter phrase turned out to be a euphemism for bribes.

In November of that year, William Becknell, father of the Santa Fe trade, was the first to learn of the new policy. Most of his men elected to stay in New Mexico and spend the winter trapping rather than return to Missouri.

The floodgate was open. On September 3, 1822, the Franklin *Missouri Intelligencer*, reported a "Company of about fifty persons, principally from St. Louis and its vicinity are now in town, on their way to Santa Fe. Their purpose is to hunt and obtain furs." The Mexicans soon recognized the possibility of their streams being depleted. In 1824 the Mexican government enacted a regulation that only native settlers should hunt beaver. However, since there were no New Mexican trappers, the governor granted licenses to American trappers in the name of Mexican citizens. The Americans were supposed to take along Mexicans to teach them the art of trapping.

The original caption on this portrayal of mountain men was "I took ye for an Injin." —Frederick Remington

In one way or another, the mountain men continued their invasion. Some married New Mexican girls, some gained Mexican citizenship, some used the names of pliant citizens to obtain licenses to trap, and others simply evaded the regulation. For example, in 1829 Ewing Young organized a party of forty men which included 20-year-old Kit Carson. They trapped their way to California, where they sold their furs to the captain of a trading schooner. On the way back they trapped the Gila River and stashed their catch in the Santa Rita mine. Then Young and Carson went to Santa Fe and got a license to trade with the Indians on the Gila River. They quickly returned to Santa Fe with the pelts, supposedly obtained by trading with the Indians. They sold 2,000 pounds of furs for $12 a pound.

Of all the mountain men in New Mexico, Kit Carson had the most impact upon the future of the Territory. Carson was born in 1809 in Kentucky. In 1826 he joined a caravan bound for New Mexico. From 1828 to 1831 he learned trapping under Ewing Young. After that, he wandered up and down the spine of the Rockies and throughout the West, gaining extensive knowledge of Western trails and Indian ways.

In 1835 he attended the fur-trading rendezvous at Green River with Jim Bridger. Along the way he married an Arapaho girl who died and a Cheyenne girl who is reputed to have divorced him Indian style by throwing his belongings out of the tepee. After serving as a trapper for Bent's Fort on the Arkansas River and as a guide for John C. Frémont, he married fifteen-year-old Josefa Jaramillo of Taos on February 6, 1843.

After performing courier and guide service for Frémont and Gen. Stephen W. Kearny during the Mexican War, he returned to New Mexico where he took up ranching. From 1853 until 1861 he was an Indian agent. During the Civil War he became a colonel in the First New Mexico Volunteer Infantry. After the Civil War he was called upon to subdue the Apaches, the Navajos, and the Kiowas. Carson was a reluctant campaigner against Indians because of his sympathy for their plight. He mastered Spanish, patois French, and a number of Indian dialects, but he never learned to read and write English. He spent his later years in Colorado. After his death, his body along with the remains of his wife were removed to Taos for burial near his old home.

By the mid-1830s the demand for furs was beginning to decline, as was the supply. By the beginning of the Mexican War many mountain men had gone into buffalo hunting, trading with the Indians, and other pursuits.

Taos

There is confusion regarding the origin of the name Taos (pronounced to rhyme with "house"). The commonest explanation is that it derived from the Tewa word *towih*, meaning "red willows," common to the area. But there are those who insist the term came across the Bering Strait from ancient China and means "The Way" or "The Right Way." *Taos* has referred to three separate communities: San Gerónimo de Taos, the Indian Pueblo north of present-day Taos; Don Fernando de Taos, the central commercial center; and Ranchos de Taos, a residential and agricultural community to the south.

The Taos Pueblo was known to the Spaniards from 1540 when Hernando de Alvarado, a captain in Coronado's army, explored the area. About 1617 a Spanish settlement developed close to the Indian Pueblo, and Fray Pedro de Miranda built a church on the edge of the pueblo. But friction developed between the two communities and the Indians asked the Spaniards to move. It has been suggested the Indians objected to intermarriage between Spaniards and Indians.

Fray Miranda and two Spanish soldiers who served as his guards were killed in 1631, and relations between the Spaniards and the Indians did not improve over the years. The Taos pueblo was the central point from which Popé planned the Pueblo Revolt of 1680, and Don Fernando de Taos was the first to feel the brunt. Only two Spaniards escaped, one of whom was Don Fernando de Chávez for whom the village had been named. He never came back to occupy his land. In 1696, after de Vargas' return, there was an attempted reenactment of the Pueblo Revolt. Taos was not at peace until after 1700.

Taos was the scene of an annual trade fair to which Indians brought their wares. The fairs were attended by Utes, Apaches, and Comanches who bartered with the Pueblo Indians and the Spaniards.

Trappers began to filter into Taos about 1820 and, as they expanded their activities in northern New Mexico, made the village their headquarters. They were within easy distance of the beaver-laden headwaters of the Arkansas, Rio Grande, Platte, and San Juan rivers. Here they could sell their pelts, obtain supplies, and spend the winter. They could gamble and dance with local señoritas, and there were distilleries to supply Taos Lightning. Some would blow a year's earnings in one grand and glorious spree; others were more conservative. In *Pioneer Life in the West,* the Rev. James B. Finley told of seeing a trapper come into a bank:

> His dress and appearance were those of a backwoods trapper and the bank room being filled with the gentry they looked upon his greasy buckskin hunting shirt and leggins as though they feared he would touch them and spoil or soil their delicate clothing, and after looking around the room, he threw down his first check—then his second, third. Then the cashier said, "Where are you from, Sir?"
>
> The trapper replied, "Just from the moon, Sir!"
>
> "How did you get down, Sir?"
>
> "Why, I just greased my hunting shirt, Sir, and slid down the rainbow!"

To the mountain men, the village may have seemed a bustling metropolis and its fleshpots the Saturnalia supreme, but most American visitors of the day penned a different picture. Albert Pike found "a few dirty, irregular lanes, and a quantity of mud houses."

William Sherley Williams, better known as Old Bill Williams, was one of the most colorful of the Taos mountain men. Before going West, Williams had been a circuit preacher in Missouri, but he became so captivated with Indian ways that he was adopted by the Utes. His drinking exploits became legendary. On one occasion he exchanged his winter's catch for a new trapping outfit and spent the remainder of his earnings on a barrel of Taos Lightning. He opened the barrel, invited other trappers to "jine in," and did not leave his place beside the barrel until it was empty. The next day he headed back to the mountains.

On another occasion Bill Williams tried his hand at being a merchant. He opened a store in Taos. After a few days of arguing with women about the price of dollar-a-yard calico, he threw his entire stock out into the street and watched as his former customers fought for a share. When the melee was over, he headed for his beloved mountains. Bill Williams met his death at the hands of the Utes, the tribe that had adopted him.

After Mexico gained independence from Spain, New Mexicans revolted against high taxes and unpopular governors. Contentious Taoseños took their place in the forefront of the action. They continued their insurrectionist ways by leading one of the few reactions against the American occupation in 1847. Pueblo Indians were incited to riot by local malcontents. Governor Charles Bent was attacked in his Taos home, shot with arrows and scalped while still alive. Other civil officials were similarly slaughtered.

Today, visitors to Taos wonder at the American flag which flies over the plaza day and night. This is because of a right earned during the Civil War. A large element of Southern sympathizers lived in Taos. They were bent upon tearing down the flag and destroying it. Kit Carson and others went to the mountains for a tall cottonwood pole. They nailed the flag to the pole and erected it in the plaza. Capt. Smith H. Simpson and a friend retired to a store on the south side of the plaza with guns in hand to see that the flag stayed in place. After a short time, the Southern sympathizers left town by joining deserting Union officers who came through Taos from a fort in Colorado. Subsequently Congress authorized Taos to fly the Stars and Stripes day and night in recognition of the loyalty of its early citizens.

During the twentieth century, Taos has steadily grown in reputation as a mecca for artists. The start of the movement has been traced to a broken wagon wheel. Before the turn of the century a couple of artists passed through Taos, but the first painter of note was Joseph Henry Sharp, who settled down in an old Penitente church in 1908. Sharp's enthusiasm over the Indian way of life caused two other artists to come to the Southwest.

Bert G. Phillips and Ernest L. Blumenschein were on their way between Denver and Mexico, painting along the way, when their wagon broke down outside of Taos. Blumenschein lost the flip of a coin and had to carry a broken wagon wheel into Taos for repairs.

Kit Carson's home in Taos was not an imposing structure.
—Courtesy New Mexico Department of Development, No. 2776

On returning, his report about the town was so enthusiastic that the pair went no farther. That was the beginning of the Taos art colony.

In 1916 a very bored and very rich Mabel Ganson Evans Dodge Sterne arrived in Taos. She was once widowed and once divorced; she had spent the preceding fourteen years presiding over literary salons in Italy, Paris, and New York. Mabel's third husband was Maurice Sterne, artist and sculptor. He had gone to New Mexico to paint Indians. Mabel followed his suggestion to come "Save the Indians, their art-culture—reveal it to the world!" Maurice went back to New York; Mabel stayed in Taos and chalked up her second divorce.

Perhaps she stayed because she met Antonio Lujan, a blanket-clad Pueblo Indian. She bought a plot of ground adjoining Taos Pueblo and employed Antonio to build on it. In 1923 she married Tony Lujan, (anglicized her new name,) and became Mabel Dodge Luhan. Her home became a mecca for artists and writers, the likes of D. H. Lawrence, Georgia O'Keeffe, Ansel Adams, Marsden Hartley, and John Marin. Mabel Dodge Luhan's house has since become a conference center and a bed and breakfast establishment.

D. H. Lawrence died of tuberculosis in Italy in 1930, but his wife brought the author's ashes back to New Mexico for burial on the D. H. Lawrence ranch on the outskirts of Taos. The ranch is now owned by the University of New Mexico, and visitors can climb the mountainside to the shrine and pay their respects to the English author who shook the literary world by writing *Lady Chatterley's Lover* in 1928 to pave the way for a host of steamy romances.

During the 1960s, Taos saw another invasion. Members of the hippie culture arrived, attracted by the town's widely advertised reputation for free-spirited living. They occupied rundown houses, converted buses, and tepees. Some tried to stake out spots in the plaza and in hotel lobbies. They put a considerable strain on the welfare budget. There were misunderstandings and a few incidents. As winter approached, most moved on to more temperate climates. A few stayed to join the colony of painters, weavers, writers, jewelers, and potters who still live in Taos.

Today, Taos remains largely unspoiled by glitz, at least in the central plaza area. It is now free of conflict, unless a scramble for parking space can be termed conflict. Pickup trucks emblazoned with the names of Taos Valley ranches cruise around the ancient plaza, vying with tourists for space in front of favorite cafes. Most of the mercantile establishments which formerly supplied local ranchers and Indians have moved to the outskirts of town, supplanted by galleries, boutiques, and souvenir shops.

Ranchos de Taos

The site of Ranchos de Taos was a pre-Spanish farming settlement for Taos Indians. Spaniards began to populate the community in 1716. Apache raids caused abandonment on at least one occasion, and the Spanish settlers accompanied the Indians to live for a time with them in the pueblo north of Taos.

By the end of the eighteenth century they had returned to Ranchos de Taos. The community was then called Río de las Trampas de Taos. Subsequently the name was changed to Ranchos de Don Fernando de Taos and then shortened to Ranchos de Taos, as it remains today.

Ranchos de Taos is the location of the Church of St. Francis of Assisi, one of the most frequently photographed churches in the United States. The fortress-like structure was built during the 1770s as a mission for the conversion of Taos Indians, but it now serves parishioners of the community who care for their church with loving hands. In 1967 a hard, harsh cement stucco coating was applied to the exterior of the church as a means of preservation. In 1979 the parishioners replastered the exterior with adobe mud, the traditional way of protecting adobe walls.

The massive buttresses of the church loom just off the highway to the east in the center of town, an unmistakable landmark. The huge twin towers and entrance face east behind a time-worn adobe wall. The church's walls are four feet thick, surrounding the interior which stretches a hundred and eight feet in length. Enormous vigas rest upon carved supports which are imbedded in the walls. Among a collection of artwork there is a painting which is said to emit a miraculous glow during the dark of night.

The church of St. Francis of Assisi at Ranchos de Taos was built during the 1770s. —Photo by the authors

The feast of St. Francis is celebrated at the church and in the village on October 4. The church is always open to visitors and guides are sometime available to conduct tours and take pictures of visitors standing in front of the historic landmark. NM 68 bisects the town. A tour of the dirt roads which wander off on either side of the highway will reveal many fine old adobe buildings and fences.

Pilar

A primitive Jicarilla Apache farming community occupied this site in pre-Spanish times. Their village was burned by de Vargas in 1694. A century later Governor Fernando Chacón granted the area to twenty Spanish families. In the meantime, the Apaches to whom the land really belonged were in dire straits. In 1822 Don Facundo Melgares, the last Spanish governor, ordered that the Apaches be allowed to live and farm in the area. The order was not enforced because of protest from the settlers. Originally called Cieneguilla (little marsh), the area was renamed Pilar, presumably after Nuestra Señora de Pilar, a shrine in Zaragoza, Spain.

Both sides of the Rio Grande are farmed. The bridge which crosses the river was built during the 1880s. The earliest bridge at this spot is believed to have been built in 1598.

The Rio Grande Gorge State Park, just up-river from Pilar, provides campsites, picnic facilities, restrooms, fishing, and a place from which to watch white-water rafting parties.

Glen-Woody Suspension Bridge

Three miles south of Pilar a suspension bridge spans the Rio Grande. In 1902 a town was laid out on the west bank of the river as part of an elaborate mining venture, the Glen-Woody Mining Camp. A large flume was constructed just north of the bridge with a 160-horsepower turbine to power mining equipment. A hotel was built and hopes ran high. The mine never developed and the would-be town rotted away. The land is now privately owned.

Embudo

This former Indian pueblo and Spanish farming community was given the name Embudo (funnel) by early Spanish settlers because Embudo Creek flows through a constricted opening resembling a funnel. Little remains of this once-bustling farming and ranching community.

A wooden trestle bridge spans the river to an abandoned railroad station on the Denver & Rio Grande Western Railroad. It was the old "chile line" which was constructed to carry wool, hides, piñons, chiles, and other agricultural products out of the valley. There was a turntable for the helper engines which were used to boost trains up the steep grades. The railroad station and the turntable have been declared a historic district.

Prior to the turn of the century, John Wesley Powell, pioneer Western explorer, built the Embudo Gauging Station to measure the depth of the river. It was the first of its kind, but it still measures the depth of the river. The gauging station is included in the Historic District which is privately owned.

Embudo was the scene of an incident which generated one of the strangest railroad regulations on record. The *New Mexico Daily Examiner* told about it:

DENTAL MISHAP FAILS TO DELAY

Lost time and teeth seem to be of equal value to the D&RGW.

The Saturday afternoon train, right on time, was coming down the Embudo hill on its way to Santa Fe. Engineer Albee of Alamosa, Colo., felt an urge to cough, and inadvertently faced the cab window when he did so. As a result his false teeth sailed out the window.

Engineer Albee immediately stopped the train, then backed it up to the hill to the place where the accident happened. The train crew and some of the passengers joined the search, and finally F. D. Casan of Chicago found the missing dental work.

Albee wiped off his teeth with his machine rag, replaced them, and raced the train into Santa Fe, arriving promptly on schedule.

On hearing yesterday of the dental mishap on the D&RGW, State Corporation Commissioner Bob Valdez announced that plans would be made to issue orders to all railroads, asking them to clear brush from the vicinity of the tracks in order that wigs, teeth, and other detachable objects might be more easily found.

Velarde

This agricultural community was called La Jolla in 1875 when it was founded by the Velarde family but was later renamed after Matías Velarde. It is the center of a farming community which raises apples and peaches. During the harvest season, the highway is lined with fruit stands. Chiles and gourds are offered during the winter season. The town is close to the river and not observable from the highway.

Los Luceros

Also off NM 68, five miles south of Velarde, Los Luceros was the capital of the Rio Arriba *departmento* when New Mexico was under Mexican rule. The community was the county seat of Rio Arriba County from 1855 to 1860. The old county courthouse is now a private residence. One of the state's original territorial residences, it is open to the public by appointment only.

Alcalde

In 1860 the county seat of Rio Arriba County was transferred from Los Luceros to Alcalde, at that time called Plaza del Alcalde. The county seat was again transferred in 1880 to Tierra Amarilla. This once thriving trading post now consists of a scattering of houses.

A turnoff connects with the Old Velarde Road, NM 582, which runs along the Rio Grande to San Juan Pueblo. Along the way it passes the Swan Lake Ranch, at one time a luxurious hacienda which was owned by a dancer. It became known for the parties and literary events given by the dancer and Hamlin Garland, an author who wrote primarily about the hardships of Middle-Western farm life. The road continues to the San Juan Pueblo.

San Juan Pueblo

The San Juan Pueblo can be reached from either NM 68 or the Old Velarde Road. San Juan Pueblo has roots deep in New Mexico's history. The original Indian name was O'ke. It was occupied by Don Juan de Oñate in July, 1598. Oñate displaced the Tewa Indians as he moved in his men and 7,000 head of livestock. He renamed the pueblo San Juan de los Caballeros and confiscated the Indians' possessions. They were forced to go to neighboring villages. A month later he moved to another pueblo, which he renamed San Gabriel, and the Tewas returned to their looted village.

The pueblo still bears the name given by Oñate, though its site has been moved across the river. For three-quarters of a century the people of San Juan endured indignities from the Spaniards. In 1675 forty-seven religious leaders from several pueblos in the area were arrested on charges of witchcraft. Some were hanged and some were

A nineteenth-century view of San Juan Pueblo. In 1598 Juan de Oñate established the first capital of New Mexico nearby. —Ritch, 1882-3

flogged. One of those who were flogged was a medicine man named Popé of San Juan Pueblo. It was he who plotted the overthrow of the Spaniards and led the Pueblo Revolt of 1680.

After the Reconquest a mission church was built, probably just after the turn of the eighteenth century. On his inspection tour of New Mexico missions Fray Francisco Atanasio Domínguez noted of the mission: "Above the main door is a poor arch containing two good middle-sized bells without clappers, but they are rung with stones." The mission stood until 1913 when it was replaced by a brick structure.

Some of the pueblo's old adobe homes still exist, interspersed with modern houses of the HUD variety. The reservation encompasses 12,000 acres. Farming and stock-raising are still important sources of revenue, but many of the pueblo's residents work at jobs off the reservation.

Santa Cruz

This was the second villa to be established in New Mexico. It was founded by de Vargas in 1695 with the impressive name La Villa Nueva de Santa Cruz de los Españoles Mejicanos del Rey Nuestro Señor Carlos Segundo. Understandably, the name was shortened to Santa Cruz de la Cañada or simply Santa Cruz.

The original settlement was by families from Zacatecas, Mexico. In spite of the villa being made the military headquarters of the district, it had to be abandoned for a time with crops left standing in the fields because of inadequate military protection. Resettlement began in 1706. When Zebulon Pike passed through the village a century later he reported a population of more than 2,000.

Santa Cruz has had a turbulent past. In 1837 it was the scene of the so-called Chimayó Rebellion. On July 1 Governor Albino Pérez announced a policy of direct taxation. Under the policy citizens could be cast into jail for nonperformance of military service, even when pleading poverty, or subjected to a forced loan when ordinary revenue was inadequate.

A mob of about 2,000 assembled in Santa Cruz to march on Santa Fe. Governor Pérez countermarched with a force of 200, the majority of whom were Indians. Most of the force deserted at the first shot. Seven were killed and many wounded. The governor escaped. However, on the following day when he was trying to flee the country he was met by a group of rebellious Santo Domingo Indians and assassinated. His head was carried back to the rebel camp at Santa Cruz on a pike.

When Col. Sterling Price was marching on Taos to avenge the death of Governor Bent and suppress the Taos Revolt of 1847 he was met at Santa Cruz by a force of Mexicans and Indians. Two Americans were killed and several wounded during the engagement.

During Territorial days, Santa Cruz's reputation for violence increased. Thomas A. Janvier wrote in the *Santa Fe Partner*:

> Santa Cruz de la Cañada . . . was said to have took the cake for toughness before railroad times. It was a holy terror Santa Cruz was! The only decent folks in it was the French Padre— who outclassed most saints—and hadn't a fly on him—and a German named Becker. He had the government forage station, Becker had; and he used to say he'd had a fresh surprise every morning of the five years he'd been forage agent—when he woke up and found nobody'd knifed him in the night and he was keeping on being alive.

The plaza in Santa Cruz is dominated by the old Spanish Mission, a massive cruciform church built in 1733, one of the largest in the state. The church originally had a flat roof. After a number of heavy rains, a pitched roof was added. In 1979-80, the church was renovated. The church has records dating back to 1695 and is particularly rich in religious art of the Spanish colonial period.

There is a legend concerning a santo which has two missing fingers. According to the story, the Santa Cruz River overflowed and was threatening the town. A finger was broken off the statue and thrown into the flooding river. The sun came out and the water subsided. At a later date the village was being ravaged by a smallpox epidemic. Another finger was taken from the santo. It was burned and the ashes were rubbed on the foreheads of the faithful on Ash Wednesday.

For more than three centuries, Santa Cruz was on the main road between Santa Fe and Taos. It was bypassed by the modernization of the highways and is located a half a mile east of NM 68.

US 64
Shady Brook—Cimarron

Shady Brook

US 64 leaves Taos as Kit Carson Road, winding through the Taos River valley past galleries and small hotels into the Carson National Forest, where the roadside is punctuated by campgrounds and picnic areas beside the rippling stream. The area is dotted with summer homes. Numerous hiking trails lead off into the mountains.

Historical Excursion

NM 434
Angel Fire—Guadalupita

Angel Fire

After a rather uncertain start as a ski resort, Angel Fire took a second breath and developed into a year-around resort community, complete with summer homes, condominiums, an 18-hole golf course, and glitzy restaurants. Thirty miles of ski slopes and trails range in difficulty from beginner-level to a 2,180-foot drop to test the talents of experts.

Black Lake

The community had its beginning with settlement by José María Mares and his wife Doña Jenara Trujillo in 1886. José and his brother were hunting in 1857 when they were captured by Indians and sold into slavery. They were luckier than most slaves. The brothers were taken to Taos and sold to Don Juan Mares who adopted them and brought them up as his own children.

Today Black Lake is nothing more than a popular fishing spot. It was so named because dense timber surrounding the water made it look black instead of blue.

Guadalupita

Beyond Black Lake, NM 434 becomes somewhat primitive. It wends through pasture land, then past an occasional housing development and a Christmas-tree farm as it nears Guadalupita. During the late nineteenth century, Guadalupita was a farming, lumbering, and sheep-raising community. Now, except for cemeteries, it is virtually abandoned.

The road continues on past Coyote Creek State Park to intersect NM 518 at Mora. Coyote Creek has camping facilities and visitors with the required licenses can fish for rainbow and brown trout in a secluded stream which is dotted with beaver ponds.

————Historical Sidebar————————————

Vietnam Veterans National Memorial

As US 64 descends from Palo Flechado Pass and crosses the Moreno Valley, a gull-like structure sweeps up out of the hillside to the south, silhouetted against the Sangre de Cristo Mountains: Vietnam Veterans National Memorial.

During a period when the Vietnam conflict was a less-than-popular issue, the family of Dr. Victor Westphall constructed the memorial as a tribute to the memory of Westphall's son, who was killed in a 1968 enemy ambush in Vietnam. The Westphalls completed the shrine in 1971.

The walls sweep to a height of fifty feet at the front of the building in a chapel from which visitors can contemplate the tranquility of Moreno Valley through a narrow window which stretches to the top of the building.

Eagle Nest

In pre-Spanish days, Taos, Picurís, and Pecos tribesmen frequented the area to obtain golden eagle feathers for use during ceremonial worship. Later mountain men took beaver from the Cimarron River, in spite of Spanish dictates against trapping in New Mexican streams. In 1841 the area became part of the vast Maxwell Land Grant.

Charles Springer acquired land in Moreno Valley and built a dam at the head of Cimarron Canyon to impound water for irrigation. Eagle Nest Lake was completed in 1919 and fishermen began to arrive. Springer stocked the lake with trout, and by 1922 there was a garage, a store, a hotel, and a few summer homes. The growing town was called "Therma." By the early 1930s the community was wide open. Big-time gamblers ran the circuit from Las Vegas to Therma. Stakes were in the tens of thousands of dollars. Visiting gamblers slept all day and played all night.

Stores featured slot machines, and Julio's, the Gold Pan, and the El Monte Hotel (later the Laguna Vista Lodge) had gaming tables. Old-timers will tell you that most of the games were rigged: a row of buttons back of the roulette table would stop the roll of the ball, dice were doctored with mercury spots, and cards were marked. The El Monte featured a house of prostitution with a hidden staircase leading upstairs to the ladies of the evening.

In 1935 the town's name was changed to Eagle Nest and gambling was outlawed, with dire predictions that the ban was a rash act which would end the tourist trade. The prediction came to naught as those who wanted to gamble retired behind closed doors.

Eagle Nest with Baldy Mountain in the background. An exploration tunnel was cut through the mountain during a 30-year period beginning in 1900.
—Courtesy New Mexico Economic Development & Tourism, No. 43,590

Ute Park

US 64 leaves Eagle Nest by way of Cimarron Canyon, a narrow twisting gorge where crenelated granite formations known as the Palisades come down to the road. As Cimarron Canyon State Park, it is dotted with picnic and camping sites, and the Cimarron River provides good fishing.

About five miles after US 64 breaks out of the canyon, it comes to Ute Park, named for the Indians who used to live on the slopes of nearby Mount Baldy, convenient to the agency at Cimarron which supplied them with provisions. Settlers moved into Ute Park about 1867, and the St. Louis, Rocky Mountain & Pacific Railroad (later taken over by the Santa Fe) built a branch line to Cimarron and Ute Park.

Cimarron

The town dates from 1841, the year the vast Beaubien-Miranda Land Grant was filed. The village became a gathering place for ranchers and miners from a wide area and was headquarters for the Maxwell Land Grant Company which took over the Beaubien-Miranda Grant. By means of inheritance from his father-in-law, Carlos Beaubien, and purchase from other partners, Lucien Bonaparte Maxwell accumulated 1,714,765 acres. His holding included the towns of Springer, Maxwell, French, Raton, Vermejo Park, Ute Park, and Elizabethtown, plus a large area in Colorado.

At the age of eighteen, Maxwell accompanied John C. Frémont on his Oregon expedition. He married 13-year-old Luz Beaubien, daughter of Carlos Beaubien, owner of the land grant. They had nine children. Maxwell cast aside the life of a mountain man and adopted the life of a feudal lord, living first at Rayado and then moving into Cimarron. His mansion had two grand pianos and luxurious furnishings.

Maxwell was a powerful man and an expert horseman. He loved gambling; it was said he would bet on anything. About 1864 he built the Maxwell House, as large as a city block. It housed a gambling room, a billiard room, and a dance hall, as well as a rear section for ladies of the evening. They were not allowed to leave the area. Every night large sums of money changed hands as gunmen and ranchers gathered to play faro, roulette, monte, cunquién, poker, and dice.

Soon Maxwell's became the principal stopping place for travelers on the Santa Fe Trail. It was a jumping-off point for prospectors, hunters, and trappers. Guests are said to have included Kit Carson,

Ceran St. Vrain, Charles Bent, Davy Crockett, Clay Allison, Buffalo Bill Cody, and Tom Boggs (grandson of Daniel Boone).

The 40-room St. James Hotel was built across from the Maxwell House and run by Henry Lambert. Before coming to New Mexico Lambert had been a chef for Gen. Ulysses S. Grant and Abraham Lincoln. This inn was a hangout for outlaws; it was the scene of twenty-six killings. Whenever a man was shot in the hotel, the townspeople would say, "Lambert had a man for breakfast." The *Las Vegas Gazette* once reported, "Everything is quiet in Cimarron. Nobody has been killed for three days."

As the community continued to grow, it accumulated fifteen saloons, four hotels, a post office, and a newspaper. On one occasion when Clay Allison and a number of his cohorts were in town, Allison became angered by an item in the Cimarron *News and Press*. He and his men battered in the door of the warehouse where the paper was published, smashed the press with a sledge hammer, and dumped type cases and office equipment into the Cimarron River. The next morning Allison went back to the newspaper office, found a stack of papers which had already been printed, scrawled "Clay Allison's Edition" across the back, and went from bar to bar selling them at 25¢ a copy. Allison later apologized and paid the newspaper $200 for the damage.

According to Agnes Morley Cleaveland in *No Life for a Lady*, the next morning her mother stood in the midst of the newspaper office and accosted Allison: "Now see what you've done. You ought to be ashamed of yourself!"

Allison pulled out a roll of greenbacks and said: "Well, go buy yourself another printing press. I don't fight women."

In 1860-61 Maxwell was associated with Buffalo Bill Cody in a goat and sheep ranch near Cimarron. Buffalo Bill organized his famous Wild West Show in Cimarron, rounding up Indians and pinto ponies in the area. On occasion Buffalo Bill would return to Cimarron for Christmas and give a Christmas party for children at the St. James Hotel. On one occasion he gave each child a plush-seated tricycle and for many years some of the recipients were displaying their presents as cherished mementoes.

Owners of the St. James Hotel, operated for a while as the Don Diego Tavern, have taken back its original name and restored the establishment to its former glory. However, no attempt was made to patch or cover the bullet holes in the dining room ceiling. The dining room was the former saloon. The latest ceiling was installed

The jail at Cimarron was built to hold the likes of Clay Allison.
—Photo by the Authors

in 1903 after three layers of oak flooring were laid in the room above to protect the guests from bullets.

Rooms at the St. James have been occupied by the likes of Buffalo Bill, Annie Oakley, Jesse James, and Zane Grey, who occupied a room while writing a book. Old guest books display notes about guests and meals in spidery handwriting. Some of the rooms are said to be haunted by the spirits of those who lost their lives at the St. James.

Cimarron was the county seat of Colfax County from 1872 to 1882 but declined with the transfer of the county seat to Springer. However, mining and lumbering continued to be important industries. There was a new wave of prosperity in 1905 when the railroad built the branch line to Cimarron and Ute Park. The Cimarron Townsite Company bought a tract of land on the north side of the river called New Town and sold lots to homeseekers who came in with the railroad. In the 1930s a fire destroyed five blocks in the business section of New Town.

With the arrival of the railroad, Cimarron had played out its role in the opening of the West. Today, the sleepy village basks in its historical past as tourists wander about town reading historical markers. The museum is located in the old Aztec Mill, a grist mill where Utes and Jicarilla Apaches received government flour rations from 1864 to 1870.

Outlaws and Desperados

During the height of its frontier days, Cimarron probably saw more outlaws than any other community in New Mexico. Clay Allison was in many ways typical of the lot. He was a cattleman and a gunfighter. He lived on the fringes of legality. He lived by a personal code which placed a higher value on personal honor than on legal restraints.

Born on a Tennessee farm, he grew up among talk of states' rights and slavery. The Civil War divided his state, and young Allison chose to join the Southern forces. In January, 1862, he was discharged because of emotional instability resulting from a head injury received as a child, but he reenlisted and served until the end of the war as a scout for Gen. Nathan Bedford Forrest.

After the war he migrated to Texas and became a cowhand for Oliver Loving and Charles Goodnight. By 1870 he was ranching in Colfax County and earning a reputation for getting into drunken brawls and shooting sprees. Legend insists that he killed a man named Johnson in a knife duel which was fought in an open grave to be occupied by the loser. Also in 1870, he was the leader of a lynch mob; he decapitated the victim and displayed the head in a Cimarron saloon.

This magazine illustration depicting a stagecoach holdup was drawn from an actual event which took place at Tecolote near Las Vegas.
—Hayes, 1880

Allison was also subject to erratic behavior. On one occasion he rode nude through the streets of a town. While on a cattle drive to Wyoming he developed a toothache. He visited a dentist in Cheyenne. The hapless doctor drilled the wrong tooth. Allison went to another dentist to have the work completed. Then he returned to the first dentist and pulled one of his teeth.

Allison met his death in a freak accident. He was thrown from a wagon and the rear wheel rolled over his head.

Miguel Otero, who became acquainted with Allison shortly after his arrival in New Mexico, probably put his finger on Allison's problem: "When sober Clay Allison was well mannered and extremely likeable, but under the influence of liquor he was a terror to the whole neighborhood and a good man to avoid."

In 1965 Peter Hertzog compiled *A Directory of New Mexico Desperadoes*. His list totaled 567. The individuals named ranged from out-and-out criminals to politicians and lawyers who occupied high places in government and society. Many were involved in political or economic feuding or warfare, as opposed to outright criminal activity. An examination of early-day newspapers and of court testimony reveals that much of the frontier violence resulted from drunken brawls and sprees.

US 64
Taos Pueblo—Tres Piedras

Taos Pueblo

US 64 becomes North Pueblo Road as it passes through the business district of Taos. The road to the pueblo veers off to the east about a mile north of the plaza.

The Taos Pueblo is the gemstone of New Mexico's Indian pueblos; it a trademark of the state and the mecca of every tourist who visits Taos. San Gerónimo de Taos was the name the Spanish missionaries gave it.

Hernando de Alvarado, a captain in Coronado's force, was the first European to see it, in 1540. After Oñate's visit to Taos in July, 1598, a priest began work on a mission church which was completed in 1617 and destroyed during the Pueblo Revolt of 1680.

Taos Pueblo had not yet been spruced up to entertain tourists when this early-day photograph was taken. —Courtesy New Mexico Department of Development, No. 2748

The Taos Pueblo has long been a seat of revolt. A Spanish priest and two Spanish soldiers were killed in 1631. Taos was the central point from which Popé sowed seeds for the Pueblo Revolt. After de Vargas' Reconquest, in 1696 the inhabitants joined another revolt in which five priests and twenty-one other Spaniards were killed.

In January, 1847, dissident Mexicans refused to recognize American authority in New Mexico. They aroused the Taos Indians, and Governor Bent and other Americans were slain in an attack upon the nearby village of Don Fernandez de Taos. In February Col. Sterling Price arrived with an avenging army and 700 Indians barricaded themselves within the San Gerónimo mission. Colonel Price battered down the walls of the ancient church with a furious cannonade and the Indians fled to the mountains, leaving a hundred and fifty dead. Price demanded the surrender of fifteen leaders of the insurrection. They were hung, martyrs to the Indians' cause. Today the ruined church serves as a memorial to those who gave their lives.

The Taos Indians were not through with protest. Early in this century a sacred site in the mountains to the east known as Blue Lake was included in the Carson National Forest. Immediately it began to be overrun by campers. The Indians objected strenuously and launched another battle, this time in court. The fight lasted for more than fifty years. In 1971 the land was returned to the tribe.

Each August the Taos Indians journey up Pueblo Creek to Blue Lake for rituals which are not open to outsiders.

Snuggled beneath the sweeping slopes of 13,160-foot Wheeler Peak, the multistoried apartment houses of Taos Pueblo must closely resemble the prehistoric pueblos. By tribal consent, electricity and telephones are prohibited. Many of the upper-story rooms are still reached only by ladders, ladders which the dogs have learned to negotiate as readily as the people.

Various dances, footraces, and religious-oriented ceremonies are open to the public on varying dates through the year. The highlight of the year is the San Gerónimo Feast Day. It is accompanied by an arts and crafts fair, a pole-climbing contest, and various dances.

The modern fairs during San Gerónimo Day celebrations are actually extensions of the trade fairs that were held at the pueblo before and during the Spanish colonial period when the Plains Indians came to trade. Spanish governors and officials attended those early fairs. Early during the eighteenth century it was the practice of some governors to reserve this trading for themselves, punishing ordinary Spanish citizens who attempted to profit from the trade. Fray Francisco Atanasio Domínguez gave some idea of the pricing schedule:

> The Comanches usually sell to our people at this rate: a buffalo hide for a *belduque*, or broad knife made entirely of iron which they call a trading knife here; . . . an Indian slave, according to the individual, because if it is an Indian girl from twelve to twenty years old, two good horses and some trifles in addition, such as a short cloak, a horse cloth, a red lapel are given; or a she-mule and a scarlet cover, or other things are given for her. If the slave is male, he is worth less.

Multistoried Taos Pueblo has become a trademark of the state.
—Photo by the authors

Rio Grande Gorge Bridge

This bridge links the eastern and western parts of northern New Mexico. Before its construction in 1965, in order to cross the Rio Grande travelers had to negotiate steep banks to cross primitive bridges several miles away. The bridge is 600 feet above the river. The height of the concrete piers is equivalent to an eight-story building. When the bridge was constructed it was the second tallest in the world. It was built to withstand winds in excess of ninety miles an hour.

Tres Piedras

Named for the three large extrusions of granite which can be seen from miles away, this lumbering and ranching community was settled in 1879. This area was a favorite Tewa Indian hunting ground; their name for it was "mountain sheep rock place." Although the antelope herds have been depleted, many New Mexicans still come to hunt.

NM 522
Arroyo Hondo—Costilla

Arroyo Hondo

On February 28, 1813, Spanish officials issued a proclamation inviting settlers to occupy vacant land, and Nerio Sisneros and forty-two others petitioned for plots in the Arroyo Hondo area. *Moradas*, recognizable by their wooden crosses, testify to the strength of the Penitentes in the region. Simeon Turley, an American, came to Taos in 1830 and soon developed a flourishing ranch with its headquarters at Arroyo Hondo. He dammed the Hondo River and built a grist mill. Eventually he added looms and spinning wheels. His establishment employed many New Mexicans and Indians. However, he was perhaps better known for his distillery which supplied Taos Lightning.

During the insurrection of 1847, when warned that a party of raiders was approaching his establishment, he barricaded the ranch. During a two-day battle the raiders set fire to his ranch. Turley escaped but confided to a neighbor whom he had befriended where he was going to hide. His neighbor betrayed him and Turley was killed.

Sheep have right of way in the area around Arroyo Hondo.

—Photo by the authors

At the turn of the century a mining boom attracted prospectors and gold-seekers, but the output was limited and Arroyo Hondo settled back to its former way of life.

Historical Excursion

NM 577-150
Arroyo Seco—Taos Ski Valley

Two Spanish farmers, Cristóbal and José Martínez, founded Arroyo Seco (dry ditch) in 1804 by planting crops. They commuted to their fields for three years before building houses. It was 1881 before the community got a post office.

Taos Ski Valley

NM 150 follows the route of an old toll road as it goes to Taos Ski Valley, one of the most popular ski resorts in the state, complete with chalets, condominiums, and hotels which can accommodate more than 1,100 skiers.

In 1880 gold was discovered at the site now occupied by the ski resort. The town was called Amizette, after the wife of the prospector who made the strike. The gold played out in 1895, but Walter Frazer found copper and gold farther east in the canyon. He interested Albert C. Twining, a New Jersey banker, in the enterprise. Twining invested money, and the town was named in his honor.

Frazer built a $300,000 smelter to handle the output of the mine. Unfortunately, when the smelter was fired the molten ore froze to the sides of the furnace and the enterprise went bankrupt. Twining remained a ghost town, cluttered with rusting machinery, until Ernie Blake arrived in the 1950s. Blake was a European in search of the perfect site for a ski slope. Blake became a leader in bringing the ski industry to New Mexico.

D. H. Lawrence Ranch

Between Arroyo Hondo and San Cristobal a dirt road leads eastward to the D. H. Lawrence Ranch, now the property of the University of New Mexico. Originally known as the Kiowa Ranch, it was owned by Mabel Dodge Luhan. She traded it to Frieda Lawrence in exchange for the manuscript of her husband's novel *Sons and Lovers*.

The Lawrences spent two years in Taos during the 1920s, much of that time at the ranch. Three of Lawrence's books derived from his stay in Taos: *The Plumed Serpent*, *David*, and *Mornings in Mexico*. D. H. Lawrence died in France in 1930. His ashes were sent back to Taos a number of years later.

By that time, Frieda Lawrence had remarried. According to the story, she and her friends went to Lamy, the closest railroad station, to meet the train carrying her former husband's ashes. Since the train was late, the party went to the nearest saloon to wait. The merriment continued, even after they had picked up the urn containing the ashes.

Finally, the group returned to Taos. It was then that they remembered leaving the urn containing Lawrence's ashes under a table in a saloon in Lamy. A messenger was sent for the urn which now reposes in a mausoleum near the ranch house.

Frieda willed the ranch to the University of New Mexico, and it is now used by the university as a conference center and vacation facility.

Questa

This farming and mining town was originally called San Antonio del Rio Colorado. Farming was a chancy business in 1829 when Don Francisco Laforet built a house on the fertile river bottom. The Utes and Apaches took a dim view of intrusion into one of their favorite hunting grounds. Laforet had to move up to the ridge to keep an eye out for marauders. But the settlers prevailed.

Old records show that a hundred families were living in the area in 1849. They eagerly greeted mountain men and traders who came over the old Taos Trail in covered wagons. In 1854 the Indians struck again, and a six-foot wall with only one entrance was built around the town. In 1872 the settlers obtained rights to a grant containing 115,000 acres. In 1883, when the town acquired a post office, the name was changed to Questa.

Questa continued its agricultural pursuits with little change until early in the twentieth century when a molybdenum mine began operation a few miles east on NM 38. Farming still continues in the valley, but Questa has acquired motels, restaurants, and filling stations to cater to the passing public.

Historical Excursion

NM 378
Cerro—Rio Grande

Cerro

The farming community of Cerro, just west of NM 522, was settled in 1854 by families from Taos and Questa. Even though it is the gateway to the Rio Grande Wild River Recreation Area, it offers limited services to travelers.

Rio Grande Wild River Recreation Area

The visitors' center for the Rio Grande Wild River Recreation Area is about fourteen miles beyond Cerro on NM 378.

From its source in the high plains of Colorado, the Rio Grande stretches 1,885 miles to the Gulf of Mexico. Over the eons, its waters have worn a deep gorge through volcanic rock and gravelly plain. Seventy miles of the gorge lies within New Mexico. Here, at the La

Junta Campground and Overlook, is the most exciting stretch of the gorge.

The Bureau of Land Management, a division of the U.S. Department of the Interior, became responsible for administering the gorge when the Rio Grande became the first river to be placed under the protection of the National Wild and Scenic Rivers Act in 1970.

Petroglyphs in the area are believed to date from 8,000 years ago. They depict religious and hunting scenes.

Costilla

Only a mile from the Colorado border, Costilla is named for the Rio Costilla (Rib River), which curves through town. Instead of having one plaza, Costilla had four. In 1852 an expedition of settlers from Taos and Arroyo Hondo laid out four plazas on land acquired by Carlos Beaubien, who had also filed the Maxwell Land Grant.

The town proper is reached by turning east on NM 196, the old road which used to form the main street of the town. The four plazas originally stretched the length of the village into Colorado. One of the plazas had a torreón, a tower from which to watch for Utes and Apaches who made repeated attempts to steal horses and sheep. The surrounding area, known as Sunshine Valley, raises beans, corn, and chile.

NM 38
Elizabethtown—Red River

Elizabethtown

About 1866 a band of Utes appeared at Fort Union to trade rich copper float, ore which had washed to the surface. William Kroenig and W. H. Moore hired the Indians to lead them to the source. The ore had come from Baldy Mountain. The strike resulted in the famous Mystic Mine near the peak of the mountain.

Gold—lots of it—was discovered in Willow Creek in the late fall. By the summer of 1867 the secret was out. Willow Gulch swarmed with prospectors; so did Mexican Gulch, Anniseta Gulch, Grouse Gulch, Humbug Gulch, Big Nigger Gulch, and Pine Gulch. As the mountain and streams yielded gold, a thriving community sprung up nearby. Streets were surveyed in 1867, and the town was named Elizabethtown after the daughter of one of the promoters. It was incorporated in 1870, and "E-town," as it was called, became the county seat of Colfax County.

Placer mining and dredging equipment required more water than the creeks provided. A 42-mile ditch was built to bring water around mountaintops from Red River, only eleven miles away as the crow flies. The "Big Ditch" proved to be a disappointment; however, millions were taken from mines with names such as Aztec, Paragon, Montezuma, Rebel Chief, French Henry, Red Bandana, Legal Tender, and Ajax. Then, a lawsuit was filed challenging the right to divert water from the Red River. Further diversion was banned, and within a few years Elizabethtown was practically deserted. Today, as a result of fires and vandalism, it is a gaunt spectacle of a once thriving community.

Red River Pass

At 9,852 feet above sea level, Red River Pass is the highest in New Mexico, the division between the Red River and the Moreno valleys. From the top, a series of switchback turns lowers westbound traffic to the floor of Red River Valley. Each turn unfolds a new view of distant mountain ranges, and buildings at the bottom take on a dollhouse appearance. Prior to paving and the removal of some of the early hairpin turns, the gravel road washed out with almost every rain. Drivers searched for wide spots to let cars going in the opposite direction pass.

Timid tourists from the East missed most of the scenery because of their attention to the road, and the most common remark was, "I don't know how we are going back, but it will not be by this road."

Red River

The Taos Indians called the stream *pee ho ghay po* (red river creek) because of the sediment which has stained the water as far back as man remembers. The town was laid out in 1894 and the area was the site of many attempts at mining around the turn of the century. The mines—Carabel, Midnight, Anchor, and Eddison—were only moderately successful.

Red River had to await the development of New Mexico's tourist industry to hit its stride. An active chamber of commerce keeps the spirit of the Old West alive. During the summer visitors can watch the robbery of the bank every afternoon at 4:30. The spectacle concludes just in time for Happy Hour at the watering spots strung along the main street.

This is all that is left of Midnight, once a booming gold-mining town northwest of Red River. The town was abandoned when local factions fought over the belle of the dance hall. The community was named Midnight because from the miners' viewpoint midnight was the liveliest time of the day. —Courtesy New Mexico Economic Development & Tourism, No. 63.

History buffs can visit historic buildings: the Little Red School House, built in 1915; the Brigham J. Young House; Pierce-Fuller House; Sylvester Mallette Cabin; Orin Mallette House; and Elson-Oldham Cabin—all on the National Register of Historic Places. One can pan for gold or fish in either of two public lakes, and Red River is a jumping off point for hikes on more than a hundred miles of trails, including backpacking into the Wheeler Peak Wilderness area. It is a popular winter sports area. Dominoes and bridge in the Community Center await those with less energetic aspirations.

US 285
Ojo Caliente

Ojo Caliente

The hot springs of Ojo Caliente, on US 285 some 25 miles north of Española, have attracted health seekers since prehistoric times. The ruins of three ancient Tewa pueblos are on the mesa above town and, according to Tewa legend, Poseyemu, a mythical hero, was born of piñon nuts gathered by a virgin at the spring. He returns annually to visit his grandmother, who lives in the curative water of the springs.

During the latter half of the seventeenth century, Spaniards established a settlement but in 1748 petitioned the governor to be allowed to abandon the village because of Ute and Comanche attacks. In 1790 eighteen families from Bernalillo petitioned to establish a new settlement. Permission was granted provided it was "a well-ordered and regular settlement on the outskirts of the Cañada de los Comanches." It had to be heavily fortified "since experience has proven that nobody can last there because of its fatal position."

In 1807, after his capture by the Spaniards near Taos, Lt. Zebulon M. Pike was brought through Ojo Caliente. He described the community:

> The village consisted of civilized Indians, but much mixed blood. Here we had a dance which is called the Fandango, but there was one which was copied from the Mexicans, and is now danced in the first societies of New Spain, and has even been introduced at the court of Madrid. This village may contain 500 souls. The greatest natural curiosity is the warm springs, which are two in number [actually five], about 10 yards apart, and each affords sufficient water for a mill seat. They appear to be impregnated with copper, and were more than 33° above blood heat.

The hot springs at Ojo Caliente were used by the Indians for many years before the Spaniards arrived. —Ritch, 1885

Like the Tewas, Utes, Comanches, Apaches, and Spaniards, bathers continue to visit Ojo Caliente.

─────── Historical Excursion

NM 554
El Rito

Two miles north of Ojo Caliente, NM 111 heads northward. NM 554 branches off to El Rito, nine miles east.

This ranching community on the El Rito River grew from a series of Spanish settlements which were scattered along the river early in the nineteenth century, known collectively as El Rito. In March, 1909, the Spanish-American Normal School was established. The legislature became convinced that low salaries did not attract teachers to mountain communities, and that local boys and girls must be trained to teach in rural schools. In 1947 the name was changed to Northern New Mexico State School. Today it is the Northern New Mexico Community College, serving a varied student population.

─────── Historical Excursion

NM 111
La Madera—Cañon Plaza

La Madera

The name of the town means "wood" or "lumber," a mainstay of its economy. The community was settled in 1820 by Juan de Dios Chacón. The Halleck and Howard Lumber Co. of Denver mounted a sawmill operation in the ponderosa pine forest. The Denver and Rio Grande Railroad built a narrow-gauge line from Taos Junction, a distance of sixteen miles. As soon as the timber played out the line was abandoned.

Vallecitos

This tiny farming and ranching community was established in 1776, during the Spanish colonial period. It did not get a post office until more than a century later, in 1886.

248

Cañon Plaza

This village also dates back to the Spanish colonial period. A four-wheel-drive vehicle is advisable. The road is impassable during bad weather.

Philmont Scout Ranch—Miami

Philmont Scout Ranch

Every summer brings a fresh crop of Boy Scouts to Philmont Scout Ranch for exposure to life in the West. They come from all over the United States and assorted foreign countries. On any given summer day as many as 2,000 may be scattered among the various camps on the ranch. It is Kit Carson's old ranch.

In 1849 Kit Carson constructed a home where the Santa Fe Trail crossed the Rayado River. He built a trading post and took up farming and ranching. The ranch passed through various hands until it was purchased by Waite Phillips, an Oklahoma oilman.

Phillips bought a third of a million acres of the old Maxwell Land Grant. Through the mountainous back country he strung a chain of fishing and hunting camps for himself and his guests. Recognizing the value of scouting to the youth of America, Phillips gave one third of his ranch to the Boy Scouts of America, 127,000 acres. It is a working ranch. Scouts come to observe and join in the work.

Carson's home is still there, a Spanish type adobe building. The outer walls are almost devoid of openings. Thick-set windows look inward on a patio. There is a loopholed watchtower at one corner. Kit Carson's bed is on exhibit, a bed that was allegedly too comfortable for his Spartan tastes. According to the story he slept on it for only two nights before taking his buffalo robes and spreading them on a hard adobe couch in the corner.

The old house was restored in 1949 by the Boy Scouts. It now serves as a museum. Kit Carson's rifle hangs on the wall, its stock studded with brass tacks. Legend has it that each tack represents a man he killed. There are eighty-seven. The ranch has herds of buffalo; beaver build dams in the streams.

Christopher Carson. The painting by Blanche C. Grant hangs in the chamber of Commerce at Taos. —Courtesy New Mexico Economic Development & Tourism, No. 656

Rayado

Kit Carson was the first Anglo settler in 1849 in this community closeby the old stage relay station on the mountain branch of the Santa Fe Trail. Carson came to establish a ranch, hoping that the government would have no further need for his services. In 1850 ten dragoons under Sergeant William Holbrook were sent to protect the settlement. They remained until Fort Union was established forty miles to the south.

Here at Rayado, Lucien Maxwell, who had married Luz Beaubien, built his ranch house. Later Maxwell moved to Cimarron where he built a grand mansion, and Kit Carson gave up ranching to go back into government service.

Miami

This farming and ranching community was settled in 1908 by colonists from Miami, Ohio. Consequently, a town in New Mexico's Ute and Apache country echoes the name of an Indian tribe that lived in Ohio and Indiana. Some years ago an Ohio newspaperman who took a whirlwind trip through New Mexico informed his readers that the Miami Indians had "ranged as far west as New Mexico."

Talpa

This community near the mouth of the Rio Chiquito was settled early in the eighteenth century as part of the general occupation of the Ranchos de Taos area. Prior to the arrival of the Spaniards, it was the site of prehistoric pit houses and small pueblos during the period 1100 to 1300 A.D.

A village weaver named Juan Pedro Cruz lived in Talpa. Before the era of machine-made blankets and carpets, he supplied the Taos Indians with serapes and the surrounding villages with small brown, black, and white rugs with which they covered their dirt floors. He wove the white foundation cloths used for elaborately embroidered colchas (bedspreads), now eagerly sought by collectors of Spanish handicrafts.

The Ponce de León Hot Springs were close by. Before Taos had plumbing, they were known as the Taos Bathtub because the town's citizens would go there to take baths.

Fort Burgwin Research Center

The Fort Burgwin Research Center is a research facility of Southern Methodist University which is constructed at the site of Cantonment Burgwin.

Cantonment Burgwin was never officially a fort. Cantonment Burgwin was built in 1852 fifty miles west of Fort Union on the only wagon road to Santa Fe. It was named to honor Capt. John H. K. Burgwin, who was killed during the Taos uprising of 1847. The installation's mission was to protect the Taos area from the Jicarilla Apaches and the Utes. The troops who were stationed there had their hands full.

In 1853 a detachment from Cantonment Burgwin was on an expedition chasing a band of Navajos who had murdered seven civilians. They found 400 of the troublemakers near the San Juan River and sat down with them for a council of peace. One of the chiefs was given a bag of flour as a gift. Another chief felt he had been slighted. He grabbed the bag of flour and swung it around his head until everyone in the council looked like a snowman. He was captured and held until he bought his freedom with a dozen sheep. That night the soldiers ate mutton.

All expeditions from the post did not end in peace councils. The following year a band of miscreant Indians were captured. A guard of sixty troopers set out to take them to Fort Union. En route, the Indians escaped. During pursuit, the soldiers rode into an ambush and were surrounded by some 400 Utes and Jicarilla Apaches. More than forty soldiers were killed during a day-long battle before the tattered unit made it back to the post under the cover of darkness.

On a tour of western forts in 1853, the inspector general found that the troops at Cantonment Burgwin had not been paid for five months. He noted that ten new recruits had recently joined the company: one was near-sighted, one was left-handed, and at least one could not speak English. The inspector general doubted the wisdom of having a left-handed trooper. He could pose a danger wielding a saber in ranks.

Cantonment Burgwin was abandoned in 1860, and the log and adobe buildings sat vacant for many years. In the 1950s a Kansas businessman established a lumber mill in the area. He became interested in the history of the fort. The original foundations were excavated and some of the buildings reconstructed.

The facility was acquired by Southern Methodist University. It is now used by the university in furtherance of archaeological research programs. In selecting a name for the installation, Cantonment Burgwin was given the status of a fort, a distinction it never achieved during its service against the Indian menace.

Tres Ritos

Now a resort community, Tres Ritos (three rivers) was established about 1900 as a mining and lumber camp. It got its name from being at the confluence of the Rio La Junta, Agua Piedra Creek, and Rio Pueblo. Tres Ritos was used as a camping ground for freighters on the old Taos-Las Vegas Trail. It now has summer houses, gas stations, restaurants, and lodges.

Holman

This farming and sheep-raising community was established in the latter part of the nineteenth century and named after Charles W. Holman, the first postmaster. It experienced a flurry of excitement during the 1970s. Residents began to see holy images on the cracked walls of its adobe church. Both skeptics and believers came to see the miracle. Newspaper reporters and television crews came to record the event. The streets were lined with refreshment stands. Then, as suddenly as they had started, the sightings ceased.

Cleveland

Under the influence of Governor Alberto Maynez's policy of encouraging new settlements, about 1816 a group of families moved into the Mora Valley. They established two plazas, one of which was called San Antonio de la Mora, now known as Cleveland. In the late 1800s Dan Cassidy and a group of his countrymen from Donegal, Ireland, came to Cleveland. Cassidy opened a general store and the rest of his group were farmers and merchants. By the turn of the century the population exceeded six hundred.

Mora

The community had its beginnings as Santa Gertrudis de lo de Mora about 1816; however, French trappers would call it L'eau des Morts (Water of the Dead) after finding a dead body in what is now called the Mora River. During its early days, Mora was seldom a peaceful place. Comanche raids caused the settlers to build their houses close together and keep constant watch while clearing their lands.

Mora developed into a thriving business center with sawmills, flour mills, hotels, saloons, and mercantile establishments. It also attracted the overflow of outlaws and criminals from Las Vegas and was noted for feuds, murders, lynchings, and terrorism.

─────── **Historical Excursion**

NM 94
Ledoux

This small isolated Hispanic village was established before the turn of the century. It was named for an early French fur trapper. It got a post office in 1902.

Morphy Lake State Park, seven miles west of Ledoux, is a popular wilderness camping and fishing spot. Designated as a "primitive-use area," it is accessible to backpackers and four-wheel-drive vehicles, trucks, or horses.

NM 105
Gascon—Rociada

Both of these small communities were settled by Jean Pendaries, a Frenchman who named the village of Gascon after his native French province. Rociada apparently got its name from the fact that the area is subject to exceptionally heavy dew; Rociada means "dewy." Pendaries started a large ranch, the Baca Ranch.

New Mexico author Oliver LaFarge married Pendaries's great-granddaughter and wrote about life on the Baca Ranch in his book *Behind the Mountain*. A large tract of land near Rociada has been incorporated into a recreation-oriented development called Pendaries Village, complete with a golf course, a motel, and other facilities.

La Cueva

Built shortly after the construction of Fort Union, La Cueva was founded by Vincente Romero as a ranch to provide forage and grains to Fort Union. Romero slept in caves while he was building his ranch, hence the name of the community. He built a mill to provide flour to Fort Union. The mill generated electricity until 1949. La Cueva is now dedicated as a national historic district; it belongs to the owners of a nearby ranch.

NM 442
Rainsville—Ocate

Rainsville

Both Rainsville and Ojo Feliz are ranching and lumbering communities which were settled after the turn of the nineteenth century. The former was originally called Coyote. Its name was probably changed upon application for a post office because the designation was preempted by another New Mexico town. About that time at least four settlements, three creeks, two canyons, an arroyo, a draw, and a valley were called "Coyote." Ocate was established at an earlier date.

Sapello

This farming community was settled prior to 1874 and possibly as early as the late 1830s. Historians and linguists have had a field day trying to divine the origin of the community's name. Spanish, French, and Kiowa have been suggested as possible sources from words meaning "toad," "hairbrush," and "burial." A resident was queried: *"Yo no say,"* (I don't know). Then he shrugged and added a testimonial to the village, "Knowing would not make it any better."

NM 75
Peñasco

Peñasco

This village, originally composed of three small settlements, was founded in 1796. Three families from San José petitioned Governor Fernando Chacón to build two towns in the valley. The governor agreed under the provision that "at least 50 individuals must repopulate the place and hold the land against sale for ten years."

Peñasco residences were once considered showplaces in the Embudo Valley, but life styles changed during the twentieth century as the children of farmers found easier ways to make their livings in nearby communities. Many have moved away; others commute to nearby towns. However, summer residents have found the area as real-estate developers tout the Embudo Valley.

NM 76
Las Trampas—Chimayó

Las Trampas

The village of Las Trampas (the traps) was established in 1751 by twelve families from Santa Fe, led by Juan de Argüello who received a land grant from Governor Tomás Velés Cachupín. The most notable feature of the town is the church, San José de Gracia, one of the finest surviving eighteenth-century churches in New Mexico.

The church was first known as the Church of the Twelve Apostles, and legend has it that only twelve men were allowed to work on the building at one time. It is built of adobe with walls four feet thick and thirty-four feet high, relieved of severity by small towers on the front facade. An outside choir balcony stretches across the front of the church between the two towers. The choir moved outside to sing during religious processions.

The church had two bells, one of which was exceptionally sweet in tone. It was called María del Gracia and tolled for mass and the deaths of infants. The other, called María del Refugio, had a heavier tone. It was rung for masses and for the death of adults. Since María del Gracia was stolen, María del Refugio tolls for all occasions.

Las Trampas has long been a strong center for the Penitentes. Formerly there was a Penitente "death cart" at the church. It was a carved skeleton draped in black and mounted on a two-wheeled cart with three-foot wheels hewn from a solid log. She was named Doña Sebastiana. Doña Sebastiana held a bow and arrow in her bony fingers. The cart was trundled in Holy Week processions by the Order of the Penitentes. It was said she had been known to shoot arrows at unrepentant sinners. The cart has disappeared.

In 1966 the fine old San José de Gracia almost became a victim of progress. State highway department engineers were surveying to widen and pave the highway through Las Trampas. The church was in the way. The villagers needed the road so badly that they were about to agree to the church's destruction when a group of conservationists in Santa Fe heard about the problem.

During restoration of the church at Las Trampas an old photograph was discovered from which the long-lost wooden belfries were reconstructed.
—Photo by the authors

The church was placed on the National Register of Historic Places to save it from destruction. Then the venerable church was refurbished. The two wooden belfries were rebuilt from an old photograph which was discovered in the possession of one of the villagers.

Until recently Las Trampas was a predominately Spanish-speaking community. Now many of the residents are summer visitors who have bought and restored many of the old adobe homes some of which date back to the eighteenth century.

──Historical Sidebar────────────────────────

The Penitentes

In traveling through northern and central New Mexico, particularly on back roads, one frequently sees squarish buildings with small crosses on the roofs above the entrance. The older ones are built of stone and have no windows; newer ones are usually built of adobe and may have windows. These are *moradas*, meeting places of the Hermanos de Luz (Brothers of Light) commonly called Penitentes.

The Penitentes of the Southwest descended from the Flagellantes that swept southern Europe during the Middle Ages, first appearing in Italy in 1210. In a document in the cathedral of Saint Francis in Santa Fe, dated September 17, 1794, reference is made to the founding of the "Venerable Third Order of Penitente," founded in Santa Fe and Santa Cruz. The Penitentes have long been a powerful political force in northern New Mexico.

The principal services took place during Lent. Each night during Lent the brothers met in a *morada* for prayer and instruction. The Penitentes were divided into two groups: Brothers of Light, the organizers and readers, and Brothers of Blood, men in their first years of membership who performed penances.

On Friday nights a procession of self-whippers marched from the *morada* to the Calvario cross at the end of a path, usually on a nearby hill symbolizing Mount Calvary. The door of the *morada* opened and the Piper came out, playing a doleful tune on a wailing reed pipe. The Piper was followed by a line of Brothers of Blood, naked to the waist. Each carried a whip made of Spanish bayonet fibers with a knot of cholla cactus spines at the end. Moving slowly, a step at a time, the flagellants swung the whips upon themselves, over first one shoulder and then the other.

On Ash Wednesday a "Christ" was selected by drawing lots in preparation for a reenactment of the passion of Christ on Good Friday. On Good Friday the individual selected for the role of Christ carried a heavy cross. Others carried smaller crosses in a literal interpretation of Christ's words: "Whosoever will come after me, let him deny himself, and take up his cross, and follow me." As the procession moved toward Calvario, those doing penance brought up the rear, still enduring the agony of self-torture. A simulation of Christ's meeting with his mother on the way to Calvary took place.

When the permanent cross at Calvario was reached a circle of fourteen crosses was formed, and the Penitentes stopped for prayer at each of these traditional stations of the cross. The Christ was then fastened to the cross which was raised with its human burden. At a signal from the Chief Brother, the Christ was taken down and carried back to the *morada*. If he had not survived the ordeal, his body was secretly buried, and his boots or shoes were placed on the doorstep of his home, the only word his relatives received of his fate.

When Archbishop Lamy arrived on the scene, he viewed the Penitente practices with horror and, in 1899, the Church placed a ban on the Penitente societies. This effectively drove the practices underground. Official condemnation remained until 1947 when the archbishop publicly accepted the practice under the provision that the penances did not do bodily harm. Thus, in present-day ceremonies the Penitente taking the part of Christ in the reenactment would be tied to the cross.

The Penitente "death cart" in the church at Las Trampas. Doña Sebastiana is poised to shoot arrows at unrepenitent sinners. This photograph was taken about 1935. The cart has since disappeared.
—Photo by T. Harmon Parkhurst, courtesy Museum of New Mexico, neg. no. 11529

The rules of the order, as published in 1221, are stringent. A Penitente must be a member of the Roman Catholic Church, of good repute and live a blameless life. Newly initiated members must restore all ill-gotten goods, must renounce all evil practices, and must abandon feuds and enmities with their neighbors.

A gracious and very patient priest who was being quizzed on the subject of the Penitente brotherhood was asked the inevitable question:

"But this is the twentieth century! Surely people don't do that sort of thing now in a civilized world, do they?"

A twinkle lighted the priest's eye. "I would not know. When the archbishop lifted the ban he also forbade the curious to spy on Penitente services." Then his expression became serious. "I will say that I don't believe it would be advisable to greet a member of my congregation on Easter Sunday morning by slapping him on the back."

Truchas

A document in the Spanish archives, dated 1752, refers to Truchas (trout) as Nuestra Señora de Rosario de las Truchas, a name as long as the main street of the village. In the 1770s it was listed as having twenty-six families, 122 persons. In 1772 the people requested twelve muskets and powder to provide protection from the Comanches. The request was denied. The people were told to build their houses around a central plaza rather than living in scattered ranchos.

Chimayó

The community was founded on the site of an old Tewa pueblo called tsimayo, meaning "good flaking stone"—i.e., obsidian. The Tewas were expert weavers, and it has been assumed that the early Spaniards learned the craft from the Indians.

From 1598 until 1695 Chimayó was the eastern boundary of the province of New Mexico, a place of banishment for offenders, in those days a punishment worse than prison. After the Reconquest in 1692 it was called San Buenaventura de Chimayó (Chimayó of the Good Venture).

For more than two centuries Chimayó has been known for its weaving. During the early days, most Spanish residents could weave, if only to make their own clothing. However, by the beginning of the nineteenth century the craft had deteriorated. In 1805 residents of Santa Fe sent to Spain for weavers to teach the art. Two master weavers came, Don Ignacio and Don Juan Bazán, under a six-year contract to teach the youth. But the two brothers found conditions in Santa Fe not to their liking, they moved to Chimayó and the community became the capital of the weaving industry in New Mexico, a status it still maintains.

The Santuario de Nuestro Señor de Esquipulas is Chimayó's other claim to fame. The sanctuary was built between 1813 and 1816 by Don Bernardo Abeyta in what was then a separate community called El Potrero. A legend claims that when Don Bernardo was deathly ill a vision led him to the spot now occupied by the sanctuary. He was immediately cured.

The sanctuary is now cherished for the healing power of the earth in the floor of a room to the left of the altar. The anteroom is lined with crutches and braces. Letters of thanksgiving attest to the curative power of the holy mud. People make pilgrimages from miles away to take part in the Easter pilgrimage to the shrine.

Legend has it that during early days priests who visited the sanctuary would carry back some of the holy earth with which to allay violent storms. A small portion thrown into a fire would subdue the most violent tempest.

The chapel remained in the Abeytas family until 1929.

The Santuario de Nuestro Señor Esquipulas at Chimayó has a reputation as a healing place. —Courtesy New Mexico Economic Development & Tourism, No. 737

Cundiyó

This hill-top village seems to have survived intact from an earlier century. The name is derived from a Tewa word, kudijo, meaning "round hill of the little bells." It perches above the Rio Frijoles looking down upon the fields in the valley below. Just above the town are the ruins of an old adobe pueblo, probably ancient Nambé. The post office dates from 1922; however, the land grant surrounding Cundiyó was awarded in 1743 by Governor Gaspar Domingo de Mendoza to Joseph Isidro de Medina, Manuel de Quintana, Marcial Martínez, and Miguel Martínez.

Nambé Pueblo

One of the first missions in New Mexico after the settlement of San Gabriel was founded by Friar Cristóbal de Salazar at the Tewa pueblo of Nambé. The old church was destroyed during the Pueblo Revolt of 1680, and in 1729 Governor Juan Domingo de Bustamente had a church erected at his own expense. This church fell victim to a modernization program. Early in the twentieth century, the old flat roof was removed and a new one erected. This weakened the walls and the church collapsed during a storm in 1909. The old kiva in the center of the plaza is still in use.

The name of the pueblo derives from Tewa, *nambay-onghwee* (people of the roundish earth). It applied to an earlier pueblo, the ruins of which are some distance northeast on a mound.

With the encroachment of trailer houses and HUD housing, few of the early buildings have survived. Intermarriage with Hispanics has reduced tribal purity and, consequently, traditional beliefs and ceremonies. Work in nearby Española and Los Alamos has largely replaced agricultural pursuits. Nambé artists are known for their pottery made of brown micaceous clay studded with mica specks. They are also known for handwoven leggings and ceremonial belts.

Pojoaque Pueblo

This pueblo has almost lost its identity as a pueblo. The ancient Tewa pueblo was abandoned after the Pueblo Revolt and partially resettled in 1706 with only five families. A new mission named Nuestra Señora de Guadalupe de Pojoaque was founded. However, in 1760 it was reduced to a *visita* of Nambé. On an inspection tour of missions in 1776, Fray Francisco Atanasio Domínguez noted that a priest from Nambé sometimes came to say Mass, "and when they go to Nambé to hear it, they take small loads of firewood."

Today the village is without a definable center. As is the case at Nambé, most of the inhabitants work at nearby industrial facilities.

VII. The Cattle Country

Development of the cattle industry in New Mexico came by way of an invasion from Texas. After the Civil War, millions of longhorns were roaming South Texas. War had depleted the supply of cattle in the North. A succession of drives began to railheads in Kansas, but Charles Goodnight had a different idea.

He believed a better market existed to the west: forts, mining camps, and railroad towns in northern New Mexico, Colorado, and other areas. In June, 1866, Charles Goodnight and Oliver Loving left Fort Worth with a trail herd.

They drove the herd west to the Pecos River. Following the Pecos, they entered New Mexico near Pope's Well and went north to Fort Sumner, where they sold a goodly share of their herd for $12,000 in gold. The government purchased the cattle to feed Indians on the Bosque Redondo reservation. While Goodnight hurried back to Texas for more cattle, Loving drove the remainder of the herd to Colorado.

New Mexico became a trade route for cattle: John Chisum, John C. Dawson, John Slaughter, and others joined the parade. As Texas cattlemen discovered the lush grama grass pastures of New Mexico, they moved in with their herds. Chisum established headquarters near the Bosque Grande to control a range which extended 150 miles along the Pecos from the Texas border to Fort Sumner. At the height of his career he had 80,000 head on the range. He became involved in the Lincoln County War, a conflict pitting large ranchers against small cattlemen and merchants.

By judicious control of water holes, backed by well-armed riders to protect "grazing rights" on state and federal lands, cattle barons controlled vast domains, dealing frontier justice to rustlers and interlopers alike. By the turn of the century, large operators were

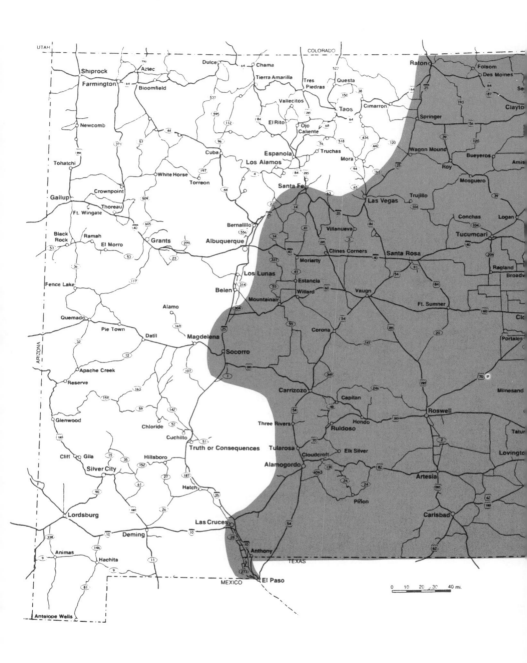

The Cattle Country

selling out, drift fences were removed, and barbed wire took the place of six-shooters for the protection of small ranches.

Cowboy-author Max Evans grew up in northeastern New Mexico where traditions of early-day ranching continue into the twentieth century. Evans dubbed his land the "Hi Lo Country," a name that caught on. He captured life on the range and in the cowtowns during the 1930s, '40s, and '50s in a series of novels: *The Rounders, The Hi Lo Country,* and *The Great Wedding,* to name a few. He described the country and its impact upon the people who live there:

> In the Hi Lo country the wind blows hot or freezing about three hundred days a year. Fighting just that alone would cause a man to have a tendency to turn loose when he had a chance, not to mention the bucking horses, the kicking calves, the poor wages, the fence building and windmill repairing, the hay hauling in blizzards, and the chopping of ice with an axe from a tank so the stock could water. Then there are droughts that shrivel everything on earth: the grass, the wild animals, the cattle, the horses, the insects, the birds, bank accounts, and of course, the men and women responsible for the survival of all.
>
> The Hi Lo country is not just made up of cowboys. There are merchants, mechanics, railroaders, miners, bartenders, poets, inventors, whores, semi-whores, and elegant, dedicated, long-suffering women, every kind that's anywhere else on the globe. I think here, though, the land and the elements are finally in control. It is a country of extremes. You adapt or die, in body or spirit. Because of this, the inhabitants laugh and play to extremes; they speak with descriptive comparisons in extremes; and as some old cowboy once said, "What the hell, you just live till you die anyway, and the rest of the time you spend shoveling manure so you can get the cows in the barn."

The cattlemen were followed by farmers. With the coming of the railroads between 1879 and 1882, trains from Iowa, Kansas, Missouri, and Arkansas brought homesteaders—nesters, the ranchers called them. The ranchers tried to convince them that a 160-acre homestead of semiarid land was not big enough to support a family.

The homesteaders kept coming, bringing with them the tools and techniques of farming in the Midwest. They had learned nothing from the drought of the 1890s which had driven them from land in western Kansas and the Texas Panhandle. Hope made them believe promoters who made vague promises of irrigation.

Settlers were attracted to New Mexico by brochures containing fanciful illustrations of lush farming communities. —Ritch, 1885

Settlers huddled about abandoned railroad construction camps and at the intersections of their homesteads. The abundant supply of hope built schools, stocked stores, and even printed newspapers. Then Mother Nature repeated the inevitable cycle. Drought set in, beginning in 1909 and lasting until 1912. A few learned to raise dryland crops such as sorghum grains, millet, kafir corn, and wheat. The rest gave up. Some went to mining towns in Colfax County, only to delay their fates until oil superseded the use of coal; some returned to the East, from whence they had come.

The history of Roosevelt County is typical. In 1900 it tallied some 350 residents. By 1904 there were more than 3,000; in 1910 the count was in excess of 12,000. Shanties and dugouts speckled the land. However, by 1912 a homestead which sold for as much as $1,000 in 1906 could be bought for $200, but there were few takers.

Farming land returned to grazing cattle, awaiting irrigation water to be provided by the construction of dams and reservoirs and improved pumping methods. These things would not come until after World War II, and they were not a force in driving cattle from the ranges until politicians began enticing rural voters with crop subsidy programs.

Capulin—Clayton

Capulin

This minuscule community on the Santa Fe Railroad was initially named Dedman in 1909 to honor E. J. Dedman, a railroad superintendent. When Mr. Dedman died in 1914, the town was renamed Capulin because of its proximity to nearby Capulin Mountain.

--- Historical Excursion

NM 325
Capulin Mountain National Monument—Folsom

Capulin Mountain National Monument

The mountain has been a national monument since 1916. It was an active volcano about 10,000 years ago, only a matter of seconds on the geological time clock. Volcanologists consider any volcano less than 25,000 years old as geologically recent and potentially active. Nevertheless, visitors can go down to the bottom of the crater and look into the vent.

In this area of volcanic activity, lava erupted in three flows, separated by long periods of inactivity. The last of this series created Capulin Mountain, which rises more than 1,000 feet from its base.

Capulin Mountain is considred a "potentially active" volcano.
—Courtesy New Mexico Economic Development & Tourism, No. 826

Folsom

NM 325 continues through lava-speckled cattle country to Folsom, named for Frances Folsom, the wife of President Grover Cleveland. Folsom was preceded by a town named Madison, located eight miles to the northeast, a rough-and-ready village which was settled in 1865. The coming of the Colorado & Southern Railroad in 1887-88 marked the beginning of Folsom and the end of Madison.

Initially, the railroad construction camp was called Ragtown because the saloons, restaurants, and dwellings were all housed in tents. From that beginning, Folsom became a bustling town with the largest stockyards north of Fort Worth. By 1895 it had two mercantile stores and three saloons. The latter provided a plentitude of gunplay.

The Gem Saloon was owned by W. A. Thompson who had arrived in Folsom from Missouri with a price on his head, charged with the murder of a man in his home town. In spite of dubious qualifications for the job, he was appointed deputy sheriff. On one occasion he shot a man because he "had the nerve" to become intoxicated in a rival saloon.

The decline of Folsom as a shipping center began in 1908 with a disastrous flood which swept away most of its buildings and drowned seventeen people. Many more would have died had it not been for Sarah J. Rooke.

Sarah was a telephone operator. One August night in 1908 her switchboard buzzed: "The river has broken loose! Run for your life!" Sarah did not run. She called people, one by one, to warn them. She stayed at her switchboard until the flood swept her cottage away. Her body was found in the wreckage of her house eight miles below town. Four thousand contributors paid for the granite monument which marks her grave in the Folsom cemetery.

The old Folsom Hotel, built in 1888, is still standing in Folsom, a reminder of boom times.

In 1926 an event occurred which trumpeted the name of Folsom around the scientific world. Back in 1893, George McJunkin, a black cowboy on Lige Johnson's Crowfoot Ranch, had found some curious chipped stone darts among some very, very large bones in Dead Horse Gulch. Few people paid attention to George's story. But McJunkin was no ordinary cowboy. Although self-educated, he was well-educated. He not only persisted in telling his story, he displayed samples of his find. Finally in 1926 archaeologists from the Denver Museum of Natural History arrived in Folsom to begin the Folsom dig.

The result was proof that a hunting culture had thrived in the area from 10,000 to 11,000 years earlier. Nineteen projectile points, now known as "Folsom points," were found in association with the bones of twenty-three bison. Not only had man lived in the area at that time, he chipped distinctive spear points out of stone and used them to hunt beasts which are now extinct. That man became known as the Folsom Man.

The excursion to Capulin Mountain and Folsom is completed by continuing on NM 325 to rejoin US 64-87 at Des Moines.

Des Moines

Named for Des Moines, Iowa, this community began life as a railroad shipping point with the construction of the Colorado & Southern in 1888. For a time it was on two railroads.

In 1920 it reached its peak with a population of 800. With drought and the economic depression of 1929 it shrank to half that size. The crowning blow came in 1940 when the Santa Fe, Raton and Eastern Railway was abandoned and the tracks removed. Des Moines is still an important shipping point on the Colorado & Southern.

Unbeknownst to its residents, Des Moines gained anonymous fame as the setting for a novel by cowboy-author Max Evans. It was the town of Hi Lo in *The Rounders* published in 1960, a comic Western novel about modern working cowboys. In 1965 the novel was made into a movie starring Henry Fonda and Glenn Ford. It also had a short run as a TV series.

Grenville

This community developed as a station on the Colorado & Southern Railroad, serving ranchers and farmers. It got a post office in 1888. The town experienced a boom in 1919 when the Snorty Gobbler oil well was brought in five miles to the north. Its growth stopped in 1925 when the oil company failed.

——Historical Sidebar——————————————

Rabbit Ear Mountains

A roadside historical marker on US 64-87 pointing out Rabbit Ear Mountains is likely to be misconstrued by strangers who look for something more closely resembling the ears of a rabbit. The twin mounds were named after a Comanche chief called Rabbit Ears, *Las*

Orejas de Conejo, because his ears had been frozen. Rabbit Ears was killed in battle in 1717 and buried on the mountain which bears his name.

Rabbit Ear Mountains was a major landmark on the Santa Fe Trail. It signaled the Cimarron Cutoff with good water, wood, and grass. Caravans would often lay over a day while they sent runners ahead to Las Vegas to negotiate with Mexican customs officials. The Indians also used Rabbit Ear Mountains. From it they could watch the approach of a caravan on the trail. When the wagons reached a water hole the Indians would swoop down for a raid.

Clayton

When William Becknell established the Cimarron Cutoff for the Santa Fe Trail in 1822 his route came across the present townsite of Clayton which was at that time a large prairie lake. It was a welcome watering hole after the long dry spells during the trip from Dodge City. In 1828 a new route was opened north of Rabbit Ear Mountains.

However, the site of the present town continued to be a favorite campground for drovers and herdsmen on the northbound cattle trails. The first store was a tent from which supplies were sold to cattlemen. Gen. Granville M. Dodge, construction manager for the Denver & Fort Worth Railroad (now Colorado & Southern), was persuaded to build a line through the projected town. The first train came in 1888, and Clayton began to grow. By 1900, the population was 750. There had been a setback, however.

In October and November of 1889 a killer blizzard dealt the area a blow from which it took a year to recover. A 25-inch snow piled drifts seven feet deep. Thousands of cattle, horses, and sheep died. Train service from the north was held up for thirteen days; two passenger trains were snowbound at the Texas border for several days. When the snow melted, the bodies of several cowhands and shepherds were found. Cattle shipments from Clayton were practically discontinued for the winter—a severe blow for a railroad town in those days.

In 1901 Clayton was the scene of a macabre hanging. Thomas E. "Black Jack" Ketchum had been specializing in train robberies. On the night of August 16, 1899, Tom Ketchum was alone. His brother had been killed and his gang had broken up. On that night he attempted what he later said he thought would be the crowning

Black Jack Ketchum wore a white shirt, a white bow tie, and a black suit to his hanging. His shoes were carefully polished. —Courtesy El Paso Public Library

achievement of his career: stopping a moving train, capturing the crew, and robbing the train—single-handedly—would have given him bragging rights to be admired in his field.

But he came a cropper. Ketchum boarded the tender of an engine at Folsom and captured the front-end crew. He ordered the rear express car cut loose from the train, but since the train was stopped on a curve, they could not pull the coupling pin. During the delay, the conductor shot Black Jack Ketchum in the arm with a shotgun.

He escaped but was captured the following day. While awaiting trial, his right arm was amputated. There was not enough evidence to prove a murder case against Ketchum, but train robbery carried a death penalty under the old Territorial laws of New Mexico. He was tried in Clayton and sentenced to be hanged.

The execution took place the afternoon of April 26, 1901. According to witnesses, Ketchum obligingly moved his head from side to side to assist in proper adjustment as the noose was placed about his neck.

"Are you ready?" asked the sheriff.

"Ready, let her go!" said Black Jack.

Another version has it that Ketchum told the nervous hangman: "Hurry up; I'm due in hell for dinner."

The difficulty was that the noose was not properly adjusted and Ketchum was a heavy man. As the trap sprung he was decapitated and his head rolled toward horrified spectators.

Black Jack Ketchum was buried in an unmarked grave. After being moved from one site to another, the outlaw's remains still repose in an unmarked grave in a median between two roads.

US 56
Abbott—Gladstone

This lonely road gives the traveler an excellent feeling for the land as it was seen by travelers on the Santa Fe Trail. East of Springer the highway crosses the Cimarron Cutoff of the Santa Fe Trail. The Point of Rocks was a landmark on the trail. A spring made it a favorite stop, but the pioneers camped some distance from the spring to avoid attack by Apaches who frequented watering places. This necessitated a three-mile drive to fill water barrels. Graves and tepee rings were visible in the area for many years.

Abbott

The post office was established in 1881 and the town was named for Horace C. Abbott. Horace and his brother Jerome owned a large sheep ranch in the area. The village hung on for many years but did not prosper. The post office closed in 1963 and little of the community remains today.

Farley

This farming and ranching community on NM 193, three miles north of US 56, took its lifeblood from a branch of the Santa Fe Railroad which ran from Mt. Dora. The post office opened in 1929 and lasted only three years.

Gladstone

Founded in 1880 by William Harris, the town was said to have been named for the British statesman W. E. Gladstone, whom Harris knew. The original inhabitants were from Texas, Oklahoma, and Kansas.

Kiowa National Grasslands
—Mosquero

Travelers with a yen for exposure to the New Mexico's cattle country should take NM 39 from Abbott to Logan between US 56 and US 54, or vice versa.

Kiowa National Grasslands

Between Abbott and Roy, the highway crosses the western section of the Kiowa National Grasslands. This 136,000-acre preserve, under the administration of the U.S. Forest Service, perpetuates in an untrampled state a remnant of the vast "sea of grass" which covered the plains of New Mexico and much of the West prior to the coming of cattlemen and farmers. Ten thousand years ago it was disturbed only by the now-extinct straight-horned bison and an occasional prehistoric hunter armed with nothing but a spear.

Mills

The name of the town honors Melvin W. Mills, an early-day lawyer and rancher who was an entrepreneur par excellence. One of his projects was the development of a 10-mile-long orchard in the Canadian River canyon twenty-five miles southeast of Springer (west of NM 39). He blasted underground irrigation channels in the sandstone of the canyon; built cisterns, bunkhouses, a cider press, and a stone mansion. He planted 14,000 trees: peaches, apples, pears, cherries, plums, apricots, walnuts, almonds, and chestnuts. Additionally, he grew an assortment of vegetables. He hauled produce to Springer for shipment to Harvey Houses along the Santa Fe Railroad. In 1904, a flood ended it all by destroying Mills' orchard.

He was involved in many other enterprises, but he died a broken man. At the time of his death in 1925, he was living in a three-story, thirty-two-room mansion he had built in Springer. However, the mansion had been foreclosed upon by his former law partner, Thomas B. Catron; and Mills had to beg to be allowed to die on a cot in his old home.

Roy

Established in 1901 by Frank and William Roy, the original town was two miles west of its present site. The location changed in 1906 when the Southern Pacific Railroad built a line from Tucumcari to the Dawson coal fields west of Raton. Roy lies over the Bravo Dome carbon dioxide field and prospered from the production of dry ice during the 1920s and 1930s. At that time dry ice was not only used for refrigeration and by doctors but it was in demand by movie directors to create fog. More recently it has been used in oil fields for the tertiary recovery of oil pools not accessible by other methods.

Mosquero

In Spanish *mosquero* means "flytrap" or "flypaper," but the meaning in New Mexico is "swarm of flies." However the name came about, Mosquero originated as a Southern Pacific Railroad farming and ranching community with its post office opening in 1908. It also had dry-ice plants. In 1987 the Mosquero Municipal School District had only sixty students, the smallest enrollment of any district in the state.

US 54
Nara Visa—Logan

Nara Visa

Travelers entering the state on US 54 find the Llano Estacado slashed by ravines, arroyos, and red sandstone cliffs—country better suited for grazing than for agriculture. A sheepherder named Narvaez who lived here during the late 1880s left his name upon the land. When the Rock Island Railroad arrived in 1902, the Anglo railroad officials pronounced his name "Narvis" and the town was officially designated Nara Visa.

Logan

This ranching community at the intersection of US 54 and NM 39 was established at a trading point and station on the Rock Island Railroad. It was named for Capt. H. Logan, a Texas Ranger who filed a claim in the area. Today the community serves as a gateway to Ute Dam and Ute Lake State Park where fishing, sailing, and water-skiing is available.

Trujillo

The name of this farming and ranching community represents the family name of Diego de Trujillo who arrived in New Mexico in 1632, but there is no information as to whether there was a family connection with the town. This settlement dates from about 1836.

Mesa Rica

This trading post at the intersection of NM 129 no longer rates a mention on the state's official highway map. It took its name, meaning "rich tableland," from an old story that Indians attacked a burro train of gold. During the fight, some white men slipped away with the gold and hid it on the mesa. No one has yet reported finding the treasure.

Conchas

Conchas is a small community made up of government workers and concessionaires who serve the needs of visitors to the Conchas Lake State Park recreation area which is located to the north on NM 433.

——Historical Sidebar——

Bell Ranch

The headquarters of the historic Bell Ranch is about ten miles north of Conchas. In 1870, the ranch was designated as both a national and a state historic site.

During the two decades following the Civil War, the cattle industry was swelling out of southern Texas and spreading across the West. Eastern New Mexico was among the first regions to be taken over by the Texans. The Bell Ranch resulted from this expansion.

In a way, the Bell Ranch had its beginning in 1824 with Pablo Montoya, an alcalde from Santa Fe who wanted room for his family. He applied to the Mexican government and received a grant of 655,468 acres of grassland watered by the Canadian River. Pablo

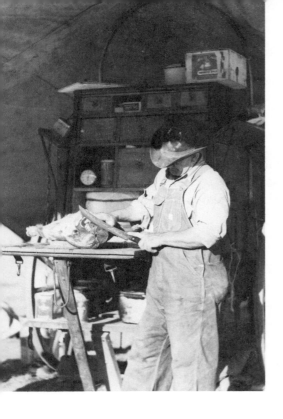

The Bell Ranch cook and chuck wagon on roundup. —Courtesy New Mexico Economic Development & Tourism, No.

died, but his sons retained rights to the land which by 1865 had fallen into the hands of John Watts, a Santa Fe attorney.

J. Wilson Waddington, a wheeler-dealer cattleman, acquired the land and began to buy up smaller ranches in the vicinity. The spread grew to three-quarters of a million acres, including several villages, but depression and drought drove the Waddington interests into receivership. The ranch was taken over by the Red River Valley Company and operated until 1947 when it was divided into six ranches and sold.

To go to work for the Bell Ranch all a cowboy needed was a bedroll and a saddle. The company furnished a mount of twelve horses, room, and board. The ranch was operated from ten line camps in addition to the headquarters. Line camps were two-room adobe or rock shacks where cowhands did their own cooking. The line camps were preferable to headquarters. Old-timers told about their work at a reunion:

Generally you went to a line camp with a pardner, looked after the cattle and checked the fences. If you wanted to go to town for two or three days, you could. Your pardner would stay in camp and keep an eye on things, then you stayed while he went to town. We went out in the spring as soon as the weather broke and we worked cattle until it started snowin' again next fall.

The first work in the spring was horse work. Then we'd gather steers for branding and after that, we'd gather the stuff to be shipped in the fall. I don't know how many cows there were on the ranch, but I know that ever' year I was there we branded between 15,000 and 20,000.

Pay for a hand averaged $25 a month. The wagon boss got $75, and the range boss was paid $125. Some men would let their pay accumulate until they had as much as a $1,000 on the books.

The ranch operated under several different names until 1889 when it took its name and the shape of its brand from a distinctive bell-shaped butte on the property.

Los Montoyas—Anton Chico

Los Montoyas

The Montoyas began arriving in New Mexico in 1600. In 1824 Salvador Montoya was awarded a land grant in this area. Pablo Montoya's 655,468-acre land grant in the valley of the Canadian River ultimately became the nucleus of the Bell Ranch. At this point, the highway roughly follows the old stage and mail route which operated between Las Vegas and Mesilla from 1860 until 1880.

Anton Chico

This historic old town is off US 84 on NM 386. The community was settled in 1822 by Don Salvador Tapia and sixteen other colonists, built around two fortress-like plazas for protection against Indians. George Kendall passed through Anton Chico with the ill-fated Texan-Santa Fe Expedition in 1841. He described the community:

A ride of another half hour brought us in sight of Anton Chico, a village seated upon a little hill overlooking the Pecos, and probably containing some two or three hundred inhabitants. . . .

The little village of Anton Chico is built on a square, the houses fronting on the inner side, although there are entrances, protected by strong doors, on the outer. The houses are of one story only, built of *adobes*, a species of large, sun-dried bricks, while the tops are flat. They have neither windows nor floors, and in point of comfort and convenience are only one degree removed from the rudest wigwam of the Indian. In case of attack from the savages, continually hovering and committing depredations upon the frontiers of New Mexico, these little hamlets serve as forts, the Indians rarely pursuing the inhabitants farther than their outer walls, as they carry on their warfare entirely on horseback.

We entered the largest house in the place. . . .We called for something to eat, suggesting a somewhat varied "bill of fare" to be spread before us, for which we manifested our readiness to pay the highest prices: our dinner consisted—substantials and extras all enumerated—of tortillas, boiled eggs, and miel, the latter somewhat resembling molasses and water, the water predominating.

Lamy—Galisteo

Lamy

From Santa Fe, Lamy is reached by taking northbound I-25 to US 285. The exit to Lamy, just east of US 285, is seven miles from the freeway. A bus ride to Lamy has been Santa Fe's only railroad link with the rest of the world since 1926. In 1878 the main line of the Santa Fe Railroad bypassed Santa Fe, leaving the Ancient City connected by a spur line to Lamy. On October 1, 1926, service over the spur line was discontinued. Passengers, mail, and baggage had to be transported by busses, "Harveycars." The town grew with the railroad and was named to honor Jean Baptiste Lamy, the first archbishop of the American Territorial period.

Bishop Lamy came to the Santa Fe diocese in 1853 and labored prodigiously among Anglos, Mexicans, and Indians to reform a religious establishment which had been allowed to grow stagnant and corrupt. He removed several priests from their posts and unfrocked them; some were members of New Mexico's leading families. Vengeful politicians attempted to oust him, but he continued on. Willa Cather immortalized Bishop Lamy in her novel *Death Comes for the Archbishop*.

Galisteo

Each Spanish explorer who came by gave the prehistoric Tano Indian pueblo at Galisteo a new name. Coronado called it Ximena. Castaño de Sosa dubbed it San Lucas. After the Pueblo Revolt Governor Valdés changed it to Santa María. When Fray Francisco Atanasio Domínguez came by on an inspection tour in 1776 it was called Nuestra Señora de los Remedios de Galisteo. There were only 41 families, 152 people. By 1782 smallpox and Comanche raids had taken a terrible toll. The remnants of the pueblo moved to Santo Domingo. Later, the old Tanos had a different explanation. They said their sacred snake left the village and disappeared into the Rio Grande. The people no longer had the food and clothing which the snake provided and so had to move.

During the period of Mexican rule Hispanic settlers recolonized the village and pastured sheep among the old pueblos. The community slumbered through the years as a stock-raising village until it was more recently discovered as a fashionable hideaway for well-heeled Anglo-Americans.

NM 14
Los Cerrillos—Golden

This scenic stretch of highway through ghost towns left from New Mexico's mining days has been promoted as the "Turquoise Trail" through a cooperative effort on the part of communities and busi-

Panning gold in the mountains near Cerrillos. —Gregg, 1844

ness establishments along the way. Restaurants, crafts shops, galleries, and antique shops have blossomed.

Los Cerrillos

More commonly known simply as Cerrillos, this former coal-mining community was built by the Santa Fe Railroad in 1879. Mines in the area yielded gold, silver, lead, zinc, and turquoise. Historical evidence indicates that the Spaniards enslaved Indians to mine turquoise with crude hand tools prior to 1680. At its peak during the 1880s the town supported twenty-one saloons and four hotels.

Madrid

Coal was mined by squatters in the area as early as 1835. Gen. Stephen W. Kearny sent to the area for fuel when he built Fort Marcy during the occupation of Santa Fe in 1846. Settlement dates from 1869. At its peak, Madrid produced 250,000 tons of coal a year, and its population exceeded that of Albuquerque.

For many years the Christmas lights of Madrid gained recognition as one of the nation's outstanding folk celebrations. There was a Christmas tree in front of every one of Madrid's 250 homes; numerous religious dioramas were displayed. Thousands of visitors came to thread their way through the barren gulch to see the exhibition. At one time, during the Christmas season, Transcontinental Airlines (later TWA) rerouted flights over Madrid so passengers could see the lights.

Company houses lined the streets of Madrid during its boom days as a mining town. —Courtesy New Mexico Economic Development & Tourism, No. 670

Today, crafts shops, galleries, and snack shops beckon. The Old Coal Mine Museum gives visitors a glimpse of Madrid's historical past.

Golden

The present town was founded in 1879, so named because it was the center of a gold-mining district. The Spaniards were reputed to have mined the area, and placer gold was discovered in 1839 at a place called Tuerto to the north. A settlement called Real de San Francisco had previously occupied the site of the present community.

Mining activity played out in a fairly short time, although unsuccessful efforts were made to dredge the area. Local residents claim to find free gold in gulches after cloud bursts.

NM 536
Placitas

This farming community on NM 536, established in 1901, was built on the site of an ancient Indian pueblo. During the 1960s the community was occupied by several counterculture communes. In the 1980s it began to attract residents of Albuquerque who want to escape city life.

The Sandia Man Cave is along the winding road to Placitas. It was discovered in 1936 by a graduate student in anthropology at the University of New Mexico who began to explore the shallow caves just off the road. He gathered a cigar-box full of artifacts and took them back to the university. Subsequent investigation turned up the jawbone of a long-extinct giant sloth and projectile points contemporary with those used by the Clovis Man.

NM 209
Tucumcari—Clovis

Around the turn of the century, the extension of railroads brought an influx of homesteaders, hopeful farmers and ranchers who paid a filing fee of ten cents per acre, $16 on a 160-acre homestead. The result was a dramatic increase in population. On January 28, 1903, the Territorial Legislature established Quay County to provide local government.

NM 209 zigzags through country that was speckled with burgeoning towns during the first decade of the twentieth century. Most of the first settlers lived in dugouts until men with an entrepreneurial bent surveyed townsites and organized schools. The tiny communities dotting the roads through this area are vestigial remains of a time when hope prevailed. Old maps include the names of towns that were casualties to drought and hard times, names such as Plain, Stockton, Kirk, and Frio. NM 209 provides a generous sample of the countryside. Quay, Ragland, Grady, and Broadview are typical of communities remaining in the area.

US 60-70-84
Texico—Scholle

Texico

On the eastern border of New Mexico, the first town's name is a blend of "Texas" and "New Mexico." The Pecos Valley and Northeastern Railroad built a siding here in 1902, and Texico experienced a brief boom until the railroad moved its division point nine miles west to Clovis. The first settler, Ira W. Taylor, was a section foreman on the railroad. He homesteaded a 160-acre plot adjoining the railroad depot.

During its early days, Texico was a typical wild-Western town. One historian noted that killings in Texico outnumbered the notoriously high slaughter rates quoted for Dodge City and Tombstone.

Clovis

In 1907 Clovis was called Riley's Switch. It consisted of a few shacks along the siding of the railroad that was reaching across New Mexico. Officials of the Santa Fe Railroad had intended to establish a division point at Portales, but some of the citizens became greedy. It was decided to move the eastern terminal of the Belen cutoff to Riley's Switch, and the railroad started looking for a more appropriate name. The daughter of an official had been reading French history. She became enchanted with Clovis, King of the Franks, who converted to Christianity in 496. And thus the town was named.

Clovis became an agricultural center in the midst of fields of grain, alfalfa, and sugar beets. Cattle feed lots have been established in the area, and weekly cattle auctions provide entertainment, even if one doesn't want to buy cattle.

Cannon Air Force Base, at first called Clovis Air Force Base, was established near Clovis in 1942, helping the population of Clovis to double within the next fifteen years.

St. Vrain

Although Ceran St. Vrain, the trapper and early settler who came from St. Louis to Taos in 1830, had little to do with this rural siding on the Santa Fe Railroad, it perpetuates his name. Most of the early settlers who attempted farming lived in dugouts. The community even had a dugout school.

Dry farming discouraged settlers. However, with irrigation and the railroad for shipment, peanuts, sugar beets, sweet potatoes, and such became viable crops. A proposed local newspaper never got off the press. The *St. Vrain Times* was published as part of the Clovis paper. On July 11, 1912, the St. Vrain correspondent reported: "The good old glorious Fourth was celebrated in our burg by a merry bunch of people. Wagon loads from north, south, east, west came."

Melrose

The settlement began in 1882 as Brownhorn, so named because it was located between Walter "Wildhorse" Brown's ranch and the Pigpen Ranch, owned by a Mr. Horn. In 1906 the Santa Fe Railroad established repair shops and laid out a townsite. Today the Melrose Bombing Range to the south is used by F-111 fighter-bombers and the 27th Tactical Fighter Wing from Cannon Air Force Base. In 1981 the Air Force invoked lively protest by proposing to take over 52,000 additional acres of grazing and crop land.

Tolar

As the railroad was being constructed after the turn of the century, Tolar provided much of the sand and gravel used in construction. The community began as a tent city with some of the earliest tents serving as saloons. Gay ladies pitched tents on the fringe of the settlement, an area known as Casanova Alley.

In November, 1944, a passing munitions train exploded, flattening the town and showering the area with shrapnel. Miraculously, only one man was killed.

At one time Tolar had three saloons. The Pink Pony lasted the longest. It boasted a snake pit for the entertainment of tourists.

Taiban

The name is an Indian word for "horsetail," selected for reasons obscured by the mist of time when the townsite was laid out in 1906.

Stinking Springs is located nearby. It was there that Sheriff Pat Garrett captured Billy the Kid on a bitterly cold day in December, 1880. Garrett cornered Billy the Kid and his men in an abandoned rock house which had been an overnight stop for cattle drivers and sheepherders. The members of Garrett's posse did not know the Kid by sight; he was to be identified by his hat. Garrett would give the signal to fire.

Charlie Bowdre came out of the house to feed his horse, wearing Billy the Kid's sombrero. Garrett raised his gun and Bowdre died in a hail of gunfire. After a day-long siege during which Garrett taunted the fugitives with the smell of cooking food, the outlaws were starved out and Billy the Kid was taken to the Las Vegas jail in handcuffs and leg irons which were attached en route by a blacksmith at Fort Sumner.

La Lande

This forlorn ghost town was founded March 10, 1906. On May 12, 1906, John C. Light, the first postmaster wrote:

> Two months ago not a house or tent marked the spot of our townsite. Now we have a thriving little town. Homes and tents of various descriptions dot the prairie. Trees have been planted on Main Street.

Southwestern Holiness College was constructed. A newspaper began publication and a bank opened. At one time La Lande was said to have the largest swimming pool in New Mexico; the town vied with Fort Sumner to be the county seat of De Baca County. But the homesteaders found the land too barren to support crops; they moved away.

Fort Sumner

Fort Sumner grew up as a tempestuous civilian settlement providing a nearby fort with meat and food staples and furnishing entertainment for the soldiers. After the army withdrew, the community continued as a cattle town on the Goodnight Trail over which cattle were driven northward to Cheyenne, Wyoming, for shipment to Chicago. With the coming of the railroad and irrigation water, it became an agricultural center.

Today the grave of Billy the Kid is the most popular tourist attraction in the area, and "Old Fort Days," a four-day festival in mid-June, is the high point of the year. The festival, named in memory of old Fort Sumner, is a time of fun and games featuring such events as a dog show, an old fiddlers' contest, and the Billy the Kid marathon. However, the museum at the nearby Fort Sumner State Monument recounts a grim story about the fort.

In 1862 Gen. James H. Carleton was bent on solving the Indian problem by a "death or captivity" policy. He sent Col. Kit Carson to destroy or capture the Navajos and the Mescalero Apaches. Then he built Fort Sumner in the Bosque Redondo where both the Navajos and the Apaches would be interned on a large reservation to learn farming.

Carson carried out his part of the mission. Some 8,000 Navajos were rounded up and marched three hundred miles to Bosque Redondo. The horror of "The Long Walk" is kept green in Navajo memory.

Carleton's "reformatory for Indians" was a fiasco from the beginning. The Navajos were not farmers. The unirrigated arid land was not suitable for farming. To make matters worse, the Apaches—traditional enemies of the Navajos—were interned closeby. Both tribes were victims of periodic raids by Kiowas and Comanches. During the night on November 3, 1865, every Apache who could travel disappeared from Bosque Redondo.

Carleton was ousted in 1866. In 1868 Gen. William T. Sherman listened to the Navajos' promise to forsake the warpath if they could return to their homeland. Since the Apaches were gone, there was no longer a need for Fort Sumner. It was abandoned in 1868.

Lucien B. Maxwell, proprietor of the vast Maxwell Land Grant, bought Fort Sumner at auction. He remodeled the officers' quarters into a twenty-room mansion and lived in it until his death in 1875 after which his son Peter continued to live there. Pat Garrett killed Billy the Kid in Pete Maxwell's bedroom in this house.

The outlaw was buried in the nearby cemetery next to his friends Tom O'Folliard and Charlie Bowdre. There is speculation that Billy the Kid's body may have been moved to the Santa Fe military cemetery years ago, but a tombstone marks a grave at Fort Sumner and it is regularly visited and photographed by tourists while historians continue to argue about the location of the outlaw's body.

In 1905 the Santa Fe Railroad built a line through the Pecos Valley six miles north of the old fort. Newcomers settled closer to the depot and named their part of town Sunnyside after the Sunnyside

This portrayal of the killing of Billy the Kid by Sheriff Pat Garrett is taken from Garrett's biography of the outlaw. —Garrett, 1882

Springs just north of the railroad. Sunnyside succeeded in getting a post office. Heated controversy over the name erupted between the newcomers and the old settlers. Pioneer ranchers who had gotten their mail at Fort Sumner for a quarter of a century voiced their wrath for five years. The long dispute ended on March 3, 1910, when the name Fort Sumner was given to the town.

Today, Fort Sumner depends heavily upon tourism, and local museums and displays make the most of Billy the Kid's activities.

Yeso

The community was established in 1906 when the railroad came through. As an end-of-track town, it harbored the usual run of hard-drinking, hard-fighting construction workers. The town took its name from Yeso ("gypsum") Creek. In 1909 on the application for a post office, the name was spelled "Yesso." It was changed three years later. As other communities wilted away, Yeso prevailed through drought and crop failures. At one time it vied to become county seat.

Vaughn

A wagon road between Las Vegas and El Paso passed through present-day Vaughn. With the coming of the Rock Island Railroad joining El Paso and Kansas City in 1902, a construction camp was established a few miles west of the present community. When the Santa Fe Railroad crossed the Rock Island line in 1907, Vaughn was founded, and Vaughn became a division point. It was named after Major C. W. Vaughn, a civil engineer. Today, motorists see little of Vaughn's residential area, which stretches along the railroad track. Most of the railroad repair shops are gone.

Willard

This community was established in 1902, and between 1900 and 1940 tremendous quantities of pinto beans were grown between Willard and Mountainair. The Santa Fe Central built a line to tap the Estancia Valley. The rails crossed the Belen cutoff at Willard. It became known as the "Bean Line."

About five miles south of Willard there was a chain of salt lakes which were used by the Spaniards as early as 1668. Burros laden with salt to be used in smelting silver ore were driven more than 700 miles to Chihuahua.

Historical Excursion

NM 41
Estancia

NM 41 leads northward out of Willard to Estancia, the county seat of Torrance County. The present town began with the coming of the railroad between 1901 and 1904, but sheepmen and cattlemen had been in the area for many years before. There was a dispute over the land.

Shortly before the Mexican War, Antonio Sandoval was granted 415,000 acres centered on the land which would become the town of Estancia. The powerful Otero family, of Los Lunas, had been granted a large portion of the same tract upon which they ran sheep. Sandoval's heirs sold their claim to a Boston millionaire and, in 1883, James Whitney and a group of men showed up to claim the land on behalf of the Bostonian.

While Don Manuel Otero was away, Whitney moved into the Otero ranch house at Estancia Springs. When Otero returned he asked Whitney by what authority he was there. Whitney picked up a pistol.

"By this authority," he said as he fired.

There is debate as to whether Otero or Whitney fired first. Otero was killed; Whitney had a portion of his jaw shot away. Before the shooting stopped, another man was killed and two more were wounded. The courts acquitted Whitney and decided neither party had claim to the land. Thus, the land in Estancia Valley was opened to homesteading and to the New Mexico Central Railroad.

Mountainair

This farming and ranching town was established in 1901 when the Santa Fe Railroad built the Belen cutoff through Abó Pass. Some of the settlers planted pinto beans, just as nearby Spanish-Mexican farmers and prehistoric Pueblo Indians had done. Soon, Mountainair was boasting of being the "Pinto Bean Capital of the World."

One of the early settlers was a free spirit named Clem "Pop" Shaffer. He gained a substantial list of titles: merchant, horse-trader, land speculator, philanthropist, patriot. But more important, he was a dreamer and a folk artist. Pop created small animals, using the blacksmith's artistry he had learned from his father and a fertile imagination. He also decorated buildings. The latter penchant created the Shaffer Hotel.

Gran Quivira National Monument (on NM 55 twenty-five miles south of Mountainair) is actually the ruins of Pueblo de Las Humanas, a Spanish name given to the Anasazi village at Gran Quivira. It was occupied for nearly nine centuries, 800 A.D. to 1672 A.D. There are 21 separate ruins in the 611 acres of the monument. —Courtesy National Park Service

Today, Pop's hotel is on the National Register of Historic Places. It no longer operates as a hotel. Pop Shaffer is no longer around, but he left memories in the Shaffer Hotel. It houses the headquarters of the Salinas National Monument which directs preservation and education work at the three pueblos, Gran Quivira, Abó, and Quarai. Pop Shaffer's Rancho Bonito is located one mile south of Mountainair on NM 55. Appointments can be made at the Shaffer Hotel to view the exhibition of Shaffer's folk art.

Historical Excursion

NM 55-337
Punta de Agua—Chilili

Punta de Agua

This tiny village at the junction of the road to the Quarai ruins was named Punta de Agua (water point) for a spring. It has long been the residence of farmers and woodcutters.

Quarai at Salinas National Monument

The Quarai ruins are a mile west of NM 55. Quarai was a thriving pueblo in 1598 when Oñate first came to "accept" its oath of allegiance to Spain. The Mission of the Immaculate Conception was founded in 1629 by Fray Francisco de Acevedo. This was northernmost of the pueblos in the Salinas Valley, and it was the first to be abandoned.

According to legend, the people of Quarai made a temporary peace with the Apaches between 1664 and 1669 and plotted with them to drive the Spaniards from the valley. The Spaniards discovered the plot and executed the leaders. The Apaches renewed their raids with increased fury and, in 1674, the Quarai were forced to flee to Tajique, twelve miles to the north.

The Apaches in Salinas Valley may have had substantial reason for their ire. During the seventeenth century, the Spaniards conducted slave raids against the Apaches with the assistance of the Pueblo Indians.

Ruins of the mission which was founded at Quarai in 1629 under the name Immaculate Conception by Fray Francisco de Acevedo. —Courtesy New Mexico Economic Development & Tourism, No. 923

Manzano

The town takes its name from the apple trees which were in the area when the village was founded in 1829. For years it was assumed the trees had been planted by Franciscan friars during the Spanish mission period prior to 1676. However, tree-ring studies spoiled this romantic story and fixed the age of the trees as dating from no earlier than 1800.

Settlers moved into the land near the south end of the Manzano Mountains as early as 1816. They built a small fort with a tower which served as an observation point and a rallying place during emergencies.

Following the Civil War, Manzano became a hotbed of political activity. For several years, Charles G. Kusz was the outspoken publisher of a newspaper called *The Gringo and the Greaser*. Kusz campaigned against many local customs, principally Penitente ceremonies and cattle rustling. He definitely made an impression; in 1884 he was assassinated in his print shop.

Torreon

The defensive towers built by the Spaniards at Manzano gave this small farming community its name. Torreon is built upon the ruins of an old Tewa pueblo not far from the salt lakes of the Salinas Valley—"The Accursed Lakes," the Tewas called them. Like other pueblos in the area, this one was abandoned because of Apache raids. The pueblos in this area have been called "The Cities that Died of Fear."

Tajique

This small farming, ranching, and lumbering community was built upon the ruins of another abandoned Tewa pueblo. The old pueblo was on the south bank of the river northwest of the present village. The name is probably as close as Spanish phonetics could come to Tashike, the Indian name. It furnished a refuge for the inhabitants of Quarai in 1674, but was abandoned the following year because of Apache raids.

The pueblos of the Salinas area came back to life years later as Spanish communities when settlers began to plant crops in the open valleys. The deserted pueblos provided a convenient source of building materials. NM 55 continues to intersect NM 41 at Estancia.

Chilili

NM 337 takes off northward from NM 55 three miles east of Tajique. Members of Oñate's expedition visited the Indian pueblo which was built along both sides of the stream that now forms the east boundary of the present village. About 1630 Fray Alonso Peinado took up residence and erected a small mission, La Nuestra Señora de Navidad. After its abandonment between 1669 and 1676, the Tewa Indians made no attempt to resettle the pueblo.

Hispanic settlers had been working the land for about fifteen years by 1839 when they received a land grant for the village of Chilili. On his exploratory trip in 1847 Lt. James W. Abert found Chilili had been abandoned.

The community rose again, closer to the old pueblo site. In 1893 Chilili was caught up in a buried treasure hunt. A large, black-whiskered Brazilian came to town, Juan de la Serda. Juan convinced the natives that he knew of gold buried beneath the ruins of the old church. For more than forty days he supervised thirty men in a dig. They found nothing more valuable than broken pottery and a few human bones.

One evening the Brazilian sent the laborers home, assuring them that they would take the gold out on the following day. The next morning the Brazilian did not appear. There was a large hole in the center of the church, presumably where the treasure had been. Immediately, the bilked laborers set out with the intention of lynching the Brazilian. They found he had spent the last night in Tajique. That was the last trace they found of Juan de la Serda.

Abó Ruins

Located nine miles west of Mountainair on NM 513 a mile north of US 60, the Abó Ruins display the remains of an early seventeenth-century church which was considered by the Spanish at the time of its construction to have been one of the finest and most architecturally advanced in the region.

The pueblo was built by the Tompiro Indians and settled by 1150 A.D. They traded salt, hides, and piñon nuts with people in the Ácoma-Zuñi area. Springs provided water for households, crops, and flocks of turkeys. Spaniards first visited in 1581, and Fray Francisco de Acevedo founded a mission and built San Gregorio de Abó alongside the pueblo. The church had a sophisticated buttressing technique. There was an organ and a trained choir. But as was the case of the other Indians in the Salinas Valley, they abandoned the pueblo between 1672 and 1678. The majority of the Abó Ruins are unexcavated.

Ruins of the old Spanish mission at Abó, once judged the finest church in the region. —Courtesy New Mexico Economic Development & Tourism, No. 991

Abó

During the early 1900s the coming of the railroad created another Abó which took its name from the nearby ruins. Many of the houses were built out of red sandstone filched from the Abó ruins. The post office lasted only a year, 1910-11, and the town deteriorated into near ghost-town status.

Scholle

The ruins of red rock buildings by the railroad signal the presence of what was once a busy railroad town with a depot, two stores, a post office, and a section gang. A 24-hour dispatcher was required to handle the railroad traffic. The town was named for Fred Scholle, an early Belen merchant. There are numerous Indian pictographs in the area.

US 285
Ramon—Mesa

Ramon

Southeast from Vaughn, US 285 crosses sparsely populated prairie land in Guadalupe and Lincoln counties to this small ranching community. The name, Spanish for "Raymond," was selected by the Post Office Department in Washington from a list of names which was submitted in 1924. The post office was discontinued in 1945.

Mesa

The Artesian Basin underlies the area beyond Mesa. Water from heavy rains and melting snow is trapped in channels of porous limestone beneath the topsoil. The underground basin extends from the eastern slope of the Sacramento Mountains to bluffs east of the Pecos River, allowing irrigation water to be tapped at an average depth of 250 feet. Depressions which are occasionally visible from the highway are sinkholes in porous Permian limestone. Irrigation has been practiced in this area since 1880.

Blackwater Draw Museum

During the Great Drought of the early 1930s, the scouring wind exposed spearpoints and gigantic mammoth bones on a ranch southwest of Clovis. Later a gravel pit was opened in the ancient Blackwater Draw lake bed, and bulldozers unearthed mammoth, bison, and other animal bones, intermingled with fluted spearpoints, crude hammerstones, scrapers, and other artifacts indicating the presence of man at a time earlier than the Folsom culture (9000-8000 B.C). The distinctive projectile points have been dubbed "Clovis points" and date back to between 10,000 and 9000 B.C.

The Blackwater Draw Museum, twelve miles south of Clovis, displays a generous sampling of the remains of the six-ton Ice-Age mammals and the weapons used by the Paleo-Indians to bring them down.

NM 70
Portales

The first permanent settler of Roosevelt County was Doak Good. a cattleman who made his home at Portales Springs about 1880. When he first arrived he lived in the caves from which the springs flowed. The caves resembled the porches or *portales* of Spanish adobe houses, hence the name.

The city owes its start to "Uncle" Josh Morrison who opened a store in a one-room building at Portales Springs. With the coming of the construction camp for the Pecos Valley and Northeastern Railroad, Uncle Josh put his store on skids and moved it to town.

Railroad promoters promised irrigation water, but the project fizzled and many homesteaders did not stay long enough to prove up on their claims.

With the coming of Eastern New Mexico University in 1934, Portales may be said to have gotten into the education business. The community centers around the university.

Elida

Elida preceded Portales as a trading center for ranchers. With the coming of the railroad, homesteaders came. However, homesteaders also left, particularly after the grasshopper infestation of

1913 when the rails became so slick with grasshoppers that trains could not run.

Kenna

The ranching town was originally named Urton for the Urton brothers from Missouri. One was foreman of the Bar V Ranch which extended west to the Pecos River. Prior to the railroad it had been called Kenna's Camp. This was where stages from Amarillo, Texas, and from the west met to transfer passengers and mail. After the coming of the railroad the name was changed to Kenna.

Bitter Lake National Wildlife Refuge

This refuge provides migratory birds with a place to stop, rest, and grab a bite to eat. Fields of grain are planted just for them; this keeps the birds from arousing the ire of farmers in the area. Canada geese, ducks, sandhill cranes, and a few white pelicans are the usual visitors although officials have counted thirty species of wildfowl. Other wildlife includes mule deer, coyotes, bobcats, badgers, quail, pheasants, roadrunners, desert cottontail rabbits, and snakes— including rattlers.

Roswell

The first serious attempt at settlement in the Roswell area was made in 1865 by a group of Missourians who gathered at Missouri Plaza fourteen miles southwest of the present city, but they soon abandoned the attempt because of its droughty condition.

Grama grass in the Pecos River Valley made the Roswell area a favorite stopover for Texas cattlemen driving herds north. There was a cattle pen, a house, and an adobe building that served as a hotel. In 1869 Van C. Smith, a professional gambler, and his partner Aaron Wilburn acquired the adobe building. They had a general store, a post office, and the hotel at what is today Fourth and Main streets. When Smith filed on the land, he called it Roswell for his father, Roswell Smith.

In 1877 Capt. Joseph C. Lea bought out Smith's claim and thereby earned the title "The Father of Roswell."

In the early days, ranching families who came to town to shop did not stay in hotels. They "put up" at the wagon yard. The first wagon yard was operated by Robert Cruse. The charge was $1.00 per day. Cecil Bonney told about it in *Looking Over My Shoulder: Seventy-five Years in the Pecos Valley*:

For this you were given a place for your team of horses; of course, you paid extra for their feed. Water was available in barrels, hauled from the North Spring River. Rooms were provided for women and children, eight-foot by eight-foot sheds with open front doorways and no windows. They barely provided protection against the weather. The facility today known as the "restroom" was located somewhere in the rear of the wagon yard, devoid of heat or running water. There were no furnishings in the rooms; you spread a bedroll on the wooden floor. The men and boys spread their beds outside on the ground. I recall that I looked upon the wagon yard as a rare treat because I was permitted to sleep with dad.

Food was prepared in a Dutch oven, frying pan, and coffeepot over an open fire built with cow chips or "prairie coal."

In 1891 Nathan Jaffe accidentally discovered that the Roswell area was located atop a source of artesian water, and thousands of acres of land came under cultivation as farmers and ranchers punctured the earth. Alas, as early as 1916 the wells started failing. Drought again became a problem.

On July 25, 1930, Dr. Robert H. Goddard arrived in Roswell to conduct rocket experiments which could have changed the course of events for the United States after World War I. Goddard was backed by banker-financier Harry Guggenheim and Charles A. Lindbergh, who was interested in the potential of rocket power for high-speed,

Harry Guggenheim, Robert H. Goddard, and Charles A. Lindbergh at the launch tower, September 25, 1935.
—Courtesy Roswell Museum and Art Center

high-altitude propulsion of aircraft and for emergency power in the event of engine failure. East-central New Mexico had been selected as a test site on the basis of terrain, climate, and weather.

Goddard rented Mescalero Ranch, three miles from town, and he found Eden Valley, some ten miles from the ranch, for a test site. In 1932-33 Goddard and Lindbergh tried to interest the U.S. military in rocketry and were ignored. Goddard continued his work in New Mexico into 1941. The U.S. military paid him little attention, but when Goddard was able to examine a German V-2 rocket he found a striking resemblance to his designs. As German rocket scientists surrendered and were questioned about rocketry, they expressed surprise that their questioners had not asked Robert H. Goddard.

The Goddard Wing of the Roswell Museum and Art Center houses a replica of Goddard's liquid fuel rocket workshop in Roswell.

NM 206
Arch—Lovington

Arch

To reach Arch, take NM 88 east from Portales. The community's post office was established September 22, 1903. The argument over how the village got its name is larger than the town. One "authority" says it was for a settler named Arch Williams. A second version cites an early sheriff, Arch Gragg—or maybe it was Arch Gregory. That wasn't it at all, says another. The Post Office Department asked for a short name; the postmistress wrote down "Arch" and sent it in. Then there is the school which says the name commemorated Archie Roosevelt, the son of the President for whom the county was named.

Rogers

Rogers is on NM 235 six miles east of NM 206. Roosevelt County was opened to settlers in 1906-1907. Rev. Andrew J. Maxwell brought his family from Rogers, Arkansas, and homesteaded on what had been the vast DZ Ranch. He laid out the townsite in 1908 and sold it to a man named Pitts in January, 1909. The early settlers were into agricultural activities. During the summer of 1909 the newspaper noted that W. S. Hamby's 80-acre field of potatoes was flourishing.

After a rain, an unpaved road could make the convenience of an automobile seem a highly debatable matter. —Courtesy El Paso Public Library

The Vaughn Automobile and Transportation Company furnished transportation for Portales people to and from Rogers. The 20-mile trip took "less than one hour." The *Portales Herald* commented: "These automobiles are proving themselves more and more a great convenience to Portales people."

Dora

The town was founded in 1905 a mile west and three-fourths mile south of its present site, the homestead of the Lee sisters, the eldest of whom was named Dora. However, the first postmaster was Frederick Humphrey, and he was said to have named the town Dora after his daughter. In any case, in 1915 when NM 18 (now NM 206) came through, the settlement moved to its present site.

Lingo (east on NM 458)

Established in 1916, the community was originally named Need. However, the Post Office Department protested the name was too much like Weed, located in Otero County. In 1918 the town moved to three miles north of its old location and the name was changed to Lingo. In spite of accusations that the new name was selected because of the way people close to Texas talked, it probably perpetuated a family name.

Pep

The name is said to have been laid upon the community during the depression days by Howard Radcliff after a breakfast cereal of the same name. The post office dates from 1936.

Milnesand

Tradition has it that the town was so designated because a windmill on the old DZ Ranch was called "Mill-in-the-Sand." Mrs. Lillian Curl established the first store in 1910 and became the postmistress in 1915. Uncle Tommy Parker, a Milnesand merchant, freighted between Milnesand and Portales with a Model-T chain-drive truck, said to be "little faster than a team." He charged $5 per passenger per trip.

Crossroads

This oil field and ranching community was so named because it was at a highway intersection when the post office was established in 1923. Today a highway sign warns: "Caution—Buggy Crossing."

A nearby building houses the only industry in town, the Wolf Wagon Works. In 1980 John Wolf and his wife, Bobbie, started turning out horse-drawn carriages, wagons, and even stagecoaches. Some are restorations of vehicles owned by the grandparents of local ranching families; others are new from the ground up.

Prices range from $1,700 for a basic no-frills buckboard to $3,250 for a sporty mountain spring-hack. "You can't find a truck for that money," said Bobbie Wolf.

Tatum

The town was founded in 1909 by James G. Tatum, who started a small general store. As a community formed, the construction of a school was financed by income from neighborhood dances and box socials. The oil boom in Lea County brought limited prosperity during the 1940s.

Lovington

In 1907 Jim B. Love moved his cattle from Texas to the area that is now Lovington. His brother had occupied a dugout here since 1903. His horses were branded LOV and his cattle wore a Lazy J. When a surveyor was laying out a townsite, he told Jim Love that he would name the town for him if he would open a store. On May 7, 1908, Love opened the first store.

High winds and the consequent sand storms plague residents of the Lovington area. On one occasion, a visitor asked why, with all the wind, there had never been a cyclone. An old-timer responded: "Humph! there couldn't be. Our straight winds would blow the hell out of a cyclone."

Humble City—Jal

Humble City

With the oil boom of the 1920s, the highway between Lovington and Hobbs became one of the most heavily traveled roads in the state. In 1930 Humble City, named for the Humble Oil Company, came into being. The road had to be expanded to a four-lane divided highway to handle the increased traffic.

Hobbs

In 1907 James Isaac Hobbs and his family of five were westbound in a covered wagon headed for Alpine, Texas, when they met a wagonload of eastbound pioneers. They told Hobbs they were leaving Alpine because they could not make a living there. Hobbs turned his wagon north and settled in the southeastern corner of New Mexico Territory. The Hobbs family occupied a dugout near what is now First and Texas streets in Hobbs. The promise of free land brought other settlers. By 1911 there were twenty-five land-owners.

James Hobbs rode from ranch to ranch enlisting support for the first rural school. His son opened a store near the school, and his wife, Grandma Hobbs, ran the post office. For the next eighteen years, Hobbs was a minuscule agrarian community.

In 1927 the Texas Production Company brought in No. 1 Rhoads well near Jal. On November 8, 1928, "Black Gold" began to flow from a Midwest Refining Company (now Amoco) well on the corner of Stanolind Road and South Grimes Street. Fortune hunters rushed in; shanties and tents blossomed. The old village became three towns: Hobbs, New Hobbs, and All Hobbs—about 12,000 people.

Hobbs united into a single town and became a brawling community as oil drillers went directly from work to taverns, brothels, domino parlors, and pool halls. A metal tank was chained to a post in which to incarcerate those who became too raucous.

Hobbs weathered this storm and the Great Depression which followed. Diversification includes feedlots for cattle, chemical production, and attractions for tourists. The latter include the Lea County Cowboy Hall of Fame and Western Heritage Center on the campus of New Mexico Junior College, and a museum for the New Mexico Wing of the Confederate Air Force.

When it was found that conditions over Hobbs are conducive to powerless flight, the National Soaring Foundation organized. A 10-knot lift and a consistent 12,000-15,000-foot cloud base have resulted in glider pilots flying at record-breaking speeds in excess of 100 miles per hour.

Eunice

Eunice is located two miles west of NM 18 on NM 207. In 1908 John N. Carson laid claim to his 320-acre homestead by plowing a furrow around it. Carson opened a store and named the town after his daughter. Homesteaders in the area started a one-teacher subscription school; they advertised for a physician for whom free living quarters would be provided, but there was not enough illness to support him.

Population dwindled during the drought years as the remaining farmers used acorns and pie melons to feed their horses. The oil business alternated with economic depression to provide a boom-and-bust economy for Eunice. Appropriately, the Eunice Chamber of Commerce has adopted the caption "Where oil flows a city grows." The citizens keep time to the slow but steady rhythm of the pumpjacks which are scattered around town like giant grasshoppers pecking at the earth.

Jal

The name comes from the brand of the old JAL Ranch in Monument Draw, six miles east of the present town. The ranch was owned by John A. Lynch. As required by Post Office Department regulation, the ranch obtained a post office in 1910 by carrying mail free for three months.

Mail wrought little improvement in the lives of the homesteaders. Most of them left because the land was too dry, and the post office moved to the present location of the town in 1916. The community led a lackluster existence until the discovery of oil in 1927, at which time it joined neighboring cities in a boom-bust cycle dependent upon the weather, the price of oil, and the national economy.

Monument—Oil Center

Monument

In 1870 two buffalo hunters named Falkner and Hill trailed a band of Indians, hoping they could follow them to water. On the fourth day they came to a hill surrounded by a pile of rocks about thirty feet square and twenty feet high. It was the marker for a spring located a mile east. In 1885 Guy Falkner sold Monument Springs to an Englishman named Kennedy for $400.

It passed through successive hands until it became the Hat Ranch. Homesteaders claimed land and the population peaked between 1909 and 1912. During the drought, the community virtually disappeared, but it was revived by discovery of oil.

From the early days, the old Hat Ranch house remains, and there is a sculptured monument of an Indian. A nearby Indian battlefield has yielded numerous projectile points, and signs were found in the area of the pottery-making Mogollons who farmed and built pit houses from 200 to 400 A.D.

Oil Center

This community is precisely what its name implies. Behemoth vehicles grunt around among a field of massive storage tanks. Giant retorts spout plumes of hissing steam, and the whole place reeks with the stench of "Black Gold." It was born of the oil boom and petitioned for a post office in 1937.

Caprock—San Pedro

Caprock

This lonely hamlet, named for the presence of cap rock in the surrounding land, was named in 1913 by Ed Charles E. Crossland, founder and first postmaster. He planted cottonwood trees around the post office. They are still visible from miles away.

Geologically speaking, cap rock is a relatively impervious layer of anhydrite, gypsum, or limestone overlying a dome of salt, oil, gas, et cetera.

Sunset

This tiny rural community does not have a post office. It is located just west of where the Chisum Trail crossed what is now US 70-380. In 1875 John S. Chisum, the "Cattle King of the Pecos," made his headquarters near present-day Roswell. In that year, 80,000 cattle wore his famous Jinglebob earmark. The Chisum Trail, not to be confused with the Chisholm Trail, wound from Roswell to Las Cruces and then roughly followed present-day I-10 west to Arizona. In 1875 Chisum sent 11,000 head of cattle over this route. In the spring of 1871 a herd of 1,100 was trailed across the Pecos, up the Rio Hondo along the Chisum Trail, and on to California. After being wintered in California, they were taken to Reno, Nevada, and sold for $30 a head. They had cost $10 a head.

Picacho

The first settlers came from the Rio Grande Valley in 1867-68 with small flocks of sheep and goats to establish a settlement on the bank of the Rio Hondo, overshadowed by nearby Picacho Peak for which the town was named. A stage road ran along the Hondo and the hill at Picacho was so steep that it was considered hazardous for inexperienced drivers.

Cattlemen were not long in discovering the fine grazing lands of the Hondo Valley. They came in the 1870s. The Circle Diamond Cattle Company adjoined Picacho on the east with pastures, corrals, and wide green alfalfa fields. Fruit trees surrounded an adobe house with three-foot-thick adobe walls. The Circle Diamond was annexed by the Diamond A Cattle Company. Both became part of the Bloom Land and Cattle Company which grew to an empire of 800,000 acres or more. During the late 1940s sale of the historic Circle Diamond Ranch began. It was broken up into scores of small tracts now in the hands of new owners. Many are "weekend ranchers" who live in Roswell.

Tinnie

This farming and ranching community has had assorted names. It began in 1876 as Analla, for José Analla, an early settler. It was also called Las Cuevas (the caves) for the caves in which the first settlers lived. For reasons unknown, it was called Cuba for a while. In 1909 the buildings were bought by the Raymond family and the town was named Tinnie for their oldest daughter.

In 1959 Robert O. Anderson, of Roswell, purchased the Tinnie Mercantile Company and added a porch, a tower, and a pavilion to the old building. He opened it as the Silver Dollar Bar and Steak House. It became a popular eating establishment.

Historical Excursion

NM 368
Arabela

During earlier days the winding dirt road that preceded present-day NM 368 north from Tinnie led to Blue Water, Pine Lodge, and Arabela. Arabela is the only name remaining on today's maps. In 1909 the site of Pine Lodge, in the Capitan Mountains, was leased by a group of Roswell businessmen for the purpose of establishing a summer resort. It did not materialize.

Arabela was established as Las Tablas (boards, planks) during the 1870s by three Hispanic families from Walsenburg, Colorado, who settled on ranches at the southeast end of the Capitan Mountains. In 1886 Andy Richardson moved to Las Tablas and opened a general store. When he was appointed postmaster in 1901 he renamed the town to honor the daughter of one of the settlers. The post office lasted until 1928.

Hondo

The settlement was originally called La Junta (junction) because it was at the confluence of the Bonito and Ruidoso rivers. The community formed at the homestead claim of W. L. Coe, cousin of Frank and George Coe who figured prominently in the Lincoln County War. The Coe brothers claimed land farther upriver.

Earlier, the Coe ranch had been occupied by Dick Brewer, who imported apple seeds from Missouri. The Coes took over the orchards. Today, fruit and vegetable growing is the backbone of Hondo's economy. There are packing sheds, refrigeration facilities, and a trucking company; roadside fruit stands dot the highway.

Lincoln

Lincoln's early settlement is attested to by *El Torreón*, the old Spanish watchtower, a reminder of earlier conflict. During Apache attacks, women and children crowded into the first floor while men went to the second floor where they fired at attackers through holes

El Torreón, *the old watchtower at Lincoln, was built for protection against attack by Apaches.* —Courtesy New Mexico Economic Development & Tourism, No. 57

or slits. Not withstanding their torreón, early settlers were driven out three times by hostile Indians. But Lincoln's early history pales beside events which took place during the Lincoln County War.

Any reasonably complete library of New Mexico history contains at least a six-foot shelf of books dealing with the Lincoln County War, and more are being written annually as new facts are brought to light and new opinions are brought to bear. Lincoln was the focal point of that bloody conflict.

Lincoln was settled in 1849 by Hispanic villagers from the east side of the Manzano Mountains. It was called Las Placitas (little settlements). Later the name was changed to Bonito after the river which flowed past the town. With the formation of the county, named to honor President Lincoln, the Territorial Legislature of 1869 changed the name of the town from Bonito to Lincoln.

Fort Stanton had been established in 1855, and the Mescalero Apaches were herded onto a reservation. The government purchased great quantities of beef to supply the needs of Fort Stanton and to fill the ration requirements of the Indians. There was a market for vegetables, fruit, hay, and grain. Settlers arrived to establish "Squatters' Rights" to the as yet unsurveyed land in the public domain. Cattlemen from Texas arrived to take advantage of the growing market for beef.

The Lincoln County War has been erroneously characterized as a range war. Although an attempt to destroy John Chisum's domination of the cattle market was involved, it was not a range war. Because of the ardent alliance of Billy the Kid with one of the warring factions, the Lincoln County War has been called a blood feud. It was not. The Lincoln County War was a fight between business competitors, abetted by political forces.

Maj. Lawrence G. Murphy came to New Mexico with the army. After he was mustered out of the service he became the post trader at Fort Stanton. The post commander fired him for questionable dealings, and Murphy moved to Lincoln where he opened a store and saloon. Soon he had a monopoly on supplying beef and flour to Fort Stanton. As long as Murphy had the only store, farmers and ranchers were forced to pay exorbitant prices in order to obtain credit.

As business grew, Murphy formed an alliance with Thomas B. Catron, a corrupt politician who headed the powerful "Santa Fe Ring." Murphy was ruthless in exercising political control. At one point he boasted, "You might as well try to stop the waves of the ocean with a fork as to try and stop me."

As Murphy's health deteriorated from drinking, he took in two partners, James J. Dolan and John H. Riley. The immediate objective was to eliminate John Chisum as a competitor for the beef market. But more formidable competition was coming from another source. Alexander McSween arrived on the scene. He bought an interest in a ranch, he opened a bank, and he built a store to challenge Murphy's trade monopoly. McSween had the support of John Chisum, and he was financed by John Henry Tunstall, a wealthy young Englishman who had come to the American West to make a fortune in the cattle business.

The first volley in the Lincoln County War was fired on February 18, 1878. Tunstall was murdered in cold blood by a group of gunmen who had been hired by the Murphy forces and deputized as possemen by the local sheriff. Since the county had no funds to pay officials, they were paid in scrip. The Murphy faction kept the sheriff under control by buying his scrip.

Members of the McSween faction, including Billy the Kid, vowed to avenge Tunstall's death. They called themselves the "Regulators." Early in March the Regulators killed two men who had been members of the posse that murdered Tunstall. On April 1 they set an ambush behind the adobe fence of a corral adjoining the Tunstall store. As Sheriff William Brady and four of his deputies walked down Lincoln's main and only street toward the Murphy store, the hidden gunmen opened fire. Sheriff Brady and one of his deputies were killed, another was wounded.

There were more confrontations and more killings. On March 4 Samuel B. Axtell, governor of the Territory, appealed to President Rutherford B. Hayes to send federal troops to assist Territorial civil officers. Soldiers from Fort Stanton showed up but did little more than observe. On June 29 the post commander announced his troops could no longer participate in civil disturbances because Congress had forbidden it in a rider attached to the army appropriations act.

The stage was thus set for a showdown. With the army out of the way, the McSween forces decided it was time to seize the initiative. On July 14 they assembled some sixty men. The McSween cause was popular because so many ranchers and farmers suffered under the monopolistic domination of the House of Murphy. What would become known as the "Five-Day Battle" began. The next day the sheriff moved about forty men into the Wortley Hotel just down the street from the McSween House. For the next two days there was sporadic fighting during which a few shots and a lot of verbal insults were exchanged.

On the fourth day, the commander of Fort Stanton arrived with a force of thirty-five men and five officers, a mountain howitzer, and a Gatling gun. The troopers camped on a vacant lot and the commander announced he was there only to protect women and children. Nevertheless, the McSween forces began to evaporate leaving McSween, his wife Susan, and about fourteen men bottled up in the McSween house.

On July 19, after five days of siege, the sheriff torched the house, and flames spread slowly from room to room, driving the roasting occupants ahead. Susan McSween ran from the building and pleaded with the commander of the troops from Fort Stanton to save the men who were in the burning building. He disregarded her plea and she returned to the building.

As darkness approached, Billy the Kid took command of plotting an escape and was among the first to put the plan into effect by dashing from the burning building. McSween stepped outside to ask a deputy to accept his surrender. He fell on his back doorstep with five bullets in his body. The deputy was also killed in the fusillade. When it was over, the bodies of McSween and two of his supporters lay in the backyard. The rest escaped into the darkness.

It should be noted that Lawrence G. Murphy, who started it all, did not play an active role in the conflict. In 1877 he sold his interest to his partners. Threatened with death by the Regulators, he fled to Fort Stanton. His continuing bout with alcoholism resulted in his death in October.

After the Five-Day Battle, President Hayes bowed to political pressure from New Mexico and replaced Governor Axtell with Lew Wallace in September, 1878. Wallace had before him a long roster of warrants for arrest including "Wm. H. Antrim, alias Kid, alias Bonney."

The governor issued an amnesty proclamation which was published in the Santa Fe *Sentinel* on November 14, 1878, in which he announced "that the disorders lately prevalent in Lincoln County . . . have been happily brought to an end":

> . . . the undersigned, by virtue of authority in him vested, further proclaims a general pardon for misdemeanors and offenses committed in the said County of Lincoln against the laws of the said Territory in connection with the aforesaid disorders, between the first day of February, 1878, and the date of this proclamation.

The amnesty aroused a flood of public criticism, and Wallace went to Lincoln on March 5 to interview participants in the conflict. The end result of the visit was to turn "Wm. H. Antrim, alias Kid, alias Bonney" into a national celebrity.

At the beginning of the Lincoln County War, Billy the Kid was a teen-age drifter with a reputation which, translated into today's terminology, would classify him as a juvenile delinquent. He was barely eighteen years old when he arrived in Lincoln County in October, 1877, a fugitive from an Arizona murder charge. He signed on as a cowhand at John H. Tunstall's ranch and was on hand at the killing of Tunstall. Thus, he became a participant in the Lincoln County War as a member of the McSween faction.

The governor's amnesty proclamation did not apply to Billy the Kid because he was under previous indictments in the Territorial court for the murder of Sheriff Brady and in a federal court for the murder of Buckshot Roberts. However, Governor Wallace was so anxious to bring an end to the troubles in Lincoln County that he promised to protect the young outlaw from prosecution: "I have authority to exempt you from prosecution if you will testify to what you say you know."

Billy the Kid kept his end of the bargain. He met the governor and told him what he knew. He submitted to a simulated arrest.

But the governor's plans went awry. The men against whom Bonney was to testify escaped from jail. Billy did testify at an army court of inquiry after which he rode out of Lincoln and settled into pursuing an outlaw career. Governor Wallace responded with a reward notice:

$500 REWARD.

NOTICE IS HEREBY GIVEN THAT FIVE HUNDRED DOLLARS REWARD WILL BE PAID FOR THE DELIVERY OF BONNEY ALIAS "THE KID," TO THE SHERIFF OF LINCOLN COUNTY.

LEW. WALLACE
GOVERNOR OF NEW MEXICO

SANTA FE, DEC. 15TH, 1880.

On December 23, 1880, Bonney alias "The Kid" was captured by Sheriff Pat Garrett and his posse at Stinking Springs. He was taken to the jail in Las Vegas. The Las Vegas *Gazette* published a midnight extra on Sunday, December 27. A *Gazette* reporter was permitted to interview Bonney:

"Billy the Kid," and Billy Wilson who were shackled together stood patiently up while a blacksmith took off their shackles and bracelets to allow them an opportunity to make a change of clothing. Both prisoners watched the operation which was to set them free for a short while, but Wilson scarcely raised his eyes, and spoke but once or twice to his compadres. Bonney on the other hand, was light and chipper, and was very communicative, laughing, joking and chattering with the bystanders.

Sheriff Pat Garrett, the slayer of Billy the Kid. —Courtesy Leon C. Metz

Billy the Kid.
—Courtesy El Paso Public Library

"You appear to take it easy," the reporter said.

"Yes! What's the use of looking on the gloomy side of everything. The laugh's on me this time," he said. Then looking about the placita, he asked: "Is the jail at Santa Fe any better than this?"

This seemed to trouble him considerably, for as he explained, "this is a terrible place to put a fellow in." He put the same question to every one who came near him and when he learned that there was nothing better in store for him, he shrugged his shoulders and said something about putting up with what he had to.

He was the attraction of the show, and as he stood there, lightly kicking the toes of his boots on the stone pavement to keep his feet warm, one would scarcely mistrust that he was the hero of "Forty Thieves," romance which this paper has been running in serial form for six weeks or more.

"There was a big crowd gazing at me wasn't there?" he exclaimed, and then smiling continued: "Well, perhaps some of them will think me half a man now; everyone seems to think I was some kind of an animal."

310

He did look human, indeed, but there was nothing very mannish about him in appearance, for he looked and acted a mere boy. He is about five feet, eight or nine inches tall, slightly built and lithe, weighing about 140; a frank and open countenance, looking like a school boy, with the traditional silky fuzz on his upper lip, clear blue eyes, with a roguish snap about them, light hair and complexion. He is, in all, quite a handsome looking fellow, the only imperfection being two prominent front teeth, slightly protruding like squirrels' teeth, and he has agreeable and winning ways.

Governor Lew Wallace did not respond to Billy the Kid's attempts to remind him of his promised protection from prosecution. On April 13, 1881, at Mesilla, Bonney was sentenced to death for the murder of Sheriff William Brady. He was taken back to Lincoln to await his execution in the county's newly acquired courthouse, the old Murphy-Dolan store. The jail was on the second floor.

Billy was swathed in chains and anchored to the floor. His guards were Deputy Sheriffs Bob Olinger and J. W. Bell. They had been with the Murphy faction during the Lincoln County War. Olinger would let his prisoner see him loading his double-barreled shotgun, reminding him that the eighteen slugs in each barrel would do a powerful lot of damage.

On the morning of April 28, Bob Olinger was on guard. At noon he was relieved by Bell. Olinger left his shotgun downstairs in the sheriff's office and went across the street to the Wortley Hotel for dinner.

Billy asked Bell for permission to use the outside privy. There he acquired a gun, previously hidden by a confederate. It took two shots to do away with Bell. Olinger heard the shooting, pushed away from the table, and dashed out of the hotel—to find himself staring down both barrels of his own shotgun. Eighteen slugs did a powerful lot of damage. Then Billy fired the second load into the lifeless body and flung the gun at his tormentor.

"Take it, damn you! You won't follow me any more with that gun."

A frightened caretaker helped Billy loosen his shackles. The fugitive took time to shake hands with a few citizens who dared show themselves. As he passed Bell's body he expressed regret at having to kill him, but he had no kind words for Olinger as he climbed on a horse and galloped away.

During the first weekend of every August, Billy the Kid's escape is reenacted in Lincoln. During his time, Lincoln had a population of 400. Today, some seventy-five people live in the sleepy adobe village nestling between wooded hillsides on the Rio Bonito, but

Billy the Kid's escape from Lincoln County jail in the courthouse on April 28, 1881. The event is reenacted annually. —Garrett, 1882

thousands of visitors trek up and down the street reading historical markers that explain the Lincoln County War. They duck in and out of Lincoln's four museums, one of which is the old courthouse from which Billy the Kid made his escape.

During the century since that escape the outlaw had been the subject of hundreds of books and some forty movies. (One of the movies was entitled *Billy the Kid vs. Dracula*.) He has been portrayed as everything from a psychotic neurotic to a heroic avenger of wrong. Indeed, "a big crowd" has gazed at him.

Historical Excursion

NM 214
Fort Stanton

Fort Stanton, about four miles southeast of Capitan on NM 214, can be reached from either US 380 or US 70. This fort was established in 1855 on the banks of the Rio Bonito for the purpose of controlling the Mescalero Apaches and encouraging settlement in the area. It was named for Capt. Henry W. Stanton, who had been killed by the Apaches on January 18 of that year.

By its mere presence, the fort may have encouraged settlers, but its value in controlling the Apaches is debatable. The Indians lived off the land; they could move farther and faster than the U.S. troops.

312

While the homesteaders and soldiers were attempting to stave off Indian depredations, another war was approaching.

As Confederate forces approached Fort Stanton, the Union troops attempted to burn the post to keep it from falling into Rebel hands, but a heavy rain put out most of the fires. Apaches and local citizens looted the buildings before the Confederate forces arrived. The Confederates stayed until September, 1861.

A year later Brig. Gen. James H. Carleton arrived on the New Mexico scene, determined to put an end to the Mescalero problem. He was convinced the solution lay in teaching the Indians to respect the white man's laws and forcing them to adopt his ways. He persuaded a reluctant Col. Christopher Carson to take command of New Mexico Volunteers in the field. After a successful campaign, Carson proceeded to Fort Stanton.

Fort Stanton's mission was to guard captured Apaches. By March, 1863, remnants of the Mescalero tribe were in Santa Fe begging for peace tempered by respect:

> You are stronger than we. We have fought you so long as we had rifles and powder; but your weapons are better than ours. Give us weapons and turn us loose, and we will fight you again; but we are worn out; we have no more heart; we have no provisions, no means to live; your troops are everywhere; our springs and water holes are either occupied or overlooked by your young men. You have driven us from our last and best stronghold, and we have no more heart. Do with us as may seem good to you, but do not forget we are men and braves.

The post was deactivated in 1896. In 1899 it became a U.S. Marine hospital for tubercular patients. In 1939 it served as an internment camp for captured German seamen. In the 1950s it was taken over by the State of New Mexico and used successively as a tubercular hospital and a school for the mentally retarded.

Fort Stanton. —Courtesy El Paso Public Library

Capitan

In 1884 Seaborn T. Gray homesteaded on the Salado Flat. He opened a small store. In 1894 a post office opened, and Gray was appointed postmaster. He named the community Gray in his own honor. In 1899 the El Paso and Northeastern Railroad (later to become the Southern Pacific) built a branch line to coal mines a mile northwest. A little mining community called Coalora sprang up there.

The railroad changed Gray's name to Capitan after the surrounding mountains. The coal mines played out in 1905. Most of the buildings in Coalora were moved to Dawson where productive mines were in operation, and Coalora faded from the map.

Capitan survived. In May, 1950, a devastating forest fire, started by a camper's carelessness, swept 17,000 acres in the Capitan Mountains. Firefighters found an orphaned bear cub. They called him Hot Foot Teddy, but the late Elliott S. Barker changed the cub's name to Smokey and was instrumental in making the bear a symbol of national concern over protection of the forests.

Smokey was flown to Santa Fe for medical care and later to Washington, D.C., where he became a fixture in the National Zoo. The town of Capitan built the Smokey Bear Motel and Cafe and a log museum to tell the story of the cub's hectic start in life. Smokey Bear Historical State Park was established in 1976. Upon his death, the body of the original Smokey was brought from Washington for burial in the park, and Smokey Junior took over the duties of representing fire prevention at the Washington National Zoo.

Capitan keeps Smokey's memory green with an annual Fourth of July Smokey Bear Stampede.

Historical Excursion

NM 37
Nogal—Bonito City

Nogal

In 1879 when prospectors found free gold in what is now Nogal they called it Dry Gulch. For a time the growing village was also called Galena because of lead in the area. And it was named Parsons for a miner who made a strike in 1892. The name was

An arrastra was powered by a horse or a burro dragging a heavy stone around a circular trough to grind ore-bearing earth. —Drake, 1887

finally changed to Nogal because of the large walnut trees growing in town. In 1900 the Secretary of the Interior told about the Nogal mining district in his *Annual Report*:

> Among the more productive mines . . . might be noted the American, where its original locator, Billy Gill, ground out a fortune with the aid of a mule and an arrastra; the Hellen Rae, from which old man Rae carried a gunny sack of ore down to his cabin daily and pounded out enough yellow metal in a mortar to wear a silk hat and a syndicate smile the remainder of his days, and then sold the claim to St. Louis parties for $10,000.

Today there is no trace of the large hotel which accommodated eager miners and fortune-hunting adventurers. The land which once yielded gold now grows orchards, and summer homes are sprinkled about the area.

Bonito City

Just down the road from Nogal, Bonito City flourished during the 1880s. Its post office closed in 1911, and it is now under seventy-five feet of water in Bonito Lake. The Southern Pacific Railroad built a dam to provide a water supply for its track-side water towers. Today, the water from Bonito Lake goes to Ruidoso and Carrizozo, and the lake provides a popular fishing spot.

Bingham

Coal was discovered in this area prior to the Civil War. With the coming of the railroads, it was needed; mining began. In 1881 the Santa Fe Railroad built a spur line to the Carthage coal fields, and Bingham grew to provide services to those engaged in mining. When the mines were no longer productive they were abandoned and the railroad tracks torn up. Bingham declined. Today only a few buildings remain.

San Pedro

This old Spanish settlement on the bank of the Rio Grande was established during the 1830s. Grapes were the principal crop, and at the turn of the century some 250 barrels of native wine were being shipped out of San Antonio. There was also a coal mine at San Pedro.

US 70
San Patricio—Mescalero

San Patricio

When the community was settled about 1875, it was called Ruidoso. An Irish priest built a church and dedicated it to St. Patrick. The name of the town was changed to honor the priest's patron saint. San Patricio became a favorite hangout for Billy the Kid during the Lincoln County War.

More recently it has been home to such notables as actress Helen Hayes, author Paul Horgan, and artists Peter Hurd and Henriette Wyeth. The late Peter Hurd grew up in Roswell and attended New Mexico Military Institute there. He bought land in San Patricio along the Rio Ruidoso and built an adobe hacienda by the river. An avid polo player, Hurd included a polo field and stables for his ponies.

Few motorists on US 70 would believe that at one time San Patricio was the largest voting precinct in Lincoln County.

Glencoe

Several brothers of the Coe family came to the Ruidoso valley from Missouri in 1875. With the help of neighbors, they constructed irrigation ditches and harvested their first crop in 1876. They grew

Frank B. Coe in 1922. During the Lincoln County War he rode and fought beside Billy the Kid. —Hertzog Collection, Acc. No. 540, U.T. El Paso Archives

produce and cut hay for market at Fort Stanton. During the summer of 1877 they employed a hand named William Bonney, who would become known as Billy the Kid. During the Lincoln County War they sided with the McSween faction and after a shoot-out in 1878 left the country for a while.

Ruidoso Downs

The race track two miles east of Ruidoso on US 70 has had a lot to do with the influx of business to the area. During the 1930s Heck Johnson sold lots and water rights around Hale Spring. The community was called Palo Verde. When application was submitted for a post office in 1946, the Post Office Department translated the name to Green Tree because there was already a Palo Verde in New Mexico.

In the meantime, Ruidoso Downs Race Track had developed across the road. It started with contests between friends and developed into a nationally known track featuring the All-American Quarter Horse Futurity, billed as the richest horse race in the world with $1,000,000 going to the winner. Eugene V. Hensley, originator of the race, persuaded the town to change its name to Ruidoso Downs so the race track would have a postmark.

Ruidoso

Originally known as Dowlin's Mill because of the grist mill which still stands, the village was located on the Chisum Trail which ran from the Pecos River to Arizona. By 1885 it had attracted a store, a blacksmith shop, and a post office named Ruidoso (noisy) after the creek which ripples through the town. Capt. Paul Dowlin had served in the New Mexico Volunteers during the Civil War, after which he became post trader at Fort Stanton. Dowlin had the right to sell liquor, which created a problem with Indians on the Mescalero reservation. Unable to oust Dowlin and halt the sale of whiskey to his charges, the post commander moved his quarters to Copeland's Ranch, eight miles away.

Dowlin prospered. He acquired a flour mill, a sawmill, livestock, a store, and other property in the area. On May 5, 1877, Dowlin was killed by Jerry Dillon, a former employee. According to the Santa Fe *New Mexican* of May 15, Dillon "lit out for Texas" and was never heard from again.

Paul Dowlin's mill is still in use, grinding small amounts of flour for souvenir packages. —Courtesy New Mexico Economic Development & Tourism, No. 673

The Ruidoso of today bears little resemblance to the explosive trading center for ranchers of the 1870s and 1880s. During the late 1940s Ruidoso was discovered as a summer resort area. Business boomed. The main street still meanders through some eight miles of pine forest, but arteries reach out into hidden cañoncitos which are speckled with summer homes. Motels, condominiums, and resort hotels abound; there are more than forty-five restaurants.

Blazer's Mill

US 70 passes the faded remains of Blazer's Mill. Here, during the Lincoln County War, a group of McSween supporters were eating on April 5, 1878. They had been deputized by a justice of the peace who favored the McSween faction. The group included Dick Brewer, their leader; George and Frank Coe; Charles Bowdre; and William Bonney, as yet an obscure figure in the conflict. Andrew L. Roberts rode up. He was one of John H. Tunstall's assassins—as historian Leon C. Metz noted, a "veteran of many fights, a scrawny fellow with a crippled arm and a body so full of lead that he was known as 'Buckshot'."

Buckshot Roberts refused to surrender to the group. He was trying to earn a $200 reward offered by the Murphy faction for capturing the killers of Sheriff Brady and George Hindman. Gunfire broke out and Roberts and Brewer were killed. Billy the Kid was eventually tried for the murder of Roberts and set free on a technicality.

Mescalero Apache Indian Reservation

The Mescalero Reservation was originally established in 1873 near Fort Stanton where disputes and quarreling broke out between the Mescaleros and the Navajos. The present reservation, established in 1883, eventually covered 460,177 acres between the White and Sacramento mountains.

Containing timbered mountains, lush pastures, and some 2,000 acres of cropland, it is one of the richest Indian reservations in the nation. The Mescaleros manage hunting and fishing preserves. They have constructed the Inn of the Mountain Gods near Ruidoso, a luxury resort which annually extracts a substantial toll from vacationing "white eyes" and patrons of Ruidoso Downs.

The Mescaleros got their name from mescal, a food staple. *Mescalero* means "mescal maker." The mescal is a large desert plant which is also called agave. It provided the Indians with food in several forms including a sort of hardtack comparable to C-rations which they could carry when on the move. Thread and fabric were made from fibers of the plant. Additionally, it could be fermented into a colorless, fiery potion which, as C. L. Sonnichsen noted in *The Mescalero Apaches*, "is supposed to give more action with fewer aftereffects."

Actually, the Mescaleros preferred *tiswin* or *tulpai*, made from fermented corn sprouts. At one time Indian agents would issue nothing but ground corn to the Mescaleros because whole corn was sure to fall into the hands of old women who kept the *tiswin* business going.

Mescalero

Reservation headquarters is located at the town of Mescalero. The tribe maintains its own police force, fish and game agency, and elementary schools. High-school students attend school in Tularosa, sixteen miles west. The Mescaleros invite tourists and neighbors to a four-day ceremonial held annually in early July. The ceremony combines celebration of the coming of age of young women in the tribe and the emergence of mountain spirits for the healing of the tribe with Fourth of July festivities.

—— Historical Sidebar ——————————————————————

St. Joseph's Mission

The tersely worded historical marker at the side of US 70 does not do justice to the story of St. Joseph's Mission. The church just off the highway is a monument to the devotion of one Franciscan friar, Albert W. Braun. Father Braun came to the Mescalero Indian Reservation after service with the infantry in France during World War I. He wanted to build a mission as a monument to those he had seen die. He had no money, but cathedrals had been built during the Middle Ages without money and machines.

He gathered a few faithful Indians and, later, refugee priests. He brought rocks from the nearby hills, some weighing as much as 1,500 pounds. He crushed and burned his own lime for mortar. He felled and hewed trees for timbers. It took seven years to lay the foundation. As the mission grew, Father Albert's friends rallied to raise money. The walls of the mission are 131 feet long, 68 feet wide,

St. Joseph's Mission is a symbol of the faith and determination of one missionary priest. —Courtesy New Mexico Economic Development & Tourism, No. 743

and 57 feet high. One wall is 8 feet 2 inches thick; here the 1,500-pound stones were used.

By the beginning of World War II, the church was completed except for the great glass windows, and there was a $3,000 indebtedness. Father Albert put aside his Franciscan habit and reported for military duty. He was one of 1,600 men from New Mexico with the 200th Coast Artillery who were taken prisoner at the fall of Corregidor. On May 3, 1942, Father Braun sent out by submarine from Corregidor the last check to pay off the $3,000 debt.

After his liberation in 1945, Father Albert returned to Mescalero to pick up work where he had left off on the construction of his personal monument to faith. After completion of St. Joseph's Mission, he returned to serve another two years in the army. After retirement he went to work with the Franciscan fathers in Phoenix, but not without making arrangements to return to Mescalero:

> We have the privilege of choosing our final resting place. I have chosen Mescalero. I want to be buried in the Indian cemetery among all those Indians I have esteemed and loved so much . . . in the same soil where the Indians are at rest.

Dexter—Artesia

Dexter

Articles of incorporation were filed in January, 1903, by Theodore Burr, a native of Denmark; Milton H. Elford, from Canada; and Albert E. Macey, an Iowa farmer, as members of the Dexter Townsite Company. Macey selected the name, after his hometown in Iowa.

Lush gardens sprang up; alfalfa was grown in the area, dehydrated, ground to powder, and sacked as stock feed. Alfalfa fields still blanket the Pecos Valley like a giant patchwork quilt.

Hagerman

This tranquil farming town of less than a thousand has been here since before the turn of the century. It was named for J. J. Hagerman, president of the Pecos Valley and Northeastern Railroad. He also became owner of the old Chisum Ranch which, after his death, was sold to Cornell University.

The crime rate in Hagerman is low, perhaps because the Town Council keeps a tight leash on the community. In 1988 several residents complained that a local beekeeper's bees were bothering people. The Town Council researched and found an ordinance on the books which said one must own one acre to have a farm animal and then have a half-acre for each animal. They ruled that bees are farm animals and the bee bother was eliminated.

Artesia

In the 1890s, John F. Truitt, a Union soldier, homesteaded along the Chisum Trail at the South Chisum Camp just three blocks from what is now Artesia's principal business district. When a stage line was running through in 1894 the stop was called Blake's Spring. When the Pecos Valley Railroad came past and built a siding they named it Miller's Siding. In 1899 a post office opened; it was called Stegman after a land promoter who married John Chisum's niece. But in 1903, after the discovery of artesian water, the name was changed to Artesia.

Well over a thousand people congregated in the area to take advantage of the fertile land and plentiful water for irrigation. Artesian water helped farmers and ranchers weather the drought which ruined so many settlers in the Southwest.

The horseless carriage replaced stagecoaches between Artesia and El Paso. —Courtesy El Paso Public Library

It was the water which led to the discovery of oil. In 1923 two men who had heard of oil traces in the artesian well water showed up with a steam-powered drilling rig. After several dry holes they were ready to pack up their rig when Martin Yates II talked them into drilling one more hole on his land. In April, 1924, the drillers brought in a producing well, setting Artesia on a course to profit from the petroleum industry.

US 82
Maljamar—La Luz

Maljamar

As New Mexican towns go, Maljamar is a latecomer. The post office was established in 1943, but the town started on December 9, 1926, when oil gushed from the ground to open the field which stretched south of town. William Mitchell, a member of the New York Stock Exchange, was president of the Maljamar Oil and Gas Company. He had named the company for his three children: MALcolm, JAnet, and MARgaret.

Hope

The first settlers, from 1884 to 1888, called the place Badgerville because they lived in dugouts, like badgers. With the coming of permanent settlers in 1888-89, the community was renamed. Two of the settlers threw a dime in the air and shot at it to determine who would have the honor of naming the town. "I hope you lose," said one. His opponent did, and the winner chose the name Hope.

In 1912 the community hoped to be on a railroad which was being built between Artesia and El Paso. Part of the roadbed was completed. However, money to complete the railroad was to come from Lord Pierson, a British financier. Lord Pierson went down on the ill-fated Titanic, sinking Hope's hopes for a railroad.

Lower Peñasco

This old farming and ranching community was named for the Rio Peñasco (rocky river), which lived up to its name. Except during periods of heavy runoff, the river frequently disappeared beneath the sand and gravel of its bed, leaving only sinkholes full of water. Early settlers dug ditches around the sinkholes and packed the river bed by driving cattle over it. In this way, they created a new river bed, a man-made river which lengthened the Rio Peñasco by some twenty-five miles.

Elk

In the early days, large herds of elk roamed the area. Established between 1885 and 1887, the town was initially called York or Yorktown for the York Ranch which was located in Elk Canyon. Eventually it took its name from the canyon. Archaeologists have removed artifacts from several sites in the area. One contained an unbroken pot full of burnt beans, indicating hasty flight by the inhabitants.

Mayhill

The community was settled as Upper Peñasco in 1876 by immigrants from Texas who were interested in lumbering, sheep ranching, farming, fruit, and truck gardening. There was an Apache stronghold in the hills west of the village. In 1854 Capt. Henry W. Stanton raided the Apaches, destroying 200 dwellings. The following year Stanton lost his life on Mayhill Mesa during a fight with the Mescalero Apaches.

The name of the town was changed to honor John F. Mahill, a pioneer settler from Missouri; however, the postmaster made a spelling error when he sent in the application, and it has been Mayhill ever since.

Cloudcroft

This mountain village was established in 1899 when Charles B. Eddy built a branch line of the El Paso & Northeastern Railroad to take timber out of the Sacramento Mountains. The railroad was dubbed the "Cloud-Climbing Railroad." All that is left of the railroad is a vestige of the curved trestle.

The railroad built a lodge for construction workers. The construction workers left, and a community grew around the lodge as it became a popular summer resort for El Pasoans. The lodge burned in 1909 but was rebuilt. Guests have included Pancho Villa, Gilbert Roland, Clark Gable, and Judy Garland. At 9,200 feet, the lodge's nine-hole golf course is the highest in the United States. Golfers are asked not to feed the bears on the ninth green.

Winter visitors have been attracted by construction of the southernmost ski area in the United States, and the cars of local residents wear bumper stickers which say: THINK SNOW.

Trestle of the "Cloud-Climbing Railroad."
—Photo by the authors

NM 6563
Sunspot

NM 6563 leads to Sunspot, where Sacramento Peak Observatory, one of the world's largest solar observation centers, studies the sun's gaseous outer envelope and sunspots. The Tower Telescope is a massive structure reaching thirteen stories above the ground. There are daily self-guided tours year-around and guided tours on Saturday afternoons May through October.

Mountain Park

Settled in the 1880s, Mountain Park was first called Fresnal. Archaeological digs in the nearby Fresnal Rock Shelter have unearthed evidence of prehistoric people from 700-800 A.D. who quarried rock with which to build hearths and fashioned stone tools, *manos* and *metates*, for grinding grain.

High Rolls

"Rolls" is local usage referring to the rapids on Fresnal Creek; however, the postmaster noted, "If you ever lie down and start rolling, you won't stop until you reach the next county—forty miles away."

The area around High Rolls and Mountain Park is noted for apples, peaches, pears, and cherries. Annually, the towns combine in the sponsorship of a Cherry Festival. If the year's crop has been good, visitors can pick cherries from the trees; otherwise, the cherries they buy may come from California.

La Luz

To visit La Luz, turn off onto NM 545 just before reaching US 54. In 1719 two Franciscans came by and founded a mission, Nuestra Señora de la Luz (Our Lady of Light). Not much happened after that until immigrants came from Mexico in 1863. Still later, Roland Hazard came from Rhode Island. He built a pottery factory which gained a national reputation. He also built an inn. Both were located up La Luz Canyon. The inn was called Mi Casa (my house) and served as a stage stop during the late 1800s and a popular eating establishment in the early 1900s.

The serenity of the present sleepy village belies its past. It became a popular stopping place for brawling soldiers from Fort Stanton. Here John Good built a ten-room adobe house. That made La Luz the focal point of the range war which erupted between Good and political power Oliver Lee.

On August 25, 1888, the newspaper reported, "The whole country is up in arms, and such a reign of terror has not been known since the Lincoln County War." Sixty citizens of La Luz sent a petition to Las Cruces, the county seat, asking the sheriff to come and disarm the factions.

US 285
Seven Rivers—Loving

Seven Rivers

If a television producer could film the events which took place in Seven Rivers, he would be assured of raw material for a series that could last a lifetime. Seven Rivers, where seven arroyos lead into the Pecos River, was settled in 1870 by Pa and Ma Jones, who came from Virginia by ox-wagon. The spot became a stopping place on the cattle trail from Texas and a trading post for Pecos Valley ranchers.

Initially it was known as Dogtown. It was renamed Seven Rivers. It soon became a truly "wild and wooly" community. One saloon boasted "a door with easy hinges": It could be removed quickly to serve as a stretcher for a customer who had been too slow on the draw. As early settlers told it, cowboys shot sheepmen and buried them in shallow graves with their toes sticking out.

At one point, Seven Rivers had aspirations to become the county seat of Eddy County. Today, nothing is left but ruins and a cemetery populated by the remains of those who helped create the Western tradition by dying with their boots on. Because of the Brantley Dam, the last remains of the old town will be covered by water.

As bodies from the old cemetery were being prepared for reinterment in the Twin Oaks Cemetery in Artesia, anthropologists and forensic scientists discovered that the reputation of Seven Rivers was not without reason. Bullet or knife fragments were found in the bodies of ten of fourteen men in the 18 to 45 age group. Two had knives still in place, a third had a knife wound in the head. Although many men may have died with their boots on, none was buried in his boots. In those days boots were too expensive to waste by burial in a grave.

Brantley Dam

McMillan Dam and Avalon Dam, north of Carlsbad, were completed by 1893, but they had to be rebuilt after extensive flood damage that year and reconstructed again in 1906 and 1908. Both the dams proved structurally incapable of holding back major floods. Additionally, there was a buildup of silt and sediment.

In 1972 Congress approved the construction of Brantley Dam, with a capability of holding back 40,000 acre feet of Pecos River flow and providing water for the Carlsbad Irrigation District. Preparation included archaeological excavation of the area to be flooded; relocation of cemeteries, highways, and railroad track; and, of course, construction. The first water flowed through the gates of the new dam in November, 1987.

Carlsbad

In 1880 Charles B. Eddy came from New York to the Seven Rivers area to go into the cattle business. Drought set in, and in 1887 Eddy teamed up with Pat Garrett, who had recently killed Billy the Kid. To solve the problem, they planned the Pecos Valley Land and Ditch Company.

This post office and store for the erstwhile ranch settlement of Queen was forty miles southwest of Carlsbad on NM137. The proprietor agreed to name the place Queen for use of water from the nearest ranch owned by the Queen brothers. —Courtesy El Paso Public Library

On September 15, 1888, Eddy was dedicating a townsite at Loving's Bend, an old ford on the Pecos River. Lillian Green, the daughter of one of the promoters, broke a bottle of champagne and named the town Eddy. (It must have been strictly ceremonial champagne, because Charles Bishop Eddy was a vehement teetotaler.)

Lots sold for $50, and the deed for each lot imposed a restriction against the manufacture, distribution, or sale of liquor. In 1891 the railroad reached Eddy, bringing construction workers with appetites for alcoholic beverages. As fast as saloonkeepers defied the restriction, Eddy won court injunctions to run them out of town. And out of town they went.

On May 7, 1892, the newspaper noted: "H. A. Bennett & Co. opened for business at 'Phenix,' Tuesday evening, having erected the first building in the new town." Eddy had a suburb. It consisted of saloons, gambling casinos, dance halls, and houses of ill repute. Before it was over with, there were reported to be underground tunnels so that prominent citizens from Eddy could make discreet visits. In 1898 a law-and-order slate of county officials was elected; the denizens of Phenix sensed the end. In September, 1895, they picked up, en masse, and moved to Arizona.

Some of the credit for Carlsbad's founding goes to the nickel cigar or, more specifically, to Robert W. Tansill whose stock in trade was the "Tansill Punch," a popular five-cent cigar of the 1880s. In 1888 Tansill left his Chicago cigar plant in charge of his son and went West for his health.

He arrived in a caravan of eighteen prairie schooners in time for the September, 1888, christening of Eddy. He was instrumental in much of Eddy's early development. He purchased a section of land ten miles south of Eddy and established a farm which was cited as a model operation. In 1894 he had 450 acres in alfalfa, 100 in Egyptian corn and sorghum, and 50 in fruit trees and grape vines. The names of a street and a dam keep his memory green in Carlsbad.

When it was learned the mineral content of water from a spring northwest of town rivaled that of the Karlsbad Springs in Czechoslovakia, agitation arose to change the name of the town from Eddy to Carlsbad. It was R. W. Tansill who suggested the name, but he died in 1902 before the change became official. The change was voted at an election on May 23, 1899, but the name was not officially changed until March 25, 1918.

The economy was primarily agricultural until nearby potash mines opened in 1931. (The potash was discovered by geologists

The town of Eddy shortly after it was established, before it was renamed Carlsbad. —Ladd, 1891

who were looking for oil.) The discovery of Carlsbad Caverns was an additional boon. Since the 1930s, Carlsbad's economy has been tied principally to potash mining and tourism.

Loving

The community was settled in 1891 by a group of fifty-four Swiss immigrants in search of irrigated farm land. Their canton in Switzerland was named Vaud (pronounced "voe"), so that is what they called their new home. They produced potatoes, wheat, barley, alfalfa, sorghum, Egyptian corn, watermelons, cantaloupes, sugar beets, and various fruits. The Swiss imported Italian laborers to work their farms.

At first the Italians lived in a nearby community called Lookout (now Malaga), but many bought farms from the Swiss and changed the name of the town to Florence in June, 1894. There was still another name-change in June, 1908, to honor Oliver Loving who, with Charles Goodnight had established the Goodnight-Loving cattle trail.

The old cemetery in Loving was witness to a bizarre incident. Joseph Jonathon Hoag died August 4, 1894. At the time of his death, the family did not erect a marker. In 1910 his son returned to place a headstone. He was not sure which grave was his father's, so he dug up bodies and examined skulls until he recognized his father's dental work and then set the marker which remains to this day.

Carlsbad Caverns National Park

In 1901 a young cowboy, James Larkin White, was riding across the Guadalupe foothills when he saw what appeared to be a cloud of smoke spiraling up in the distance. The smoke turned out to be bats, thousands of them, coming out of a cave. Two days later, White went back with coils of rope, a kerosene lantern, a canteen of water, some wire, and a hand axe. He fashioned a crude ladder with the rope and some sticks and climbed down into the cave. He told about it later in his autobiography, *The Discovery and History of Carlsbad Caverns*:

"I kept going until I found myself in the mightiest wilderness of strange formations a cowboy had ever laid eyes on."

When Jim White got back to tell other cowboys, nobody would believe him. In fact, it was years before he could interest anyone in visiting the cave. In the meantime, in 1903, he sank a shaft and began mining bat guano, a highly sought fertilizer.

After twenty years, White talked a photographer into taking pictures of the caverns. Word spread slowly. Finally, on October 25, 1923, by proclamation, President Coolidge established the Carlsbad National Monument. In January, 1924, *The National Geographic Magazine* described a visit:

Early-day visitors at Carlsbad Caverns.
—Courtesy El Paso Public Library

The cavern is reached over a road sadly in need of improvement. Like many of the roads in the sparsely settled Southwest, this one is kept passable by each vehicle following the tracks of the one that has gone before, until the ruts become too deep, when a new route is sought out among the rocks, through the thorny mesquite bushes and over the mats of prickly pear.

Two hours of jolting into the ruts and out of them brings us to the foot of a steep, rocky slope from which every vestige of soil has been washed away, leaving a barren pavement of limestone. Here the laboring machines come to a halt, while their overheated engines cool, and the much-shaken passengers stretch their cramped limbs and test the strength of the spines that cover a large melon cactus at the side of the road where we alight.

Up this rocky slope we must make our laborious way to a bench on the mountain side about 1,000 feet above the valley. Some of the party remain in the jolting machines; others prefer to walk.

Visitors entered the cavern two at a time in a steel bucket suspended on a wire cable. The real purpose of the apparatus was to bring out bat guano. In 1924, when the Department of the Interior began to keep records, there were 1,886 visitors. In 1987 there were 781,300.

There are more than seventy caves in Carlsbad Caverns National Park. Two are open for public tours, Carlsbad Caverns and "New Cave." Today, visitors either walk through the entrance or descend by elevator to a point 750 feet below the surface and begin their tour there.

A group of Carlsbad Caverns visitors admiring the formation known as the Temple of the Sun. —Courtesy New Mexico Economic Development & Tourism, No. 1069

descend by elevator to a point 750 feet below the surface and begin their tour there.

"Breakfast with the Bats" has become a popular annual event. Once a year during the summer, visitors gather to eat scrambled eggs and sausage while witnessing the return of the bats from a night of feasting on insects. The bats create an eerie whooshing sound as they fold their wings and free-fall into the entrance.

US 54
Pastura—Newman

Pastura

This tiny community on the Santa Fe Railroad was founded in 1901 by the Pastura Trading Company, an outlet of the Charles Ilfeld Company which dealt in sheep and cattle and mercantile goods. Pastura (Spanish for "pasturage" or "hay") was a fitting name for a community located in the midst of a vast stretch of grazing land.

The water at Pastura and other stops along the railroad route was unfit for use in locomotive boilers. The railroad piped water from Bonito Lake, 125 miles away, to use at water stops established along the railroad at 25-mile intervals.

Duran

The town was founded about 1901 by Hispanic families named Duran who worked for the Santa Fe Railroad. In addition to serving as a supply base for ranches in the area, Duran was a division point on the railroad, complete with repair shops and a roundhouse.

Torrance

This once-thriving town was located a half-mile west of US 54 about fifteen miles southwest of Duran. It was formerly the terminus of Francis J. Torrance's New Mexico Central Railroad, taken over by the Southern Pacific. Some 1,500 people lived in the town. The community no longer exists, but it was the location of the first U.S. mail contract for delivery of rural mail by automobile. The route was from Torrance to Roswell.

Corona

At 6,724 feet above sea level, Corona is cited by the Southern Pacific Railroad as the highest point on the line between Chicago and Los Angeles.

Greathouse's Tavern, a stage stop on the White Oaks-Las Vegas road, was located nearby. Operated by "Whiskey Jim" Greathouse, it was primarily a hideout for the likes of Billy the Kid. In November, 1880, James Carlyle, a popular White Oaks blacksmith, was killed at Greathouse's Tavern during a shoot-out. It is debatable whether Billy the Kid was responsible for the killing, but suspicion that he was guilty probably triggered Governor Lew Wallace's offer of $500 for the delivery of "Bonney alias 'The Kid' to the Sheriff of Lincoln County."

Corona was established in 1902 during construction of the El Paso & Northeastern Railroad. It became a prosperous agricultural and ranching town. During August-September, bean shellers ran sixteen hours a day processing crops from the area at the rate of a hundred pounds a minute.

Historical Excursion

NM 349
Ancho—White Oaks

Ancho

Located two miles off US 54 on NM 349, the erstwhile station on the Southern Pacific Railroad now serves to house a museum. As a town, Ancho has never amounted to much. It was established in 1899 with the coming of the railroad. It served as a trading center for ranchers who grazed cattle and sheep on the mountainsides and for miners who attempted to scratch gold out of the gullies and streams in the Jicarilla Mountains. For a time there was hope in Ancho when brick kilns were built to utilize nearby clay deposits. However, the bricks proved inferior and the project died aborning.

In 1954 Ancho's public school closed. In 1955 the main highway between Vaughn and Carrizozo bypassed the town. In 1959 the railroad canceled its stops at Ancho. But there was a savior waiting in the wings.

In 1912 a little girl named Lucy Straley was brought to Ancho. She grew up and married W. L. Silvers, a railroad man, and came to be called "Jackie." Jackie contracted a disease. She could not bear to throw anything away, and she could not refuse anything that was given to her. People allowed she was a great one for "keeping things," and gave her obsolete washing machines and rusty stoves instead of taking them to the town dump. Relatives willed her things. Friends and strangers gave her collections of rocks, cigar bands, dolls, bottles, dishes, pencils, and pens.

When the railroad station was abandoned, Jackie could not stand to see the old building and all the railroad equipment go to waste. She bought the station and had it moved next to her home to house her collections. In June, 1963, she had a grand opening of her museum, "My House of Old Things." People came from all over New Mexico. The Secretary of State was there to give the state's blessing. Newspaper reporters covered the event. Until her death in 1972, Jackie took great pleasure in conducting tours.

The museum is still there. There are no Rembrandts, no Egyptian mummies, and no crown jewels, but there is an amazing accumulation of Americana and railroad memorabilia. It provides a nostalgic trip for oldsters and an education for members of the younger generation who have little knowledge of pioneer life.

White Oaks

According to the story, in 1879 John Wilson had escaped from a Texas prison. He was heading west when he stopped off at a mining camp in the Jicarilla Mountains to visit two friends, Jack Winters and Harry Baxter. The day after his arrival, Wilson headed for the top of Baxter Mountain to reconnoiter his westward route. He took a pick with him and jokingly said he was going to find a gold mine.

Wilson returned to show Winters pieces of gold-flecked rock. Winters let out a yell, awakened Baxter, and the three set out by lantern light to where Wilson had found the rocks. The two miners planted stakes. They asked Wilson for his full name so they could stake a claim for him.

"I have no use for gold," said Wilson.

Wilson left the next day with gifts from his friends, nine silver dollars and a good pistol. Winters and Baxter eventually sold their North Homestake and South Homestake claims for $300,000 each. There were other mines with names like The Boston Boy, Lady

Godiva, Comstock, Little Mack, and the Old Abe. Old Abe produced more than $3,000,000 in gold.

During the 1880s and 1890s, White Oaks grew to be one of the "belles" of the territory. At its peak it boasted four newspapers, two hotels, three churches, a planing mill, a bank, and 4,000 people. Of course there were saloons and gambling houses. In the Little Casino, Madam Varnish, so-called because of her slick ways, dealt faro, roulette, and poker. In another saloon the proprietor sold three grades of whiskey at three different prices—all from the same barrel. The thirsty miners never caught on because each always ordered the same grade.

Emerson Hough was a newspaper reporter on the *Golden Era* during the 1880s. He dubbed White Oaks "Heart's Desire" in a novel of the same name which was published in 1903.

The bonanza lasted for twenty years. In 1898 railroad builders planned to run the main line of the El Paso and Northeastern through White Oaks, but the citizens were greedy; land prices were too high. Instead, the railroad bypassed White Oaks through Carrizozo.

After the gold boom, White Oaks survived into the 1950s as a trading center, school, and post office for communities in the area. After the town was abandoned, its buildings suffered considerable depredation; however, some are now being renovated and restored.

Motorists who wish to visit White Oaks without negotiating an unpaved road should continue on US 54 to the southern intersection of NM 349 and turn back to White Oaks on the paved portion of NM 349.

Carrizozo

This community owes its existence to high land prices in White Oaks. Prior to 1899 the Bar W and smaller outfits ran cattle on Carrizozo Flats in the upper end of the Tularosa Basin. When the El Paso and Northeastern Railroad extended its line through Carrizozo, business boomed. People came to fill jobs in the roundhouse and car repair yard and in other capacities.

The surrounding land opened for homestead and many railroad families filed on the open range, hoping to make the required improvements and receive their patents. The town was well underway, but it was not platted until 1907. "Carrizo" is the Spanish word for reed grass. It is said James Allcook, a ranch foreman, added a second *zo* to *Carrizo* to indicate abundance, making the town's name Carrizozo.

The railroad payroll lasted into the early 1940s, but it was dwindling. Diesel engines required neither water nor coal. It was no longer necessary to have track-repair crews every twelve miles. One by one, the depots requiring a 24-hour telegrapher on duty were eliminated.

Carrizozo survived the failure of the vital organ which had pumped lifeblood into the town. Today its residents are polishing up Carrizozo's association with the West, restoring buildings to their 1920s appearance, and pinning hopes on the tourist business. It advertises itself as a "Paradise in the Pines."

Oscuro

The community started life in 1899 as a pumping station on the railroad. In 1906 E. G. Rafferty of Chicago purchased land and laid out a townsite. He drilled for oil without success and Oscuro settled into an uneventful future.

Westward out of Oscuro a wispy road traces forty-five miles across lava beds, past Oscura Peak, and through Mockingbird Gap to Trinity Site where on July 16, 1945, the first atomic bomb was exploded. White Sands Missile Range was created that year and now, together with the Fort Bliss Military Reservation, occupies most of the land between Oscuro and El Paso. The road is closed to the public and nearby peaks bristle with antennas to track missiles which periodically stain a turquoise sky with contrails.

————Historical Sidebar————————————————

Trinity Site: The First A-Bomb

The first atomic-bomb test operation was known as Project Trinity. It took place early on Monday morning, July 16, 1945, in the lonely desert country some forty miles west of Oscuro. The area was being used as a bombing and gunnery range.

A 100-foot steel tower had been constructed at a point designated Ground Zero. The bomb was brought from the laboratory at Los Alamos. Scientists called it the "thing" or "gadget." Assembly of the active nuclear materials started on July 12 in the McDonald ranch house. The "thing" was installed atop the tower on Saturday, July 14, and installation of the detonators was started.

In the mean time, technicians were installing seismographic and photographic equipment at varying distances from the tower. Other instruments were set up to record radioactivity, temperature, air pressure, and other data. Three wooden shelters protected by concrete and earthen barricades were located 5.7 miles from Ground Zero. The one south of the tower was the control center. It was occupied by Dr. J. Robert Oppenheimer, head of the Los Alamos laboratory.

A fourth observation point was located at Base Camp, ten miles from Ground Zero, and a fifth was on Compania Hill, twenty miles away. Most of the scientists and observers were on Compania Hill, watching through dark glasses. The test was scheduled for four in the morning, but there was rain and lightning. Rain would increase the danger from fallout and interfere with observation. The rain stopped and the device was exploded at 5:30 a.m.

The blinding flash was visible over a radius of at least 160 miles. Glass windows were shattered 120 miles away in Silver City. Residents of Albuquerque saw the flash on the southern horizon and felt the tremor of the shock waves.

Closer to Ground Zero, a lead-lined tank ventured out to explore. It probed with instruments and scooped samples from the ground. The tower had virtually disappeared. Where it had been there was a crater about 400 yards in diameter and eight feet deep. The sand in the crater had been fused into a glass-like material the color of green jade. It would be dubbed Trinitite, after the code name of the project.

During the first open house at Trinity Site in 1953, visitors wandered among the twisted remains of the tower which had held the bomb and picked up pieces of Trinitite, sand which had been fused by the heat of the bomb, with no thought of potential radiation hazard. —Photo by the Authors

Authorities encircled Trinity Site with more than a mile of chain-link fencing. Signs were posted warning of radioactivity. The site was off-limits to military and civilian personnel of the missile range; it was closed to the public. Presently, it lies within the impact area or safety zone for missiles fired into the northern part of White Sands Missile Range.

By 1953 much of the radioactivity had subsided and in September between 600 and 700 people attended the first Trinity Site open house. A few years later a small group from Tularosa visited the site on the anniversary of the explosion to conduct a religious service and pray for peace.

Trinity Site is closed except for an annual tour under the sponsorship of the U.S. Army and the Alamogordo Chamber of Commerce. Visitors are not allowed to pick up or dig for Trinitite. Radiation emissions at the site are said to be less than those of a radium dial watch; however, organizers say pregnant women and people who bring babies on the tour do so at their own risk.

Three Rivers

In 1873, Three Rivers was a railroad station for the Tres Ritos Ranch, established by Patrick Coghlan, who found his way from Ireland to New Mexico by way of a hitch in the U.S. Army and farming and ranching in Texas. There were occasional rumors from Texas that he had acquired his obviously substantial funding by selling other people's cattle.

Pat Coghlan began to acquire land and property, earning the title "the king of Tularosa" as he rode about with his wife in a carriage behind a coachman and high-stepping buckskin horses. He established a business partnership with William Bonney, alias Billy the Kid, in which he sold stock, supposedly from his ranch at Three Rivers but in reality rustled by Billy the Kid.

Coghlan managed to avoid prison, but the cost of his defense ate away at his fortune. He sold the Three Rivers Ranch to Senator Albert B. Fall, who would later have troubles of his own. Pat Coghlan died January 22, 1911; his estate totaled $319.20. It went to a woman who claimed he owed her $1,382.26.

Like Coghlan, Albert Fall got into difficulty. As a result of the Teapot Dome Scandal, he spent six months in prison for accepting bribes from business associates in return for granting them oil drilling rights in the Elk Hills Reserve in Wyoming.

Today, the principal attraction at Three Rivers is the Three Rivers Petroglyph National Recreation Site, located about five miles off US 54. Between 1000 and 1350 the prehistoric people who occupied the pueblo and pit houses spent a great deal of time picking and scratching in the brownish patina of the rocks in the area. Their pictorial records await translation.

Tularosa

The first attempt to settle this farming and ranching community was made in 1860 by a band of settlers from washed-out villages along the Rio Grande in the Mesilla Valley. Frequent Apache raids made the settlement on the edge of the Indian reservation untenable. It was abandoned.

In 1863 another attempt was made, and the present townsite was platted. Irrigated gardens and orchards flourished, but Indian raids continued. On one occasion, some women were frying bread in an adobe house which had a narrow window high up near the ceiling. Apaches came but could not get in because the women had barred the door. They climbed to the window and began fishing for the bread with long sticks. Finally, one bulky brave decided to come in. He had squeezed halfway through the window when one of the women threw the contents of a pail of hot lard on him. His screams frightened away the rest of the band.

As Fort Stanton provided protection, the community settled into idyllic existence which has been called its Golden Age. Peace did not last. Cattlemen arrived from Texas. With the discovery of gold near White Oaks, miners came. Black troops from the Tenth Cavalry came to patronize Pat Coghlan's saloon and bathe their feet in the community's irrigation ditches. There was trouble at the *bailes* (dances) when gringos insisted upon dancing with Mexican girls.

Tularosa survived the ordeal to win a place in both fiction and nonfiction. When Eugene Manlove Rhodes wrote of the Tularosa country he called it his "Little World" and dubbed Tularosa "Oasis." Later, Southwestern historian C. L. Sonnichsen chronicled the life and times of Tularosa in *Tularosa: Last of the Frontier West*.

Alamogordo

Since 1895, Charles B. Eddy had been trying to promote a railroad through the Tularosa Basin. In April, 1897, he induced a group of Eastern capitalists to come to San Antonio, New Mexico, in a private railroad car. Then he took them cross-country in four-horse coaches to White Oaks, from whence they could trace the line of his proposed railroad to El Paso. He wanted to show them the gold, coal, timber, and cattle which would support a railroad. The visitors ate from a special chuck wagon and slept in bedrolls. In October the capitalists agreed to back Charles B. Eddy and before the month was over he incorporated the El Paso and Northeastern Railroad.

Alamogordo (large cottonwood) then settled into business with trading, ranching, and lumbering as the principal industries. By 1950 the population was 6,728. During the next three decades the population almost quadrupled. This growth was largely due to nearby military activities and the nation's program of aerospace research and development.

Alamogordo is located in the midst of a vast stretch of desert, ideal for use as a bombing range. The Alamogordo Army Air Base was established to train B-17 and B-24 bomber crews. After the war the base was virtually abandoned, but it was reactivated as Holloman Air Force Base to serve as the Air Force's Research and Development Command and later was designated a Tactical Training Center. Immediately following World War II, German rocket scientists were brought to nearby White Sands Proving Ground (now White Sands Missile Range) to work on the development of rocketry on behalf of the United States.

The International Space Hall of Fame has been built to house artifacts relating to space pioneers. Exhibits include space launch vehicles, spacecraft, satellites, moon rocks, and astronaut attire. Closeby, the Tombaugh Space Instruction Center features spectacular movies on a four-story wrap-around screen. The facility is well worth the investment of an afternoon.

—— **Historical Sidebar** ————————————————————

Oliver Lee State Park

This 180-acre hide-away is located in a box canyon about two miles east of US 54 just south of Alamogordo. Dog Canyon was an Apache stronghold, a festering thorn in the side of the U.S. Army during the 1880s.

The Apaches found it first, a lush green oasis along a sparkling stream. They established a camp. Access was by a long trail across a 2,000-foot bluff with a thousand feet of perpendicular wall above and below. "Eyebrow Trail" it was called.

The Apaches perfected the "fool hen" trick. They would pick a fight with troopers, or steal horses and leave a trail. They would then head toward the box canyon at a crippled pace with gleeful soldiers following to reach out and pick up their fluttering quarry, only to have an avalanche of rocks, gunfire, and arrows hurtle down from Eyebrow Trail. In April, 1880, Capt. Carroll Henry was chasing a band of Apaches with detachments of the Ninth Cavalry with the intent of returning the Indians to the reservation. His report told what happened:

> The men were now suffering for water. I divided what was in my canteen amongst them; I believe I never felt the heat so much before. Several were suffering from slight sun-strokes. The bluffs shut off all air that was stirring and we were in a furnace.... The pack mules had been ordered to follow our trail; but being convinced that they could not overtake us before night—if they could at all—I ordered them back.... As the head of the column passed around the bluff it was received with vollies of musketry and several tons of rock.

A Frenchman, Francois Jean Rochas, was the first to settle in Dog Canyon in the mid-1880s. He built a crude rock house and raised cattle and cultivated various fruits. Cattlemen killed him in 1894 in a disagreement over water.

Oliver M. Lee, leading figure in a cattle war, established his ranch headquarters a quarter of a mile south of "Frenchy's Cabin." The state park service took over the site and rebuilt Lee's ranch house, turning it into a museum. There are displays on the Indians, Rochas, Lee, and recent archaeological finds. One can follow the old Indian trail. It climbs 3,000 feet in four miles.

Orogrande

Halfway between Alamogordo and El Paso, Texas, Orogrande (big gold) sits southeast of the Jarilla Mountains in lonely memory of the days when prospectors and miners swarmed in. The memories are rich. Back during 1905-06, when the town was called Jarilla, there were 2,000 people. There was a 32-bed hospital, a 63-room hotel, and a weekly newspaper, *The Jarilla Enterprise*. Gold and silver were not dreams; they were reality. Oliver Lee was piping water all the way from the Sacramento Mountains for use by the town and the railroad. The ruins of the smelter are northeast of town. Since its heyday there have been a few desultory efforts to revive mining. None has provided enough color to turn a profit.

Newman

This former railroad water-stop and trading post on the Texas border was named for L. E. Newman, an El Paso real estate man who sold building sites to homeseekers. Very little came of the development, and the post office which he instigated closed in 1914. Archaeologists have identified the location as the site of a prehistoric Indian pueblo.

US 70
Holloman Air Force Base—Organ

Holloman Air Force Base

Initially established during World War II to train bomber crews, Alamogordo Army Air Base was renamed to honor Col. George V. Holloman. In 1952, it became Holloman Air Development Center, a research and development facility. It now houses a Tactical Training center and is one of the mainstays of Alamogordo's economy.

A rocket-powered sled called MASE (Multi-Axis Seat Ejection) emulates aircraft in flight to test ejection seats of the future. —Courtesy Bob Pepper, Holloman Air Force Base

White Sands National Monument

Chemically, it is hydrous calcium sulfate—gypsum or, if heated, plaster—275 square miles of it, enough to reproduce the fireproof walls of every skyscraper in America and to duplicate every sheet of wallboard that was ever made. This vast white sand pile is advancing inexorably upon Alamogordo, at the rate of about 8 to 10 inches per year over a 25- to 30-mile front.

As one drives through the trackless waste, it is not hard to believe the old Spanish legend of a beautiful woman whose lover became lost in the endless expanse of shifting sand on the eve of her wedding. Wind swirls the sand and you see her standing on the summit of the dune just ahead, standing erect, peering into the shadows—*Pavlo Blanco*, the White Wraith. She poises for an instant, dressed in her flowing wedding gown, then runs along the rippled edge of the dune, disappearing with a sound halfway between a sigh and a sob. Just the wind? Well, maybe, but—

Since the area was proclaimed a national monument in January, 1933, students have probed the mysteries of the perpetually shifting sands. They have found two distinct animal species which have evolved in the sands. The normally brown bleached earless lizard, *Hilbrookia*, is white. Over eons, lighter members had sufficient protective coloring to escape their enemies until the species evolved. Then there is the Apache pocket mouse, as white as the driven sand. In the nearby red hills the pocket mice are rusty-hued. In the black lava beds north of White Sands another race is found with very dark fur.

White Sands National Monument is a family playground and picnic area. —Courtesy New Meexico Economic Development & Tourism, No. 886

The Fountain Murders

As US 70 leaves the White Sands National Monument and starts to rise toward San Agustin Pass, it cuts through a white outcropping. This gave the place its name, Chalk Hill. This was the scene of one of New Mexico's most celebrated unsolved mysteries.

On February 1, 1896, Col. Albert J. Fountain and his son Henry were riding in a wagon past Chalk Hill on a trip from Lincoln to Las Cruces when they disappeared, never to be seen again. Subsequent examination of tracks revealed that the wagon had been forced off the road by three riders. Trackers found blood on the ground, and they found the wagon twelve miles away. Colonel Fountain's possessions had been thoroughly rifled. But they found no bodies. Nevertheless, it was clearly a case of murder.

Colonel Fountain had gone to Lincoln to press charges against Oliver Lee and William McNew for "unlawful branding of cattle." Lee and McNew were ringleaders of what Fountain called the "Tularosa gang." During the court session thirty-two indictments were handed down, and Fountain was handed a slip of paper which told him that if he did not drop the cases he would never reach home alive. Such was the case.

Pat Garrett, the slayer of Billy the Kid, was called out of retirement to gather evidence and make arrests. Evidence pointed toward Oliver Lee, Jim Gilliland, and William McNew as prime suspects, and Pat Garrett took to the trail. It was a long trail fraught

Col. Albert J. Fountain: the murder of Colonel Fountain and his son is one of New Mexico's prime unsolved mysteries. —
Courtesy Leon C. Metz

with gunfire which resulted in the death of one of Garrett's deputies. Oliver Lee went into hiding and wrote letters to the Las Cruces *Independent Democrat* explaining his side of the affair. He would not surrender to Pat Garrett because Garrett had publicly threatened to kill him.

Ultimately, when Garrett appeared to be closing in, politicians took a hand in the game. In 1898 a new county, Otero County, was created out of the eastern half of Doña Ana County. It included the site of the Fountains's disappearance. The case was thus removed from Pat Garrett's jurisdiction.

Lee, Gilliland, and McNew then surrendered. In May and June, 1899, they were tried in Hillsboro and acquitted. The Fountains' disappearance remained a mystery. US 70 crosses the Otero-Doña Ana county line just west of the scene of that disappearance.

White Sands Missile Range

On February 20, 1945, White Sands Proving Ground was born out of necessity. The United States discovered it was ten years behind Germany as the Germans began to level London block by block with V-2 rockets. The lonely pastures of New Mexico were selected as a testing ground.

Among the European invasion force, a group of officers were assigned the task of rounding up knowledgeable German scientists and their equipment. At the rocket works at Peenemünde, Dr. Wernher von Braun and his associates gathered up files and headed

Making final adjustments to flight-control instrumentation prior to firing a captured German V-2 rocket.—U.S. Army Photo, courtesy Monte Marlin

for the American lines just ahead of the Russians. The total harvest was 118 scientists; they had 25 captured V-2 rockets to work on.

What had once been a lonely cattle range was dotted with firing areas and blockhouses, observation stations, laboratories, and barracks. Missiles with names like Falcon, Matador, Rascal, Nike, Aerobee, Honest John, Little John, Sergeant, Lacrosse, Hawk, and Dart were tested.

As missiles reached higher and farther, more land was needed. Cattlemen who had occupied the land for more than half a century took a dim view of being dispossessed. However, by 1956 the ranchers had seen the futility of further resistance against the government and were preparing to clear out—all except one.

John Prather was a vigorous eighty-two years of age. He had come from Texas in 1883 and established a ranch in the Sacramentos consisting of 4,000 acres of deeded land and 20,000 acres of state and federal land. In July, 1956, after the condemnation proceedings he announced, "I'm not moving." He let it be known that anybody who tried to put him off his land was liable to get hurt.

When the U.S. District Court at Albuquerque ordered the ranchers to move by March 30, 1957, John Prather said, "I'm going to die at home."

The Army sweetened the pot. They would give Prather $200,000 for his land and let him keep his ranch house with fifteen acres as long as he lived. Prather allowed he would go home and think it over. The negotiators asked him if he wasn't afraid to live in the midst of all that shooting.

"I am not afraid of missiles. I've raised mules all my life," said Prather.

The Army named August 1, 1957, as the final date for John Prather's evacuation and sat back to await developments. Prather was quoted in the El Paso *Times* on July 19 and 24:

> "We've fought a hard battle against low cattle markets and droughts and depressions and big cow outfits for fifty years, and we don't know anything else to do but fight. And I've always figured I had a right to be buried here at home, where I've always worked. . . ."

The Army shied away from the encounter. They sent civilians, U.S. marshals. They caught Prather in the yard with nothing but a knife with which to defend himself. He kept it in his hand and defied the three men to touch him: "Just let me get my gun and we'll square off and have at it. I'm ready any time you are."

The civilians tossed the hot potato back to the Army. Officers mounted jeeps and went to visit Prather. The newspaper quoted him as saying, "I will kill the first man that steps into the door of my house." On August 9, 1957, the El Paso *Herald-Post* reported that District Judge Waldo Rogers of Albuquerque had issued a writ exempting Prather's ranch house and fifteen acres of land from seizure.

One determined 82-year-old New Mexican rancher had fronted the might of the Pentagon in single-handed battle and won.

Organ

Just west of the top of San Agustin Pass, Organ comes into view. It was rescued from ghost-town status as employees from White Sands Missile Range took up residence. The community began its life as a mining camp during the 1870s and yielded tons of lead, copper, and silver. One of the last businesses from the boom days was the L. B. Bentley Store. The store opened in 1903. During 1907, when the Torpedo Mine was running full blast, Bentley employed four clerks. That year, he grossed $50,000.

Bentley was an opportunist. He sold Green River and Old Taylor whiskey. His rival across the street sold Yellowstone. One day Bentley came across the body of an alcoholic miner who had died, his hand outstretched. Bentley put an empty Yellowstone whiskey bottle in the outstretched hand. He then broadcast the information, "If you look carefully, you'll see what killed him." His competitor experienced a drop in sales.

On February 29, 1908, Pat Garrett was murdered on the road between Organ and Las Cruces. It resulted from an argument over goats. Garrett, a cattleman, hated goats. Wayne Brazel and Carl Adamson leased ranch land from Garrett and then started raising goats on it. To make matters worse, they drove their goats past the front door of the Garrett ranch.

In December, 1907, Garrett found an old New Mexico law on the books making it illegal to herd livestock near a residence. He swore out a complaint with the justice of the peace in Organ. Brazel and Adamson were arrested. Since there was no courthouse in Organ, the trial was held in a butcher shop. An impartial jury could not be found, so court was recessed until spring.

Brazel and Adamson attempted to resolve the issue by selling the goats to Garrett. They met to discuss the deal on February 29, 1908. Garrett, Brazel, and Adamson were riding toward Las Cruces in a buggy. Near Alameda Arroyo they stopped the buggy and got out to urinate. Pat Garrett was shot in the back of the head while he was urinating.

Adamson and Brazel hurried to Las Cruces where Wayne Brazel surrendered to Deputy Sheriff Felipe Lucero:

"Lock me up. I've just killed Pat Garrett." Brazel pointed to Adamson. "He saw the whole thing and knows that I shot in self-defense."

When Brazel was indicted, the examining doctor called the slaying "murder" in "cold blood and in the first degree." When the trial was held, April 19, 1909, it took the jury only fifteen minutes to find Brazel not guilty. Frontier justice was indeed blind.

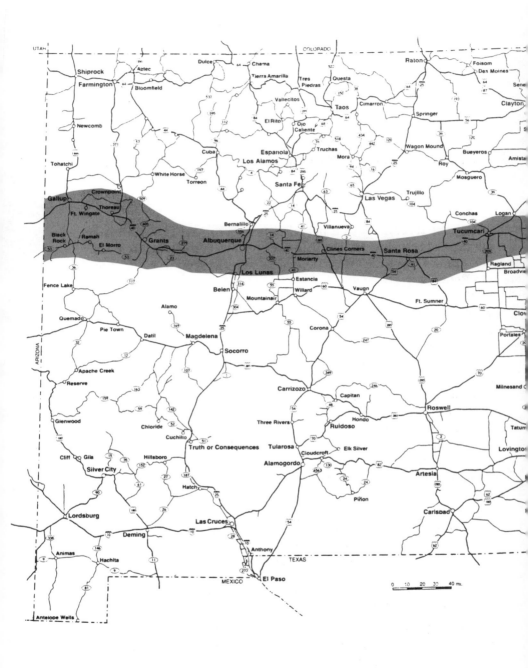

"MAIN STREET 66" IS NOW I-40

VIII. "Main Street 66" Is Now I-40

For the traveler with a nostalgic bent who participated in the opening of the West to motorized tourism or the exodus from the Dust Bowl during the Great Depression, I-40 is a poor substitute for old Route 66.

The old highway left the corner of Michigan Avenue and Jackson Boulevard in Chicago and spanned the nation's heartland through Illinois, Missouri, Oklahoma, and the Texas Panhandle. It entered New Mexico at Glenrio, a dusty cluster of stores and filling stations, passed through downtown Tucumcari and Albuquerque, dawdled along past Indian trading posts and reservations to Gallup, and continued on through Arizona to Santa Monica, California.

It formed the main streets of towns along the way. Traffic through those towns was slow, and you could pull over to the curb to negotiate with an Indian who was hawking turquoise-studded silver necklaces from the sidewalk.

John Steinbeck called it the "mother road." Ma and Pa Joad traveled it in *The Grapes of Wrath*:

> Highway 66 is the main migrant road. 66—the long concrete path across the country, waving gently up and down on the map, from the Mississippi to Bakersfield—over the red lands and the gray lands, twisting up and down into the mountains, crossing the Divide and down into the bright and terrible desert, and across the desert to the mountains again, and into the rich California valleys.

Route 66 was a friendly road, lined with small cafes, mom-and-pop tourist courts, and operators of two-pump filling stations who would *give* you a map if you were lost. The old road spawned songs and a TV show that caused viewers to nudge each other and point: "Do you remember—"

But it's gone now, a victim of "improving the flow of high-volume traffic." Route 66 was widened, repaved, straightened, and carefully routed around towns to avoid the retarding influence of civilization. Then, one day in 1984, the last of the old signs was taken down. I-40 is now a freeway that can be negotiated through New Mexico from border to border by a determined motorist in less that six hours.

Thomas W. Pew, Jr., the Editor-in-Chief of *American West,* bid the old road a sad farewell:

> No more homemade apple pie, real milk shakes, coffee that tastes like coffee. No more places to skinny-dip in a creek on a hot afternoon on the road, no more farms with a ramshackle fruit stand run by the youngest kid in the family, and no more "rooms for rent" for the families that are making the trek with some really hard times tugging them on toward California. In place of the color and adventure—the human experiences—on the old road are the familiar, sanitized rest stops, smelling of a pervasive, chemical, rest-room Gardenia that permeates the clothes and follows the traveler back to his car and for miles down the road.

The only way today's traveler can recapture the history and heritage of New Mexico that used to be visible from border to border along old Route 66 is to leave I-40 and prowl about the towns which have been bypassed.

Most towns have adapted to the transformation and found new life by luring motorists from the concrete ribbons of I-40 with towering signs advertising self-service stations and fast-food establishments; a few steadfastly persist in their old ways, keeping their quiet charm a secret from passengers in the cars that scream past; others stand as decaying examples of Americana, gradually falling prey to the same people who have expropriated all of the Burma Shave signs which used to furnish periodic amusement as one drove from Glenrio to Gallup.

I-40
The Staked Plain—Manuelito

The Staked Plain

From the east, I-40 enters New Mexico on the Staked Plain or Llano Estacado. This expanse of "high plain" includes some 30,000 square miles about one-third of which is in New Mexico. It stretches

This artistic rendition of the Staked Plain was made in 1853 during Lt. A.W. Whipple's exploration for a railroad route to the Pacific Ocean.

—Whipple, 1856

400 miles southward from the Canadian River in New Mexico and Oklahoma. The Staked Plain is reputed to be "as flat as any land surface in nature."

There is debate as to how the area got its name. In Spanish *estacada* means "palisade" or "fence," a term which could have been applied to the bordering escarpment. Others say the name came from men driving stakes into the ground to mark a route across the desolate stretch. A variation of this story concerns a group of Spanish padres who drove stakes into the ground and marked them with buffalo skulls so that they could be seen from a distance. A motorist on I-40 has no difficulty believing a third theory that the name derived from the thousands upon thousands of yuccas which thrust spear-like stalks into the air.

In 1849 Capt. Randolph B. Marcy described the Staked Plain as "a vast illimitable expanse of desert prairie . . . the great Zahara of North America. . . . even the savages dare not venture to cross it except at two or three places where they know water can be found."

Captain Marcy was grossly ill-informed. Traversed by the Great Comanche War Trail just east of what is now New Mexico, the Staked Plain teemed with Comanches. Early in the eighteenth century Spanish traders from Santa Fe, *comancheros*, began carrying on a lively trade with the Indians. At first they bartered for buffalo robes. Later, Josiah Gregg wrote that traders would "collect together several times a year, and launch upon the plains with a few trinkets and trumperies of all kinds, and perhaps a bag of bread and another of *pinole*, which they bartered for horses and mules."

As trade improved, the *comancheros* increased their stock: ammunition, lead, paint, knives, calico, and other items for the Indians' toilet and boudoir. The Comanches raided ranchers in West Texas and northern New Mexico, sometimes stealing as many as five hundred head of cattle at a time. They also mounted forays against caravans on the Santa Fe Trail.

The majority of the *comancheros* were native Spanish-Americans who knew the country well and had excellent rapport with the Indians. A few retired U.S. Army officers were in the trade, as well as some renegade Anglo-Americans. There were stories of them loaning guns and horses and waiting in Comanche camps for the Indians to return with stolen horses and cattle. Profits were tremendous. A loaf of bread would buy a cow; a keg of whiskey would get a whole herd.

In 1863 Fort Bascom was built some eight miles north of what is now Tucumcari to protect settlers and the Navajos at Bosque Redondo. With only eighty-eight men, the commander of Fort Bascom was sorely pressed to carry out his mission. One historian noted that Fort Bascom had three enemies: Comanches, *comancheros*, and Army red tape.

Parties would go out to intercept traders and arrest them if they had no licenses or had been trading in guns and ammunition. Frequently, soldiers would confiscate the trade goods for themselves, sometimes selling the contraband and putting the money into a fund to purchase supplies the Army would not buy for the desolate frontier post. Whiskey was consumed on the spot.

Civilian courts frustrated the Army's efforts to control the traders. On one occasion, soldiers arrested twenty traders who were tried in Santa Fe courts and promptly turned loose by juries composed of their sympathetic countrymen. In 1867, on Gallinas Creek in New Mexico, Charles Goodnight found six hundred head of cattle which had been stolen from his ranch near Fort Belknap, Texas. He went to court in Las Vegas to recover them. In spite of the fact that he proved by the *comancheros* themselves that they had brought three hundred thousand head of stolen cattle from Texas into New Mexico, his efforts were fruitless. He was assessed seventy-five dollars in court costs.

Finally, the beleaguered post commander complained that he could not control both the Comanches and the *comancheros* with only eighty-eight men. The Army responded by abandoning the post in December, 1870.

In the early days, car trouble in the desert could be a terrifying experience. —Courtesy El Paso Public Library

Operating out of Fort Concho, Texas, hard-bitten Col. Ranald S. Mackenzie finally put a damper on the business, using old Fort Bascom as a supply base during his campaign against the Comanches. He captured one of the traders, José Piedad Tafoya who knew the Staked Plain from border to border. Tafoya would not talk for fear of the Comanches. Mackenzie propped up a wagon tongue and hanged Tafoya from it until his tongue loosened. As a result, Mackenzie located the Indians' camp in Palo Duro Cañon and administered a crushing defeat.

Fort Bascom was a scrabbly frontier post on the south bank of the Canadian River. The officers' quarters were of sandstone, roofed with poles and earth. The remaining buildings were leaky adobe structures with earthen floors. Water for the garrison had to be hauled from the river and stored in barrels until the red mud settled.

It was no wonder the soldiers preferred whiskey, but it was illegal to sell spirits within five miles of a military post. A village began to grow to the south on Pajarito Creek, just outside the five-mile limit. Whiskey flowed like water. The soldiers named the burgeoning town Liberty. It became a stage stop between Las Vegas and Tascosa, Texas, and a gathering place for traders, sheepherders, *comancheros*, rustlers, and horse thieves.

Liberty outlived Fort Bascom to became a roaring cowtown, an oasis for thirsty cowpunchers from miles around. The settlement moved to what is now Tucumcari when the railroad came in 1901.

Today few traces remain of either Fort Bascom or Liberty. The sandstone of the officers' quarters crumbled or was hauled away, and the adobe washed back to the earth from whence it came. Liberty vanished completely from its location three miles north of Tucumcari.

Glenrio

Established on the Rock Island Railroad in 1903, Glenrio served as a railroad siding. After the opening of Route 66, it became the first stop in New Mexico for westbound motorists. It now serves the same function for motorists on I-40. Its name is a rare English-Spanish combination: English "glen" plus Spanish *rio* "river."

Endee (Exit 372)

The town is now little more than fading memories, but it had its day. It was located on the railroad, just south of Glenrio where NM 93 crosses the railroad. The name was the brand of the ND Ranch, established by the Day brothers, John E. and George, in 1882. It was a "blowoff" town for cowboys on a weekend spree. There were frequent Sunday morning burials for those who had been too slow on the draw the night before.

Bard (Exit 364)

This trading point on the railroad was never more than a few shacks and houses clustered around a store. The name is said to have been a transfer from a Texas town which had been so named because of a group of wandering musicians who held dances.

San Jon (Exit 356)

The name is probably a corruption of Spanish *zanjon* (deep gully). The first building was constructed in 1902, and the coming of the railroad in 1904 caused the town to boom as a trading center for farmers and ranchers.

Tucumcari (Exit 335)

Tucumcari was born out of a railroad construction camp in 1901 when the Rock Island Railroad was pushing a line toward the west coast. Merchants, gamblers, saloonkeepers, and madams in the hell-roaring cowtown of Liberty dismantled their establishments and moved three miles south to take advantage of the payrolls of the hard-working, hard-playing railroad gangs. At first, the railroad camp was called Six-Shooter Siding.

As the camp became a division point on the railroad, a more respectable name was needed, and Tucumcari was borrowed from a nearby mountain when the town was incorporated in 1903. The mountain was reputed to have been a Comanche lookout, gaining its name from the Comanche *tukamukaru*, "to lie in wait for someone or something to approach." However, even though it does not hold water historically, the tragic folktale which is frequently related to inquisitive tourists is more intriguing.

According to the yarn, an Apache maiden named Kari had a lover named Tocom. Tocom was killed by a rival, one Tonapon, who then went to claim his bride. Rather than submit to a man she did not love, Kari killed Tonapon and then took her own life. Kari's father, Wautonomah, was so distraught at the death of his daughter that he stabbed himself. As he expired, he cried, *"Tocom! Kari!"*

After Indian Territory was opened in Oklahoma, the Tucumcari area got an overflow of homesteaders who had arrived in Indian Territory too late to get land. By 1907 there were twenty small towns scattered about Tucumcari with names such as Ogle's Flats and Endee. In 1908 and 1909 Nara Visa, located on the railroad, had three weekly newspapers; Logan and Montoya had two each. But it was a hard-scrabble life for a dry-land farmer during the Great Depression and the Dust Bowl Era. Most of the towns reverted to cow pastures. Today few of them remain and none is large enough to support a newspaper.

The area owes its life to Conchas Dam. The dam across the South Canadian River was authorized in 1935 and completed in 1940 to irrigate some 40,000 acres of land around Tucumcari. As cow pastures were broken up and sold for irrigated farms, the town lost its place as a ranching center and most of the flavor of a western community.

With the demise of Route 66, I-40 bypassed Tucumcari to the south, and development has gravitated toward the interstate, causing the old historic heart of the town to die on the vine.

Fort Butler

Some old maps of New Mexico show "Fort Butler" in the vicinity of present-day Tucumcari, and it is designated on some lists as a "ghost town." The fort is indeed a ghost. It never existed. Fort Butler was authorized but it was never built.

Newkirk (Exit 300)

This community started as a trading post on the railroad in 1901. It was called Conant after James P. Conant, an early rancher. A settler from Newkirk, Oklahoma, renamed it in 1910. Today it draws most of its traffic from travelers who are taking NM 129 north to Conchas Lake State Park.

Santa Rosa (Exit 276)

Ranching began in the Santa Rosa area in 1824 when the Hacienda de Agua Negra Land Grant (Dark Water Estate) was bestowed upon Don Antonio Sandoval and his wife, Doña Ursula Chávez Sandoval by the Republic of Mexico.

In 1865 Don Celso Baca was an officer in Col. Kit Carson's First Regiment of New Mexico Volunteers. During Carson's campaign to intern Navajos at Bosque Redondo about fifty miles south of present-day Santa Rosa, Baca started a ranching operation on El Rito Creek just east of the Pecos River.

Don Celso controlled a large area of land, including much of the Sandoval land grant, in a cattle empire which lasted until 1910. His headquarters on the south edge of town, the Don Celso Territorial House, has been restored and may be viewed by appointment. Don Celso also built a private chapel, dedicated to Santa Rosa de Lima, the first saint canonized from the New World. The chapel, now in ruins, is across the road from Don Celso's hacienda. The town took its name from the patron saint of the chapel.

Railroads arrived in Santa Rosa, the Rock Island connected with what would become the Southern Pacific. The railroads brought a smallpox epidemic and prosperity to offset the pestilence. In 1901 there were approximately 4,000 members of construction crews and hangers-on. There was a proliferation of saloons with lunch counters and poker tables. Card sharks and tinhorn gamblers abounded.

Santa Rosa had its share of characters. There was Cherokee Dora, a hard-riding, hard-drinking, bronco-busting lady. She toted a six-shooter and wore cowboy clothing with a split skirt rather than chaps. She was reported to have the proverbial heart of gold. On one occasion she made a round-trip ride to Las Vegas for medical supplies needed for an injured construction worker.

Another lady, Six-Shooter Fannie, livened the community. She earned her name by periodically shooting up the town. However, since she took careful aim at the sky, she did no harm and no one bothered her. By 1910 the railroad shops and the workers were gone, and the town's population stabilized at about 1,000. More solid citizens took over.

Santa Rosa subsisted on ranching and farming until Route 66 began to bring tourists in the 1930s. The Flood Control Act of 1954 authorized the Santa Rosa Dam and Lake. This resulted in a recreational area only seven miles away. In the 1970s the community was panic-stricken when I-40 bypassed the city.

The most notable of these is the Blue Hole, located almost in the center of town. It is a mecca for scuba divers. The Blue Hole is sixty feet in diameter and eighty-one feet deep. It delivers 3,000 gallons-per-minute of water at a constant temperature of 61°. At the bottom of the Blue Hole, a colossal cave system yawns into blackness. The opening is barred by a 12-foot steel grate for the safety of divers.

Historical Excursion

NM 91
Puerto de Luna

It is a ten-mile drive along the Pecos River to Puerto de Luna (gate of the moon) at the end of NM 91. The town was founded in 1862 and was the county seat of Guadalupe County until the railroad came to Santa Rosa. Early settlers had to contend with frequent Indian raids.

There is no historical documentation, but down through the years it has been stoutly maintained that Coronado camped at Puerto de Luna in 1541 on his way to Kansas in search of Quivira. He is supposed to have bridged the Pecos River on his way, the first bridge to be built in New Mexico.

Clines Corners (Exit 218)

In spite of many billboards scattered along the interstate, this community is nothing but a service center for travelers—a filling station, restaurant, and souvenir shop—at the intersection of I-40 and US 285. Ray Cline opened a filling station here in 1934; it has served millions of travelers, first on Route 66 and now I-40.

Moriarty (Exit 197)

This small ranching community south of I-40 on NM 41 was established prior to the turn of the century. Michael Timothy Moriarty left Indianapolis in the early 1880s seeking a cure for rheumatism. He intended to return when his condition cleared. He settled on a sheep ranch in the Estancia Valley. He died in 1932, and it is not recorded whether he still suffered from rheumatism. However, his memory is perpetuated. Because his name was the same as Sherlock Holmes's archenemy, Professor Moriarty, a group of Sherlock Holmes enthusiasts meet annually in a local bar.

Edgewood (Exit 187)

This tiny bean- and wheat-farming community is south of I-40. The bean crop was at one time the most important feature of its economy. It was located on the New Mexico Central Railroad which connected Santa Fe and Corona, the "Bean Line." More recently, Edgewood is serving as a bedroom community for people who work in Albuquerque.

Tijeras (Exit 175)

Tijeras (scissors) on NM 337, just south of I-40, began as a settlement in Tijeras Canyon in 1856. For many years, imaginative investigators speculated that the name originated because two canyons intersect in such a way as to form an outline of an open pair of scissors. However, in reality it was more likely the family name of early settlers. Today the town is dominated by a cement plant.

Cañoncito Indian Reservation (Exit 131)

The Cañoncito Indian Reservation lies north of I-40. The band of some 1,200 Navajos occupying this small reservation has been separated from the main body of Navajos since early in the nineteenth century. They are called Diné Anai (the people who are enemies) by the Navajos on the large reservation to the northwest.

In 1818 the Navajos were in rebellion against the Spaniards. Joaquín, the leader of a small group, reported to the alcalde at Laguna that a large band of Navajos planned to attack the Spanish settlers. He claimed to have attempted unsuccessfully to prevent the attack. He then placed himself and his band of some two hundred followers under protection of the Spaniards. They settled at Cebolleta, near their present location.

As a result of Joaquín's betrayal, the Diné Anai were viewed with suspicion by the Spaniards and have never been fully trusted by the main Navajo tribe. Since 1818 they have lived apart from the rest of their tribesmen and have always existed in a comparatively impoverished state.

Mesita (Exit 117)

This small settlement of people from the Laguna Pueblo was established in the late 1870s by conservative Lagunas who felt their old ways and ceremonies were threatened by the dominant faction in the pueblo. They took their ritual equipment, altars, and an image of their patron saint. Later, the governor of the pueblo retrieved the image and ordered some of the altars destroyed.

Laguna (Exit 114)

Laguna Pueblo lies across the San Jose River from I-40 on NM 124. It was named for a lake that has disappeared. The pueblo was established in July, 1699, by order of the Spanish governor Pedro Rodríguez Cubero. The mission church, San José de Laguna, was built later that year. The church was used as a stable during and after the Pueblo Revolt and allowed to fall into ruins under Mexican rule. It was restored in 1935-36.

One of New Mexico's most famous lawsuits took place between Laguna Pueblo and nearby Ácoma Pueblo. A painting of St. Joseph which was believed to have miraculous powers was the focal point of the suit.

According to legend, this painting was given to Fray Juan Ramírez by King Charles II of Spain. Father Ramírez took the painting with him to Ácoma in 1629 when he founded the mission. Through this painting, the Indians appealed to St. Joseph in times of drought, pestilence, and illness or when an attack was expected from the Apaches or Navajos. Ácoma prospered. In the meantime, the neighboring Laguna Pueblo suffered from droughts, epidemics, floods, and disasters of all kinds. The people of Laguna finally sent

A Mexican carreta at Laguna Pueblo.
—Courtesy New Mexico Department of Development, No. 2014

a delegation to Ácoma asking to borrow the painting. There are two versions of the story regarding the loan.

One story is that the painting was loaned under condition that it be returned within a month, but at the end of that time the people of Laguna refused to give it up. The other version holds that the request to borrow was referred to the priests of both pueblos for decision. Fray Mariano de Jesús López, superior of the Franciscans, ordered that lots be drawn to determine if the painting should be loaned. The decision was against the loan.

However, warriors from Laguna stole the painting from Ácoma. Father López avoided a bloody war by convincing the Ácomas that they should allow the Lagunas to keep the painting for a short time. The people of Laguna began to prosper, and they refused to return the painting lest hard times return. A guard was placed over the painting day and night to keep the Ácomas from stealing it back.

The matter finally went to court in 1852 with Ácoma Pueblo the plaintiff and Laguna Pueblo the defendant. The United States District Court at Santa Fe ruled in Ácoma's favor. Laguna appealed the case to the Supreme Court. Through the long legal battle, attorneys' fees kept both pueblos poor. In 1857 the final decision went to Ácoma.

The Ácomas sent a delegation to Laguna to bring the sacred painting back home, but halfway there they found it resting under a tree. The Lagunas never told how it got there, and the Ácomas believe that when St. Joseph heard the court's decision he set out for home. The painting now hangs in the ancient mission church in Ácoma.

Historical Excursion

NM 279
Paguate—Cebolleta

Paguate

En route to Paguate, one passes the gigantic wasteland of Anaconda's Jackpile Mine. Until it closed in 1981, it was the largest open-pit uranium mine in the world. For more than twenty-five years, it provided jobs for residents of Laguna, Paguate, and other towns in the area.

Paguate grew out of a summer colony for the Laguna Indians. Prior to 1870 it was a temporary settlement. The old stone and adobe houses of the community were augmented by more modern dwellings during the uranium boom.

Bibo

Were it not for the church one would hardly notice the ruins of this old settlement. It was operated as a trading post and post office by Benjamin Bibo. Benjamin was one of six Bibo brothers, German-Jewish immigrants who were prominent in the mercantile trade in New Mexico. The post office was active from 1905 until 1920. There are several abandoned uranium mines in the area.

Cebolleta

On old maps the name is spelled Seboyeta. *Cebolleta* (small onion) comes from the old Spanish name for nearby Mount Taylor. Cebolleta was one of the few missions which the Franciscans attempted to establish among the warlike Navajos, hoping to wean them from their nomadic ways. It was not successful.

In 1749, after the decision was made to found the mission, two priests got into a jurisdictional dispute over whether a visiting priest had the right over the resident friar to baptize. They also disputed over selecting a name for the mission. Meanwhile, the Navajos claimed that if they consented to settle under the auspices of a missionary they would be prevented from hunting. Further, they feared they would be punished for not being able to learn the doctrine of the church.

A resident priest lived at Cebolleta for five months under primitive conditions while he tried to teach the catechism to the Indians. The Navajos told him they did not want to stay in pueblos. They "could not become Christians or stay in one place because they had been raised like deer." An interpreter told the priests, "I know all these people well, for they are my people and my relatives, and I say that neither now nor ever will they be Christians. They may say yes in order to get what is offered them, but afterwards they say no."

The Spaniards committed a tactical error. In building the mission at Cebolleta they used forced labor by Indians from the Laguna Pueblo. The Navajos could see themselves in the same situation as the Lagunas. By 1750 the Navajos were tired of sedentary life and the mission at Cebolleta was abandoned.

Spanish colonists arrived to establish Cebolleta as a military outpost. An uneasy situation developed. The Navajos raided the colonists' crops and herds, and the colonists took part in slave raids among the Navajos. In 1804 the Navajos besieged the town and the governor had to obtain reinforcements from Mexico to subdue them.

Historical Excursion

NM 23
Ácoma Pueblo (Exit 108)

From I-40 some fifty miles from Albuquerque, to the south one sees a great sandstone rock, or *peñol*, looming almost 400 feet high. Atop that mesa is Ácoma Pueblo. Some say it is the oldest continuously occupied community in the United States. Archaeologists have confirmed habitation of the mesa back to 1075.

Today, only from ten to thirteen families live on the mesa. Life there is primitive: no electricity, no running water. Even dirt for the cemetery by the church must be brought from below. A few TV antennas indicate houses which have generators. "They cannot get along without their soap operas," explains a guide. Most of the Indians in the tribe have settled in nearby villages: Acomita, Laguna, McCartys, and Paraje.

Ácoma Pueblo may be the oldest continuously inhabited community in the United States, dating back to 1075 A.D. —Photo by Mark Nohl

The Ácomas called themselves *Akomi*, "People of the White Rock," and the pueblo on top of the mesa became known as "The Sky City." The village was first reported in the fall of 1540 by Hernando de Alvarado, one of Coronado's soldiers. This stronghold, accessible by a staircase cut in rock, remained impregnable against the Spaniards until 1599, when Don Juan de Oñate's men finally fought their way up to the pueblo.

The Spaniards vented their frustration from earlier defeat by killing the warriors in their kivas and taking away 500 women and children for "trial." The few surviving men over 25 were sentenced to the loss of one foot and "personal service" for 20 years; women and children over 12 were condemned to 20 years of slavery. Children under 12 were put in the care of priests. Ultimately, Oñate was tried and convicted for a variety of crimes against the Indians, but that did the Ácomas atop their faraway mesa no good. This harsh treatment notwithstanding, the Ácomas survived and flourish to this day.

According to a legend of the Ácoma people, one night far, far in the misty past atop a high mesa, their forebearers crawled from a hole in the earth, creeping like freshly hatched grasshoppers, their vulnerable bodies naked and soft, their eyes sightless. Iatik, the

365

mother, lined these helpless creatures up in a row facing east. Then she caused the sun to rise above the horizon. When its light shone on the babies' eyes they opened. From that time, the Ácomas practiced one of the most elaborate and poetical rites for introducing a newborn child into the world.

At the birth of a child, its father made a *wabani*, a long eagle feather with four smaller feathers attached. He took this fetish to the medicine man and asked him to come to his house and take his baby out to see the sun and to give it a name.

About two o'clock in the morning of the fourth day after birth, the medicine man and his wife arrived. While his wife was bathing the mother and the baby, the medicine man prepared an altar. First he made a sand painting, usually a turtle although it might be a horned toad, depending upon which he deemed to have the strongest medicine; then he laid out assorted fetishes and paraphernalia including a gourd rattle, perhaps a bear paw, a medicine bowl, a basket of prayer sticks, and several perfect ears of corn, full-kerneled to their tips and decorated with beads and parrot feathers.

The medicine man sat by the turtle's head and began to sing, keeping time with his rattle, until his wife finished the bathing. His wife then took a place on the floor with the baby on her lap, and the mother sat beside her. The medicine man continued singing, dipping the eagle plumes into the medicine bowl and sprinkling the baby from time to time.

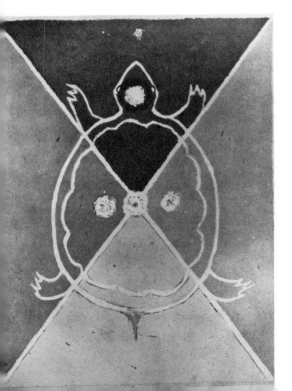

Sand painting for the Ácoma child-naming ceremony.
—Bureau of American Ethnology

Shortly before sunrise the medicine man asked the parents if they had prepared *wabani*, and the mother and father hurried to fetch the sacred eagle feathers. Standing on either side of the turtle's head, they said a lengthy prayer at the end of which they laid the *wabani* in the basket of prayer sticks.

Then the medicine man asked the parents if they had selected a name. If not, he provided one, such as "Laughs in the Morning" for a happy little girl or "Flying Wolf" for a boy who might become a fleet-footed hunter. It could not be the name of a recently dead relative lest, when pronounced aloud, his spirit and the hearts of those who mourned him would be disturbed. Just before sunrise, all went outdoors, the wife of the medicine man carrying the baby. She followed her husband to the east rim of the towering mesa. The parents waited a few steps outside the door of their house.

Armed with his eagle feathers, basket of prayer sticks, and other accoutrements of his station, the medicine man sat on the edge of the cliff praying to the sun. As the glowing ball rose out of the east, the medicine man's wife held the baby out toward him. After another prayer, the medicine man cast the basket of prayer sticks over the edge of the cliff to float down and carry his prayers to Iatik.

He then came toward the baby, gathering all the air that he could hold in his arms. He blew the air toward the baby. He repeated this from the north, the west, the south, and the east, speaking the child's name, thus giving the new arrival in the world the breath of life. The medicine man and his wife then returned to the house with the child.

"*K'aiya!*" "Hello!" the medicine man called out.

"*Hai yeh!*" answered the father.

"*Heh O!*" answered the mother.

"Baby Flying Wolf, this is his home," intoned the medicine man. "Here he comes; he is going to live here. May he have long life and all kinds of crops, fruits, game, and beads with him. He is coming in."

"Let him come in!" cried the parents.

The mother stood just inside the door to welcome the infant into her arms as the family gathered around. There were more prayers as the medicine man took the medicine bowl and poured a tiny bit into the baby's mouth. He also gave the mother and father a drink. Finally, his wife and he drank before performing ceremonial anointment of others who were present.

Before departure the medicine man prayed over the baby's cradle and sprinkled it with medicine. The mother selected one of the perfect ears of corn. The medicine man prayed over it and anointed it from the medicine bowl.

After the medicine man and his wife left, the parents shelled some of the perfect ear of corn, put the kernels into a bag, and tied it on the cradle board to the left side of the infant. The remainder of the ear was kept to be planted at planting time.

During the following months, the mother carefully monitored the development of her child. If it seemed slow in learning to talk, a few kernels of the corn were taken from the buckskin bag and placed in a mockingbird's nest. After a few days they were removed from the nest, ground, moistened, and put into the child's mouth.

Few whites ever hear the child's Indian name. Later he or she is christened by another name in the nearby Catholic mission church, San Esteban Rey. Construction of this massive adobe structure with ten-foot thick walls was started by Fray Juan Ramírez in 1629 and completed in 1640. Some historians say the present church was not built until toward the end of the century, but there is no doubt that it is the same structure described by Fray Francisco Atanasio Domínguez who made an inspection of New Mexican missions in 1776.

Feast day at Ácoma Pueblo in 1890. —Lummis, 1893

San Fidel (Exit 96)

On NM 124 north of I-40, San Fidel was once a trading center for ranchers. The community was originally called La Vega de San José. The first settlers were Baltazar Jaramillo and his family, about 1868. Today, the community is dominated by a church complex.

McCartys (Exit 96)

This Indian community with the very Anglo name came into being with the construction of the Santa Fe Railroad and took its name from a contractor who camped in the area. It is also called Santa María de Ácoma. Just above the settlement is a half-size replica of the old mission church in Ácoma Pueblo.

Grants (Exit 85)

The history of Grants began in 1872 when Jesús Blea homesteaded on the south side of San Jose Creek. He built his home in a grove of cottonwood trees and called it Los Alamitos (little cottonwoods). In 1881 the Atlantic and Pacific Railroad (later the Santa Fe) came and three brothers—Angus A., Lewis A., and John R. Grant—had a contract to build the section from Isleta Pueblo to Needles, California.

They employed about 4,000 men, mostly Irish, and used 2,000 mules. The first settlement was known as Grant's Camp, and the community embarked upon a boom-bust history. With its first trading post, the incipient town acquired a social center complete with a saloon, post office, and general store. The owners, Sol Block and Emil Bibo tended store and refereed barroom brawls. They were assisted by Emil's brother Simon. Simon was deputy sheriff. He lived about sixty yards away and, on call, would come running, armed with a Winchester rifle.

On the afternoon of June 20, 1889, three beer-drinking cowboys came to town to celebrate having shipped a herd of cattle. In due time, they were told they had had enough to drink. They insisted upon sitting on the bar instead of in chairs. Block went for his gun and the cowboys jumped him. Emil went to get his brother. When it was all over, one of the cowboys was dead and another wounded. Passengers on the train through Grants that night reported the entire town was in darkness with armed men guarding the Block-Bibo store to prevent trouble.

In 1897, the last robbery of a Santa Fe train took place just east of Grants. The loot—$100,000—was never recovered. It was reported to have been buried under a juniper tree.

After the construction of the railroad, the population dwindled to a mere 350 in the late 1920s, but another boom was coming. With the construction of the Bluewater Dam, agriculture became a major factor in the local economy. Carrots were the principal crop. Because those grown in the area had unusually lush tops they were sought by Eastern markets. The first crop was shipped in 1939, and by 1941 an ice plant and several large packing sheds had been built. About 2,000 carloads a year were shipped at a value of $2,500,000. But the use of cellophane bagging nullified the value of the luxuriant carrot tops, and Grants was in for another bust.

Grants' next boom started in 1950. Paddy Martinez, a Navajo Indian who knew nothing about uranium, heard two prospectors talking about the subject at a lunch counter in Grants. One showed the other a dusty yellow rock which he said was carnotite. Paddy pastured sheep near Haystack Mountain, a butte resembling a haystack located about eighteen miles west of Grants. He remembered seeing similar rocks in an outcrop near Haystack Mountain. He brought some in to be assayed.

And that's how New Mexico's uranium boom got its start. It mushroomed to a modern-day gold rush. Grants got new schools, housing, and churches. In 1960, with a population of 10,274, it was designated a city. In 1981, it became the county seat of Cibola County, the first new county in New Mexico in thirty-two years. But the following year brought a decline in the uranium industry.

Big wages, big spenders, and big dreams evaporated. The citizens of Grants are waiting for another boom.

Historical Excursion

NM 53
San Rafael—
Zuñi Indian Reservation

NM 53 roughly follows one of the oldest roads in America, the Zuñi-Cíbola Trail, sometimes called "The Ancient Way." It was a trade route for Indians between Ácoma and Zuñi long before the arrival of the Spaniards. It passes the Malpais, named "bad land" by the Spaniards, now a national monument. It goes to El Morro—the water hole where Indians, Spaniards, Mexicans, and Americans left graffiti—and on to Zuñi, one of the Seven Cities of Cíbola. The U.S. Army surveyed it as a possible transcontinental railroad route in 1853. Parts of the Ancient Way became NM 53 in 1914.

San Rafael

On NM 53 four miles southwest of Grants, San Rafael was developed by settlers who homesteaded a meadow watered by Ojo del Gallo, a spring named after turkeys that came for water. At first the settlement was called El Gallo or simply Gallo. The community took its present name after the coming of the Catholic church. Historical evidence indicates that the site was visited by Francisco Vásquez de Coronado's expedition in 1540.

The settlement got its big boost in 1862 when the area was selected as the site of the original Fort Wingate. The fort provided a market for hay which the settlers grew on the rich meadow. Hay was baled by tamping it into a hole in the ground and tying the bundles with leather thongs.

The greatest obstacle to agriculture was lava rocks which had been strewn across the land by a nearby volcano. Don Sylvestre Mirabel, son of one of the original homesteaders, eventually became one of the richest men in the state. When asked how his family had cleared the land of rocks, he explained that they had placed one rock in each bale of hay that was sent to Fort Wingate.

The mission church in San Rafael.
—Photo by the authors

At that time, Fort Wingate was probably the only military post in the Southwest where ice was served year-around. Wagons were regularly sent to the nearby perpetual ice caves.

In 1868 Fort Wingate was moved to a site near present-day Gallup to be closer to the Navajo reservation. Today, in sleepy San Rafael, boarded-up vestiges of adobe and rock buildings testify to the town's age. The best preserved building is Mission San Rafael.

Bandera Crater—Ice Cave

Some 1,000 years ago a volcano on the lower tip of the Zuñi Mountains, now known as Bandera Crater, erupted, spreading jagged, broken lava over a strip some ten miles wide and twenty-five miles long. Indian legends tell of "fire rock" that buried their ancestors' fields. Molten lava flowed through tubes under the hardening crust, leaving caves in portions where the tubes have not collapsed. During the winters, cold air sinks into the caves and remains, insulated during the summers by the beds of porous lava on top. Over the years, water has seeped into the caves and frozen in centuries-deep layers of blue-green ice.

In 1540, Coronado was the first European visitor, brought by Zuñi guides. Since his visit, soldiers have used it as an ice supply, and countless travelers have paused to cool their heels in this "Icebox of the Desert." Only one of the several ice caves in the Malpais is developed for public visitation. A path leads to the cindery rim of Bandera Crater, 800 feet deep and 1,500 feet across.

Inside Bandera Crater. —Photo by the authors

The massive formation of El Morro is visible for miles. There are ruins of an Indian pueblo on top of the mesa. —Photo by the authors

El Morro National Monument

The gemstone of the excursion along NM 53 is El Morro (bluff or headland in Spanish), a massive sandstone mesa which rises 200 feet above the valley floor to form a landmark. At the base of the cliff is a pool fed by summer rains, twelve feet deep and holding about 200,000 gallons of water. Nearby on the cliff is a series of Indian petroglyphs: hand prints, foot prints, and a zigzag line pointing to a hole in the cliff. This has been translated to mean "Follow the hand and foot trail to the pool of water."

Two years before the founding of Jamestown and fifteen years before the Pilgrims landed at Plymouth Rock, Don Juan de Oñate left the first message on the rock:

> *Paso por aquí el adelantado Don Juan de Oñate del descubrimiento de la mar del sur a 16 de Abril de 1605.*

> Passed by here the Governor Don Juan de Oñate, from the discovery of the Sea of the South on the 16th of April, 1605.

By "Sea of the South," Oñate meant Gulf of California. Many Spaniards left a record of their passing. One of the most interesting involves a revision of an inscription by Don Juan de Eulate, governor of New Mexico 1618-1625. He left a somewhat self-serving message:

373

I am the captain General of the Providence of New Mexico for the King our Lord, passed by here on the return from the pueblos of Zuñi on the 29th of July the year 1620, and put them at peace at their humble petition, they asking favor as vassals of his Majesty and promising anew their obedience, all of which he did, with clemency, zeal, and prudence, as a most Christian-like XXXXXXX extraordinary and gallant soldier of enduring and praised memory.

The word which is crossed out appears to have been "gentleman." The assumption is that a later traveler who knew Governor Eulate took exception to the high-flown praise.

The first inscription in English was written in September, 1849. Lt. J. H. Simpson, an engineer for the U.S. Army and R. H. Kern, a Philadelphia artist, wrote: "Lt. J. H. Simpson USA & R. H. Kern Artist, visited and copied these inscriptions, September 17th 18th 1849."

Other Americans left records of their passing. In 1857 Lt. Edward Beale watered the twenty-five camels he was testing for the U.S. Army in the pool. He took time to make his mark upon the cliff. The next year John Udell, Holland, and Williamson scratched their names. They were members of the first emigrant train to try this new route to California. And there were more: Indian agents, traders, soldiers, surveyors, and settlers. The monument is not called Inscription Rock without reason.

At one point, some twelve feet above the ground, a series of notches has been cut in the sandstone, a precarious set of toeholds leading to the top of the mesa. On top are the ruins of Atsinna ("writing on rock" in Zuñi), a pueblo that was occupied during the

In 1849 an artist with James H. Simpson's expedition copied the Spanish inscriptions at El Morro. —Simpson, 1850

The pool at the base of the cliff at El Morro. The formation was called "the funnel." —Courtesy New Mexico Economic Development & Tourism, No. 24

thirteenth and fourteenth centuries. It was close to water and it could be defended easily. Some of the houses were three stories high. The communal complex sloped down the southern end of the mesa to take advantage of the sun. The Indians abandoned it during the fourteenth century, probably in order to move to better farmland around Zuñi.

Ramah

The town was settled in 1876 by Mormon missionaries to the Navajos. The original settlement was located at Savoya, six miles away, but that site was abandoned in favor of the present location. Originally, the community was called Navajo, but there was another town in New Mexico Territory with that name. Ramah was the hill cited in the Book of Mormon as the place where sacred records were hidden.

Men in Mormon colonies were selected to meet community needs for skilled manpower: a blacksmith, a tanner, and a stonemason. A midwife and, wherever possible, a teacher were also included. The

375

Mormons' practice of polygamy was a matter of concern to the nation.

It did no good for them to explain that only three percent of Mormon men entered into "plural marriage," as they preferred to call the practice, or that it was unusual for a man to keep more than one wife under a single roof. Each wife had her own home, and they saw to it that the husband's time was divided equally, usually in one-week intervals. The ire and indignation of the nation was aroused.

In 1862 an antipolygamy bill was passed by Congress. In 1882 the Edmunds law prohibited all who lived in polygamy from voting, holding public office, or serving on a jury. Effectively, this required that men with multiple wives choose between them. It also set zealous local lawmen to rooting out the evil.

In 1890 the president of the Latter-Day Saints church issued a Manifesto urging all members to comply with the laws of the land regarding marriage, ushering in an "era of good feeling" between the Mormons and the nation. Indictments against offenders were quashed and sentences commuted. Apparently this feeling did not seep into New Mexico. On February 27, 1900, an editorial in *The New Mexican* said:

> The Mormon colony at Ramah, Valencia county, seems to be a blot upon New Mexico that should be obliterated. . . . New Mexico cannot let this imputation of allowing polygamy within its borders to rest upon it, and the officers are called upon to investigate and sift the matter thoroughly. If the Mormons at Ramah are a peaceful, law-abiding people the world should be assured of it, but if they practice polygamy and other crimes against the law of the land the sooner the colony is transplanted to the penitentiary the better for the reputation of New Mexico.

Ramah generated one of the many stories about Billy the Kid's escape from death, according to Gary Tietjen in *Encounter With The Frontier*. When Billy the Kid was shot by Pat Garrett at Fort Sumner, his "body" was turned over to some Mexican women for burial. They substituted the body of a Mexican man who had died the night before. Billy the Kid was nursed back to life. He went to Ramah to live under the alias of John Miller.

In addition to religious persecution, Ramah suffered the problems common to most frontier communities. There were outlaws and rustlers, floods and droughts, grasshoppers and plagues. There were no doctors or medicines in early-day Ramah. Midwives did their best at nursing and using herbal remedies common to the frontier. Yarrow tea could be depended upon to break a fever;

graperoot was used for chancre and as a spring tonic; peppermint and sage tea treated stomach troubles. Infections were treated with kerosene. Turpentine was applied to wounds, and insect bites were eased with onion juice. Cocklebur tea would force measles to break out. Persistent open sores were treated with poultices of cow manure, still steaming with animal heat. The warm flesh of a freshly killed chicken would draw the poison from a rattlesnake bite.

In spite of or because of such practices, Ramah continued as a small town in the midst of the Ramah Navajo Indian Reservation, and so it is today.

Upper Nutria

West of the Zuñi farming village of Pescado, where US 53 crosses the Rio Pescado, a road leads north to Upper Nutria. Nutria Lake lies in a long, grassy valley; a nearby canyon is known to the Zuñis as *Yu' ashah kwi* (Lonesome Place). It is roamed mostly by fishermen, shepherds, and tourists with four-wheel drive vehicles.

At the end of the valley is an archaeological site known as the Village of the Great Kivas. It has a ceremonial room two feet wider in diameter than the largest at the Chaco Canyon ruins. The Village of the Great Kivas was once a major Anasazi dwelling, an outlier to Chaco Canyon.

The site was excavated by Frank Roberts in 1930-31. It was dated as being occupied from 1050 until the late 1100s. The area is noted for rock art in the nearby cliffs. Petroglyphs include drawings of insects, centipedes and ants, and a friendly-looking little creature known as the humpbacked flute player. There are drawings of half-moons and four-pointed stars. A researcher has noted that the astral etchings could have been made at the time a supernova explosion was recorded in China and Europe about 1056.

Zuñi Indian Reservation

The Zuñi Pueblo received its first visit from Europeans in 1539 when Fray Marcos de Niza saw Hawikúh village, apparently from a distance. The ruins of that village are fifteen miles southwest of present-day Zuñi. In 1539 the multistoried adobe buildings reflected the golden desert sunlight, and de Niza hastened back to Mexico with glowing tales of golden cities with treasure-laden streets. This prompted Coronado's search for the fabled Seven Cities of Cíbola. He arrived in July, 1540, and found nothing but

Ruins of the mission at Zuñi Pueblo. The church was completed in 1705.
—Courtesy New Mexico Economic Development & Tourism, No. 451

impoverished villages built of mud and stone. Of Fray Marcos de Niza he said, "I can assure you that he has not told you the truth in a single thing that he said."

Juan de Oñate arrived in 1598. Two priests were with him and they began to build missions in 1629. But the Zuñis did not cotton to Spanish religion. They killed two priests in 1632, abandoned their villages and fled to Thunder Mountain, now called Corn Mountain. After three years another set of priests enticed them back to the villages.

Even today, the white man's religion plays a minor role in the lives of the Zuñis, and the Zuñis still guard their tribal rites as zealously as they did in 1880 when Frank H. Cushing lived among them and attempted to gather information for the newly created Bureau of American Ethnology. Cushing was a self-invited guest in the governor's house. He announced his intention of watching the Keá-k'ok-shi, a sacred dance:

> "And *I* think," said he [the governor], as he set his mouth and glared at me with his black eyes, "that you will not see the *Keá-k'ok-shi* when it comes tomorrow."
>
> "*I* think I *shall*," was my reply.
>
> Next morning before I was awake, the herald and two or three *tinieutes* had come in, and, as I arose, were sitting along

The Dance of the Great Knife as witnessed by Frank H. Cushing at the Zuñi Pueblo in 1879.

—Cushing, Aug., 1893

the side of the house. The old chief had just prepared my morning meal, and gone out after something. I greeted all pleasantly and sat down to eat. Before I had half finished I heard the rattle and drum of the coming dance. I hastily jumped up, took my leather book-pouch from the antlers, and strapping it across my shoulder, started for the door. Two of the chiefs rushed ahead of me, caught me by the arms, and quietly remarked that it would be well for me to finish my breakfast. I asked them if the dance was coming. They said they didn't know. I replied that I did, and that I was going out to see it.

"Leave your books and pencils behind, then," said they.

"No, I must carry them wherever I go."

"If you put the shadows of the great dance down on the leaves of your books to-day, we shall cut them to pieces," they threatened.

Cushing learned to speak Zuñi fluently. Eventually he was initiated into the secret Priesthood of the Bow, "in many ways strangely like the Masonic Order, of which I have since become a member." He also became a Zuñi war chief and aided the Zuñis in fending off the encroachments of Navajos and Anglos. But in the end he violated the trust of his adopted tribe by publishing secret legends and ceremonial practices.

Frank H. Cushing in Zuñi attire after his initiation into the Bow Society. —Cushing, May, 1883

Like many ancient peoples, the Zuñis have a flood legend. It centers around Corn Mountain—*Dowa Yalanne* to the Zuñis—a sacred place. When water started to cover the earth, the Zuñis fled to their sanctuary atop the mountain. They watched the water rise higher and higher until it was ready to crest the top. Then it was revealed to them that they should sacrifice a male and female virgin.

A boy and girl were selected and dressed in traditional attire. Prayer sticks were prepared for them to take. They were led down a path lined with people who sprinkled them with sacred corn meal and invoked them with prayer as they went to the north rim of the mesa. As they entered the water, the flood began to recede. In time, two large stone spires formed where they touched the bottom of the mesa. Those spires are still at the north end of *Dowa Yalanne*.

At first glance, the Zuñi Pueblo looks like any small New Mexican town, but there are startling contrasts between the old and the new. Television antennas sprout from roofs while women bake outdoors in the traditional "beehive" ovens. The old mission was rebuilt in 1968 and is used by the villagers today. However, inside, the walls are decorated with murals of Zuñi religious figures; beneath the colorful rain dancers, Mudhead, the Father of the Kivas, and the masked Shalakos, traditional Stations of the Cross line the wall. Unlike most other New Mexican Indian pueblos, little remains of the ancient villages. The crumbling remains of the old adobe and stone structures have been replaced or hidden by cut-stone dwellings topped by tin roofs and new HUD houses. Grocery stores, arts and craft shops, and filling stations line the main street.

The Zuñis have the most elaborate ritual of any pueblo in New Mexico, the Shalako ceremony. It is a year-long celebration of life. The public portion takes place in late November or early December. Mudheads, clowns smeared with mud, announce the arrival of gods and the Shalako. The Shalako are ten-foot-tall masked dancers who are bedecked with raven and eagle feathers. Their final dance is the culmination of a year of planning and forty-nine days of ceremony. As during Frank Cushing's time, cameras, tape recorders, and sketch pads are not welcome.

Historical Excursion:

NM 605—NM 509
San Mateo—Ambrosia Lake

San Mateo

NM 605 (Exit 79) leads northward from Milan to San Mateo. One story says the town was founded in 1835 by Col. Manuel Cháves who rested under a tree here while on his way to Seboyeta (Cebolleta) from fighting Indians. The colonel decided to build a home and a chapel dedicated to St. Matthew. Another version has it that Roman A. Baca, Cháves's half-brother, led a band of colonists to the site after the Navajo campaign of 1855.

In either case, the community remained a sleepy trading center for sheep ranchers—a few adobe houses clustered about a small chapel—for more than a century. Then, uranium was found in the surrounding hills, and workers came to scar the countryside and set up trailers and build houses.

Ambrosia Lake

NM 509 takes off NM 605 eight miles west of San Mateo to Ambrosia Lake. This was a ranching area until uranium miners pierced the earth to remove the dusty, yellow radioactive rock and process it in a nearby milling operation.

The original name was La Laguna del Difunto Ambrosio, so named because the body of a man named Ambrosio was found floating in the lake; his body was pierced with arrows. The lake is now dry.

Thoreau (Exit 53)

This lumbering and ranching community on Route 66 and the Santa Fe Railroad was originally called Mitchell. When the railroad established a station it was renamed Thoreau, probably after the author Henry David Thoreau. However, the name of the community is pronounced locally as "through."

Coolidge (Exit 44)

The sleepy appearance of this community belies its turbulent past. Newspaper stories refer to a shooting and a hanging in Coolidge in 1882. The town was named for Thomas Jefferson Coolidge, a director of the old Atlantic and Pacific Railroad which became part of the Santa Fe Railroad.

Historical Excursion

NM 400
Fort Wingate

Fort Wingate, south of I-40 via Exit 33 to NM 400, has had two locations and a variety of names. In 1860 Fort Fauntleroy was established at Ojo del Oso (Bear Springs). It was named after Col. Thomas T. (Little Lord) Fauntleroy, who established the fort.

In 1862 Fauntleroy resigned from the U.S. Army to join the Confederate army. The fort was quickly renamed, Fort Lyon, for Brig. Gen. Nathaniel Lyon about whom there was no doubt of loyalty. He had recently lost his life fighting on the Union side.

Fort Lyon was partially abandoned during the Civil War, but in 1868 when the Navajos returned to the reservation in their original homeland, additional troops were needed. Troops from Fort Win-

Officers' row at Fort Wingate during the 1870s. —Beadle, 1873

homeland, additional troops were needed. Troops from Fort Wingate were moved from its location near present-day San Rafael, and Fort Lyon was renamed. Troops were continuously stationed there until 1911.

Some famous names have served: Douglas A. MacArthur was born there while his father commanded the post in 1880. John J. Pershing was stationed at Fort Wingate.

One of the regular duties of troops at Fort Wingate was to provide entertainment at the New Mexico Territorial Fair in Albuquerque. In 1903 the manager of the fair thought a battle between cavalry troops and Navajos would provide a lively spectacle. A sham battle was scheduled for Albuquerque's Old Town.

Both sides were issued blank cartridges. The cavalry was to ride past the grandstand toward a clump of bushes where the Indians were waiting in ambush. However, some of the Indians had substituted live ammunition for the blanks which they had been issued. They planned to shoot down as many of the cavalry as they could and escape in the confusion. An interpreter discovered the plot. The perpetrators were arrested and the cavalry troop rode thoughtfully back to Fort Wingate. The War Department issued an order forbidding future mock battles between U.S. troops and Indians.

Fort Wingate was deactivated in 1911, but it was reopened from 1912 to 1918 to house 4,000 Mexican refugees from the Pancho Villa revolution in Mexico. In 1918 the U.S. Army Ordnance Department took over the fort for munitions storage, and it still serves in that capacity. Many hogans and houses in the area have been built with ammunition cases from the fort.

Gallup (Exit 22)

First there was the Blue Goose Saloon; then came Gallup. The saloon was built in the 1860s close by a little adobe building which was the station for the Overland Mail, the Pony Express, and Wells Fargo. By 1881 the Iron Horse was on its way to replace the stagecoaches, freight wagons, and express riders which had provided the West with transportation. In 1882 the village was the end of the track, and the Blue Goose had a great deal of competition: twenty-two saloons and two dance halls. The patrons lived in tents and a few houses, and the town was in the process of getting a name.

David L. Gallup was the paymaster of the Atlantic and Pacific Railroad. On payday, railroad workers would say, "I'm going to Gallup's," meaning they were going to collect their wages. The name stuck; the Post Office Department made it official.

During its early days, Gallup acquired all the trappings of a frontier town, including Kitchen's Opera House and Bar. It was a two-story building with a hall and stage on the second floor and a

Joe Crazy Horse, a Zuñi war chief, at the Gallup ceremonial, August, 1939. It was Joe Crazy Horse who told another actor after two hard days of working in a movie, "Me tired playing Indian." —Courtesy New Mexico Economic Development & Tourism, No. 12,125

An exhibition of sand painting at the Gallup Indian Ceremonial.

bar on the first, known locally as "The Bucket of Blood." It served as an arena for prize fights, attracting some of the nation's top talent. Later it offered such plays as "Ten Nights in a Bar Room," "Quo Vadis," and "Uncle Tom's Cabin."

Prostitution and gambling, though illegal, were wide open to the patronage of soldiers, lumberjacks, miners, cowboys, and railroad employees. Frequent assessment of fines made taxation unnecessary. In December, 1892, the town board discovered the constable had been withholding half the fines he collected. One member of the board suggested the practice be stopped. Another member took a more positive approach:

"The only thing to be done is to chop off his head!" declared Frank Reitz.

The constable resigned immediately.

The Harvey House brought a measure of respectability to Gallup. The railroad restaurant offered travelers in the West good food served by pretty women. The Harvey Girls were recognized by their crisp white aprons and "Elsie collar" bows topping well-fitted black shirtwaist dresses. A number of these women married and settled in Gallup. When the Santa Fe train would stop, a porter would strike a brass gong announcing the first seating for dinner. The Harvey meals had as many as seven courses and even seconds—all for 75 cents.

A Navajo family on their way to shop in Gallup.
—Courtesy New Mexico Economic Development & Tourism, No. 936

Prior to the coming of the railroad, sheep- and cattlemen occupied the territory. The Government granted the railroad alternate sections of land on both sides of the tracks in a forty-mile strip. Ranchers were forced to graze their stock farther inland. The Atchison, Topeka & Santa Fe Railway had sent mining engineers to prospect for coal in 1879. The railroad supplied a ready market for coal, and mining to the north of Gallup became the most important factor in the local economy. However, as the United States moved toward the use of oil after World War II, the coal mines were closed in 1950.

The proliferation of highways, cheap motor fuel, and increased use of air transportation contributed to the decline of the railroads. During the 1940s, twenty-two passenger trains a day came through Gallup. By 1983 there were only two and they were in the endangered species category. Gallup's economic emphasis shifted to the tourist business and promotion of its long-time status as an Indian trading center. It advertised itself as "The Indian Capital."

Prior to 1978, the annual Intertribal Indian Ceremonial had been held in Gallup for fifty-six years. In 1978 the old ceremonial grounds were razed to make way for I-40, and the ceremonial was moved to Red Rock State Park on NM 556, in a spectacular canyon

386

six miles north of Gallup. Held in mid-August, the four-day ceremonial features Indian sports and rodeo, Indian dances, and exhibitions of arts and crafts.

Indian dances are the highlight of the affair with performances by Navajos, Pueblo tribes, Plains Indians, and a tribe from Mexico. The event begins with a parade through Gallup with frequent stops for dances to the accompaniment of throbbing drums. If one plans to attend the Intertribal Ceremonial, it is well to make reservations for lodgings far in advance.

Manuelito (Exit 8)

This Navajo settlement and trading post is more than a century old. It was named for Manuelito, a prominent Navajo chief who was elected in 1855 when a treaty, not ratified by Congress, was arranged with the Navajos to end their depredations. Lawlessness on their part continued for another eight years. When they were finally subjugated, Manuelito was made head of the police force and proved loyal to his trust

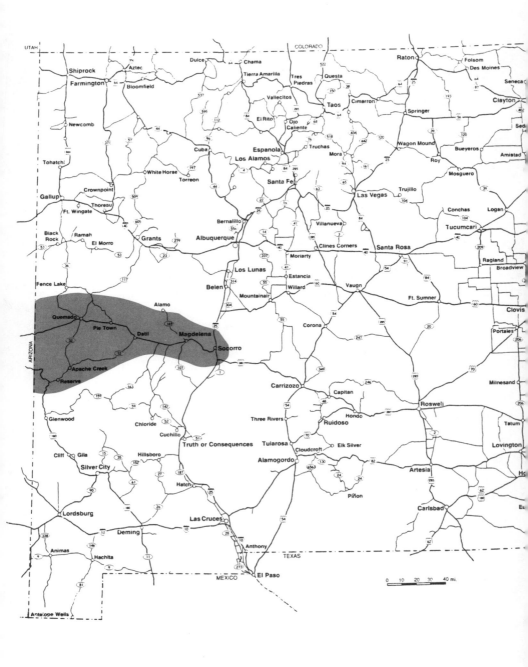

The Beefsteak Trail

IX. The Beefsteak Trail

The last regularly used cattle trail in the United States stretched 125 miles westward from Magdalena across the San Agustin Plains to Datil where the trail forked. One branch went northwest to Quemado and the other branch headed southwest through Horse Springs. With the coming of the railroad to Magdalena in 1884, the town began to flourish as a shipping point for cattle and sheep.

After the Apaches were subdued and placed on reservations, the cattle industry began to move into southwestern New Mexico. Marketing cattle involved trail drives to the railhead at Magdalena. The route was over what became known formally as the Magdalena Livestock Driveway. Informally it was the "Beefsteak Trail" or a "hoof highway." Its use began in January, 1885, and extended into the 1950s.

Annually, herds were gathered in the western part of New Mexico and in eastern Arizona for the drive to Magdalena. The driveway varied from a few hundred yards to five or six miles in width. The route went through timber land, over mesas, up and down canyons, and across the headwaters of Apache Creek where stock and horses were watered. The cattle were alternately driven and grazed.

The peak trailway year was 1919 when 21,677 cattle and 150,000 sheep were driven over the trail. Cattle usually moved at the rate of about ten miles a day and sheep at five, grazing as they went.

During times when the feed was good, cattle were allowed to graze by the hour. After they had eaten their fill and were ready to lie down, they were driven on.

During the days of the Civilian Conservation Corps, in the 1930s, the trailway across the San Agustin Plains was fenced and water wells were drilled at ten-mile intervals. With the coming of paved highways, problems developed because the herds had to cross the highway three times between Datil and Magdalena. The problem was not with the paving but with the white stripe down the middle.

When wild cattle who had spent their lives on mountain ranges came to the white line, they refused to cross. A bull would stand on the highway, paw at the white line, smell the paving on the other side, and refuse to cross. When a cowboy attempted forceful herding, the bull would duck under the horse's neck and head to the rear.

Various ploys were worked out. The herd would be nosed up to the highway with cowboys pressing close behind. Suddenly someone would rattle a tin can containing a rock and everybody would shout. If they were lucky the bellowing, frightened cattle would stampede across the road. More often, the cowboys would have to resort to hard labor. They would break out shovels and cover a stretch of the highway with sand in order to hide the white line.

Even after shipping cattle by transport truck became prevalent, old-time cattlemen preferred trail driving. Their stock arrived at market in better condition from grazing during the drive and would bring a better price than cattle which had been trucked. Cattle cannot graze during a truck ride, and they are "choused about," as the cattlemen put it. Knowing the condition of trail-driven cattle, buyers would write into their contracts that cattle must stand a twelve-hour shrink period in the pens before they were weighed.

In any herd there are "natural leaders." These were placed at the beginning or point of the herd and accompanied by a couple of experienced cowhands to keep the herd headed in the right direction. Flankers rode up and down the sides of the trail herd to head off revolutionaries who wanted to wander off on their own. Sore-footed cattle, skin and bones specimens, and lazy "all brawn and no brains" bulls gravitated to the rear of the herd where they were urged along by drag riders. The dusty job of riding drag fell to inexperienced riders or to the newest hands in the outfit.

The Beefsteak Trail roughly parallels US 60 between Magdalena and Datil and NM 12 from about ten miles northeast of Old Horse Springs.

Magdalena—Red Hill

Magdalena

Magdalena lies twenty-seven miles west of Socorro on US 60. The community had its beginning in the 1880s when prospectors came to probe the mountainsides in the area. They found lead and zinc. In 1884 the railroad built a spur line to haul the ore away, and Magdalena was on its way to becoming one of the largest cattle-shipping centers in the Southwest. It had a monopoly; there was no other station at which to load cattle between Magdalena and Arizona. The highway between Socorro and Magdalena approximates the old railroad line, called "The Elevator" because it climbed 2,000 feet in some sixteen miles.

Money was free and easy and liquor was abundant. During cattle-shipping time cattlemen arrived with their herds. While waiting for chugging switch engines to bring cars to load their cattle, the cowboys formed a contentious mixture with miners in local saloons. In June, sheepmen brought the "season's clip" to Magdalena in long wagon trains packed with bags of wool.

Agnes Morley Cleaveland, in her book *No Life for a Lady*, told of her mother's stipulation when renting a hotel room in Magdalena in 1886: "Please give us a room that is not directly over the barroom. I'm afraid those bullets will come up through the floor."

Most of Magdalena's early-day buildings are gone. However, the old railroad depot survives; it houses the city hall and the public library.

Kelly

The erstwhile town of Kelly, three miles southeast of Magdalena, had been there for almost a decade when Magdalena was settled. Kelly was laid out in 1870 by Andy Kelly, who owned a sawmill and worked a lead-zinc mine. Mining sustained the community until 1931. Kelly once had a population of 3,000 people who supported two churches, seven saloons, two dance halls, and two hotels.

As Magdalena grew, a lively rivalry developed between the two towns. Cowboys from Magdalena took delight in riding over to Kelly to shoot up dances. The railroad reached Kelly while Apaches were still active in the area; a string of railroad cars was kept on a siding to rush women and children to safety if the Indians attacked; however, the Indians contented themselves with stealing horses.

After the mines closed down, people came to salvage building materials from abandoned buildings, and Kelly became a vandalized ghost town that is now scarcely visible.

Historical Excursion

NM 169
Alamo Band Navajo Tribe

NM 169 leads northwest out of Magdalena through the Gallinas Mountains to the reservation of the Alamo Band Navajo Tribe where the Indians are not really Navajos at all. Most of the members of the Alamo Band are actually descended from Chiricahua Apaches who now live in Arizona. During the confusion of the 1870s, when the reservation system was established, this group apparently decided to let themselves be considered Navajo in order to keep their land and be recognized as an organized tribe. There are about 2,000 Indians on the reservation. The primary activity is raising sheep.

Very Large Array

As one drives west on US 60 from Magdalena, the Plains of San Agustin come into view, stretching out beyond the Magdalena Mountains. One's first impression is that he has come upon the setting for a multimillion-dollar science-fiction movie. Twenty-seven giant antennas with dishes 82 feet in diameter spread across the floor of the ancient lake bed. They are usually arranged in a gigantic Y-shape with each arm of the Y thirteen miles in length.

The highway map carries the cryptic notation "Nat'l Radio Astronomy Observatory, VLA Telescope," a masterpiece of understatement. The Very Large Array is high tech of the highest order, a gargantuan radio telescope which is used to "listen" to the stars. Just as an astronomer with an optical telescope can record an optical image of a stellar object, scientists at the Very Large Array can create an image from the radio waves emitted by quasars and galaxies which are far, far away in both space and time.

The radio waves from the violently pulsating quasars which formed the inner-cores of galaxies started their journeys to the earth billions of years ago. Thus, the scientists are not only looking out into the farthermost reaches of space but back into time to

At the Very Large Array 235-ton antennas are cocked to "listen" to distant stars. —Phtot by the authors

obtain information on the physical conditions, past history, and the evolution of celestial objects. The goal of the various experiments which are carried out is "a greater understanding of the cosmos."

In order to achieve results comparable to the multiple antennas in this vast array by use of a single antenna, its dish would have to be seventeen miles in diameter. By changing the separation of the antennas, the arms of the array can be varied from 2,000 feet to thirteen miles. This changes the resolution of the array, an effect somewhat similar to use of a zoom lens on a camera.

Each of the antennas weighs 235 tons. The antennas are carried along the array arms by a special self-propelled transporter on two parallel sets of railroad tracks. Each cleat on the treads of the huge transporter weighs a ton. During operation, the inner electronic workings of the antennas have to be cooled to 427° below zero.

The National Radio Astronomy Observatory began planning for the project in the early 1960s. The Very Large Array was completed in January, 1981, at a total cost of $78,600,000. The site on the Plains of San Agustin was chosen because of the absence of electrical interference.

Datil

Datil started in 1884 as Baldwin's, a stop on the wagon road between Magdalena and Quemado. The army established Camp Datil on Datil Creek a mile and a half to the north, manned by a unit of the 6th Cavalry. The mission was to check raids by the Gila Apaches. The camp remained until September, 1886.

In 1886 the stage stop became Datil by decree of the Post Office Department, named for the nearby mountains and canyon. The Spaniards had dubbed portions of the landscape datil ("date") after the date-like fruit of a species of yucca which has since disappeared because cattle liked the fruit.

The area around Datil was occupied by Indians of the Mogollon culture. Most of the early-day ranchers had an "Injun pot" or two which they had dug up from the ruins of Mogollon pit houses which dotted the country.

Datil is still a tiny village serving ranchers in the area. West of Datil just off US 66, the Bureau of Land Management has built a camp ground for motorists at Datil Well, which used to be a watering stop on the Beefsteak Highway.

Pie Town

Just west of where US 60 tops the Continental Divide at 7,796 feet above sea level, Pie Town has caused many a curious motorist to stop and ask the origin of the name. The community began with a filling station owner who had a mining claim on the site. When it appeared that US 60 would become a transcontinental route, he opened a roadside eating establishment and put up signs advertising his specialty. His first customers were road workers; motorists followed, and the Post Office Department approved use of the name.

Omega

This lonely gas-stop on the highway was established in 1870 as Rito (ceremony or little river) by Felipe Padilla. It was later called Sweazeville by a filling station owner named Sweaze. The name was changed to Omega, the final letter of the Greek alphabet, in 1938.

Quemado

Quemado was on the Beefsteak Trail between Springerville, Arizona, and the railhead at Magdalena. The community was founded by José Antonio Padilla who came from Belen with his family to homestead about 1880. He called the place Rito Quemado.

As with many communities, there is variance as to the origin of the name. *Quemado* means "burnt" in Spanish. One version says the village was so named because the sage and rabbit bush on both sides of the creek had been burned off by the Apaches. A second explanation is that the town is located near an extinct volcanic area and the land appears to have been scorched. Then there is a story about an Apache chief who had burned his hand in a campfire.

In any case, Padilla brought sheep with him and started the stock industry in this part of the territory. Other homesteaders followed, laboring against the harsh land to be able to send their annual herds to market over the trail to Magdalena. Then the Depression came, and by 1937 seventy percent of the residents of Catron County had gone on relief. The Government came up with a resettlement program. Better lands would be given to the homesteaders in exchange for their patents, land on which they could raise their own food and where their children would have easier access to schools. The homesteaders viewed this as a plot on the part of predatory cattle barons to get the land back.

The imminent arrival of a Government representative to explain the advantages of the resettlement program precipitated a near-riot in Quemado. Agnes Morley Cleaveland told about it in *No Life for a Lady*:

> In 1937 angry men muttered darkly in the streets of Quemado. On many a previous occasion in Quemado the muttering had given place to the spit of gunfire and men lying dead. But these angry men carried no six-shooters and they did not wear high-heeled boots and broad-brimmed hats. No saddled ponies stood at hitching-racks. These men had come to town in rickety automobiles over roads that had been surveyed and graded, even if not surfaced, roads which were 'maintained' and upon which they would not have to wait long before help reached them should the unforeseen mishap befall.

The Government's spokesman arrived to meet with the local Planning Board, ready to explain that the Government had made a mistake in inviting settlement of such "submarginal" lands in the first place. The Government had a new sense of social responsibility and was going to rectify past fumbles by giving the people a fair opportunity to make a living. The spokesman was met by a deputy sheriff who hustled him off to jail for his own protection. The mob finally dispersed and the Planning Board held its meeting in jail, confining their business to checking the current list of relief applicants. The issue of resettlement was left for later decision.

There was some bitterness on the part of the "predatory cattle barons." They had been there before the homesteaders. In a test against the land, many had lost; others had survived the Depression so far.

Today Quemado is a small trading town. The highway is strung with filling stations, cafes, and a few stores. The busy season comes in the fall when ranchers are rounding up their herds and visitors come to seek their help in hunting deer, antelope, elk, bear, and wild turkeys. Highway signs warn that the country is open range, and windmills stand against the sky turning fitfully to provide water for huddling clusters of cattle.

Red Hill

The post office of this ranching and lumbering community, eleven miles from the Arizona border, was active from 1935 until 1957. The community has since deteriorated to a single business establishment and a rest-stop on the highway.

During earlier days of ranching, New Mexican cattlemen along the Arizona border were particularly vulnerable to rustling. The story is told of an ex-inmate of the Arizona Territory penitentiary who managed to build a sizeable herd without rustling. He registered a brand according to law with the Arizona Live Stock Sanitary Board and moved to Graham County, close to the New Mexico Territory border. There he waited, branding iron dangling from his saddle, for New Mexican steers to drift across the boundary. By 1897 he had accumulated a foundation herd of some 1,100 head.

NM 12
Old Horse Springs—Reserve

Old Horse Springs

This small ranching community was just plain Horse Springs when the large, bubbling spring about a mile west of the present settlement served as a watering stop on the cattle trail to Magdalena. It got its name because some soldiers on their way from Socorro to Fort Tularosa lost a horse. On their return trip they found it at the spring.

Ranch roads frequently left something to be desired.
—Courtesy New Mexico Department of Development, No. 2295

Aragon

The little village in the Tularosa Valley about fifty miles south-east of Datil on NM 12 took its name from a Spanish family that arrived in New Mexico in 1693 to settle in the area. In 1872 it became the scene of an attempt to secure an armistice between the Chiricahua Apache chief Cochise and the United States.

Cochise had long carried out raids against Mexicans on both sides of the United States-Mexican border. Until 1860, he refrained from attacks upon Anglo-Americans and, thus, did not attract the ire of the U.S. Army. In January, 1861, an inexperienced lieutenant named George N. Bascom feigned friendship and captured Cochise to falsely accuse him of kidnapping a rancher's son. Cochise escaped, but six of his warriors were captured and hung. This episode, known as the "Bascom Affair," was followed by a twelve-year vendetta during which Cochise launched a war of retaliation against all whites, leaving a trail of plunder and pillage which terrorized the Southwest.

In 1871, as a solution to the problem, the Tularosa Apache Reservation was laid out. It stretched along the Tularosa River and its tributaries from the Datil Mountains south. A small adobe fort was built where Aragon is today, Fort Tularosa. By April, 1872, two companies of troops were ready to guard the Indians and about 500 Apaches arrived, but Cochise and his warriors were not among them.

A peace commission headed by Gen. Gordon Granger met with Cochise at Cañada Alamosa, along the Rio Alamosa northwest of present-day Truth or Consequences, to tell him and his warriors about the reservation which was offered. Cochise informed General Granger that he would never go to the Tularosa reservation:

> That is a long ways off. The flies in those mountains eat out the eyes of the horses. The bad spirits live there. I have drunk of those waters. . . . I do not want to leave here.

Less than half of the Apaches who were at Cañada Alamosa went to the Tularosa reservation. The remainder returned to the war-path with Cochise. In 1874 the Indians were moved to the Ojo Caliente Reservation and Fort Tularosa was abandoned. Today, Aragon is a picturesque village. An old burial ground for soldiers is the only remaining trace of Fort Tularosa.

Tularosa Cave is located a mile east of Aragon on the north side of Tularosa Canyon. Ancestors of today's Pueblo Indians occupied it from 400 B.C. to 1100 A.D.

Reserve

Reserve, the county seat of Catron County, was founded by Mormon cattlemen during the 1860s. Originally, the settlement along the San Francisco River consisted of three plazas about half a mile apart. Individually, they were known as the Upper, Middle, and Lower Plaza. Collectively, they were known as San Francisco Plaza or simply Frisco. The old Upper Plaza is today's town of Reserve.

The designation changed to Reserve when a U.S. forest ranger established the headquarters of the forest reserve in the town. Reserve's main street follows the San Francisco River and comes to an end just beyond the old Lower Plaza, now designated as San Francisco Plaza.

By the 1880s, a number of Texas cattlemen had ranches in the area, particularly John B. Slaughter. This was a period when there was considerable ill feeling between Anglos, particularly Texans, and individuals of Mexican ancestry. This was illustrated by the commonly voiced measurement of a gunman's prowess. It would be pointed out that a lawman or an outlaw had however-many notches on the grip of his gun indicating the number of men he had killed, "not counting Mexicans and Indians."

Frisco was a magnet for the cowboys on surrounding ranches when they were in a mood to celebrate. When they came to town, local citizens learned to stay indoors or out of the way.

One night in October, 1884, a group from the Slaughter ranch was on the prowl. After consuming a goodly quantity of nose-paint at the whiskey bar of Milligan's store, six or seven cowboys got hold of a Mexican called El Burro who had been so indiscreet as to venture out. The cowboys captured El Burro and laid him out on a counter; while one sat on his chest and arms and another on his lap, the others castrated the man. Epitacio Martínez, who happened to be present, objected. The cowboys tied Epitacio and measured off twenty or thirty paces. From that distance, they conducted target practice, betting drinks on who was the best shot. Epitacio was shot four times.

Pedro Sarracino, the deputy sheriff, knew that if he tried to arrest anybody, his life would be in immediate danger. Instead, he rode to Socorro and told Elfego Baca about the atrocities, thereby setting the stage for one of the West's epic gunfights.

Nineteen-year-old Elfego Baca was a champion of the Mexican underdog. He was also very handy with a pair of six-shooters. Baca put on a Prince Albert coat, loaded his six-shooters, and accompanied Sarracino to Frisco where they sought out the justice of the peace. While they were talking to the justice of the peace, two cowboys rode by "shooting up the town." The cowboys adjourned to Milligan's place for more drinking.

> I asked the J.P. why that should be allowed there. The judge told me that it couldn't be stopped, because the Slaughter outfit had about 150 cowboys. When a bunch of them came into town they shot dogs, chickens, cats, etc. Just then I saw a cowboy butt another on the head about three or four times. I walked up to the fellow using the gun, and he had already fired five shots. I commanded him to quit; that I was a self-made deputy in order to keep order. He turned around and shot my hat off.

Elfego Baca caught the miscreant and arrested him. A dozen cowboys came and demanded the release of their friend. Baca told them that he would count to three before he shot. The cowboys started to draw. Baca started to count:

"One, two, three."

Baca fired. The cowboys ran, but one man and his horse did not make it.

The cowboys returned with reinforcements about nine o'clock the next morning. Later testimony in court placed the number at about eighty. Baca recognized one of them.

"Hello, Mr. Wilson."

"Hello, you little Mexican."

Someone behind Wilson fired a gun. Baca drew his guns and backed into a small log *jacal*. It was a rickety structure with chinks as wide as the logs.

Bert Herne, from the Spur Ranch, rode forward and dismounted, "I'll get the little Mexican out of there."

Elfego Baca told about it years later: "I could see him when he got off his horse through the cracks of the door. I shot him with both guns at the same time." Subsequent court testimony indicated Herne was a Texas outlaw with a price on his head.

For thirty-three hours, the Texans alternated between going to a saloon to bolster their courage and shooting through the walls of the *jacal*. They attempted to burn the shed but could not because it had a thick dirt roof. They dynamited one corner. Still, Elfego Baca could shoot back. When it was all over, thirty-three hours later, Baca had killed four and wounded eight. He finally surrendered on his own terms.

He would not give up his guns. He and the deputy to whom he agreed to surrender would ride in a buckboard to Socorro. His "guards" would ride horseback ahead of him where he could keep an eye on them. Elfego spent four months in jail before the trial was moved to Albuquerque on a change of venue.

Testimony indicated that some 4,000 shots had been fired into the *jacal*. Everything inside, even a broomstick, had holes through it except for Elfego Baca and a statue of Saint Ann which he called Mi Señora Santa Ana. The door of the *jacal* was introduced in evidence; it had almost four hundred bullet holes. Elfego Baca was acquitted.

Today, Reserve continues to serve ranchers and farmers in the area, much as it did a century ago with a few changes. Instead of tethering horses to hitching rails, today's cowboys nose their pickups into curbstones.

X. Butterfield Overland Mail

In 1845, Congress turned its attention to the necessity for establishing postal communications with newly acquired territories in California and Oregon. Ocean traffic was painfully slow. A ship carrying mail by way of the Straits of Magellan cleared the New York harbor on October 8, 1848, and did not arrive in San Francisco, the first post office on the Pacific coast, until February 28, 1849.

After the discovery of gold in California, overland routes were investigated. By using a railroad across the Isthmus of Panama, the time could be cut to thirty days. But the isthmus was rife with cholera, and costs were inordinately high. Travel by overland routes across the northern and central United States was unreliable during the winter months when the high mountain passes were clogged with snow.

In order to use the southern all-weather pass cut by the Rio Grande through the Rockies at El Paso, Texas, it was essential for the United States to have the Mesilla Valley. Through the efforts of James Gadsden, minister to Mexico, the strip of territory through southern New Mexico known as the Gadsden Purchase was ceded to the United States on June 29, 1854.

The first contract for overland coach travel by the southern route was awarded on June 22, 1857, for semi-monthly trips between San Antonio, Texas, and San Diego, California. The company employed sixty-five men; it owned fifty four-horse coaches and four hundred mules. Coaches left San Antonio and San Diego on the 9th and the 24th of each month. They averaged about forty miles a day over the 1,476-mile route. The service did not prove satisfactory; it was curtailed after about forty trips.

On September 16, 1857, the Post Office Department inked a contract with John Butterfield and his associates to provide service

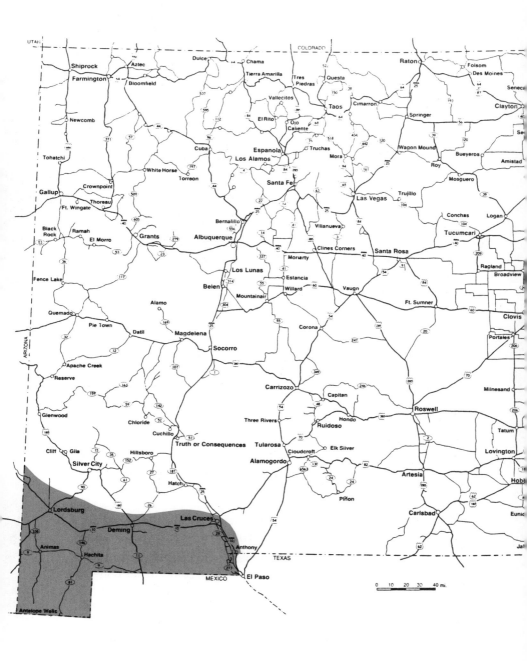

Butterfield Overland Mail

Mail delivery on the Butterfield Trail.
Harper's Weekly *commented: "In the
Eastern States the old-fashioned
stagecoach is remembered as a thing of
the past . . . but in the West it may be
called the advance-guard of invading
civilization."* —Harper's Weekly, 1874

for six years at $600,000 a year, the largest contract for land mail service ever given. The route started at St. Louis, Missouri, and Memphis, Tennessee, and converged at Fort Smith, Arkansas. It proceeded to El Paso and crossed the Rio Grande north of El Paso near Fort Fillmore. The road crossed southern New Mexico "along the new road being opened and constructed under direction of the Secretary of the Interior" and continued on to San Francisco. Service was to be provided "twice a week in good four-horse post-coaches or spring wagons, suitable for the conveyance of passengers as well as the safety and security of the mails."

Butterfield spent a year and approximately $1,000,000 in preparation. He laid out his route over existing trails and opened new ones; he located fords and ferrying places over streams and built stations. More than 1,800 horses and mules were purchased and distributed along the route. Orders were placed for two hundred fifty regular coaches and special mail wagons, harness sets and accessories, as well as a fleet of freight wagons and specially constructed tank wagons for water. The operating force consisted of conductors, drivers, station-keepers, blacksmiths, mechanics, helpers, and herders.

Stations averaged twenty miles apart over the 2,800-mile route. From two to four employees were boarded and lodged at the stations with the force increased to eight or ten at larger stations and in Indian country. The price of meals varied from forty cents to a dollar. William Tallack reported on the meals in his book *The California Overland Express*:

> Meals are provided for passengers twice a day. The fare though rough, is better than could be expected so far from civilized districts, and consists of bread, tea, and fried steaks of bacon, venison, antelope, or mule flesh—the latter tough enough. Milk, butter, and vegetables can only be met towards the two ends of the route—that is, in California and at the "stations" in the settled parts of the western Mississippi valley.

The first westbound mail left St. Louis on the morning of September 16, 1858. It passed through Mesilla, New Mexico, on September 30 and arrived in San Francisco on Sunday morning, October 10 at seven-thirty: twenty-three days, twenty-three hours, and thirty minutes from St. Louis—the fastest time yet recorded for the overland journey.

Initial passenger fare was $200 from St. Louis to San Francisco and $100 from San Francisco to St. Louis. As a result of criticism of rates favoring eastbound passengers, in 1859 the fare was fixed at $200 each way and later reduced to $150. Passengers were allowed forty pounds of baggage free. Additional weight was charged for at a dollar a pound. However, all passengers were encouraged to bring along a rifle; they were expected to help fight Indians if necessary and to help push the stage when it became stuck in the mud or mired down at river crossings. The postal rate was ten cents for each letter.

John Butterfield laid down a maxim: *"Remember boys, nothing on God's earth must stop the United States mail!"*

Consequently, the coaches rolled along both day and night. Any attempt to sleep was periodically interrupted by jolting on rough roads in coaches which were cushioned by leather thoroughbraces instead of springs. The coaches had three seats designed for nine passengers, but some rode on the outside preferring dust and open air to the crowded interior. Tallack described conditions on an eastbound trip:

> At starting, our conveyance was not a mere waggon as afterwards, but a regular coach, holding nine inside (three behind, three in front, and three on a movable seat, with a leather strap for a back), by dint of close sitting and tightly dovetailed knees. Outside the driver, the conductor, and an indefinite number of passengers, as, by popular permission, an American vehicle is never "full" there being always room for "one more." With these,

their luggage, and a heavy mail in strong sacks, stowed away under and between our feet, or overhead and elsewhere, we started from the Plaza or Grand Square of San Francisco.

Understandably, there were complaints. The most common included lack of toilet and bathing facilities, extensive use of whiskey by fellow passengers and stage attendants, drunken and profane stage drivers, and "miserable and expensive food." Some reported a fixed menu of jerked beef, mesquite beans, corn cake baked in hot ashes, black coffee, and a mysterious concoction known as "slumgullion."

Butterfield had been promised military protection for the line, but it was never supplied in sufficient strength to forestall Indian raids, so the company provided arms and ammunition for all stations in Indian country. At first the Indians confined their activities to running off the company's horses at isolated stations in Texas, New Mexico, and Arizona. This abated when horses were replaced with mules. The greatest deterrent to Indians was the knowledge that each station was a small arsenal bristling with Sharps rifles in the hands of men who knew how to use them.

The only open attack on a stage occurred at Apache Pass in Arizona in 1861. This was during the early Civil War period when Indians were encouraged by the gradual withdrawal of troops from Southwestern posts. With the outbreak of the Civil War, service to Texas, New Mexico, and Arizona was cancelled in July, 1861, in accordance with a general order to cut the secessionist states off from the privileges of the United States postal service. Contracts for delivery of mail by both stagecoach and Pony Express were awarded over northern routes to California.

At the abandonment of the stage stations and forts in the Southwest, the Indians believed they had at last driven both soldiers and the mail company off their land. They launched a wild campaign of looting and burning virtually every station in Indian country.

The Butterfield stage road looped briefly into New Mexico at two points on the southeastern border at Pope's Well southeast of Carlsbad and at the Cornudas Stage Station at the base of Cornudas Mountains near Thorne's Well. The road proceeded sixty-six miles southwest to El Paso, then north to enter New Mexico and pass through what would become the northwestern outskirts of present-day Anthony. The old road would have been less than a mile east of US 80 going north to Fort Fillmore. It crossed the Rio Grande about a mile and a half southeast of Mesilla and proceeded on to the station at Mesilla. From Mesilla it bent westward to stations named Picacho, Rough and Ready, Goodsight, Cooke's Spring, past Fort Cummings to the Mimbres River Station, Ojo de la Vaca ("Cow Spring," an ancient watering place), Soldier's Farewell, Barney's Stand, through the site of present-day Lordsburg, to Stein's Peak, the last station in New Mexico.

The route of the old Butterfield road was north of and roughly parallel to I-25, crossed by NM 26 between Hatch and Deming near the old Florida whistle stop on the Santa Fe Railroad. It is also crossed by US 180 between Deming and Silver City. Indian depredations, vandalism, and the wear of time and weather have combined to obliterate virtually all traces of those old rock and adobe stage stations which served the Butterfield Overland Mail.

———Historical Sidebar ————————————————————

Fort Cummings

A lonely historical marker at a roadside pull-off frequented by truckers is all that remains to commemorate the fort which was established to protect travelers between Mesilla and California.

On July 23, 1861, after the outbreak of the Civil War, Mangas Colorados and a large band of Chiricahua Apaches attacked seven men who were on a stagecoach in Cooke's Canyon to the north of present-day I-10. All seven were killed, but one managed to leave a blood-stained note under a rock telling of a two-day fight during which the Indians lost forty warriors. Continuing depredations emphasized the need for military action.

Fort Cummings was established in 1863 at the mouth of Cooke's Canyon near a Butterfield Overland Mail station to protect mail carriers, emigrant trains, and freighters from bands of Apaches. The fort covered an area 365x320 feet. It was built of adobe and surrounded by a wall twelve feet high. Historian Andy Gregg summed up the situation: "Life was hell inside the walls of Fort Cummings, but it was worse outside the walls."

On a four-mile "gauntlet of death" along the Butterfield Trail northeast of present-day Deming an estimated 400 emigrants, soldiers, and civilians were killed. In 1867 the road was littered with sun-bleached skeletons lying within sight of passengers riding the stages. Pressure was brought to bear upon the authorities and a detail was sent out from Fort Cummings to gather up the bones

Fort Cummings was built in 1863 to protect travelers on the Mesilla to Tucson stage road. —Bell, 1870

for burial in the post cemetery. Troops from the fort escorted wagon trains through this defile until they reached open country where the California-bound travelers could at least see hostile Indians and take defensive action.

Soldiers could not venture more than a mile from the fort without danger of attack. Inside the fort, rubber sheets were hung above tents to keep tarantulas, scorpions, and centipedes off sleeping soldiers; the place teemed with rattlesnakes.

In 1867, the post was manned by the 38th United States Infantry, Negro troops recruited largely from the cotton fields of Georgia. During their march westward, they had suffered the usual privations and dangers and were stricken with cholera. Even the army surgeon and his wife fell victims. Shortly after arrival at Fort Cummings, the troops planned a revolt. The plot was discovered by a servant girl.

The Negroes planned to kill all the white soldiers and make slaves of their wives. Tragedy was averted by announcing the impending arrival of the paymaster. All troops were assembled on the parade ground, unarmed. Their arms were confiscated by the white soldiers and officers; the ringleaders of the plot were punished.

On several occasions Apaches became so bold that they breached the wall of Fort Cummings and drove off stock almost under the eyes of the guard in the fort's observation tower. The guard did not know what was going on until he heard their Indian whoops and the pounding of horses' hooves after the stealthy marauders were inside the fort.

Fort Cummings was abandoned in 1873, but it had to be reactivated in 1880 when Victorio went on the warpath and again in 1886 during the last Indian war when Geronimo was ravaging the Southwest. After permanent abandonment in 1891, it was used as a corral by the Carpenter-Stanley Cattle Company. Today, few traces of the old fort remain and they are on private land.

I-10
Deming—Steins

Deming (Exit 85)

In late 1880 the Southern Pacific Railroad reached this point, and in 1881 the construction of a roundhouse and repair shops was started. Tents and shanties sprouted. The community was named for Mary Ann Deming, the daughter of a sawmill owner in Indiana. Six months later, the Santá Fe Railroad completed its junction with the Southern Pacific. During 1882 settlers flocked in, and the tents and shanties were replaced with more substantial buildings. Sitting on the flat Mimbres Valley, Deming was in the center of cattle ranges and cotton and milo farms.

There was a plentiful supply of water just underground. About twenty miles north of Deming, the Mimbres River disappears below the surface and continues its flow until it resurfaces near Chihuahua, Mexico, to drain into a lake. For more than a century, Deming has had access to this water supply, highly advertised as "99.9 percent pure." Before the advent of electrical power for pumps, Deming was called "the city of windmills."

Deming has become a winter-time haven for "snowbirds," retirees who come to escape the rigors of winters in the North and East. An active chamber of commerce labors to make sure there will be plenty for them to see and do. The most unique of the festivities is the Great American Duck Race.

Widely advertised as "The World's Richest Duck Race," this event takes place during the fourth week in August. Owners bring their web-footed pets from across the country to "Ducktown USA," to participate for a $7,500 purse at "Deming Duck Downs," over a 16-foot course. (To date, the record is 1.7 seconds.) The affair started in 1980. Since that time, punning members of the media from near and far have enjoyed ducking in to cover this fowl event.

Prizes are awarded for the Best-Dressed Duck, Wackiest-Dressed Duck, Most Elegant Duck, and Raciest-Dressed Duck. A Duck Queen, selected in part upon her ability to perform a duck walk, is crowned at a Duck Ball. Deming advertises itself as the "Home of Pure Water and Fast Ducks."

Historical Excursion

NM 11
Rockhound State Park
—Columbus

Rockhound State Park

About twelve miles southeast of Deming on the western slopes of the Little Florida Mountains, visitors to New Mexico's Rockhound State Park are invited to search for and take home up to fifteen pounds of rock and mineral samples. The possibilities include agate, jasper, quartz, and perlite. Even if one is not inclined to gathering rocks, the scenery from within this 250-acre park is worth a picnic stop or a hiking trip. On a trip to Spring Canyon, two miles south of the park headquarters, one may spot a Persian Ibex, an exotic species of wild goat from the Middle East introduced in the early 1970s.

Columbus

This sleepy village of perhaps 500 people was the scene of the only invasion of the United States by a foreign power. At 4:15 on the morning of March 9, 1916, Pancho Villa headed a band of between 900 and 1,100 bandits in an attack upon Columbus, New Mexico, and nearby Camp Furlong, manned by the 13th Cavalry. Villa wanted to embarrass President Woodrow Wilson for having recognized Carranza as president of Mexico and to show his contempt for Americans in general.

The bandits shot out windows and looted stores of their contents. They robbed and killed the owner and guests of the Commercial Hotel and torched buildings. By the time U.S. Cavalrymen gathered

A bullet stopped the clock in the railroad station at Columbus to mark the exact time of Pancho Villa's raid. —Courtesy El Paso Public Library

their wits and their weapons, the fires provided adequate light by which they could test their marksmanship. When the smoke and dust had settled, American casualties tallied 10 civilians killed and 4 wounded; 8 soldiers killed and 8 wounded. A hundred and forty-two Mexicans were killed in Camp Furlong, in Columbus, and on the way to the Mexican border.

On the following day, President Wilson ordered Gen. John J. Pershing to lead a punitive expedition against Villa. For the first time in history, motorized vehicles and aircraft were used in warfare. A fleet of trucks and the 1st Aero Squadron, consisting of eight obsolete biplanes then under the Signal Corps, converged upon Columbus to aid National Guard and regular troops on a foray into Mexico to capture Villa. Between 75 and 100 Mexicans were killed, but Villa lived to be assassinated in Parral, Mexico, on July 20, 1923, and to have his name added to the roster of Mexico's revolutionary leaders.

Columbus keeps Pancho Villa's memory green with two museums. New Mexico has established Pancho Villa State Park, which

Pancho Villa: The state park was named for him because villains attract more visitors than heroes. —Courtesy El Paso Public Library

is primarily a botanical garden displaying Southwestern desert plants. The park does contain the ruins of the headquarters of old Camp Furlong, the first grease rack installed to service U.S. Army automotive equipment, and other artifacts. Visitors can view a documentary film describing the Columbus Raid and its aftermath.

Naming the park after Pancho Villa did not occur without controversy. A local community booster explained the rationale: "Heroes do not attract people; villains do. If this place were named after General Pershing, we would have very few taking the trouble to visit us."

The main attractions of Columbus are secluded living, a pleasant climate, low taxes, and freedom from smog and congestion. Located only three miles from the border, it provides quick access to Mexico. Recently, plans have been initiated to convert the old Southern Pacific Railroad bed along the international boundary with Mexico between Columbus and El Paso into a highway.

Even after the U.S. Army took to a fleet of trucks, Pancho Villa eluded capture. —Courtesy El Paso Public Library

At last report, it was a gravel road paved with ballast from the railroad bead. During the past decade, an occasional brave motorist has attempted to negotiate the route over the old railroad bed in order to establish bragging rights for the performance of his off-the-road vehicle.

Historical Excursion

NM 146-81-9
Hachita—Antelope
Wells—Playas

Hachita

NM 81 (Exit 49 from I-10) leads to Hachita (little hatchet or little torch). The community has been described as "a semi-ghost town"; it has seen better and wilder days.

In 1901 the Arizona Copper Company extended its railroad line from Lordsburg to connect with the El Paso and Southwestern at Hachita. Hachita became a thriving little town with two hotels and many other places of business. It was a loading point for cattle.

The story is told of a cowboy who rode into town and reported a sizeable trail herd of Diamond A cattle at Twelve Mile Well to the south of town. Local accommodations were presumed inadequate for a crowd of pleasure-starved cowboys. The Southern Pacific Railroad agent telegraphed El Paso to send "a carload of girls from Juarez" in Mexico.

When the Southern Pacific purchased the El Paso and Southwestern it abandoned the line between Lordsburg and Hachita, and Hachita began to shrivel.

Antelope Wells

NM 81 crosses the Sonora desert from Hachita to Antelope Wells. This area was haunted by bands of Apaches under Cochise and Mangas Colorados from 1862 until 1886 when the Indian wars subsided with the surrender of Geronimo to Gen. N. A. Miles. Today, it is a prime area for hunting javelina and other game.

Antelope Wells serves as a crossing point for cattle from Mexico, and the United States maintains a 24-hour port of entry to Mexico.

The area is rife with stories of early-day outlaws, including the notorious Clanton Gang. For example, there was the time that stockmen around the Animas Mountains began to miss cattle which they suspected were leaving New Mexico by way of Antelope Wells. They looked in vain for the hoofprints of rustlers' horses. Finally, they learned of a visiting Mexican who rode a strange mount, a steer which had been broken to saddle—a big, rangy, tireless beast. He left no telltale horse tracks. The disappearance of cattle ceased for a while after the ranchers ran him out of the "bootheel" of New Mexico.

Playas

Playas is on NM 9, west from Hachita. The town's name, Spanish for "beaches," is given to dry concave drainage basins which collect water after rains. Playas Lake, just south of Playas, is such a closed basin, about a mile wide and some fourteen miles long. The village developed on the Southern Pacific Railroad and experienced an indifferent existence until it was recently selected as the site for an ultra-modern Phelps-Dodge copper smelter.

Separ (Exit 42)

Here the Janos Trail crosses I-10. This trade route was established by the Spaniards in the early 1800s after copper was discovered at Santa Rita. The trail extended from the mines and a Spanish fort at Santa Rita into Chihuahua and Sonora in northern Mexico. A portion of the trail was also used during the Mexican War by the Mormon Battalion under Lt. Col. Philip St. George Cooke when he established the first wagon road across the continent in 1846-47.

With the coming of the railroad, Separ became a cattle-loading station for nearby ranches. It now serves motorists as a stop for supplies.

———Historical Sidebar———————————————

The Mormon Battalion

The Mormon Battalion was organized soon after the beginning of the Mexican War. The Church of Latter-day Saints had become involved in difficulties in Missouri and Illinois; they were refused admission to Arkansas. On January 26, 1846, Brigham Young appointed an agent to take advantage of any facilities the U.S. Government might offer the Saints to migrate to the Pacific coast. President Polk was asked "to stretch forth the federal arm in their behalf."

The result was the Mormon Battalion. Gen. Stephen W. Kearny was ordered to enlist volunteers for service in the occupation of California. The recruiting circular read:

> Thus is offered to the Mormon people now—this year—an opportunity of sending a portion of their young and intelligent men, to the ultimate destination of their whole people, and entirely at the expense of the United States; and this advance party can thus pave the way, and look out the land for their brethren to come after them.

The Saints enlisted, some 400 strong, in five companies of infantry. They marched out of Council Bluffs, Iowa, on July 21-22, 1846, for Ft. Leavenworth. They arrived in Santa Fe, via the Santa Fe Trail, October 9 and 12. Under Philip St. George Cooke, the battalion marched down the Rio Grande, the length of New Mexico, and turned west across Arizona. Cooke's instructions were to open a wagon road to the Pacific.

The Mormon Battalion left Santa Fe with no knowledge of military tactics. It was drilled on the way and marched into the Mission of San Diego on January 29, 1847, a well-organized unit of the U.S. Army.

"Cooke's Wagon Road," as it was called, became the potential route for railroad construction. It was one of the reasons for the Gadsden Purchase in 1854. And the trek served the Saints. Their future interest in New Mexico and even northern Mexico was undoubtedly the result of information received during service with the Mormon Battalion during the Mexican War.

In seeking to expand their faith, many members of the battalion were among those who established mission stations at Kirtland, Fruitland, Ramah, Blue Water, Luna, and Virden. By their system of communal living and by the understanding they had gained of control of the water supply in an arid land, the Mormons made a lasting contribution to the development of New Mexico.

Lordsburg (Exit 24)

October 18, 1880, was a glorious day in Lordsburg. Railroad employees, prospectors, freighters, stage drivers, cowboys, gamblers, and just plain citizens gathered in the crude railroad construction camp. They came from stage stations, mining camps, ranches, and villages. They came on foot, on burros, on horseback, in buckboards, and in ox wagons drawn by ten to sixteen horses or mules. They came for one purpose: to see the "Iron Horse."

They watched to the west until they saw a curl of smoke and then watched the little engine pull a string of coaches into town. The coaches were lighted by coal oil lamps and heated with stoves. The seats were covered with rattan.

The town was forthwith named for a Mr. Lord in Tucson. Some say he was a construction engineer; others say he was in charge of the commissary; still others say he had a wholesale food distributing firm. The effects of the train were immediate. Tents and tent houses sprouted along Railroad Avenue and signs went up: "General Merchandise, Colonel Bennell, proprietor"; "O. Z. Boon's Saloon and Gautier's Restaurant."

The first telephone line in Lordsburg was the top strand of a barbed wire fence. A Southern Pacific Railroad agent got the idea. He installed two phones, one in town and the other on the Muir

Ranch fifteen miles away with barbed wire between. It worked perfectly in dry weather and was eventfully incorporated into Lordsburg's telephone system, later to be sold to the Bell Telephone Company.

The chief occupations were mining, ranching, farming, and trucking. For a time, all transcontinental trains on the Southern Pacific line stopped at Lordsburg, and one Col. Willard Holt was on hand to meet all trains. Whether they were Presidents, potentates, or Eastern financiers, Colonel Holt collared the most important passengers and told them about Lordsburg. In 1927, after his New York-to-Paris flight, Charles Lindbergh stopped by to dedicate Lordsburg's new airport, the only stop the *Spirit of St. Louis* made in New Mexico. . . . But change was on the way.

With the increase in air travel, the number of passenger trains dwindled. With the construction of I-10, Lordsburg was bypassed; no longer does a transcontinental highway go right along Railroad Avenue through the central business district. Lordsburg now advertises itself as the "Gateway to Enchantment," a place to stay while visiting nearby tourist attractions.

Historical Excursion

NM 494
Shakespeare (Exit 22)

Take the Main Street exit from I-10 at Lordsburg and turn south on NM 494 to reach Shakespeare; but, before going, if you wish to tour this old ghost town, inquire at the Lordsburg Chamber of Commerce to find out if it is open. This ghost town is now privately owned and touring is limited to certain days of the week.

Shakespeare began life in the 1850s as a watering spot known as Mexican Springs. A stage station was established there in 1858 on an alternate route of the Butterfield Overland Mail. In 1867, the National Mail and Transportation Co. made it a stage stop and called the place Grant, in honor of Gen. U. S. Grant.

In 1870 a prospector found silver in the Pyramid Mountains. William C. Ralston, a San Francisco banker, backed mining in the area. A brief boom resulted, and the name of the town was changed to Ralston to honor its benefactor. Ralston was a company town. Employees of the company staked all claims and laid out the townsite. When independent miners came in they were told all the claims were taken. Settlers had to buy lots from the company. However, not much silver materialized and, eventually, both Ralston and his bank would be ruined.

Two men salted the area with diamonds which were appraised for Ralston by Tiffany's at $150,000. Ralston formed a new company. It attracted investors such as Horace Greeley and Baron Rothschild. Alas! The diamonds played out and the "great diamond hoax" came to light.

There is controversy over whether Ralston was a party to the scam. In any case, he repaid the stockholders out of his own pocket. When the depression of 1875 struck, his bank failed; and he went for a swim in the San Francisco Bay from which he never returned.

Col. John Boyle came along in the late 1870s to change the town's name and its luck. His Shakespeare Mining Company found silver in the area. He built the Stratford Hotel on the main street, called Avon Avenue of course. At first it was a frame building with unbleached muslin sides. Later it attracted such notables as Robert Ingersoll and Lew Wallace. According to old-timers, Billy the Kid washed dishes there for a spell after getting into trouble in Silver City. During its heyday in the 1870s, there were fifteen or sixteen saloons. The red light district was called Poverty Flat.

One night, two desperados, Sandy King and Russian Bill, came to town. Vigilantes hung them from the rafters of the Grant Hotel. The next morning when the stagecoach made a breakfast stop, the passengers found the swinging bodies. They cut them down and buried them before breakfast. The graves are in Shakespeare's Boot Hill. This time, Shakespeare's prosperity lasted until the depression of 1893.

The next silver boom started in 1908 and petered out in 1932. Since 1935, the town has been owned by the Hill family. The remains consist of the Stratford Hotel, part of the Grant House, one of the saloons, a few other rusty-roofed adobe buildings, and of course Boot Hill.

NM 338
Animas—Gray Ranch

Animas

This community, deriving its name from the Spanish word for "departed souls," was settled and named by Hispanic people in 1843. Sometime in 1901, the Phelps Dodge Company completed a railroad line known as the Arizona and New Mexico through Animas to connect with the Santa Fe in Deming. As a ranching and farming community on the railroad, Animas acquired pens for shipping cattle, a grocery store, a post office, a one-room school, and a five-room hotel.

The railroad was eventually acquired by the Southern Pacific Railroad. Service was terminated in 1962 and the tracks were removed in 1965.

Gray Ranch

The 300,000-acre Gray Ranch occupies a goodly portion of southwestern New Mexico, the "bootheel." It was the subject of much misinformation and folklore until New Mexico historian Marc Simmons uncovered the facts and published them in his syndicated newspaper column in 1988.

The name of the ranch goes back to Michael Gray, a Tennessean who became a Texas Ranger and eventually migrated to California where he served for a time as a sheriff. In 1880 Gray and his two sons were in the Animas Valley where Gray found a lush meadow which was kept green by a copious spring. Curly Bill Brocius, an outlaw, claimed this oasis. Gray bought squatter's rights from Brocius for $300.

Mike Gray built a ranch house, but in 1881 one of his sons was killed. The following year, James B. Haggin entered the territory buying up small ranches on behalf of George Hearst, the father of William Randolph Hearst. Thus, the Gray Ranch became part of the new Diamond A Ranch, a huge spread owned by Californians. Gray went to Arizona, but his name has continued to be associated with the ranch. More recently, the ranch fell into the hands of the Phelps Dodge Development Corporation.

The vast area contains many rich archaeological sites relating to the Animas Phase of the Casas Grandes culture of northern Chihuahua. This vast empire of mountains and basins contains three endangered species—the bald eagle, the ridge-nosed rattlesnake, and the peregrine falcon—and seventy-five species of mammals, more than any wildlife refuge in the nation. The Archaeological Society of New Mexico urged protection of the area, and the U.S. Fish and Wildlife Service expressed an interest in acquisition by sale or trade.

Historical Excursion

US 80
Rodeo

This town on US S80 near the border of Arizona came into existence shortly after the turn of the century with the coming of the railroad. It earned its name because cowmen used to come every year to separate, brand, and ship their cattle.

When the railroad came, a man named Charlie Bond was settled where the town now stands. He did not believe the railroad was paying enough to cross his property, so he decided to blow up the railroad water tank. The blast made only a small dent. Later, Bond fought a losing battle in the local saloon and occupied the first grave in the vicinity of Rodeo.

Steins (Exit 3)

It is easy to miss the ruins of the old adobe buildings between the interstate and the railroad tracks unless you know they are there. Steins (pronounced "Steens" locally) was founded in 1880 with the building of the Southern Pacific Railroad through the Peloncillo Mountains.

The town boomed in 1905 when the railroad built a rock-crushing plant and a large depot on the site. Enough rock was blasted out of Steins Pass to ballast a 300-mile stretch of track. At that time, emigrants were still coming through to California in covered wagons on the Butterfield Trail, and Steins was serving as a supply point.

During its heyday, Steins had a two-story hotel, two saloons, and a dance hall. Killings and stabbings were commonplace in the latter establishments. Black Jack Ketchum and other outlaws held up trains in Steins Pass on several occasions during the late 1880s and early 1890s.

The town of Steins has always suffered for want of a water supply. Early settlers caught and stored rainwater. The railroad drilled for water unsuccessfully and then resorted to the use of tank cars.

The old buildings at Steins are slowly being restored and an interesting museum of artifacts from the town's past has been assembled. Water still has to be trucked in.

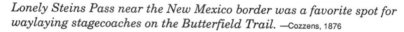

—— Historical Sidebar ——————————————

Steins Station

The railroad town of Steins or Steins Pass on the railroad is not to be confused with Steins Station or Steins Pass on the Butterfield Overland Mail route. The latter are on private land some fourteen miles north of the town of Steins. The only connection is that they were all named for the same person.

The pass which was used by coaches on the early El Paso-San Diego stage line went through Doubtful Canyon, so named because passengers were doubtful about getting through it alive. In 1854,

Lonely Steins Pass near the New Mexico border was a favorite spot for waylaying stagecoaches on the Butterfield Trail. —Cozzens, 1876

Major Enoch Stein was leading a troop of dragoons through the canyon on his way to occupy Tucson after the Gadsden Treaty. In defending Doubtful Canyon during an Indian attack, Stein gave his life to the canyon and his name to the pass.

After coming up the steep grade to the pass, horses or mules pulling the coaches were easy prey to waiting Apaches, and many victims were claimed. In later years, Cochise told of leading an attack in 1861 during which his Apaches hid above the trail and shot flaming arrows into the stagecoaches as they passed.

As result of an attack in 1859, there may be a treasure waiting to be found. Three miners from California were carrying $37,000 in gold. Their stage was waylaid by a band of Apaches led by a renegade white named Pegleg Pete and two other white men. The stage was guarded by twelve soldiers.

The melee resulted in wholesale slaughter. The three miners, the twelve soldiers, the stage driver, Pegleg and his two accomplices, and a considerable number of Indians died. The victims were buried on the spot, but the sacks containing the gold were never found. Did the fleeing miners live long enough to bury them? Did the Indians get the gold? Those questions have never been answered.

Then, the story had another nagging question. On his wooden leg, Pegleg Pete was supposed to have had a map showing where he had hidden $70,000 from a previous robbery. Some soldiers came back to unearth his body in order to find that map, but they were never able to locate his grave.

Historical Excursion

NM 92
Virden

NM 92 makes an eleven-mile detour off US 70, northwest of Lordsburg, for the express purpose of going through Virden, as well it should. Virden has been there for more than a century. It was called Richmond in the beginning.

When the New Mexico Mining Company, backed by William Ralston of the Bank of California, created the town of Ralston the promoters had bigger plans than their water supply permitted. Springs and wells provided water for normal use, but there was none for irrigation, and the hills were too rough for farming.

The promoters looked some thirty miles north to the Gila River as a source of water for a stamp mill and for irrigation. After all, Indians had used the Gila to irrigate the valley centuries before. They picked a place where the Gila flowed out of the canyons into a valley. They called the area the Virginia Mining District and named the town Richmond. Big plans were afoot. A tramway was to be built from Ralston to Richmond to carry silver ore from the mines to a stamp mill; an irrigation ditch would water the valley.

Most of the plans fell through when the pockets of ore upon which Ralston depended played out and the town became embroiled in the diamond swindle. However, a ten-mile irrigation ditch was built, and farmers did settle in Richmond. Theirs was a hard scrabble existence, and by the turn of the century most of the original settlers had sold their land and moved away.

In 1916 Mormon colonists who had been living in Chihuahua, Mexico, were forced out by the revolutionists. Some of the Mormons had friends or relatives in the Gila Valley. Earnest W. Virden, president of the Gila Ranch Company, sold them farm land and they renamed the town in his honor.

XI. In Pursuit of Quivira

Without a doubt, the lure of gold was the primary incentive which brought the Spaniards to New Mexico. The name they gave the territory grew from the hope that the northern province would produce treasures comparable to those found in the land of the Aztecs.

In 1528 Alvar Núñez Cabeza de Vaca survived a shipwreck on the Texas coast. After a trek across present-day Texas, southern New Mexico, Arizona, and the Mexican states of Chihuahua, Durango, Sonora, and Sinaloa, he and his companions met Spanish slave traders near the town of Culiacán in Sinaloa on April 11, 1536. Cabeza de Vaca became the first white man to report on a visit to what would become the province of New Mexico.

He told of populous cities. He stimulated the Spanish thirst for riches with reports of silver, antimony, emeralds, and copper. The pouches of "silver" he mentioned probably contained powdered mica. The powdered "antimony" was indisputably manganese ore, which the Indians commonly used to paint their faces. The ceremonial arrowheads made of "emeralds" were undoubtedly malachite. The only part of Cabeza de Vaca's narrative which would eventually hold water was his story of a copper rattle and of the Indians' reports that there were many sheets of the material buried in the ground.

Based upon their experiences in Mexico and Peru, the Spaniards were not prone to doubt; they wanted to believe everything Cabeza de Vaca said and more. They wanted to believe they could find the seven rich and beautiful cities which had become known in the medieval folklore of southern Europe as "The Cities of the Seven Bishops" or "The Seven Cities of Antilia." One map of the day placed it on an island in the middle of the Atlantic.

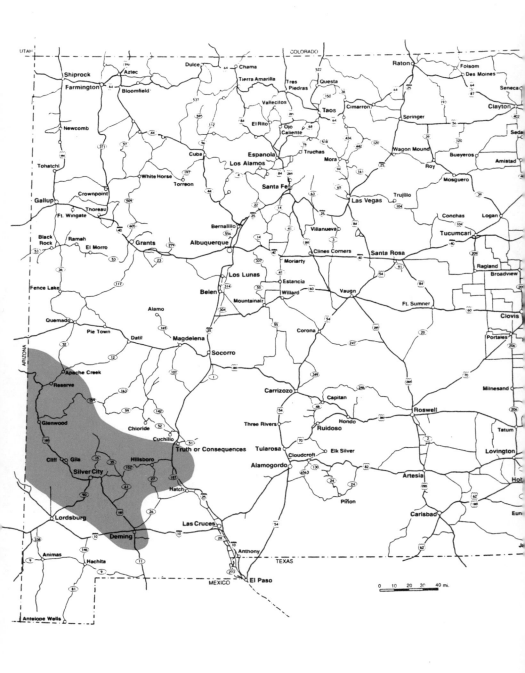

In Pursuit of Quivira

Viceroy Don Antonio de Mendoza dispatched Fray Marcos de Niza to investigate. He sent Estévan Dorantes, a Moorish slave who had accompanied Cabeza de Vaca, along as a guide. The Viceroy instructed Fray Marcos:

> You shall take much care to observe the people who are there, if they be many or few, and if they are scattered or live in communities; the quality and fertility, the temperature of the country, the trees and plants and domestic and feral animals which may be there, the nature of the ground, whether rough or level; the rivers, if they are large or small, and the minerals and metals which are there.

Fray Marcos de Niza knew exactly what Viceroy Mendoza wanted to hear. Upon his return he told of golden vessels and bejeweled ear ornaments, of pearls, and of a beautiful city called Cíbola which he had seen from a distance. Indians had told him there were seven such cities in the province.

Fray Marcos turned back without visiting those fabled Seven Cities of Cíbola. Estévan, his guide, had been killed and he feared for his own life, "which I had offered to God the day I commenced the journey. At the end I feared, considering my danger and that, if I died, I would not be able to make report of this country, which to me appears the greatest and best of the discoveries."

Obviously, Fray Marcos magnified and slanted his findings to suit his audience. At this distance in time, we do not know why. He may have been a congenital liar. He may have believed a glowing report would enhance the opportunities for the clergy to go forth and establish missions.

In an exhaustive analysis of Fray Marcos de Niza's narrative in relation to the time it would have taken him to reach Cíbola—then called Hawikúh, today's Zuñi Pueblo—Cleve Hallenbeck concluded that the monk never viewed the "very beautiful town" he claimed to have seen. He scarcely had time to reach what is now the southern border of Arizona.

But at that time nothing tarnished Fray Marcos de Niza's report. Within months, Francisco Vásquez Coronado was on the road to Cíbola with Fray Marcos along as a guide. The magnificent promise soon faded.

The fabled cities turned out to be nothing but squalid little pueblos. Castañeda described "Cíbola" as "a little unattractive village, looking as though it had been all crumpled up together." Fray Marcos was branded "The Lying Monk" and sent back, probably to keep Coronado's soldiers from killing him.

Coronado later reported to Viceroy Mendoza, "everything the friar said was found to be quite the reverse. I can assure you that in reality he has not told the truth in a single thing he said."

The Indians were learning, but the Spaniards were not. The Indians were learning that the Spaniards were looking for gold. If they told the bearded men with fire-belching sticks that it was farther along, they would leave. As Coronado proceeded in his search, he fell victim to another liar, a Pawnee Indian slave whom the Spaniards called *El Turco* because he looked like one.

The Turk told about a fabulous country to the east which was called Quivira. There, the Indians not only paved the streets with gold but drank water from jugs made of gold. Forthwith, Coronado set out. In July, 1541, near present-day Lyons, Kansas, he found Quivira. The residents were living in grass huts and there was not a fleck of gold to be seen. The Turk was issued a one-way ticket to visit his ancestors.

Coronado returned to New Spain in 1542, and his report put a damper on Spanish exploration. It was more than half a century before the next serious expedition set out for New Mexico. In 1598 Oñate's colonial expedition embarked. They professed to be colonists, but Oñate's father was a wealthy Zacatecas mine owner, and Oñate was jolly well looking for more than a good place to establish an agricultural community, as were most of those who accompanied him. Cíbola had proven a false seductress, but there was always the hope of finding the real Quivira.

But it remained as elusive as ever. By 1608 King Philip would have given up the province of New Mexico as a bad job had not a couple of priests shown up with samples of silver ore. During the next two hundred years, there were scattered attempts at mining. None was sufficiently successful to write back to Spain about. American mining engineers have been prone to categorize early Spanish mining ventures as "gopher holes."

Toward the end of the eighteenth century, near present-day Silver City, Apaches revealed copper deposits to Col. Don Manuel Carrasco. Don Manuel had found Quivira, but he did not recognize it. He filed a claim, but sold it to Don Francisco Manuel de Elguea of Chihuahua, who worked the deposits until his death in 1809.

Subsequently, gold, silver, lead, zinc, coal, potash, uranium, natural gas, and petroleum have been found beneath the earth of New Mexico; but none of them has had a more sustained impact upon New Mexico's economy than those sheets of copper that the Indians told Cabeza de Vaca about—the Quivira that the Spaniards passed up in favor of gold they could never find.

—— **Historical Sidebar** ————————————————————

Fort McLane

In October, 1860, Maj. Isaac Lynde of the 7th U.S. Infantry established a military post on the bank of a small stream flowing out of Apache Springs, about four miles south of present-day Hurley where the road leads to the Grant County Airport. The post was named Fort Floyd, after Secretary of War John B. Floyd. Its mission was to protect mines at Santa Rita and Pinos Altos as well as the overland stage route to the south.

Secretary Floyd defected to the Confederacy, and on January 15, 1861, the fort was renamed to honor Capt. George McLane who had been killed by Navajos that year. The fort was never more than a few log buildings. It was abandoned in July, 1861, when its troops were moved to Fort Fillmore.

However, in its abandonment, Fort McLane lived on to become the scene of a black page in New Mexico's history. It was at Fort McLane that Mangas Colorados was killed. The Chiricahua Apache chieftain was infamous for raids against Mexicans and Mexican settlements and for harassing miners near present-day Silver City. In January, 1863, he was captured near Pinos Altos by Capt. Edmund D. Shirland and twenty men of the 1st California Volunteers and taken to abandoned Fort McLane where he was killed. There are a number of versions of the story about his death.

One says he was captured when he walked into an army camp to talk about a truce with the soldiers. He was offered safe conduct if he came alone. He waved the warriors who accompanied him back. As soon as they were out of the way, Mangas Colorados was seized and bound. The next morning an officer told his guards he wanted the Apache chief "dead or alive," putting unmistakable emphasis on *dead*. One of his guards thrust a bayonet into the Indian's leg. When he jumped up the two guards emptied revolvers into his body. His head was reported to have been severed from his body and sent to the Smithsonian Institution.

Another version has it that the soldiers were burning Mangas Colorados' feet and legs with heated bayonets. When he objected they shot him. The official army version is that he was killed while trying to escape captivity.

Whatever the truth of the affair, it is perhaps just as well that Fort McLane left no remains and that there is no historical marker to commemorate its location.

Hurley

This is a company town. The size of the population and the fortunes of its residents are directly tied to the price of copper and to corporate machinations and high-level financial dealings which are far beyond the reach of those who live here.

The village began as a railroad siding named Hurley Siding for J. E. Hurley, one-time general manager of the Atchison, Topeka & Santa Fe Railroad. The town was started in 1910 as a result of the purchase of the Santa Rita Mining Company by the Chino Copper Company. A smelting operation and management offices provide stability to the community.

Vestiges of the Cameron Creek ruins are located about two miles west of Hurley. This was a Mogollon village which was occupied about 700 A.D. Archaeologists excavated the village between 1923 and 1928, and little remains today. The scientists found that the dead had been buried under the floors of the rooms in a flexed position. Their effects were buried with them. The ceramic pots had holes drilled in their bottoms to allow the spirit of the jar to escape with the soul of the dead.

Bayard

The waste dumps from the Santa Rita mining operation loom over this community from the east where copper is separated from the earth by a leaching process. The copper precipitate recovered during the leaching process is sent to the smelter at Hurley and the waste is deposited in the dump. As is the case with Hurley, most of the residents are employed in the mining operation.

Fort Bayard

The discovery of gold at Pinos Altos in 1859 brought miners and more prospectors. The invasion aroused the ire of the Warm Springs Apaches, who considered the land theirs. Fort Bayard was built in 1866 to protect the mines. It was manned by "Buffalo Soldiers," an all-black regiment of the Ninth Cavalry. The fort was named for Brig. Gen. George D. Bayard, who served on the frontier with the First Cavalry and was badly wounded in an engagement with

At Fort Bayard Sixth Cavalry soldiers practiced a new technique to be employed against the Indians, using their mounts as breastwork during a skirmish. The drawing was made from a photograph. —Harper's Weekly, 1885

Kiowa Indians. Bayard was killed during a Civil War battle at Fredericksburg, Virginia.

Initially, the fort was a cluster of adobe and log huts which provided little protection. The first Apache attack took place in 1867. In a predawn raid, the Indians caught the soldiers asleep. They rode through the fort, shooting into the buildings.

Fort Bayard grew slowly over the years as the soldiers built offices and barracks when they were not busy fighting Indians. The post served as a base for campaigns against Mangas Colorados, Victorio, and Geronimo. Pursuits and skirmishes lasted until Geronimo's final surrender in 1886.

The post remained active until 1900 when it became an army hospital for treatment of tubercular patients. It is now used by the New Mexico Department of Public Welfare to care for elderly and handicapped patients. Few traces of the original fort remain, but later buildings have been maintained and are still in use.

There is a game preserve behind the hospital where elk, deer, wild turkeys, and javelinas can be seen. It is a favorite spot for picnics, jogging, and walking.

Central

Just across the road from Fort Bayard, the village of Santa Clara began to develop during the early 1860s, populated by people who provided services to soldiers stationed at the fort. In February, 1868, the Territorial Legislature created Grant County out of a portion of Doña Ana County. By this time Santa Clara had been redesignated Central City.

Central City was named the county seat, a distinction probably earned because of proximity to the fort. A courthouse and jail were promptly built, followed by the establishment of businesses and pleasure houses to accommodate the miners and soldiers who came into town seeking relaxation. The boom was short-lived.

By May, 1869, Central City ceased to be the hub of Grant County. The county seat was moved to Pinos Altos and the courthouse was put up for sale. During the early 1900s the community experienced another boom when some of the old mining claims were rediscovered. On May 5, 1947, a hundred and fifty-four property owners presented a petition asking the county commissioners to incorporate the community of Central into a village. There were 1,609 residents.

About 1965 there was a third period of growth. Residents of nearby Santa Rita had to remove their homes from the path of the expanding open-pit copper mining operation of the Kennecott Copper Corporation. Some built new homes; others moved their old homes and remodeled them in the new locations. In 1976 Central celebrated its one hundredth anniversary.

Silver City

On January 1, 1869, William M. Milby, of San Antonio, Texas, and John M. Bullard, an immigrant from Missouri, started ranching at a Spanish settlement called La Cienega de San Vicente (St. Vincent's Marsh). Two soldiers from Fort Bayard provided protection from the Apaches to them and other pioneer farmers.

The following year, Bullard heard about a silver strike at Ralston. Bullard headed a party of eight who joined the stampede. The ore-bearing rocks they saw at Ralston looked similar to the rocks back home. They returned to La Cienega de San Vicente, formed the Bullard Mining Company, and began to dig. They located the same kind of ore on the hill behind the present courthouse. They staked a claim and called it the Legal Tender. The ore assayed 100 ounces of silver per ton. Soon the surrounding hills and valleys were dotted with shacks and tents.

Wagon trains in Silver City on their way to mines in the Mogollons.
—Courtesy El Paso Public Library

A townsite was laid out and christened Silver City. The community began to flourish as the county seat of Grant County was moved from Pinos Altos. There were two banks and eight saloons. Twelve retail stores, 4 restaurants, 2 meat markets, 2 drug stores, 3 billiard halls, 2 fur dealers, 2 dressmakers, 2 tailors, and a milliner catered to the needs of the citizenry. Four doctors and 7 lawyers opened offices and hung out their shingles. A circulating library opened to disseminate learning. By the end of 1882 an oversupply of newspapers had developed; six were being published concurrently.

Visitors had a choice between the Exchange, said to be the largest hotel in the Territory, or Peter Ott's Tremont House. Neither establishment provided bathing facilities, but one could rent a tub of hot water at either of the two barber shops in town.

As to John Bullard, who started it all: in 1871 he went into the hills after an Apache war party. While he was bending over a supposedly dead Indian, the Indian grabbed his gun and shot him through the heart. The mountain upon which Bullard died was named after him, and Silver City perpetuates his memory with a street name.

Before the railroads, prior to 1881, 12- and 14-horse teams hauled ore and bullion into Silver City from mining camps in the

431

Mogollon Mountains. Bricks of gold and silver were stacked on boardwalks outside stage and freight offices. Attempts at robbery were discouraged by frequent hangings.

Like most Western mining towns, Silver City had its gambling houses. Soft-handed gamblers in wide-brimmed black hats, frock coats, and diamond-studded cravats presided at the tables. Cowboys swaggered up to bars and demanded shots of red eye, bug juice, or mescal for themselves and their companions from Shady Lane. If response was not immediate, they were prone to such playful antics as shooting out lights, perforating bar mirrors, and turning over roulette tables.

As a boy, Billy the Kid lived in Silver City. His mother, Catherine McCarty Antrim, is buried in Memory Lane Cemetery at the western city limits. There are few hard facts available about Billy's life in Silver City. After his mother's death he left town to pursue his career as an outlaw.

As the rich pockets of high-grade ore played out, Silver City proved more durable than most of the mining communities in the area. The town declined, but it gained new life as modern irrigation and farming methods were introduced into the Mimbres and Gila river valleys. The copper industry and cattle ranching contributed to the town's survival.

The old Hotel Southern was a stagecoach stop in Silver City. Billy the Kid killed his first man just across the street; he made his first escape from the jail which was located next door to the hotel.

—Courtesy New Mexico Department of Development, No. 2781

During the late 1890s, Dr. Earl Sprague Bullock was stationed at Fort Bayard. Dr. Bullock was afflicted with tuberculosis. He developed a goal of providing care within the reach of people of modest means who came West for their health "contingent, of course, upon my own recovery."

During the period 1900 to 1920, Silver City became a mecca for "poor lungers," "consumptives," or "tuberculars" as they were variously called. That is probably responsible for the predominance of sleeping porches on Silver City homes built during that era. The notion developed that "sleeping out" was good for the body. It was not uncommon for entire families to sleep out on porches year-around with only canvas sheets to protect them from the elements.

By 1895 mining had pretty well denuded the hills around Silver City. That year the rains were heavy, and a 12-foot wall of water swept through town. It washed out Main Street and gouged a 35-foot-deep ditch in its place, to become known as the Big Ditch. After another flood in 1903, Main Street was dug to fifty-five feet below its original level. In 1936 the Civilian Conservation Corps lined the ditch with masonry, and in 1980 the citizens of Silver City dedicated it as a park, a river walk decorated with shade trees and waterfalls.

Silver City's central historic district contains many fine old Victorian homes. The Silver City Museum, located in the old H. B. Altman House, is a good starting point for a walking tour.

Historical Excursion

NM 15-35-61
Pinos Altos—
Faywood Hot Springs

A loop drive from Silver City north via NM 15, then southeast on NM 35 and NM 61 back to intersection with US 180 south of Silver City takes one through a historical time period spanning from the Mogollon culture of 700 A.D. through New Mexico's tumultuous mining days to the peaceful quiet of modern agricultural communities.

Pinos Altos

This community dates from May, 1860, when three prospectors—Birch, Hicks, and Snively—were camped in the area. One version of the story has it that one of them went to Bear Creek to get water and found gold. They went back to Santa Rita for supplies, told a few people, and by December some 1,500 miners swarmed to the diggings which was dubbed Birchville in honor of one of the discoverers.

Miners were camped in tents and lean-tos up canyons and along streams. They were panning from $10 to $15 worth of gold a day and entertaining hope that this would be another Sutterville. With the discovery of each new hole, more miners came with picks, shovels, and dynamite. The mines were given names like Wild Bill, Deep-Down Atlantic, and Kept Woman. Thomas Mastin found the first quartz vein and built an arrastra to crush the ore-bearing rock.

On the morning of September 22, 1861, the Apaches came, some 400 strong under Cochise and Mangas Colorados. They rode right into town and miners came from their claims. The battle raged all morning. When the Indians withdrew they left fifteen bodies behind; three miners were killed, including Thomas Mastin. Capt. Thomas J. Mastin's grave is in the Pinos Altos cemetery; his name is spelled "Marston" on the marker. When Hollywood producers made him the subject of a movie they filmed it in Colorado.

The Indians continued to harass the community, and the bulk of the miners and their families left for more promising diggings. By 1862 the town was virtually deserted. A few held on during the Civil War, and the name Birchville yielded to Pinos Altos (high pines).

A second stampede occurred in 1866. The people entered into a pact with the Apaches. Both the Indians and the whites agreed that a large cross should be erected on a hill north of town. As long as the cross stayed on the mountain there would be no killings. The pact lasted for twenty years.

Surface ore was quickly exhausted, but stamping mills brought $250,000 in gold out of the earth from the Pacific Queen and the Atlantic yielded $3,000,000 during thirty years. In 1890 optimists were predicting a future yield of that much every year, but it proved a vain hope. The miners migrated to easier diggings, leaving Pinos Altos with scarred hillsides and crumbling mine shafts.

But Pinos Altos had its day. It was county seat of Grant County for a while. Sam and Roy Bean operated a store in the 1860s before Judge Roy Bean went on to establish Law West of the Pecos in West Texas. The William Randolph Hearst fortune was represented.

The Hearsts started ranching with headquarters east of Deming near Cow Springs, they briefly owned the Santa Rita copper mine, and they opened a store in Pinos Altos. The Phoebe Hearst mine was named for the mother of William Randolph Hearst. In 1898 the adobe Methodist-Episcopal church was built with Hearst money. It now houses the Grant County Art Guild.

As a ghost town, Pinos Altos suffered deterioration for many years, but it has made another comeback. The old opera house was "rebuilt from old-time materials"; the Buckhorn Saloon, originally built in 1865, was refurbished and has become a popular eating establishment. *The San Francisco Examiner* dubbed it "One of the best Old Time Watering Holes West of the Mississippi."

Signs point to the location of historical memorabilia including the courthouse; the old cemetery with the graves of those who died fighting Apaches; the John McDonald house, where the old Indian fighter lived before the gold strike; and a scale model of the Santa Rita del Cobre Fort and trading post, geographically awry but nevertheless interesting.

Gila Cliff Dwellings National Monument

About three miles from Pinos Altos, NM 15 passes the parking area for a monument to Ben V. Lilly, legendary mountain man who was employed by ranchers to rid the area of the mountain lions and bears which preyed upon their cattle. He was noted for his knowledge of animal trails in the region.

Lilly was a deeply religious man. If he was hot on a lion's trail on Saturday evening, he would abandon the chase until Monday morning. H. A. Hoover, a pioneer resident of the Southwest, wrote about Lilly in his book *Early Days in the Mogollons*:

> One day Ben killed a female lion and upon cutting her open found two cubs "haired out" and "to be born soon." Lilly skinned them and brought in the hides. "They were about ten inches long and three wide," and Ben thought he should be paid for them too. As Louis would not take it upon himself to do so, he put the matter up to some of the cowmen, several of whom declined payment. Then he saw Hugh McKeen, the largest individual cattle owner at that time. McKeen said that if the lion had not been killed there would have been two more, and he was willing to pay his part. The others then agreed. "So Ben got $150 for that lion." During the three-year period Louis Jones paid Lilly a total of $5500.

Ben Lilly received $50 each for "ridding" the country of mountain lions. —Hertzog
collection, Acc. No., U.T. El Paso Archives

The road continues through the Gila National Forest to the Gila Wilderness area. At the urging of Aldo Leopold, a forester with the National Forest Service, the Gila Wilderness was set aside in 1924 to be kept in its natural state, the first unit in the National Forest Wilderness System.

Early settlers in this area came across pottery fragments and ruins, artifacts left by prehistoric people who lived and farmed in the narrow valley of the Gila River. In 1884 Adolph Bandelier wrote of finding the Gila cliff dwellings, and in 1907 President Theodore Roosevelt signed a bill designating the cliff dwellings as a national monument.

The earliest ruin within the monument is a circular pit house from the Mogollon culture, 100-1000 A.D. The Mogollon people grew corn and beans, hunted, and gathered wild plant food. They made plain brown pottery. Other pit houses from toward the end of the period were rectangular, built entirely above ground of masonry or adobe. Some were of interwoven twigs or wattle. It was during this time that they developed white pottery with black designs.

Sometime after 1000 they started building their homes in natural caves. There are seven caves in a side-canyon cliff which faces southeast. Five contain caves, a total of about 40 rooms. Tree-ring analysis of timbers dates the structures through the 1280s. They raised squash, corn, and beans and probably amaranth and tobacco. They traded for pottery, cotton, obsidian for arrow points, and shells for ornaments.

The men were about five-feet-five and the women averaged five-foot-one. The women wore small cotton blankets about their shoulders, "skirts" or "aprons" of yucca cord, and sandals plaited of yucca, agave, and bark. The men wore headbands, small cotton blankets, breechclouts of woven cotton, and plaited sandals.

For generations, their voices echoed in the canyons, and then there were only the sounds of the streams and birds. By the early 1300s they had abandoned their homes and their fields. Why and where they went is not known.

Mimbres

About twenty miles south of the Gila cliff dwellings, at Lake Roberts, NM 35 turns south off NM 15 to go down the Mimbres Valley along the Mimbres River. Here there were also ruins left by people known to archaeologists as the Mimbres branch of the Mogollon culture. Unfortunately, the Mimbres ruins were overrun by early-day "pothunters," and they have not been restored.

Mimbres (willow) was once the site of the Georgetown Milling Company which processed ore from the erstwhile town of Georgetown, just down the road. It was also an agricultural community. In July, 1871, the people of Mimbres traced some of their stolen stock to the Indian reservation at Cañada Alamosa. They notified the superintendent of the agency they were going to organize a posse to recover their stock, "even at the sacrifice of every Indian in the tribe." If agents, traders or soldiers intervened, they would be treated as "common enemies of New Mexico." The people of Mimbres got their stock back.

Mimbres Hot Springs was once a health resort. The community is now occupied primarily by potters and other artisans.

Georgetown

The faint remainder of what was once the second richest mining camp in the Territory is located three miles east of Mimbres on a nondescript road. Georgetown flourished from 1876 until 1886. Two disasters destroyed its prosperity: smallpox drove out many families and the price of silver fell.

The town was named for George Magruder who came from Georgetown in the District of Columbia in 1872. Ore from mines such as the Naiad Queen, the Commercial, the Silver Bell, the MacGregor, and the Quien Sabe was shipped to stamp mills located at Mimbres on the river.

The town sprawled across a gulch and was divided into three sections. The commercial area was in the center. To the south were miners' quarters, saloons, a jail, bawdy houses, and shacks. Gambling was wide open and there were many killings. In the north part of town there were churches, schools, and better residences. Georgetown had the distinction of erecting the first free public school building in the Territory of New Mexico.

Today it is all gone. Only foundations remain. The town's bleak history is incised on headstones in a lonely cemetery on a hillside under a thick grove of piñons. Grave after grave displays sentimental inscriptions lamenting the passing of children, victims of a silent plague which was infinitely more devastating than the blazing six-shooters of quarreling miners and cowboys.

Fort Webster

In 1804, Francisco Manuel Elguea built a fort near the Santa Rita copper mines to protect them from the Apaches, a triangular structure with towers and loopholes. It was abandoned in 1835 but occupied by the U.S. Boundary Commission and a company of infantry in 1851 during a survey of the new boundary between the United States and Mexico.

After the old presidio was repaired, it was named Cantonment Dawson. In January, 1852, Maj. Governeur Morris of the 3rd U.S. Infantry arrived and constructed a more permanent post, named Fort Webster for Secretary of War Daniel Webster. Its mission was to protect local mines and settlements from the Apaches.

In less than eight months the troops were moved to a more favorable location near the Mimbres River to protect the road to the mines. When 300 troopers arrived they found fifty scared soldiers barricaded within a wall of old wagons, logs, barrels, and rocks. Apaches had killed four men and wounded three more within sight of the fort. The soldiers were happy to see relief arrive.

The soil in the area was fertile, and the soldiers raised some corn and oats. The natural resources of the area attracted some of Mangas Colorados' Apaches, who settled near Fort Webster and took up farming. This caused Territorial Governor William Carr Lane to decide that farming was a means whereby the Apaches could be pacified. The soldiers knew better. They knew that only old men, women, and children settled on the farms in the Mimbres Valley.

Inspector General Joseph K. F. Mansfield inspected Fort Webster in 1853. He was gratified to learn that most of the men of one company had joined the "Temperance Society." Colonel Mansfield recommended that the post be moved to a location on the Gila River on the trail to California. Instead, in December, the troops at Fort Webster were transferred to Fort Thorn on the Rio Grande, and the post on the Mimbres was abandoned.

Today, near San Lorenzo, where NM 35 intersects NM 152, there is a heap of rubble that was Fort Webster. However, a better view can be had; a three-quarter scale replica was constructed in 1980 by Frank Tatsch in Pinos Altos.

San Lorenzo

This peaceful agricultural community has roots deep in New Mexico's Spanish colonial period. It was founded in 1714 by Gov. Juan Ignacio Flores Mogollón and named in honor of St. Lawrence.

City of Rocks State Park

More than thirty-three million years ago, southwestern New Mexico underwent a baptism of fire. Volcanoes laid down thick blankets of ash which hardened into the rock called tuff. Over

Visitors to the City of Rocks are dwarfed by the massive formations.
—Courtesy New Mexico Economic Development & Tourism, No. 49

intervening centuries the rock has been wind-carved and rain-worn into shapes that hint of streets and houses, temples and towers, hence the name City of Rocks. It was dedicated as a state park in May, 1956.

Arrowheads and shards of Indian pottery reveal that it was a favorite Indian haunt. A rusted buckler has testified that at least one Spanish conquistador came this way. There are mysterious crosses carved on the rocks; some say they point to buried treasure, but no one has reported a find.

Faywood Hot Springs

Prehistoric artifacts indicated that the Mimbres Indians had long known of the hot springs bubbling from the ground. The area was settled in 1850 by a Dutch family. Col. Richard Hudson came to New Mexico in 1862 with the California column and returned to settle in Grant County. He built a hotel with the name Hudson Hot Springs Sanitarium Company. Stages brought health-seekers from afar.

The hotel burned in 1891 and the property was taken over by J. C. Fay, William Lockwood, and T. C. McDermott. A combination of Fay's and Lockwood's name became the postmark. The clientele did not return in sufficient numbers to make it a profitable enterprise. Today all that remains are the mineral springs. Water flows out of the ground at 129° and is piped to troughs serving four large three-foot-deep cement-lined pools. The water averages 115° when it reaches the pools. There is no charge for use.

Hanover—Hillsboro

Hanover

When the Silver City and Northern Railroad was built to the Hanover Mines in 1891, shipments of iron ore averaged nine carloads a day, and the mining fraternity predicted a bright future. However, the depression of 1893 spoiled the picture. All that remains are slag heaps, rusty machinery, and a few old Victorian houses.

Santa Rita Open Pit Copper Mine

The Indians told Cabeza de Vaca about the copper at Santa Rita in 1535. They gave him a rattle made of copper. But the Spanish conquistadors were blinded by the glitter of gold. It was more than 250 years later that a Spanish soldier, Don Manuel Carrasco, listened to the Indians and found strips of almost-pure copper lying in stream beds.

Colonel Carrasco brought a force of miners, and they soon found the main lode. Curious Indians came to watch the bearded white men digging their small holes in the earth, and the Spaniards promptly captured the Indians and used them as slaves.

The horizontal tunnels were some thirty-six inches in diameter. The Spaniards sent children in to dig the ore with their hands and small tools. They shoved it back between their legs to the next child, and so on until it arrived at a wider vertical shaft. There it was loaded into cowhide bags and carried up to the surface on swaying "chicken ladders"—logs with notches in the sides for footholds.

With the mining operation underway, the Spaniards turned their attention to building a fort. It was triangular with a thick-walled adobe tower at each of the three corners. Each side of the triangle was more than two hundred feet. A church was built close to the fort, and other buildings were added as time passed. The community was called Santa Rita del Cobre.

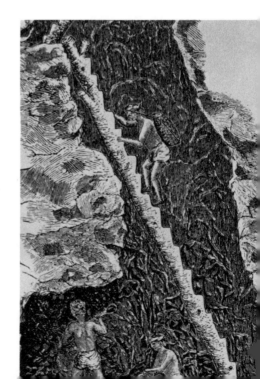

During operation by the Spaniards, Indian slaves carried ore out of the Santa Rita copper mine in bags on their backs. The ladders were notched logs called "chicken ladders ." —Ritch, 1885

Colonel Carrasco sold the mine to Don Francisco Elguea, a Chihuahua businessman. The inevitable priest attempted the conversion of Indians at Santa Rita del Cobre. The priest was particularly successful in teaching one bright-eyed Apache boy named Juan José to read Spanish. But the boy rejected Christianity and left to become a leader among the Mimbreño Apaches.

The Spaniards made a deal with Chief Juan José. As long as the miners stayed close to the mines, they could take out copper without molestation and in return the Mimbreño Apaches would receive cloth and needed supplies. But other Apache tribes were party to no such agreement. They raided into Chihuahua and Sonora at will.

In 1837 the Mexican government adopted the *Projecto de Guerra* (project for total war). The objective was to eliminate the Apaches. The state would pay bounties for Apache scalps: the equivalent of $100 for each brave, $50 for each squaw, and $25 for each child.

James Johnson, a miner, and a renegade trapper named Gleason devised a scheme to collect bounties en masse. They approached the alcalde of Santa Rita. They needed to know more about the country, and the Indians could tell them. If the alcalde would invite Indians to the fort, they would throw a feast. The mayor agreed and passed the word.

In the meantime, the two made preparations to collect scalps. They concealed a howitzer under a pile of hides in one corner of the fort. Across the room they piled trinkets, bright cloth, and dried meat. Chief Juan José was suspicious. He went into the fort along with the women and children, but posted his braves outside.

When the women and children were tightly packed around the pile of trade items, Johnson touched off the howitzer. At the same time, Gleason shot Juan José in the back. Johnson finished him off. Then Johnson and Gleason waded into the carnage to take scalps. It should be recorded that the Mexican government refused to pay Johnson; he fled to California where he died in poverty. However, the affair touched off warfare with the Apaches under Cochise, Mangas Colorados, Victorio, and Geronimo which would last almost eighty years. Needless to say, there was a long hiatus in mining activities at Santa Rita.

By 1910 most of the high-grade ore that could be reached by way of the shafts and tunnels had been removed, and Santa Rita was in a fair way to become a ghost town. A young mining engineer named John M. Sully advised open-pit mining. The Chino Copper Company brought in steam shovels to cut into the hills. After the Santa Fe Railroad laid tracks to the mine, Santa Rita began to grow. The

Prior to the use of trucks, a railroad hauled ore-bearing earth from the Santa Rita mine. —Courtesy New Mexico Economic Development & Tourism, No. 366

population was 500 in 1884. It grew to 1,500 by 1915 and eventually reached 6,000.

By 1950 the town was sitting on an island in the middle of the open pit. Copper ore in substantial quantities was found at the base of the island, and the Kennecott Copper Corporation, owner of both the town and the pit, ordered the town moved. Today what used to be the town of Santa Rita is part of the gaping hole that forms the Santa Rita mine.

The Santa Rita mine is now operated by a Phelps-Dodge-Mitsubishi partnership. The corporation maintains an observation point from which visitors can look at the vast open pit through a wire mesh fence and visit a nearby museum containing historical memorabilia. The vast cavity is a mile and three-fourths long, a mile wide, and a quarter of a mile deep. It is ringed by a series of fifty-foot-high multicolored terraces on which huge trucks, shovels, and drills work. From the observation point on the rim of the vast pit, they look like toys.

At the touch of a button, a tape-recorded voice describes the operation. Ore-bearing earth is gouged from the ground at the rate of 165,000 tons per day, processed at nearby installations to form a concentrate which is piped to the smelter at Hurley, nine miles away. The hearty-voiced speaker finishes by thanking observers for taking time to look at "the world's most beautiful copper mine," a statement which is challenged by every environmentalist who hears it. Nevertheless, nobody should pass the Santa Rita Open Pit Copper Mine without stopping to view its vastness.

————Historical Sidebar————

The Kneeling Nun

On a nearby mountain, a rock formation known as the Kneeling Nun (*La Monja Arrodillada*) overlooks operations at the Santa Rita del Cobre. Legend has it that Sister Teresa worked in an Indian mission. One day a soldier named Diego staggered into the mission, the only survivor from his party. As Sister Teresa nursed Diego back to health they fell in love, and she renounced her vow of chastity. She was turned to stone as she knelt to pray, forming the spire that is the Kneeling Nun.

Kingston

For a time it seemed that one could not scratch the ground in the Black Range without uncovering evidence of mineral wealth. Silver was first discovered near Kingston in 1880. A man named Barnaby pitched a tent under a big cottonwood tree and opened a store. Within five years the settlement grew to 7,000, as fortune hunters followed the rumor that the streets were paved with silver.

The town was laid out by the Kingston Townsite Company, deriving its name from the Iron King Mine. Other mines were the Brush Heap, Empire, Bullion, Comstock, and Miner's Dream. Ore was close to the surface and working the mines was comparatively cheap and easy. More than $10,000,000 in rich pay dirt was taken from the earth in less than fifteen years.

The tents that started the town were soon supplemented by lean-tos and shanties. Later, substantial houses of solid stone and brick appeared as residents built on the canyon sides. There were twenty-two saloons, three hotels, and a theater. Lillian Russell brought a troupe to perform in the theater.

It finally occurred to someone that the town did not have a church; sponsors of the idea went where money flowed the easiest, to the saloons, and passed their hats. Gamblers threw in money and diamond stud-pins; dance hall girls gave jewelry; and miners contributed gold dust and nuggets. Some of the girls worked for

Sadie Orchard, who plied her trade on "Virtue Avenue," which paralleled Main Street. The collection totaled $1,500. An appropriate sign was placed behind the altar of the resulting house of worship: *The Golden Gate*.

Kingston had some well-known figures. As a young man, A. B. Fall, future Secretary of the Interior, taught school there; Edward L. Doheny, who would join Fall in precipitating the Teapot Dome Scandal, did odd jobs around town. From early in the town's history, the Spit and Whittle Club met every Sunday afternoon at nearby Pickett's Springs.

As miners and prospectors moved on to look for better diggings, the Spit and Whittle Club had fewer members and more time to meet. However, Kingston did not completely expire, as was the case with so many of New Mexico's mining camps. It has hung on to become a popular destination for the Sunday-drive crowd, and a few artists have settled into the old homes.

Hillsboro

In Box Canyon, between Kingston and Hillsboro, the road along Percha Creek squeezes down to a narrow passage. This was the route of freighters and stagecoaches during the 1880s, and Apaches used the huge rocks along the canyon walls to hide and await their prey. Summer rains could turn the dry creek into a deathtrap. Businessmen in Kingston and Hillsboro strung telegraph wires between the two towns so stage drivers and freighters could be warned of flash floods. Even this did not always save men and horses from drowning in Box Canyon.

Hillsboro's history began in 1877 when two prospectors discovered gold nearby. Each wrote his choice of a name for the town on a slip of paper and put it in a hat. One drew. The selection was Hillsborough, later contracted to Hillsboro. The town became the county seat of Sierra County, and miners came to register their claims. Irish names seemed to be in vogue: St. Patrick, Donegal Slasher, Erin Go Braugh, Galloway Slugger, and Tara Hall were among the list.

Madame Sadie Orchard owned the Ocean Grove Hotel. She provided miners and prospectors with entertainment in the form of wine and women. The hotel is now occupied by the Black Range Museum, which displays memorabilia of mining days, some of Sadie Orchard's effects, as well as equipment used in the Tom Ying House, a cafe which was better known as the "Chinaman's Place."

Tom Ying died in 1959. Estimates of his age at the time of his death range from 104 to 116 years.

Sadie Orchard came to New Mexico Territory in 1886 from London. She operated brothels in both Kingston and Hillsboro and, later, more respectable establishments. With her husband she ran a stage and freight line serving outlying mining camps and was said to be capable of taking the reins when it became necessary. She remained in the community until her death in 1943.

Hillsboro did not depend entirely upon mining. It was also a frontier cow town. The Ladder Ranch was the largest outfit in the area. One of Eugene Manlove Rhodes's novels, *The Proud Sheriff*, was laid in Hillsboro at the turn of the century.

Hillsboro had its day in the sun in May and June of 1899 when Oliver M. Lee and Jim Gililland were tried for the murder of Judge Albert J. Fountain and his son. The trial placed a strain upon Hillsboro's meager facilities. The only connection to the outside world was by Sadie Orchard's stage eighteen miles south to the railroad spur at Lake Valley. There were no telephones or telegraph. Some seventy-five witnesses had been subpoenaed. Reporters and correspondents from El Paso, the Hearst papers, the

Breakfast around the chuck wagon at a roundup on the Ladder Ranch.
—Courtesy New Mexico Economic Development & Tourism, No. 16,155

Associated Press, and small newspapers from about the Territory were moving in.

The Western Union Telegraph Company ran a wire from Lake Valley and provided two operators to man the key. Witnesses for the Territory were established in a tent city on the north side of town with cooks, waiters, and guards. The defense established a similar village south of town with a chuck wagon to supply meals to the supporters of Lee and Gililland. The Little Corner Saloon, the Union Hotel Bar, and the Parlor Saloon catered to all comers without discrimination.

Oliver Lee's friends brought an air of tenseness to the courtroom. It was rumored that three of his cowboys were prepared to get him out of the country if the verdict went against him. The presentation of witnesses and their cross-examination dragged on and on, with spectators waiting for the final showdown between prosecuting attorney Thomas Benton Catron of Santa Fe and Albert Bacon Fall, the defense lawyer from Las Cruces.

The trial had strong political ramifications. Democrats hated Catron because he represented the Santa Fe Ring, for which reason they believed Oliver Lee and Jim Gililland innocent. Republicans automatically believed them guilty for equally strong political reasons. The prosecution presented damning evidence. The defense countered that it was circumstantial; after all, there were no bodies. Harry Daugherty drove the point home:

"It is customary to bring into court some part of the body, or something that carries absolute conviction that the crime has been committed. I never heard of a case where men were put on trial before a jury for murder when there was not a scintilla of evidence that a crime had been committed."

Albert Fall finished off the defense with a startling accusation: "The prosecution of Oliver Lee is the result of a conspiracy to send an innocent man to the gallows. The District Attorney is involved in that conspiracy; the Honorable Thomas B. Catron is involved in that conspiracy. His honor on the bench is involved in that conspiracy. . . . Our defense is an alibi, clearly proved. You would not hang a yellow dog on the evidence that has been presented here, much less two men."

Cheering and applause broke out, and Judge Frank W. Parker had some difficulty restoring order. The courtroom was full that night at eight o'clock for Catron's final speech. He reviewed the prosecution's evidence in detail. At 11:20 the jury retired, expecting to complete their work the next morning.

Albert Fall insisted upon an immediate verdict. He wanted a decision while his speech was fresh in the minds of the jury. The jurymen were called back. The ending was anticlimactic. It took them only eight minutes to find the defendants "Not guilty."

There has not been as much excitement in Hillsboro since that day. Today, Hillsboro appears on some lists of New Mexico ghost towns, much to the chagrin of a few hundred people who still live there, mostly retired people and a number of artists and writers. The town is now best known for its annual apple festival. The Hillsboro General Store serves tourists and is the gathering place for a morning coffee klatch among local residents. It opened in 1879 and has never ceased operation. A sign on the front advertises that it still sells gold pans.

NM 27
Lake Valley—Nutt

Lake Valley

The ghostly remains of Lake Valley are eighteen miles south of Hillsboro. The Lake Valley region was one of the richest silver-producing districts in New Mexico. George W. Lufkin discovered ore in August, 1878, and a rush followed. He chose the name Daly for the community after George Daly who was killed by the Apaches, but the site was renamed for a small lake near the settlement.

The ore in the Lake Valley district was fabulously rich. A chunk valued at $7,000 was displayed at a Denver exposition in 1882. That same year water was brought in and a reducing works was built at a cost of $200,000. In less than six months, the Sierra Grande produced $735,260 worth of bullion.

Two miners struck a vein and sold out for $100,000. Two days after they sold the claim the lead ran into what became known as the Bridal Chamber, a subterranean room. The Bridal Chamber yielded $3,000,000 in silver. The railroad built a spur track into the room so that silver could be loaded directly into cars. The expense of working this cavity was so small that one man offered the owners a handsome sum for the privilege of entering the mine and taking down all the silver he could pick single-handed in one day.

Lake Valley was a thriving mining camp while the ore lasted. The booming town died during the panic of 1893. —Ritch, 1882-1883.

But mining activity declined and even the lake dried up. Today Lake Valley is a true ghost town, in spite of renewed activities from time to time by small operators.

Nutt

This former station and trading point on the Santa Fe Railroad dates from 1881. It was named for a Colonel Nutt, an original stockholder and director of the railroad. When the line was being built from Rincon to Deming, many mines opened up at Lake Valley and Hillsboro, presenting the prospects for heavy ore shipments from the Black Range. Nutt was the logical point of shipment to refineries. However, when the railroad was extended to Lake Valley in 1884 nearly all of the people moved there. At the present time, Nutt's only business establishment is the Middle of Nowhere Cafe and Bar, operated by Nutt's only two residents.

Historical Excursion

NM 90
Tyrone

This turquoise and copper mining area in the Burro Mountains was named by a Mr. Honeyky for Tyrone, Ireland. It was acquired by Phelps-Dodge in 1909 when they started buying up mining claims. By 1916 the corporation had accumulated 300.

The corporation planned a "dream city"—a mining town without saloons or brothels. Management commissioned architect Bertram Goodhue to plan this paradise; he had designed the 1915 San Diego Exposition. The result was truly a showplace.

Spanish-type architecture was the motif for homes and office buildings alike. The hospital had an air-conditioned X-ray laboratory; a mercantile with colonnades and planters was dubbed the "Western Wanamaker." A $100,000 railroad station had a marble drinking fountain, handcrafted benches with hot-air vents under them, carved ceiling beams, and an elaborate chandelier.

The 7,000 inhabitants had a school for 1,000 students, a library with 5,000 books, churches of various denominations, a bank, a Masonic lodge, and a jail. Utilities were artfully concealed underground. The price tag was $1,000,000, a massive expenditure for the time. The associated mine had a shaft which probed 800 feet deep to seventy-five miles of tunnels.

After World War I the copper bubble burst. The price of copper dropped and Tyrone became known as a "million-dollar ghost town." And so it moldered until 1966, when the mine was reactivated as an open-pit operation. With the removal of millions of tons of overburden, Tyrone—with all of its Spanish-style homes—was sacrificed. Today a visitors' lookout provides a view of the mining operation and where Tyrone used to be.

US 180
Chloride Flat—Luna

Chloride Flat (Silver City)

On September 2, 1870, the discovery of La Providencia lode on Chloride Flat started a boom which overshadowed the rest of the area. Within a year and a half, more than three hundred claims were filed, and an abandoned mine was discovered which had apparently been worked in the pre-American era.

In March, 1871, 1,900 pounds of ore from La Providencia were shipped to Newark, New Jersey, in rawhide sacks to be refined. The profit was $752.55. During the week ending June 22, 1872, four rather crude and inefficient local mills powered by blacksmith's bellows produced a total of $6,990.60. As improvements continued, the "first perfect silver mill in the Territory" was operating in 1874. The "76" mine became the outstanding producer. Its output filled "giant" wagons with boiler-plated beds to keep the Chloride Flat smelter running twenty-four hours a day. In twelve years the "76" yielded $1,260,000.

Chloride Flat was named by John Bullard and his party in 1870. The area is now on private property within the city limits of Silver City on the west edge of town.

Historical Excursion

NM 211
Gila—Fort West

Gila

This community has long been an outfitting point for trips into the Gila Wilderness and the Mogollon Mountains. It was once the headquarters of the Lyons-Campbell Ranch. In 1884 the ranch was advertised as the largest ranch in the world, stretching sixty miles from north to south and forty miles east to west. Thomas Lyons dreamed of an operation which would make Grant County the biggest cattle market west of Kansas City. His dream did not become reality. In 1917 he was mysteriously murdered in El Paso, Texas.

Kwilleykia Ruins

Saladoan people farmed this fertile valley from 1325 until 1475. They abandoned their homes because of a flash flood. Because of the emergency, the inhabitants had to leave their belongings behind, giving archaeologists a rare opportunity to study their tools, utensils, and weapons. After the departure of the Saladoans, passing bands of Apaches camped in the ruins of their community. The Apaches abandoned the bodies of those who died there, and later visitors found entire skeletons leaning against the walls of rooms.

Fort West

In January, 1863, Gen. Joseph West established the fort that bore his name on a bluff on the Gila River as a base for operations against the Apaches. The construction was not to interfere with their primary mission of campaigning against the Indians; nevertheless, the soldiers were ordered to plant corn, cultivate a garden, and gather hay.

In March, 1863, a band of Apaches ran off the post's horses, and Maj. William Van Cleave chased them all the way to Dog Canyon near present-day Alamogordo. The troopers killed two dozen Apaches in fifteen minutes. The remainder of the Indians rode to Fort Stanton to surrender to Kit Carson and live on a reservation.

Fort West was occupied for less than a year. The order for its abandonment was given on Christmas Day, 1863. At the turn of the century, many of the post's buildings were salvaged for use in building a nearby ranch headquarters.

Pleasanton

This was a Mormon settlement, founded in the 1870s on the San Francisco River and named for an Army officer. It is surrounded by small farms, orchards, and ranches.

As the highway proceeds to Glenwood, it passes Soldier's Hill, the scene of a massacre in 1885. U.S. troops were pursuing a band of Apaches. The Indians divided into three groups and caught the soldiers in a deadly triple cross fire. The dead were buried in a hillside cemetery on the WS Ranch, some eighteen miles farther down the road. The cemetery can be seen from the highway.

The WS Ranch was a sprawling ranch operated in the 1880s by Capt. William French. Butch Cassidy and his men once worked as hands on the WS Ranch, using aliases. Captain French wrote a lively book about his experiences, *Some Recollections of a Western Ranchman: New Mexico, 1883-1899.*

Glenwood

The town of Glenwood started as Whitewater, about five miles above the present location. Then it was called Graham when a mill was constructed to treat ore from the Confidence Mine. The creek often dried up, so a pipeline was built to reach about three miles up Whitewater Creek to where there was always water in order to have water power for the milling operation. In 1904 the name of the community was changed to Clear Creek. On September 11, 1906, the name was again changed to Glenwood and the post office was moved to its present site.

452

Today Glenwood is a small resort village, almost hidden by trees. It serves as a jumping off point for hunting and fishing trips and for camping trips in the wilderness area. It is the site of a state-operated fish hatchery with a plentitude of picnic facilities.

Historical Excursion

NM 174
The Catwalk

The path of the old wooden pipeline down Whitewater Canyon has been traced by a walkway between the towering walls of the rugged box canyon. When the pipeline was built during the 1880s to bring water to the mill that processed ore from the Confidence Mine, it was necessary to walk on the slick wooden pipe in order to perform maintenance chores, hence the name Catwalk.

In 1935 the Civilian Conservation Corps built a wooden walkway so that visitors could look down upon the rushing water. Subsequently, the Forest Service replaced the wooden structure with a sturdy metal walk. In places the canyon narrows to a width of only twenty feet. It towers 250 feet overhead. In many spots a hiker can leave the walkway and relax on the grassy banks of Whitewater Creek.

The walls of Whitewater Canyon tower above the Catwalk.
—Photo by the authors

NM 159
Mogollon

As prospectors probed the hills and panned the creeks, the activity shifted to Mogollon (pronounced *Muggy-yone*). The name, taken from the surrounding mountains, commemorates Don Juan Ignacio Flores Mogollón, governor of New Mexico from 1712 to 1715. Mogollon quickly became a thriving, rowdy mining town with the usual quota of saloons. One was called the Bloated Goat.

It also attracted outlaws who preyed upon passengers on stagecoaches which negotiated the precipitous road in and out of Mogollon. In 1906 three transient girls from Silver City went to Mogollon to ply their trade. A highwayman held up the stage and took the girls' money—except for one. As her sisters wept over their loss, she took money from where she had concealed it in the long hair on top of her head.

On one occasion a stage was waylaid for the purpose of collecting a debt. Bob Hollimon had worked for a rancher named Hannigan on the promise of receiving a percentage of the calves branded. Hannigan sold out and was apparently leaving Mogollon without making arrangements to pay Hollimon. H. A. Hoover told how the debt was collected:

> The stage left Mogollon after midnight in those days and likely got out of Glenwood before daylight that time of year. In the early morning of February 16, 1906, on that first hill below Glenwood, Bob stopped the stage and at gun's point made Hannigan get out. The stage then proceeded, unmolested. To prevent easy tracking, Bob wrapped gunny sacks around Hannigan's feet and then marched him to the Little Whitewater country east of Glenwood. He then took a chain and padlocked Hannigan to a tree.
>
> The chain was long enough to reach a small stream; there was a cup so he could get a drink. For food a bag of hard sourdough biscuits was left within reach. During February it can get pretty cold in those foothills. Fortunately Hannigan had on a heavy overcoat. He and Bob must have had some sort of a settlement then and there, for Bob rode over to Alma with an order on Hannigan to pay him $1000. . . .
>
> The code of frontier justice conceded that Hannigan "had it coming to him." Desultory attempts were made to apprehend Bob Hollimon without results. Years later his nephew stated

that he "got away on the best horse in the country, which is the same as getting out today in a Cadillac." Bob Hollimon resided in California unmolested for many years.

Mines in the Mogollon area produced more than $15,000,000 in gold, silver, and copper. In 1913, Mogollon's mines accounted for forty percent of New Mexico's gold and silver production. But high production costs and a dwindling supply of ore brought the bonanza to an end. Mines such as the Bloomer Girl, Little Charlie, the Maud S., the Last Chance, and the Leap Year played out.

The residents moved away, leaving schools, churches, saloons, gambling halls, and pleasure palaces behind. H. A. Hoover was left at the Little Fanney Mine as a caretaker, awaiting better times. He stayed into the 1950s, but better times never came.

However, tourists "discovered" Mogollon. They negotiated the tortuous nine-mile road off US 180 carrying cameras instead of six-shooters. They looked for trout in the streams instead of gold. Artists came to sketch the weathered buildings, snaggle-toothed chimneys, and rusting equipment; crafts people came to claim squatters' rights on old buildings in which to work; and Mogollon experienced a minor rejuvenation.

The Little Fanney Mine. —Hetzog Collection, Acc. No. 540, U.T. El Paso Archives

Freighting in the Mountains

The steep, narrow road with hairpin turns presented a problem to freighters who had to negotiate the eighty miles between Mogollon and Silver City. Tons of equipment and ore required several teams to pull a single freight wagon. On hairpin turns the lead team was often going in the opposite direction of the load to which they were attached.

An ingenious hitching arrangement provided that all teams would always be helping to pull the load. A heavy chain long enough to accommodate the number of teams was attached to the axle of the wagon. The team closest to the wagon was hitched to the wagon's tongue in the customary manner in order that they could steer the vehicle. Other teams were hitched at intervals to the long chain by means of doubletrees attached to short lengths of chain. Thus, their pulling force was transmitted to the long chain which was fastened directly to the wagon axle.

The driver mounted an animal on the left-hand side of the teams. He maintained control by means of a check line which passed through a ring on the hame of each left-hand animal and was fastened to the lead. By manipulation of this check line, the driver controlled the lead team, keeping it on the road.

Freight teams and ore wagons in the Mogollons during the mining days.
—Hertzog Collection, Acc. No. 540, U.T. El Paso Archives

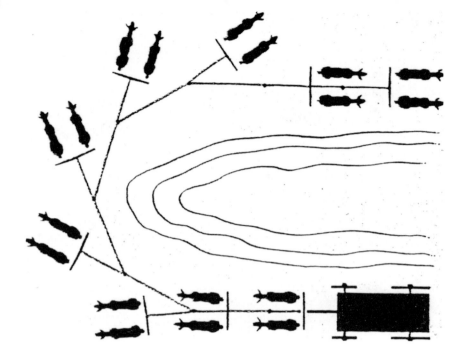

As the front team went around turns, the long chain would rub the legs of one of the animals in the team behind—the right or left, depending upon the direction of the curve—and that animal would jump over the chain to get out of its way. Thus, the animals were kept on the road and at the same time maintained a pull on the long chain which was attached to the wagon.

Alma

This once prosperous trading post for ranches and mining camps is now occupied by few residents. It was established in 1881 and named for the wife of one of the original settlers. It was once a stop on the "outlaw trail" to and from Mexico. The WS Ranch spreads out around Alma. While working on the WS Ranch a member of Butch Cassidy's gang apparently developed an affinity for the area. After serving time in the penitentiary he came back to live in Alma for two years before moving on to Wyoming.

Cooney's Tomb

James C. Cooney was a Quartermaster Sergeant of the 8th Cavalry, stationed at Fort Bayard in 1870. While on a scout through the Mogollon Mountains in 1875, he found signs of silver on Mineral

Creek. He waited until his discharge the following year and returned to work his claim, the Silver Bar. Others followed, and mining camps sprung up along Mineral Creek. The whole area became known as the Cooney Mining District. Then, the Apaches struck, and Cooney was killed in 1880.

His friends blasted a hole in a immense boulder, deposited the body, and sealed the opening. The tomb is about five miles off US 180 on Mineral Creek.

Luna

This community was named for Don Solomon Luna who was for more than a quarter of a century a leader of the Republican party in the Territory and the state. He grazed sheep in the valleys and on mountainsides. In the heyday of their business, the Luna family was credited with owning 150,000 sheep. Luna was a prime mover in organization of the Sheep Sanitary Board and served as its first president. Later, this region was populated by Mormon families who journeyed from Salt Lake City and prospered. The post office dates from 1886.

Bibliography for Additional Reading

Abert, James William. *Abert's New Mexico Report 1846-47*. Albuquerque: Horn & Wallace, 1962.

Bandelier, Adolf F. *The Delight Makers*. Reprinted, New York: Harcourt Brace Jovanovich, Inc., 1971.

Beachum, Larry. *William Becknell, Father of the Santa Fe Trail*. El Paso: Texas Western Press, 1982.

Beadle, J. H. *The Undeveloped West; or, Five Years in the Territories*. Philadelphia: National Publishing Co., 1873.

Beck, Warren A. *New Mexico: A History of Four Centuries*. Norman: University of Oklahoma Press, 1962.

Bolton, Herbert E. *Coronado: Knight of Pueblos and Plains*. New York: Whittlesby House & Albuquerque: University of New Mexico Press, 1949.

Bonney, Cecil. *Looking Over My Shoulder: Seventy-five Years in the Pecos Valley*. Roswell, New Mexico: Hall-Poorbaugh Press, Inc., 1971.

Cather, Willa. *Death Comes for the Archbishop*. New York: A. A. Knopf, 1959.

Charles, Mrs. Tom. *Tales of the Tularosa*. Alamogordo: 1953.

Chilton, Lance et al. *New Mexico: A new guide to the colorful state*. Albuquerque: University of New Mexico Press, 1984.

Chronic, Halka. *Roadside Geology of New Mexico*. Missoula: Mountain Press Publishing Co., 1987.

Cleaveland, Agnes Morley. *No Life for a Lady*. Boston: Houghton Mifflin Company, 1941.

Cleland, Robert Glass. *This Reckless Breed of Men: The Trappers and Fur Traders of the Southwest*. Reprint, Albuquerque: University of New Mexico Press, 1976.

Coe, Wilbur. *Ranch on the Ruidoso: The Story of a Pioneer Family in New Mexico, 1871-1968*. New York: Alfred A. Knopf, 1968.

Colton, Ray C. *The Civil War in the Western Territories: Arizona, Colorado, New Mexico, and Utah*. Norman: University of Oklahoma Press, 1959.

Conkling, Roscoe P. & Margaret B. *The Butterfield Overland Mail, 1857-1869*. 3 vols. Glendale, California: Arthur H. Clark Co., 1947.

Connelley, William Elsey. *Doniphan's Expedition and the Conquest of New Mexico and California*. Topeka, Kansas: 1907.

Cooke, Philip St. George, William Henry Chase Whiting, Francois Xavier Aubry. Ralph B. Bieber, ed. *Exploring Southwestern Trails, 1846-1854*. Glendale: Arthur H. Clark Co., 1938.

Copeland, Fayette. *Kendall of the Picayune: Being His Adventures in New Orleans, on the Texan Santa Fe Expedition, in the Mexican War, and in the Colonization of the Texas Frontier*. Norman: University of Oklahoma Press, 1943.

Cozzens, Samuel Woodworth. *The Marvelous Country, or Three Years in Arizona and New Mexico, The Apaches' Home . . .* Boston: Lee and Shepard, 1876.

Cremony, John C. *Life Among the Apaches*. San Francisco: A. Roman & Company, 1868.

Crichton, Kyle S. *Law and Order, Ltd.: The Rousing Life of Elfego Baca of New Mexico*. Glorieta, New Mexico: Rio Grande Press, 1970.

Davis, W. W. H. *El Gringo, or New Mexico and Her People*. New York: 1857. Reprint, Lincoln: University of Nebraska Press, 1982.

Domínguez, Francisco Atanasio. *The Missions of New Mexico, 1776*. Trans. and ed. by Eleanor B. Adams and Fray Angelico Chavez. Albuquerque: University of New Mexico Press, 1956.

Downey, Fairfax. *Indian-Fighting Army*. New York: Charles Scribner's Sons, 1941.

Dutton, Bertha P. *Sun Father's Way: The Kiva Murals of Kuaua*. Albuquerque: University of New Mexico Press, 1963.

Ebright, Malcolm. *The Tierra Amarilla Grant: A History of Chicanery*. Santa Fe: The Center for Land Grant Studies, 1980.

Evans, Max. *The Hi Lo Country*. Reprint, Albuquerque: University of New Mexico Press, 1983.

——————. *Long John Dunn of Taos*. Los Angeles: Westernlore Press, 1959.

——————. *The Rounders*. New York: The Macmillan Co., 1960.

Federal Writers' Program. *New Mexico: A Guide to the Colorful State*. Revised edition, ed. by Joseph Miller. New York: Hastings House, 1962.

Fierman, Floyd S. *The Impact of the Frontier on a Jewish Family*. El Paso: Texas Western College Press, 1961.

Finley, James Bradley. *Autobiography of Rev. James B. Finley; or, Pioneer Life in the West*. Cincinnati: 1853.

Forrest, Earle R. *Missions and Pueblos of the Old Southwest*. Cleveland: Arthur H. Clark Co., 1929.

Frazer, Robert W., ed. *Mansfield [Joseph King Fenno] on the Condition of the Western Forts, 1853-54*. Norman: University of Oklahoma Press, 1963.

French, William. *Some Recollections of a Western Ranchman: New Mexico, 1883-1899*. New York: Frederick A. Stokes Company, 1928.

Fugate, Francis L. *The Spanish Heritage of the Southwest*. El Paso: Texas Western Press, 1952.

Garrard, Lewis H. *Wah-To-Yah and the Taos Trail*. Norman: University of Oklahoma Press, 1955.

Gerald, Rex E. & Olympia Caudillo. "Bravo 1795: An Inventory of the Missions of Senecú, Ysleta, and Socorro by Fray José Bravo in the Year 1795," *Password*, Spring, 1988.

Granjon, Monsignor Henry. *Along the Rio Grande: A Pastoral Visit to Southwest New Mexico in 1902*. Albuquerque: University of New Mexico Press, 1986.

Grant, Blanche C. *When Old Trails Were New: The Story of Taos*. New York: The Press of the Pioneers, Inc., 1934.

Gregg, Andrew K. *New Mexico In the Nineteenth Century*. Albuquerque: University of New Mexico Press, 1968.

Gregg, Andy. *Drums of Yesterday: The Forts of New Mexico*. Santa Fe: Press of the Territorian, 1968.

Gregg, Josiah. *Commerce of the Prairies*. New York: H. G. Langley, 1844. Reprint, Norman: University of Oklahoma Press, 1974.

Griggs, George. *History of Mesilla Valley, or The Gadsen Purchase*. Mesilla, New Mexico, 1930.

Hackett, Charles W., ed. *Revolt of the Pueblo Indians of New Mexico and Otermín's Attempted Reconquest, 1680-1682*. Albuquerque: University of New Mexico Press, 1942.

Hafen, LeRoy R. & Ann W., *Old Spanish Trail: Santa Fe to Los Angeles*. Glendale: Arthur H. Clark Co., 1954.

——————, eds. *Rufus B. Sage: His Letters and Papers, 1836-1847, with Annotated Reprint of his "Scenes in the Rocky Mountains . . ."* 2 vols. Glendale: Arthur H. Clark Co., 1956.

Hall, Martin Hardwick. *Sibley's New Mexico Campaign*. Austin: University of Texas Press, 1960.

Hallenbeck, Cleve. *Land of the Conquistadores*. Caldwell, Idaho: Caxton Printers, 1950.

Hallenbeck, Cleve & Juanita H. Williams. *Legends of the Spanish Southwest*. Glendale: Arthur H. Clark Co., 1938.

Hammond, George P. *Don Juan de Oñate and the Founding of New Mexico*. Santa Fe: 1927.

—————— & Agapito Ray, eds. & trans. *Narratives of the Coronado Expedition*. Albuquerque: 1940.

Hart, E. Richard. "Historic Zuñi Land Use," *Zuñi History*. Sun Valley, Idaho: Institute of the American West, May, 1983.

Hendron, J. W. "We Found America's Oldest Tobacco," *New Mexico*, November, 1946.

Hertzog, Peter. *A Directory of New Mexico Desperados*. Santa Fe: The Press of the Territorian, 1965.

Hewett, Edgar L. & Wayne L. Mauzy. *Landmarks of New Mexico*. Albuquerque: University of New Mexico Press, 1953.

Hilton, Conrad N. *Be My Guest*. Englewood Cliffs, N. J.: Prentice-Hall, 1957.

Hollister, Ovando J. *History of the First Regiment of Colorado Volunteers*. Denver: Thos. Gibson & Co., 1863. Reprinted as *Boldly They Rode*. Lakewood, Colo.: The Golden Press, 1949.

Hordes, Stanley M. & Carol Joiner. *Historical Markers in New Mexico*. Santa Fe: Delgado Studios, 1984.

Horgan, Paul. *Great River: The Rio Grande in North American History*. New York: Rinehart & Company, Inc., 1954.

James, General Thomas. Milo Milton Quaife, ed. *Three Years Among the Indians and Mexicans*. Chicago: R. R. Donnelley & Sons, 1953.

Keleher, William A. *The Fabulous Frontier*. Albuquerque: University of New Mexico Press, 1962.

——————. *Violence in Lincoln County, 1869-1881*. Albuquerque: University of New Mexico Press, 1957.

Kessell, John L. *The Missions of New Mexico Since 1776*. Albuquerque: University of New Mexico Press, 1980.

Kropp, Simon F. *That All May Learn: New Mexico State University, 1888-1964*. Las Cruces: New Mexico State University, 1972.

LaFarge, Oliver. *Santa Fe: The Autobiography of a Southwestern Town*. Norman: University of Oklahoma Press, 1959.

Lane, Lydia Spencer. *I Married a Soldier or Old Days in the Old Army*. Albuquerque: Horn & Wallace, 1964.

Lecompte, Janet. *Rebellion in Rio Arriba*. Albuquerque: University of New Mexico Press, 1985.

Lee, Willis T. "A Visit to Carlsbad Cavern," *The National Geographic Magazine*, January, 1924.

Lockwood, Frank C. *The Apache Indians*. New York: The Macmillan Co., 1938.

Magoffin, Susan Shelby. Stella M. Drum, ed. *Down the Santa Fe Trail into Mexico: The Diary of Susan Shelby Magoffin, 1846-1847*. New Haven: Yale University Press, 1926.

Marshall, Michael P. & Henry J. Walt. *Rio Abajo: Prehistory and History of a Rio Grande Province*. Santa Fe: Historic Preservation Division, 1984.

McDowell, Bart. "New Mexico: Between Frontier and Future," *The National Geographic Magazine*, November, 1987.

Metz, Leon C. *Pat Garrett: The Story of a Western Lawman*. Norman: University of Oklahoma Press, 1974.

Minge, Ward Alan. *Ácoma: Pueblo in the Sky*. Albuquerque: University of New Mexico Press, 1926.

Morand, Sheila. *Santa Fe Then and Now*. Santa Fe: Sunstone Press, 1984.

Nabokov, Peter. *Tijerina and the Courthouse Raid*. Albuquerque: University of New Mexico Press, 1969.

Naegle, Conrad Keeler. "The History of Silver City, New Mexico, 1870-1886." Master's Thesis: University of New Mexico, 1943.

Pack, Arthur N. *The Ghost Ranch Story*. Philadelphia: Board of Christian Education of the United Presbyterian Church in the U.S.A., 1960.

Pearce, T. M., ed. *New Mexico Place Names: A Geographical Dictionary*. Albuquerque: University of New Mexico Press, 1965.

Pearson, Jim Berry. *The Maxwell Land Grant*. Norman: University of Oklahoma Press, 1961.

——————. "A New Mexico Gold Story—The Elizabethtown-Red River Area." Doctoral dissertation: University of Texas, 1955.

Perrigo, Lynn. *Gateway to Glorieta: A History of Las Vegas, New Mexico*. Boulder: Pruett Publishing Company, 1982.

Peters, Dewitt C. *Kit Carson's Life and Adventures, . . .* Hartford: Dustin, Gilman & Co., 1874.

Pew, Thomas W., Jr. "Goodbye to Main Street 66," *American West,* September/October, 1984.

Reiter, Robert Louis. "The History of Fort Union, New Mexico." Master's Thesis: University of California, 1953.

Robie, Edward H. "Carlsbad N. M.: Largest, Deepest, Oldest, Newest, Best Lighted of the World's Caves." *Engineering and Mining Journal,* May 23, 1930.

Robinson, Mary L. "History of Roosevelt County, New Mexico." Master's Thesis: University of Texas, 1947.

Ruxton, George F. *Adventures in Mexico and the Rocky Mountains.* New York: Harper & Brothers, 1848.

Sandoval, Richard C. *One of Our Fifty Is Missing.* Santa Fe: New Mexico Magazine Publications Group, 1986.

Simmons, Marc. *Albuquerque: A Narrative History.* Albuquerque: University of New Mexico Press, 1982.

—————. (Joan Myers, photographs). *Along the Santa Fe Trail.* Albuquerque: University of New Mexico Press, 1986.

—————. *Spanish Government in New Mexico.* Albuquerque: University of New Mexico Press, 1968.

Sloane, Eric. *Return to Taos: A Sketchbook of Roadside America.* Wilfred Funk, 1960.

Sonnichsen, C. L. *The Mescalero Apaches.* Norman: University of Oklahoma Press, 1958.

—————. *Tularosa: Last of the Frontier West.* New York: Devin-Adair Company, 1960.

Stanley, F. [Stanley Francis Crocchioli]. *Desperadoes of New Mexico.* Denver: The World Press, Inc., 1953.

Tallack, William. *The California Overland Express.* London: 1865.

Tamarín y Romeral, Pedro. Eleanor B. Adams, ed. *Bishop Tamarín's Visitation of New Mexico, 1760.* Albuquerque: Historical Society of New Mexico, 1954.

Tietjen, Gary L. *Encounter with the Frontier.* Los Alamos: 1969.

Twitchell, Ralph Emerson. *Old Santa Fe: The Story of New Mexico's Ancient Capital.* Chicago: The Rio Grande Press, Inc., 1925.

Webb, James Josiah. *Adventures in the Santa Fe Trade, 1844-1847.* Glendale: Arthur H. Clark Co., 1951.

Wellman, Paul I. *Death on Horseback.* Philadelphia: J. B. Lippincott Co., 1947.

Wislezwenus, Adolphus. *Memoir of a Tour to Northern Mexico.* Washington: Tippin & Streeter, 1848. Reprint, Albuquerque: University of New Mexico Press, 1969.

Wroth, William. *The Chapel of Our Lady of Talpa.* Colorado Springs: Taylor Museum, Colorado Springs Fine Arts Center, 1979.

Sources of Illustrations

Illustrations from early New Mexico histories and accounts of travels in the Territory are from the following sources:

Atchison, Topeka, and Santa Fe Railroad. *Las Vegas Hot Springs, New Mexico.* (Chicago, 1887).

Beadle, John H. *The Undeveloped West.* (Philadelphia, 1873).

Bell, William A. *New Tracks in North America.* (New York, 1870).

Conard, Howard L. *Uncle Dick Wootton.* (Chicago, 1891).

Cozzens, Samuel W. *The Marvelous Country.* (Boston, 1876).

Cushing, Frank H. "My Adventures in Zuñi," *The Century Magazine,* Dec., 1882; Feb., May, 1883.

Davis, W. W. H. *El Gringo.* (New York, 1857).

Drake, Samuel Adams. *The Making of the Great West.* (New York, 1887).

Emory, W. H. *Notes on a Military Reconnoissance from Fort Leavenworth to San Diego.* (Washington, 1848).

Frank Leslie's Illustrated Newspaper, Aug. 9, 1879.

Frost, Max. *New Mexico.* (Santa Fe, 1894).

Garrett, Pat F. *The Authentic Life of Billy the Kid.* (Santa Fe, 1882).

Gregg, Josiah. *Commerce of the Prairies.* (New York, 1844).

Hayes, A. A. *New Colorado and the Santa Fe Trail.* (New York, 1880).

Hughes, John T. *Doniphan's Expedition.* (Cincinnati, 1850).

Ladd, Horatio. *The Story of New Mexico.* (Boston, 1891).

London Illustrated News, December 2, 1854.

Lummis, Charles F. *The Land of Poco Tiempo.* (New York, 1893).

Matthews, Dr. Washington, "Navajo Weavers," Bureau of Ethnology, 1881-82.

"A New Cavalry Drill," *Harper's Weekly,* April 4, 1885.

Ritch, William. *Aztlan.* (Boston, 1885).

———. *Official Report of the Territory of New Mexico.* (Santa Fe, 1882-3).

Simpson, James H. *Report and Map of the Route from Fort Smith, Arkansas, to Santa Fe, New Mexico.* (Washington, 1850).

"Staging in the Far West," *Harper's Weekly,* July 4, 1874.

Tassé, Joseph. *Les Canadiens de l'Ouest.* (Montreal, 1878).

Tenney, E. P. *Colorado and Homes in the New West.* (Boston, 1880).

"A Texas Ranger," *Harper's Weekly,* July 6, 1861.

Thayer, William. *Marvels of the West.* (Norwich, Conn., 1888).

U.S. Bureau of Census. *Report on Indians Taxed and Indians Not Taxed.* (Washington, 1890).

Whipple, Lt. A. W. *Report of Exploration and Surveys to Ascertain the Most Practicable and Economical Route for a Railroad from the Mississippi River to the Pacific Ocean.* (Washington, 1856).

Wilson, H. T. *Historical Sketch of Las Vegas.* (Chicago, 1880).

Index

NOTE: Because of multiple geographical and place names in New Mexico, place names are followed by their county locations in parentheses.

472

482